Da Capo Press Music Reprint Series

MUSIC EDITOR
BEA FRIEDLAND
*Ph.D., City University of New York*

This title was recommended for Da Capo reprint by
**Dr. Léonie Rosenstiel**

# TERESA CARREÑO

## *"by the grace of God"*

MARTA MILINOWSKI

DA CAPO PRESS • NEW YORK • 1977

Library of Congress Cataloging in Publication Data

Milinowski, Marta, 1885-
  Teresa Carreño: "by the grace of God"

  (Da Capo Press music reprint series)
  Reprint of the 1940 ed. published by Yale University Press, New Haven.
  Bibliography: p.
  1. Carreño, Teresa, 1853-1917. 2. Pianists—Venezuela—Biography.
ML417.C4M6 1977   786.1'092'4 [B]      76-58931
ISBN 0-306-70870-1

√ ML
417
. C 4
. M 6

This Da Capo Press edition of *Teresa Carreño* is
an unabridged republication of the first edition
published in New Haven and London in 1940.

Published by Da Capo Press, Inc.
A Subsidiary of Plenum Publishing Corporation
227 West 17th Street, New York, N. Y. 10011

Manufactured in the United States of America

# TERESA CARREÑO

*"by the grace of God"*

*Mme. Teresa Carreño*

*von Gottes Gnaden.*

*Immer, immer Ihre treue*

*Schumann-Heink*

Excerpts taken from a letter to Carreño in explanation of the
sub-title of this book

# TERESA CARREÑO
## *"by the grace of God"*

### MARTA MILINOWSKI

PROFESSOR OF MUSIC AT VASSAR COLLEGE

NEW HAVEN

YALE UNIVERSITY PRESS

LONDON · HUMPHREY MILFORD · OXFORD UNIVERSITY PRESS

1940

PUBLISHED IN CELEBRATION OF
THE SEVENTY-FIFTH ANNIVERSARY
OF
VASSAR COLLEGE
AND IN HONOR OF
HENRY NOBLE MacCRACKEN
IN THE TWENTY-FIFTH YEAR
OF HIS PRESIDENCY

*This book is affectionately dedicated*
*to my little friend*

TERESITA CARREÑO HARRIS

*true heir to her grandmother's musical gifts.*
*By right of this inheritance*
*she promises to keep alive in her own way*
*the tradition which is Teresa Carreño.*

# CONTENTS

# ILLUSTRATIONS

# PRELUDE

NONE is more vibrantly alive than the performing artist with the floodlight of fame full upon him; none more swiftly enters the labyrinth of hearsay whose only outlet is oblivion. That even a Teresa Carreño shares this common destiny was brought home to me recently by a young musician: "Carreño, who is he?" she asked. Thirty years ago she would have known. For the chance of a standing-room ticket to hear the "Walküre of the Piano" she might have waited in line for hours with others of her kind who had hitched their wagons, often too lightly freighted, to the *fata morgana* of a concert career. It was then still the piano's golden age. That austere and sinister-looking tripod of shining black dominated the concert stage night upon night, sleek and quiet in suspense, like a fireside cat waiting for the touch of a hand to caress or chastise it into responsive sound. A concert could be as exciting as a conflagration. It became so when Carreño played. Students forgot their aching feet and listened to her message: "Music is the very essence of living. Making music is as easy as picking flowers and as rewarding. You can do it as well as I if you try hard enough." Each one of them fell asleep uplifted and dreamed herself a Carreño. To be hailed by critics as a *coming Carreño* was the culminating compliment for a young artist. Carreño herself could afford to make fun of these potential rivals. "These Carreños," she was often heard to say. "They are always *coming*. Where do they hide themselves? Why don't they come?"

This book was brought into being out of the conviction that a figure so significant in musical America and Europe during more than half a century has meaning for this day and beyond. During her life, dramatic enough to be recorded for itself alone, important changes were taking place in the concert field, in musical taste, in musical criticism. Carreño reflected these changes. She was an example of that rare phenomenon so fascinating to the psychologist, a prodigy who came true as an artist. Gottschalk, Rossini, Liszt, and Gounod believed in her genius. Rubinstein took it upon himself to be her mentor. Von Bülow, Grieg, and Brahms learned to respect her as a colleague. In her turn she decisively furthered the career of Edward Mac-Dowell, the most famous of her pupils.

Since Carreño's death in 1917 a number of persons have felt the call to write her biography. All were deterred by lack of material ready at hand. Carreño took little comfort in making order in the cluttered attic of her past. She kept no comprehensive or consecutive diary other than a meticulous record of daily expenses and concert dates. The demands of the moment were all-absorbing. Her concern was with her music, with her family. She treated herself as impersonally as she treated her public.

Shortly before her death she began to dictate reminiscences to William Armstrong. Interesting if fragmentary sketches, they were published in *The Musical Courier*. Articles and interviews treating of Carreño the artist, Carreño the teacher, Carreño the woman, and Carreño the mother, exist in profusion and confusion. With few exceptions fancy has juggled with fact to the extent of painting a distorted picture framed in a gingerbread conglomerate of adulation and anecdote. Standard musical encyclopedias disagree upon such fundamentals as the dates of her marriages and the number of her children. They have falsely labeled her the composer of the national anthem of Venezuela. Most flagrant of all is the willful misrepresentation of Carreño in Wilhelm Raupp's biography of Eugen d'Albert. A Carreño does not lose by authentic portrayal and deserves no less. This belief, quite aside from the affection of the student for the teacher of her veneration, is the force behind these words.

Carreño was no musical specialist. She was a comprehensive personality. Whether she played, or sang in opera, or took up the conductor's baton, she did so with authority. Failure was not a word in her vocabulary, not in any of the five languages she used with interchangeable ease. From the fullness of her treasure she had a gift for each and every one. That is why her life appears not as a series of happenings in the orderly sequence of time, not as an intricately tangled skein of character development, but rather as a map in topographical relief under the chiaroscuro of sun and clouds. Three mountain peaks look down upon a varied landscape which bears the marks of triumph and disaster, shipwreck and revolution. Like a ribbon of clashing colors twin factors dominated Carreño's life from babyhood, as inseparable as they were antagonistic. As music and dolls made up the world of the child, art and family became the all-absorbing concern of the woman. This unresolved dissonance is the key to the door which gives upon the essential Carreño.

The writing of this book involved much travel. Sojourns in Germany and in Venezuela were particularly fruitful. Everywhere enthusiastic and discerning coöperation gave zest to the considerable task of assembling chaotically scattered material. Without the wholehearted approval of the surviving members of Carreño's family who freely gave access to important documents, letters, criticisms, programs, articles, and photographs this undertaking would have met with insuperable obstacles. For their vote of confidence and especially for the helpful suggestions and timetaking collaboration of my friend Frau Louis Weber (the former Hertha Carreño d'Albert) I am deeply indebted.

Most gratifying was the warm welcome that greeted me, a stranger, in Caracas. Wherever I turned, valuable information and counsel stood waiting. I regret that it is impossible to make public acknowledgment to all who gave thought to my work there. Among them it was Mr. Rudolf Dolge, president of the Pan-American Society, who most generously furthered my research by acquainting me with the resources of his unique library, by hours of patient unearthing of references, by unselfish willingness to place his time and that of his secretary at my disposal during the weeks of my stay. More important still, his active initiative and perseverance are primarily responsible for the recent repatriation of Carreño's ashes by the Government of

Venezuela. Sincere appreciation is due to Señor José Antonio
Calcaño and to Señor Juan Bautista Plaza, Venezuela's enthusiastic musicologists, for their scholarly assistance, to Señor Mirábal Ponce for the use of the Carreño genealogy compiled by
him, and to the late Gertrudis Carreño, Teresa Carreño's double
first cousin, for many hours of delightful and enlightening reminiscence.

Thanks are due also to Miss Kate S. Chittenden for the use
of notes taken in Carreño's classes at the Institute of Applied
Music in New York, to Mrs. Caroline Keating Reed for sharing
with me her letters and her memories, and to Mr. James C.
Corson, Assistant Librarian of the University of Edinburgh, for
his help in establishing the date of Carreño's first appearance
in opera. Highly illuminating was a conversation with Mrs. Edward MacDowell, to whom I am indebted for permission to
publish letters of her own as well as of her husband.

To my mother, to Dr. Hannah Sasse, to Dr. Millicent Todd
Bingham and to those friends who have read the manuscript
and have helped in its preparation, allowing me to share the benefit of their literary experience, I give my affectionate gratitude.

It is beyond the range of the possible to make individual
mention of that devoted band of students, Carreño's "Berlin
Sons and Daughters." Many of them now hold high rank in
the musical profession. Carreño's influence is still a vital thing
within them, as was that intangible something they brought
her in exchange, a return too elusive for the black and white
of words. Their helpful understanding is woven into these
pages.

There is a saying: "Nothing improves with translation—unless it be a bishop." For general convenience, nevertheless, quo-
tations have been given in the original language only if meaning or flavor would otherwise suffer distortion.

Carreño has at last come into her own as honorary citizen of
her native land, a figure of lasting national import. If this
book succeeds in establishing her true place in that larger international citizenship, the world of music, it will have accomplished its purpose.

*Auch kleine Dinge können uns entzücken;*
*Auch kleine Dinge können teuer sein.*
PAUL HEYSE

PART I

PRODIGY

# TERESA CARREÑO

LITTLE Teresita stood with her nose flat against the window glass, listening to the prickling of the rain, liking the cobblestones washed bright. Rows of usually drab stone steps shone in polished and diminishing repetition, finally to disappear in the mist of lower Second Avenue. The insistent rhythms of approaching hoofs called for tunes to fit them, and Teresita hummed to herself as she watched a man crisscrossing to light the street lamps one after the other. Her own home, far away in South America, lay bathed in sunshine, as if in the mountain nest of a great *zamuro,* who had carried off some giant child's toy village in his talons, and had arranged all the pink and blue and yellow and green houses in close, straight rows. How pretty were the red roofs of Caracas! The cornices in front of them looked like decorations on a birthday cake, or even more like the lace on her best pantalettes.

All at once a familiar tightening of the throat sent out its warning. "Teresita, you are not to cry," she scolded herself, "not today when you are going to play in a real concert." Quickly she turned away from the window.

"Mamacita, will it soon be time?" All day long she had periodically interrupted whatever was going on to ask that question. At last the mother looked up from her sewing to answer: "Yes, Teresita, now it is time to be dressed."

Teresita bounded to kiss her mother's hand, then stopped for a word with her doll. "Don't cry. As soon as the concert is over I shall come back to you. Poor thing, you can't go with me, because you don't yet know how to play the piano." With that she danced from the room.

In the darkening living room Teresita's father, immaculate as always, was improvising, somewhat incoherently for him, on the Chickering. Both he and his wife were already attired in their evening best, which for her meant a gown of voluminous purple silk trimmed with precious Spanish lace. Plain gold earrings and a locket failed to lighten the impression of austerity suggested by smooth black hair, parted in the near middle and done in stiffly hanging ringlets. Crossing the room to sit beside her husband, she looked calm as an animated tea cozy.

"Do you think Teresita is nervous, Antonio?" she asked.

"No, Clorinda, she's too healthy," was the automatic rejoinder always ready for the one who asked that stupid question.

Together they sat silent thinking of Caracas three months and so many endless miles away in perpetual, temperate summer. Antonio puffed smoke rings into the air. They reminded him of the clouds that floated lightly about the Avila, of the always green and shadowed mountain ranges that encircled the city, tiered in a sort of visual counterpoint, each a perfect linear phrase. He could sing the lines. They never made him feel shut in, but rather safely shut away.

Clorinda's perspective was different. How simple was life in the land of one's own language; what precious privacy lay behind tightly shuttered, securely grilled windows, so unrevealing by day, so stinging to the imagination. At dusk the shutters might open revealing poverty or luxury in unsuspected neighborliness. At the courting hour beautiful young girls leaned upon window sills overhanging the narrow streets. Mothers laid their babies there to be admired. But most of all Clorinda missed her patio, the center of family seclusion. How could one describe these incredible gardens within houses to a New Yorker? She could sense them now, blossoming, fruitful, fragrant the year round with orchids in profusion developing miraculously overnight. She could hear the hypnotic splashing of the fountain before the old *pumaga* tree, which shed purple-red dust to make itself a regal carpet. Why did the premonition recur so often of late that never would she see her home again?

In 1862 L. F. Harrison was a well-known figure in New York. It was he who kept Irving Hall "constantly under gas with concerts, lectures, and balls." This was not his first experience with an unpredictable wonder-child, and he had reason to feel anxious. However, there was comfort in the thought that seats had

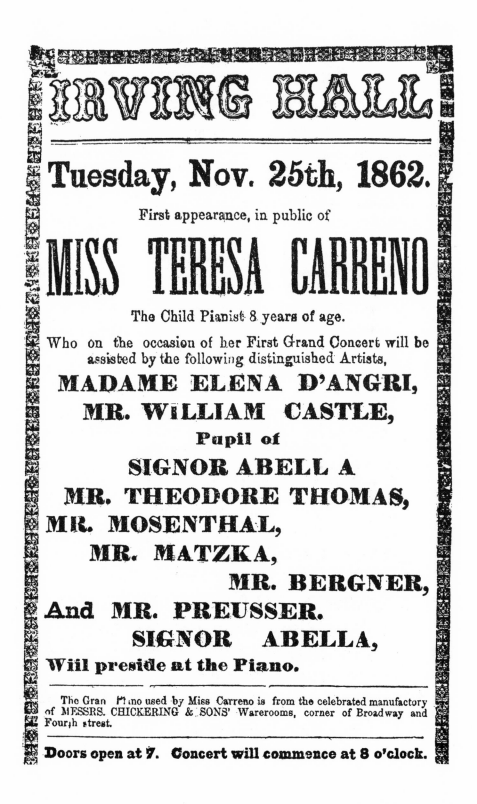

# IRVING HALL

## Tuesday, Nov. 25th, 1862.

First appearance, in public of

# MISS TERESA CARRENO

The Child Pianist 8 years of age.

Who on the occasion of her First Grand Concert will be
assisted by the following distinguished Artists,

**MADAME ELENA D'ANGRI,**

**MR. WILLIAM CASTLE,**

Pupil of

**SIGNOR ABELL A**

**MR. THEODORE THOMAS,**

**MR. MOSENTHAL,**

**MR. MATZKA,**

**MR. BERGNER,**

And **MR. PREUSSER.**

**SIGNOR ABELLA,**

Will preside at the Piano.

The Gran Piano used by Miss Carreno is from the celebrated manufactory
of MESSRS. CHICKERING & SONS' Warerooms, corner of Broadway and
Fourth street.

**Doors open at 7. Concert will commence at 8 o'clock.**

# PROGRAMME.

## PART FIRST.

1. **Rondo Brilliant**.................................................Hummel
   With accompanyments of two Violins—Viola, Violincello and double bass.
   ### MISS TERESA CARRENO.

2. **Remanza,** "Una furtiva laqrima" (Elisir d'Amore)..........Donizetti
   ### MR. WM. CASTLE.

3. **Fantasia,** "Lucia"..........................e..............Vieuxtemps
   ### MR. THEODORE THOMAS.

4. **Cavatina,** "Semiramide"........................................Rossini
   ### MADAME ELENA D'ANGRI.

5. **Fantasia,** "Moise"............................................Thalberg
   ### MISS TERESA CARRENO.

## PART SECOND.

6. **Duettino,** "Il Trovatore"......................................Verdi
   ### MADAME ELENA D'ANGRI and MR. WM. CASTLE.

7. **Nocturne**......................................................Doenier
   ### MISS TERESA CARRENO.

8. **Fantassa,** "Ernani"..........................................Vieuxtemps
   ### MR. THEODORE THOMAS.

9. **Aria,** "No no, no," (Huguenots)..............................Meyerbeer
   ### MADAME ELENA D'ANGRI.

10. **Jerusalem,** "Grand Fantasia Triumphale"..................Gottschalk
    ### MISS TERESA CARRENO.

---

# MISS TERESA CARRENO,

## Will give her

# SECOND GRAND CONCERT,

## On Saturday Evening, Nov. 29th.

HERALD PRINT.

*Irving Hall Début Program*

sold surprisingly well, and that he was not risking very much.
Señor Carreño was too gentlemanly and inexperienced to be a
good businessman. Mr. Harrison had dictated a contract to his
own liking, and he patted the pocket where it lay.

People were gathering in spite of the weather. The critics
stood grouped together, waiting for the ringing of the bell.
Those who had not heard "this last sweet thing in prodigies,"
as the *Home Journal* put it, were frankly bored at the prospect.
Mr. Harrison was everywhere in evidence, alert for remarks
that would give the temper of the audience.

A dowager was using her tortoise-shell lorgnette to best advantage: "It is the first time that I have had occasion to come
here since the hall was renovated. It is really delightful, my
dear, to hear a concert in so chaste a setting." This to a young
girl who was busily reading the program, long as a scroll.

"Yes, it is indeed, Auntie. Did you know that this child has
learned the Gottschalk piece she is playing tonight in five days?
She was running around, a mere baby, among the seats at his
last concert. He considers her a genius and means to give her
lessons when he has time to breathe between concerts."

"Does he really, my dear? But if you ask my opinion," again
the dowager's far-reaching voice, "I think it is preposterous to
allow so young a child, if she is only eight years old as they
say, to play at this hour of the night."

The critics meanwhile were engaged in argument.

A complaining one: "Another concert by one of those over-
drilled, under-nourished infants! In two years, who will remember her name?"

An enthusiastic one: "But this one is really quite different.
She has something to say, and her own compositions are in
good form and very fresh and natural."

The complaining one: "Hm! We'll soon know! I don't intend to sit this endless program through. Why can't pianists
find something to play besides opera transcriptions? They call
her the second Mozart. Why doesn't she play some of his things
then?"

The enthusiastic one: "Perhaps that's the very reason. She prefers to be Teresita the first, not Mozart the second. You'll find that she interprets every phrase as if she meant it. I heard her one morning at her own home. She improvises delightfully, making up stories as she plays. I couldn't understand them. She talks only in Spanish."

The complaining one: "Where in creation is Venezuela anyhow? One of those islands down there?—Oh, now I remember! That's the place where they are always having revolutions. The sound of the name Caracas suggests revolutions. I suppose it was too peaceful for her there, so she came up here, where something real is going on. Well, there's the call! Until later, gentlemen!"

Irving Hall, an architectural hodgepodge by day, was to Teresita on this night of her first concert a palace of jeweled light through the rain. The long row of carriages in front of theirs made progress slow, much too slow for the artist of the evening. She could not wait to begin. In a few moments she would be pleasing more people than she had pleased in all her life, and earning money to help her father and mother besides. It would not be very different from playing in the same hall three weeks ago, only so much more gay at night. Last time, when people refused to stop clapping, she ran to hide behind her father. After that she would play no more, pretending to be tired. Could anyone really get tired just playing the piano? Tonight, no matter how much noise they made, she must not hide. "Children run away, artists never!" So her father had said.

In the dressing room below stage the quintette of stringed instruments, that was to accompany Teresita in Hummel's "Rondo Brillante" under the leadership of young Theodore Thomas, was tuning. Clorinda smoothed out the points of Teresita's collar and gave an appraising look at the full skirt, which billowed becomingly to set off the lace of the pantalettes. The simple white dress, cut low and with short sleeves that puffed, was Clorinda's own contribution to the occasion, the product of her needlework. She was justly proud. From her daughter's silky black hair to the shiny black boots, which reached halfway to the pantalettes, she could find no flaw.

Now was the moment. Teresita could hardly be held back while the gentlemen of the quintette arranged themselves in their places. Vaguely, as if from a great distance, she heard her father say, "Teresita, remember not to run across the stage." It seemed so far from the door to the piano that halfway there she forgot, covering the remaining distance in a purposeful accelerando. She did remember to give a shy, appealing nod to the audience before mounting the piano stool. For her that was the really difficult part of the concert. She literally had to climb it, then arranging her feet carefully on the wooden platform, especially designed with two steel rods running through it, so that she might move the pedals she could not yet reach. Once safely mounted, she gave her miniature orchestra the *A* with so professional a gesture that the audience was hers in a common smile of tender amusement, won over before she had played a single note. Of this Teresita was unaware. Here she was at last, to play in the same place, on the same Chickering even, that had vibrated a few days before under the fingers of Gottschalk, her idol.

With the first note came a complete transformation. The child disappeared; in her place·the artist, intently, maturely concentrated. As if by electric contact the listeners were drawn into common understanding of her music. She made it sound simple, clear—and unbelievable. To play a difficult composition fluently and correctly seemed to be as easy for Teresita as saying her prayers. There she sat at ease upon her pedestal, her round arms, her short, well-cushioned fingers, moving with the freedom and grace that is the result of unconscious economy of effort. And every phrase she played she lived. The audience was baffled. How was she able at eight years of age to do that which another could not hope to do in eight years of study? Where did she get her sense of color values, of architectural balance? What gave her the power to evoke feelings she never could have had herself? Felipe Larrazábal, a musical compatriot, speaking of Teresita in Venezuela a year before, aptly quoted a Latin poet: "There is a God within me, who fills my spirit with celestial clarity. He dominates me, He moves my hands. He it is who inspires my songs of delight, my cries of pain, of passion, and of mystery. *Est Deus in Nobis.*"

The rondo at an end, Teresita, child again, responded to the stormy applause, as her father had taught her. Wall Street gentlemen and children as small as she herself brought flowers and wreaths. The wreaths she hung upon her arm; the flowers she gathered in her skirt, an improvised apron, while her parents, standing in the wings tensely aware of every gesture, wondered at her self-possession. Suddenly in the middle of a series of choppy, childishly awkward bows in embryo, she stiffened. A courtly old gentleman was holding up an enormous doll for her to take. Forgetting everything else, Teresita dropped her flowers and ran to clutch it. When she squeezed it, it cried like any live baby. Ecstatically, leaving the lesser trophies for others to pick up, Teresita ran from the stage.

A lady in the front row wiped her eyes and turned to her husband. "She reminds me of Adelina Patti. She has the same dark eyes and skin and hair, and the same bewitching expression. I have never been so moved at a concert before." Her husband was of a more matter-of-fact turn of mind. "I have heard more than I expected. She does get over the keys in tough music. Did you see that elderly gentleman try to give her a bouquet while she was running off stage? He couldn't keep up with her and was finally obliged to throw it after her."

Even the complaining critic was converted. "There seems to be nothing lacking except strength, of course, and a certain maturity of style. How those hands can stretch an octave is a mystery, and yet her octave passages are remarkably clear and accurate. I don't understand it; I just don't understand it!"

The concert continued in the approved manner of the Sixties, which called above all for variety. Teresita, absorbed in her treasure, did not bother to listen to the singing of Mr. Castle and Mme. Angri. Only once did she open the door, so that her doll might hear the violin solos of her friend Theodore Thomas, whose accompaniments she often played at home.

Soon again it was her turn. She nearly cried because she was not allowed to take her doll out upon the stage to listen to the music. In Thalberg's *Fantaisie sur Moïse en Égypte* there was chance for grand climaxes, brilliant passages, and sweet, warm melodies familiar to many of the audience. Teresita made the most of them. Enthusiasm became hysteria. Even the complaining critic surprised himself by shouting "Bravo!" to an operatic transcription. Before the first round of applause had subsided, Teresita had arranged herself upon the piano stool again, this time to play for an encore the waltz she had composed for Gottschalk. That this master would play it in his concerts was her fervent hope, one never to be realized. A nocturne by Doehler followed the intermission. Her eyes half-closed, she became serious, remote. At the end there was a momentary tribute of stillness, then the barbarous interruption of clapping, an all-too-sudden call back to childhood.

The time seemed endless until she sat before the Chickering again. Gottschalk's "Jerusalem" was worth waiting for. To surprise him she had learned it in less than a week. A single lesson taught her to interpret it as he did. Not without reason it was called a "grand triumphal fantasie." There were parts that whispered, parts that sobbed, and parts that soared to glittering pinnacles. Teresita's conviction that the music she was playing was the most beautiful in the world made it become greater than it was. The piano, the performer, and the music were completely fused. To those who listened, life for a moment seemed whole and right.

At last Teresita had said the last polite *gracias* to people, most of whom she could not understand. The hall lay in darkness. "How did you enjoy playing?" asked her father. The answer came without hesitation. "I felt I was in Heaven." The mother had a more practical question. "Suppose, Teresita, you had to choose between being a princess and an artist, which would it be?" Simply, with prophetic gravity, Teresita took her musical vows. "I shall be an artist all my life."

Overnight the little prodigy of the Andes became the marvel of New York. Without possessing its language she had made herself understood, bringing a universal message, different for each according to his state of being. Mr. Harrison, open-eyed wherever his own interests were involved, had announced a second concert on the program of the first without consulting the father. Teresita, her doll in her arms, her flowers fragrant about her, stood eager. It was great fun and so very easy to please people. Always she would like to give more pleasure to more people.

Manuel Antonio faced a crisis as important as the one that had deprived him of office in Venezuela the year before. Last night not only Teresita but he himself had succeeded. The thwarted dream of becoming an artist in his own right was now coming true in his pupil, his daughter, and the disappointment of seeing his career as Minister of Finance ended by one of Venezuela's all-too-frequent revolutions had at last found potential compensation. By nature an unselfish idealist and a teacher, Manuel Antonio might at fifty still find fulfillment as a guide to unfolding genius. The far line of his ancestors would approve such a choice.

In Spain, and later in Venezuela, the house of Carreño stood worthy of record. The family name drew its origin from a still-existing municipality of Carreño, a group of scattered farms belonging to the diocese of Oviedo in the ancient kindom of the Asturias, and lying on the Bay of Biscay west of Santander. Teresita never tired of asking her father to tell her again and again how Don Alonso Carreño helped to take Carrión de los Condes from the Moors during the reign of King Alfonso el Casto. The Christians, Don Alonso among them, taking the horse of Troy for a model, had the temerity to enter the town in carts covered with fresh vegetables. Once in the square, they surprised the infidels and drove them out. The Carreño crest, showing wheels grasped in the talons of an eagle about to take flight, bears witness to this feat and also to the derivation of the family name. On the red border of the shield appear eight crosses of San Andrés.

Emerging from the forest of tradition to the clearing of history there is mention of a certain Garcí Fernandez Carreño to whom, in return for a service, King Sancho IV of Castile gave the privilege of receiving each year the robes worn by the king on Holy Thursday. Not until the time of Carlos I of Spain was the grant revoked. A payment of 11,200 maravedises relieved the treasury of this strange obligation.

The Carreños, hidalgos of old, are not listed in the *Guía de la Grandeza*. But a number served their king intimately in the post of chamberlain, treasurer, or more remotely as city governors.

The artistic bent was characteristic of the Carreños from the first. In the middle of the fifteenth century, Fernando de Carreño built the fortress-palace, Castillo de la Mota, for the famous Dukes of Benavente. And there is mention of many others, whose gift for poetry and painting gave them passing fame in their own time. This urge reached its climax in the celebrated painter of his day, Juan Carreño de Miranda, born in Avilés, Asturias, the twenty-fifth of March, 1614. He was the one who most ably assimilated and handed down the tradition and method of Velasquez. To his misfortune he became popular as court painter and found himself obliged to take royal Hapsburgs, unprepossessing as they were, as subjects. Charles II, as vain as he was pale and vacant in expression, was one of his frequent trials. Although Carreño de Miranda solved the problem as neatly as might be by lavishing his talents on the robes, accessories, and backgrounds of his subjects, thinking it better to leave character unrevealed, and finding his devotional outlet in religious painting of uncommon beauty, it is probable that he missed true greatness in art by reason of obligatory deference to the great in lineage.

A rural quarter to the municipality of Cienfuegos in Cuba records the names and the successes of the adventurous Carreños who sailed the seas. Bartolomé Carreño, a sea captain, helped to discover the Bermudas and other Caribbean islands. His son, Francisco, became governor of Havana, improved its fortifications, increased its garrison, fought against piracy, and put into practice important means for bettering public service in the colony. He died in Cuba (1759) poisoned by the wife of a certain official dismissed by him for bad conduct.

Probably at the end of the seventeenth century the first Carreño found his way to Venezuela, perhaps a younger son with slight prospects at home in Spain, going in search of the promised Eldorado, that invention of the *Indios* meant to lead the invaders into the fastnesses of the Andes and of the Llanos where they could most easily be destroyed. These adventurous boys must have found life in this, the first and the poorest settlement on the mainland, strenuous beyond expectation. Until the late eighteenth century Spain took little interest in Venezuela, the least promising of its dependencies. Agriculture was the chief means of livelihood, gained with untold hardships in the face of uncompromising natural obstacles and other ingenious ones devised by the unfriendly natives.

In Caracas a young hidalgo was sure to be confronted by a small group of the descendants of titled Spaniards banded together in a closed circle. Excluded by birth from this, he was obliged to look for other fields in which to achieve dignified social standing. The early Venezuelan Carreños found in the position of Maestro de Coro of the Cathedral of Caracas a vocation alike congenial to their religious leanings and their musical gifts. Eventually it became a professional hereditary hierarchy in the Carreño family for generations. In unbroken succession from father to son they were devoted churchmen, able composers and organists. Although the indigent diocese of Caracas was unable to provide them with a fit salary, the Carreños did not apparently object to working tirelessly for the glory of God alone. The fact remains to their even greater credit that they played a major part in the musical development of their country.

Revered above all other musicians in the Caracas of the 1770's was Padre Pedro Palacios y Sojo. Belonging to the maternal side of Bolívar's family, he possessed considerable inherited wealth, which he used first of all to build a church, San Felipe Neri, and a monastery for the brothers of this order. His dream included an academy of music. To make it come true he brought back from Italy a library of good music, religious and secular, books of instruction, and instruments. Two visiting Austrian naturalists, Bredemeyer and Schultz by name, took an active interest in his plans. On their return to Austria, so infectious was their description that they were commissioned by their monarch to send music, among which were the string quartettes of Haydn and Mozart, and instruments, both strings and wood winds, to further Padre Sojo's undertaking. The first Societá Filarmónica had already been formed under the leadership of Don Juan Manuel Olivares. Padre Sojo wisely decided to put him in charge of the new school. Under his direction Venezuela, elementally endowed with musical riches, developed with tropical fervor and speed. Taking the European classics for a mold, eager young musicians, among them José Cayetano Carreño the younger, gathered together to learn the technique of their calling.

The Comte de Ségur on his visit to Caracas in 1776 found the men somewhat "reserved and serious," but "the Señoritas outstanding for the beauty of their faces, the richness of their dress, the elegance of their manners, and for their love of dancing and music." Alexander von Humboldt twenty-five years later reported: "I encountered in the families of Caracas a decided desire for learning, knowledge of the works of French and Italian literature, and a notable fondness for music which they cultivate with success. Like every fine art, it forms the nucleus which brings different classes of society together."

The musical life of Caracas found a center in the adjoining surburban estates of Padre Sojo, Don Bartolomé Blandín, and Padre Mohedano. There from under the orange trees with the Avila, a majestic auditor, in the background, the quartettes of Haydn and of Mozart sounded for the first time in Venezuela. Aristides Rojas, Venezuela's great historian, rhapsodized: "For the fields of Chacao the memory of the art of music and of growing coffee is what to the old castles were the legends of the troubadours."

He devoted a picturesque chapter to the celebration in honor of the first coffee harvest in that area on a scale of commercial significance. An earlier planting had failed to reach fruition, and only after two years of anxious waiting did the coffee bushes begin to blossom in their sweet-scented, breath-taking white under the shade of the higher trees planted to protect them from the sun, twice flowering themselves in blatant scarlet before the matching red of the coffee berries appeared in profusion that exceeded hope.

Finally at the end of 1786 the three neighbors were able to send out invitations for a unique festival. On the morning of the appointed day the bumpy road leading to the Blandín estate was alive with every kind of conveyance. The guests included all that was distinguished and lovely in Caracas. Entertainment began with a walk through the coffee plantation. From there the light music of an orchestra drew the young people into the huge hall for dancing, the more serious-minded preferring the orange grove where quartettes of the classic masters alternated with songs accompanied upon the clavecin, to which the birds, unaccustomed to music not of their own making, gave sweet antiphony.

Tables were laid for luncheon where fruit trees made an improvised dining room. Leisure amid beauty is a setting in which the Venezuelan feels himself at home. Laughter and easy conversation spiced the banquet from beginning to end. Come the time to serve the coffee, all the tables were removed but one in the center, whose decorations consisted of three flowering coffee bushes set in jars of porcelain. Silver platters filled with delicate pastry stood next to small cups of transparent china. The aroma of coffee, freshly distilled, insinuated itself gratefully into the consciousness of the guests standing to witness the pouring. The first cup was offered to Padre Mohedano, beloved priest of Chacao, amid great acclaim. Then spontaneously there was silence, the eloquent silence that sometimes transmits a wish more clearly than words. Padre Mohedano understood. Lifting his hand he called down the blessing of God upon this harvest, "gift of wise nature and of men of good will." Padre Sojo asked that divine favor fall upon art, "rich gift of Providence." In his turn Padre Domingo Blandín then prayed that the grace of the Lord descend upon those brought together on this occasion. The ceremony of serving a cup of coffee to each guest officially closed the festival.

A close friend of Padre Sojo was José Cayetano Carreño, Maestro de Capilla of the Cathedral of Caracas, and brother of that Juan de la Cruz Carreño, whose "Élégie" is the earliest composition by a member of this family to be preserved in its archives. Cayetano's marriage to Doña Rosalía Rodriguez resulted several generations later in the appearance of Venezuela's greatest genius, always excepting Bolívar, María Teresa Carreño y Toro, still affectionately known in the country of her birth as Teresita Carreño.

Cayetano's son, also called José Cayetano, born in 1766, was a true son of his father in more than name. He inherited his musical gifts, his kindly nature, and his probity, succeeding him in due time as Maestro de Capilla. The great pride of the Sojo-Olivares School in which he was trained, his compositions are still heard, resurrected by the young enthusiasts of today, in the setting in which they were conceived, the most famous being "La Oración en el Huerto," a master work "full of sweetness and truly celestial uplift," reminiscent of Haydn in its sincerity and purity of outline. He is remembered also for his musical high tenor, that greatly enhanced the appeal of the masses and oratorios in which he took part, for his playing of various instruments, and for his conducting of the orchestra in the Teatro Cordero. Like most of his contemporaries he was caught by the spirit of the Revolution to which a younger brother fell victim. Cayetano's contribution to the cause was the writing of patriotic songs. One, generally attributed to him, which begins: *"Caraqueños, otra época empieza,"* became so popular that it was sung *sotto voce* in the streets during the time when any form of revolutionary propaganda was punishable by death. It long remained a model for this type of composition. Cayetano did not acquire riches—he was paid ninety pesetas for a number of his compositions together—so that he found it expedient to teach, supplementing his duties as organist and choir director. His marriage with María Madre de Jesús Muñoz brought him happiness and five children, only one of whom, Manuel Antonio, father of Teresita, inherited musical talent. Cayetano died on the third of March, 1836, beloved and revered by all. Taking leave of his family, he exhorted them to virtue and high thinking. His ashes lie in the crypt of the chapel erected in the Cathedral to the honor of Our Lady of Pilar, an honor usually accorded only to priests who had become Deans of the Cathedral.

Two brothers could not be more different than Cayetano and Simón Carreño, eight years his junior, chiefly remembered for his decisive influence upon the young Bolívar as his tutor. He was an independent and erratic idealist, and a versatile one, with flashes of real vision that approached genius. The change-

ling in a devout, well-ordered family group, restless and at
odds with his father, he decided to take another name, that of
his mother. To history thereafter he is known as Simón Rodriguez, which is not, however, the last appellation of his choosing. Revolutionary ideas imported from France found ready
echo in this intelligent young eccentric. He became involved in
the uprising of Gual y España and in 1797 was forced to flee
from Venezuela to the English Antilles. There his imagination was profoundly stirred by his own isolation and by reading Robinson Crusoe whom he admired as the only true democrat. In homage he called himself, at least temporarily, Samuel
Robinson. Later in Europe he learned various languages easily,
visited France, Germany, and Austria, and made friends with
men of learning and science, drawn to him by the magnetic
warmth of his nature and his flaring intellect. In Vienna he
again chanced upon Bolívar in despair over the death of his
young wife of less than a year. One of Simón's darts of inspiration made him recognize his pupil for the genius that he
was and see in him the future liberator of Venezuela. Simón
Rodriguez was a promoter, a philosopher ahead of his time, not
a man of great courage or action. But without the force of his
personality Bolívar might never have come alive to his mission.
After months of indulgence in the most extreme pleasures,
meant to dull the edge of grief, the two friends arrived in
Rome. There in the dramatic scene on the Monte Sacro that
has so often been the subject of painting and description, Bolívar swore before his mentor to devote his life to the freeing of
Venezuela from Spanish domination. Bolívar's greater vision
made his purposes reach even further. As for Simón Rodriguez,
the oath of the sacred mountain was his great moment, his
claim to glory. For a time he wandered, absorbing the ideas of
Rousseau. Returning to South America in 1823 he felt tempted
to apply them as a teacher. When he went so far as to appear
in his classroom completely unclothed, he so shocked the parents of his pupils that he was obliged to withdraw. Improvident
and impulsive as a hummingbird, he died poverty-stricken in

a tiny Peruvian village, Ametape, in whose church he lies buried. Years after his death his last erratic wish served to identify his coffin. He had asked to be buried in sitting posture.

In Manuel Antonio, Cayetano's son, artistic inheritance was very satisfactorily blended with more practical qualities. Well educated, well mannered, and well groomed, he was something of a perfectionist. That he escaped being a stickler for the unimportant was due to his wide intellectual interests, and to his sense of affectionate obligation to his fellow men. Every mention of him is qualified by the words "distinguished gentleman." But he was ambitious, too ambitious to content himself with a profession in which he could hope for neither advancement nor wealth. A political career seemed to promise both, and, moreover, that higher social rating which he coveted before all on his wife's account.

In the days of Columbus records attest that the Toros were notable hidalgos and ancient Christians, that among them were knights who owned horses, founded towns, and inherited property, flaunting as their crest a golden bull upon a field of scarlet. A royal grant conferred upon the family the hereditary title of Marqués in 1732. Rodriguez, third Marqués del Toro, was known as Bolívar's fast friend and not-too-successful general. He was the ideal type of Spanish aristocrat with democratic leanings and readily identified himself with the ideas of the Criollo class, whom Bolívar called "stepchildren of our race" or "idle slaveholders, themselves slaves under the laws of Spain." He seemed a real menace in the royalist fold. Suspicion rested upon him. Yet he was one of the few who found it worth while to keep his title to the end. On his estate in the Aragua valley he held miniature court. Alexander von Humboldt tells of the unforgettable hours spent there "in a corner of the earth like Paradise: and such refinement of living! Such sensitive, hospitable people!"

Clorinda García de Sena y Toro, niece of Bolívar's unfortunate wife and niece also of Rodriguez del Toro, was the daughter of two famous revolutionary strains. She had undoubtedly,

*Teresita's Parents*

in the estimation of her family and friends, taken a long step downward when she married the son of a professional man. Cold and formal by nature—her children might no more than kiss her hand—she laid weight upon external graces and material rewards. The former had drawn her to the less wealthy, less noble Manuel Antonio. For material rewards she could only hope. The insecurity of banking and politics in Venezuela had played havoc with the fortunes of the Toros as with others. Of course Clorinda readily approved the choice of a career for her husband that might in time restore her to the station and affluence in keeping with del Toro tradition. When Manuel Antonio succeeded in obtaining the portfolio of Minister of Finance, the choice seemed completely justified.

The home of the Carreños, now replaced by the offices of a shipping line, became a meeting place for artists, scientists, and diplomats. A letter to the Carreños was the best of introductions for a newcomer in Caracas. Music in one form or another might be counted upon during any evening. The fountain in the patio splashed its liquid obbligato to Spanish dances, operatic arias, and even to Manuel Antonio's "La Fleur du Désert" with its too sweet melody smothered in ornamental passages of considerable difficulty. Yes, Manuel Antonio and Clorinda had every reason to be satisfied in their well-ordered household, and their peaceful, if not entirely heart-warming, family life. However, Venezuela, the incalculable, whether through the natural upheaval of earthquakes or through the less natural one of revolutions, sooner or later was sure to upset the apparently most secure state of being.

EMILIA, the first daughter, was about eight years of age when on the twenty-second of December, 1853, another little girl was born to Manuel Antonio and Clorinda. They called her María Teresa, a name not infrequent in the family genealogy. Perhaps, according to a popular superstition in Venezuela, it was a pianist who first cut her fingernails and then buried the parings in the earth. In any case, this baby, welcomed with gladness usual in a country where childhood to this day remains a cult, was the unconscious climax of generations of musicians, the predestined bearer of the stern obligation of genius.

When the baby was less than a year old, friends noticed that she kept time to music with her head and her hands, that she loved toys that made pretty noises, that she listened in absorbed silence while music was being played. It so excited her that she would sit up in her crib next to the *salón* with her eyes wide open until it stopped. She began to sing before she could talk, and as soon as she could walk, she danced. At the age of two she was heard to give a fairly accurate idea of Bellini's famous aria from *Lucia,* "Bel Alma Innamorata," in a sweet, true voice. Teresita was a friendly, happy, and healthy child. She told stories to the dolls that she loved beyond everything and sang them to sleep at night as she did her baby brother Manuel, upon whom for a time family interest centered.

There were two pianos in the *salón*. The grand, Teresita was not permitted to touch. The keys of the upright she could barely reach standing. That was her piano. When Manuel Antonio showed her how to find thirds, she discovered other combinations that pleased her for herself, playing them over and over. Soon she began to reproduce familiar melodies on the keyboard. One night there was music in the *salón* next to Teresita's bedroom. The nurse had drawn the filmy white curtains of the crib close, and had left the child, as she thought, asleep. She had forgotten that Teresita was almost a professional in the art of pretending. On this particular evening she was enchanted by a "Varsovienne" that some friends were playing for Emilia. The next morning her first thought was to try it herself. The melody she managed easily, and, with a little effort, all the chords but one. Just as she had found the missing tone needed to complete a seventh chord, her father entered to help Emilia, so he expected, with her difficulty. Totally unprepared to find four-year-old Teresita at the keyboard, he burst into tears. Teresita immediately made it a melancholy duet. "Don't cry, Papa, I'll never do it again," she sobbed, a promise that fortunately she did not keep.

Manuel Antonio was a good psychologist and an equally good pedagogue. Very wisely he left Teresita to her own devices. At the age of five she had taught herself to play dances with easy left-hand accompaniment. For her dolls and her friends she enjoyed improvising what she called operas. Meanwhile the father, methodical in everything, and urged on by his daughter's evident ambition, made a set of 500 exercises, covering all the technical and rhythmical difficulties that a pianist might be apt to encounter. Shortly after Teresita's sixth birthday lessons began in earnest. Gradually she learned how to play the exercises so that she could work through them all in rotation every three days, playing them in any key she chose. Czerny and Bertini "Études," Bach's "Inventions" and "Little Preludes" lent variety. To her practice she devoted two hours in the morning and two in the afternoon with the same spirit of playful concentration that she lavished on her dolls. Soon she found herself easily overcoming the obstacles in Thalberg's *Norma* fantasia. In five days she had made it her own. One of her daily duties consisted of ten minutes spent in reading music at sight, an accomplishment in which she acquired amazing facility. Manuel Antonio knew how to fire his daughter's ambition. Pointing to a certain exercise he would say: "Teresita, I know that you can play this study in the key of C; that is easy. But I don't believe that you can play it in the key of B; that would be too much to expect of such a little girl." The hint was enough to make Teresita determine to achieve the impossible. The next day she not only played the exercise in B, but on through other keys. Transposing her pieces became a favorite game. Somtimes she improvised so interestingly that her father took down the melodies on paper as she played. He had been carefully taught by Cayetano and was by far the most accomplished amateur musician in the city. However, it did not take him long to discover that he was being outdistanced by his daughter. So a professional pianist, Julius Hohenus, was found to supplement his teaching. It was he who first made Teresita acquainted with works of Mendelssohn and Chopin.

In everything but music Teresita was a normal child. The social distinctions upon which her father so punctiliously insisted did not exist for her. Her imagination was fertile for mischief. One night the parents were entertaining with customary formality at dinner. Teresita noticed the shiny row of top hats neatly placed, each on its own peg, in the hall. It occurred to her that they would be set off to much greater advantage by the bushes in the patio. She took infinite pains to distribute them effectively, until they looked like sleek black crows perched there for solemn conference, and together with an old servant who was always delighted to second her plans, she hid in the background, laughing to see the distinguished gentlemen picking out their property from the branches.

On another occasion Teresita confided to this same old retainer, whose duty it was to accompany Teresita to a class she attended in a private school, that she meant to give a party. The refreshments would be his problem, the entertainment hers. In the classroom she rose, and imitating in unconscious caricature the manner of her father, she asked in the name of her parents that her friends bring their fathers and mothers to her home on the next evening for some music. She did not consider it necessary to prepare her parents. On the appointed night Manuel and Clorinda were sipping after-dinner coffee in the patio. A few callers began to appear, then more and more, until there could be no question of mere coincidence. First the mother, then the father, retired to change into more suitable attire. Refreshments were ordered and miraculously appeared.

Teresita darted about, playing hostess in miniature, not caring that there were gathered in her home that evening people who for political reasons should never have been asked together. Called upon for music, she proceeded to do her part with utter enjoyment, better than ever before. Both parents rose to the occasion to make the evening as successful as it was unexpected on their part. After the last guest had departed at a very late hour the dreaded question could no longer be avoided. "Who was responsible for this?" thundered Manuel Antonio. Teresita trembled. The tone of voice promised no good for the unhappy originator. "I did," admitted a whisper. Abruptly Manuel Antonio turned his back, and with boundless relief his daughter saw that his shoulders were shaking.

MANUEL ANTONIO had a small income from a book he had been tempted to write in moments of leisure before Teresita claimed them all. He longed to make Venezuela a safe and happy place to live in, and realized that more than an honest, forward-looking political system was needed to achieve this purpose. With that meticulous thoroughness characteristic of him, and under the sign of Silvio Pellico's motto: "To rest from the honorable task of being good, refined, and courteous there is no more time than that devoted to sleep," he wrote a work of nearly four hundred pages, closely printed, on good behavior. This appeared under the title of

MANUAL OF CIVILITY AND GOOD MANNERS for the use of the youth of both sexes; in which are encountered the principal rules of politeness and etiquette which should be observed in manifold social situations, preceded by a short treatise on the moral obligations of man.

This book found wide circulation in Spanish-American countries at once. Generations of school children have memorized, if not in all cases assimilated, the rules of this Earl of Chesterfield of Venezuela. Even today the book may be bought by simply asking for "El Carreño." Manuel Antonio read profusely on his subject in the works of his predecessors in many countries, and found himself in full agreement with them, that true aristocracy is of the spirit, that there can be no question of fine manners without the basis of knowing and observing the laws of moral obligation whose source is the Bible. From this universal implication of duty toward the Deity, toward one's fellow man, and toward oneself the book narrows down to the rules of daily behavior in infinite and often amusing detail. Caracas with its mixture of race, caste, and color, needed a pioneer for the weekly bath, the moderate beard, the personal face towel, and the toothbrush. Carreño spared himself and his readers no sanitary detail, even warning those who share bedrooms with others against the impoliteness of smoking when "the windows are closed for the night."

Expanding from the particular to the general, "El Carreño" reminds us that life is very short. So it is that only by using time with the utmost economy we find the means of educating and distinguishing ourselves, and of realizing all the plans that can be useful to us and to society. "But," he adds, perhaps as a special warning for himself, "let us keep in mind that excess in method, as in everything else, comes to be an evil as well."

Disregarding details that to a freer generation in a freer land appear irrelevant and fussy, Carreño's book remains the sincere credo of a high-thinking man, concerned for the good of his country, which he sees threatened by the impulsiveness and instability of its people. Much as he demands that the individual sacrifice his own interests to those of others, of the state and of the church, he nonetheless insists upon respect for personal dignity, and, believing in man's perfectibility as of determining importance in art and industry, and in the material and moral progress of his country, he urges him on to new and greater effort.

In early 1862 solving the problem of the right musical training for Teresita was more urgent to Manuel Antonio than even the welfare of Venezuela. Should he wait, perhaps for the rest of his life, to be reinstated in the Venezuelan Cabinet, while Clorinda, dreaming of the generous living on the hacienda of her childhood, chafed under the enforced economy so foreign to her taste? He had no doubt that Teresita's talent was worthy of greater stimulus than either he or Julius Hohenus could provide. She should measure herself against a more exacting scale of standards, hear better music, better playing. For Caracas she, the spoiled darling of completely undiscriminating friends, had already arrived at a climax. Was not one of her compositions publicly performed by a band of professional musicians, and did not the daily papers erupt with long columns of extravagant praise, wherever this little girl was heard?

One listener felt moved to give his impressions of such an affair in an article published by *El Buen Senrido*. On this evening Teresita was operatically inclined. One after another she played arrangements of melodies from *Lucia, I Puritani,* and *Norma.* The effect was so electrifying that the writer spent a sleepless night in consequence. Just for the fun of it Teresita would turn phrases upside down, change a fortissimo to a whisper, correcting, improving, or just playing musical jokes on her audience. Then jumping down from her piano stool with a very definite *"aquí no hay nada de eso,"* just then her pet phrase, she would turn to the really serious business of undressing her doll, ascending her pedestal again later of her own free will to improvise on a given theme or on some fantastic idea invented by herself. One of these arguments lasted for three quarters of an hour. The listener asked himself, "Who taught this child the silence of midnight with its sombre and religious majesty, the fury of the enraged sea, the sinister noise of battle, conjugal love, maternal tenderness, the feeling of cold terror? Where did she learn to understand the human heart?" Sometimes she talked on without understanding the meaning of the words. For instance she began to illustrate a story at the piano. It started: "A youth loved a maiden. . . ." For a moment she hesitated, then asked her father: "What is it to be in love?" Not until the answer satisfied her would she go on with the intricacies of her "opera." In the words of the writer: "At times she held to mezzotints—a really vague twilight, a point between being and not being, truths that deceive, lies that promise."

After that someone gave Teresita a strangely sophisticated plot to interpret. Completely unfazed, she evoked the mezzotints remarked by the writer of the article. "It was the perfect expression of hope without trust, of happiness without understanding, of wishing in which both confidence and doubt took part. Never before have I seen something become and be perfect all at the same time."

Meanwhile Fate, shaking her kaleidoscope, was on the point of transforming the regular pattern, by which the Carreños ordered their living, into a new and frightening one. Long conferences were being held at the hacienda of pioneer-spirited Grandmother Gertrudis, a del Toro unmolested by the demon of ancestral pride. Without the wisdom of her counsel no decision of importance was reached within the family circle. More forward-looking than Clorinda, she felt in closer sympathy with her son-in-law than with this daughter, whose mouth was already set in drooping lines of disenchantment. As soon as Grandmother Gertrudis was convinced that for the sake of Teresita's future the family must be transplanted to another land, she volunteered to sell her property to make the journey possible. Moreover, suddenly possessed by a youthful urge for adventure, she had no intention of being left behind. Preparations could not go ahead fast enough for her. To add to the confusion of packing and of farewell parties, as well as to Clorinda's reluctance to leave home, Emilia, not yet sixteen, insisted upon staying in Caracas to marry her first cousin. In partial compensation, Manuel Antonio's brother, Juan de la Cruz Carreño, doubly a member of the family through his marriage with María Teresa, Clorinda's sister, resolved to join the expedition with his wife and baby, Gertrudis. This was further augmented by five faithful servants, former slaves freed by the grandmother on the day of Teresita's birth, one an old woman who had been her personal maid since the age of twelve.

On the morning of July 23, 1862, a group of fourteen strangely assorted travelers, ranging in age from one to seventy-five, jogged over one of the most majestic and terrifying of roads, zigzagging down through solemn, naked, almost unpeopled country, on one side cliffs that shaded from terra cotta to rust, dotted with scraggly trees of unhealthy-looking green, and on the other abysmal precipices at once repellent and magnetic. After endless meandering there opened before the little company, already attacked by homesickness and dread of the unknown, a vista of reassuring blue, growing deeper as the road sank to the level of the calm Caribbean at the port of La Guaira.

From there they embarked at once to visit relatives at Puerto Cabello, an overnight journey westward along the South American coast. Teresita's fame had preceded her. Night after night friends were invited to hear her play. When her infallible memory had exhausted its store, she drew upon her imagination with matching success. It was an impressive escort of new converts that gathered to watch the *barca Joseph Maxwell* fade slowly out of sight on the morning of August 1 bound for Philadelphia. Off the coast of Santo Domingo, on the name day of that Saint, a hurricane gave the adventurers anxious moments. Twenty-three days later a much subdued band found harbor at last. Sheer exhaustion called for a week of recuperation before proceeding to New York, the real objective.

Once there, the Carreños were not entirely derelict. Acquaintances who had enjoyed their hospitality in Caracas retaliated in kind. That in North America, too, there was fighting among brothers, was not especially disturbing to Venezuelans. If anything it helped to make them feel at home. So in a furnished house on Second Avenue, a quarter approved by polite society, yet within their means, the travelers settled down without delay. The fading dignity of Knickerbocker days gave it a touch of formality, to which the Carreños naturally responded. Even

Teresita felt reassured. Her great worry had been that an English-speaking God might not understand the Spanish prayers of a little girl from South America. It was exciting to them all to be a part of the noisy current of life in the busiest city of the new world, hard as it was to adjust themselves to earlier rising and longer days of work. After the war, when he had become more familiar with the English language, Manuel Antonio meant to give piano lessons. Meanwhile Teresita and her little brother were sent to a private school standing in the spot now occupied by Wanamaker's store. The burning problem was to find the right teacher for Teresita.

The pianist of the hour was the great Louis Moreau Gottschalk. War had not kept him from playing day after day to crowded houses from coast to coast, in solo recital at that, and on that most brittle of instruments, the piano. A child of Louisiana, he reaped his first laurels in France. In New York that, even then, was a talking point in his favor. Berlioz heard him and wrote: "He is a consummate musician; he knows how far in expression imagination may go; he knows the limit beyond which liberties taken in rhythm only produce disorder and confusion; and these limits he never transcends." Victor Hugo was equally eloquent in his praise. Other less discriminating critics endowed him with the power of Liszt, the correctness of Thalberg, and the expression of Chopin himself. Fiorentino, the critic of *Le Corsaire,* closed the subject with these words: *"Après Gottschalk il faut tirer l'échelle."* Teresa Carreño many years later remembered that his playing was like zephyrs sighing on a poet's harp, that none approached him in his trill. And that was the opinion of one whose own trilling left whole audiences gasping with unbelief.

To New York Gottschalk became romance personified. His love affairs were pleasant scandal over the teacups, the envy of the most fastidious debutantes. New York delighted in his mannerisms, and applauded wildly when he seated himself at the piano, lazily drawing off his glove and running his fingers over the keyboard in prelude, as if dusting it. He had a melancholy air a little at odds with a trimly pointed mustache and an impeccably tailored suit, and he was apt to play with his head thrown back—and often with a cigar in his mouth—nonchalantly pretending to be alone with himself, to the hysterical joy of the listeners he treated so highhandedly.

To have Gottschalk hear Teresita became Manuel Antonio's dream. How could it be brought about? Among his friends were some who had known the master well in Cuba. But Gottschalk was known to be wary of prodigies. There was faint hope. Meanwhile the musical evenings of Caracas were duplicated in a new setting. Friends brought critics and amateurs to hear the little genius of the tropics. Her name penetrated artistic circles by the grapevine telegraph of hearsay. Invitations to the soirées on Second Avenue were seldom refused. They received more than casual mention in papers and journals. It was Teresita's extemporizing that drew forth the most comment.

An editor of the New York *Illustrated News* tells of such an evening:

We have heard her at her father's residence play the most delicious concerted music which she composes as she goes along. On one occasion she offered to compose an opera for me which at once showed her great power and her childlike simplicity. She commenced with an overture, and introduced a little girl as heroine of the play. After some fine music for the soprano, came a young man who made love to her, but he was not in favor with Papa. So another young man makes love to her, and he is rejected. The young men meet, and as neither can marry her, they resolve to kill her. They come upon the little girl who is dreadfully frightened, and seeing death before her, commences a prayer which we think one of the most feeling bits of music we have ever listened to, strong and original. The Papa comes just in time to prevent the murder. And then she was perplexed to know what disposition to make of her characters. Suddenly her face lit up with a happy thought. "Oh, I know, Father! I think the little girl had better go home to her Mamma." She sprang from the piano stool, and seizing a great doll that had been presented to her at one of her concerts, commenced squeezing it to make it cry, screaming with delight at the result.

Mr. J. G. Maeder, composer and professor of the pianoforte, also heard Teresita play at home. He reported that

she is very lively and childlike and received her visitors with perfect ease and gracefulness. . . . First she played a nocturne of her own, then an elaborate composition, uniting at one time no less than three separate themes. She attacked *Norma* with great spirit and immense power, work enough for four hands, not to say two, and those a child's.

Another writer, who calls himself "Amphion," noticed the slightly inclined curves in her forehead and her peculiar smile.

Even when her mouth is full of it, she does not lavish it as stupid people do, but holds it back like a thread of reflection, recalls it at pleasure, and closes her lips again. This control over her smile is the indication of a superior spirit. [He notices] the certain consciousness of power, a dominating quality, and the mystery in her eyes. The space between her eyebrows opens when she is gay, but it closes up frequently, a rare thing at this age, as if thereby she tried to ignore a familiarity that hindered her thought.

Wherever Teresita appeared someone was sure to voice the wish that she might be more generally heard. That was quite in line with Teresita's own desires. She was perpetually teasing to be allowed to play in a real concert, and Manuel Antonio was himself not averse to putting his daughter to the test of a private recital, admission being, of course, by invitation only.

He was still undecided when the matter was taken out of his hands by what at the moment seemed the greatest possible personal catastrophe, nothing less than the sudden death of the trusted friend who was administering the Carreño property in Caracas. The agreement had been purely verbal. To have asked for a receipt would have been an unpardonable breach of confidence. While the whole family was still in desolation over this misadventure, it became evident that his son and heir was made of different stuff. He pretended to know nothing about the funds that had been placed in trust with his father, funds that also included the grandmother's small fortune, and he made it clear that he would assume no obligation whatsoever for future remittances. The Carreño household was in consternation. The money in the combined family treasury might last a month with the rigid economy so difficult to carry out efficiently in a foreign land. Intimate friends were willing to help. But against this the pride of Spanish and Venezuelan ancestors revolted. Taking stock of their resources, it was found that there was not a single member of the group quickly able in this emergency to earn a living for a household of fourteen, always excepting a little girl of eight. And that, of course, was out of the question. Even supposing she were able, Clorinda never would consent to let the descendant of a Marqués del Toro play in public for money. While friends were clamoring, and Teresita was begging for the private audition that had been discussed, Manuel Antonio still vacillated. Without an opinion other than his own he dreaded exposing Teresita to the cold criticism of New York. It was left to Fate again to shake her kaleidoscope.

In the Carreño circle there moved a certain Simón Camacho, a writer who chose to publish under the pen name of "Nazareno." Urged by his admiration for Teresita, he achieved the impossible. In a letter written in Spanish he managed to awaken the curiosity of Gottschalk, and the meeting, finally consummated, could be described in no more telling manner than by his own pen.

In August I wrote the following letter which, scarcely dry, took wing over the mountains:

My dear Luis: I have here a little girl of eight years who plays the piano like T. . . , I will not say like "Te." Would you like to hear her? Come soon! She is your affair, and I should be sorry if somebody else presented her to you. If Mohamet cannot go to the mountain, the mountain will come to Mohamet. One word from you and you will see us in your beautiful *Tébaide*.

Two days later Gottschalk appeared in New York. Could he have believed me?

"Here I am," said he.———"Thank you," said I.

"Who is T. . . ?"——————" 'Te' is the accusative of 'Tu.' "

"But the child?" —————"Let us go to see her."

"And to hear her?"————"As you choose."

Luis shook his head in sign of unbelief. I felt as I suppose John the Baptist did when he announced the coming of the Messiah. Prodigies had so often fooled Gottschalk, there had been so many Papas and Mammas who had promised to show him marvels in their *primogenitos* or *primogenitas,* geniuses that turned out to be nothing more than *geniecitos* or better *pergenios,* that the king of the piano had good reason for being sceptical. "And is she pretty?" he asked.

"So lovable, so childlike!"

We left and soon arrived. The piano was opened. That silence is like no other.

The piano had sounded for some minutes, but only Gottschalk, in my opinion, had heard it. All the other spectators were concentrated on one object, hanging on one thought, one verdict, one sentence of life or death.

I did not even breathe, except perhaps to count. This scene had in it something very moving; you heard the beating of the heart of a mother; you saw the severe expression of a father change in the agony of uncertainty.

The king had not spoken, but—

I remembered the story of the bolero dancers accused in the court of Rome for the freedom of their motion. When least it might be expected the judges, in spite of their severity and the prejudices by which they were dominated, began to dance to the sound of the castañuela.

A few moments only, and Gottschalk, the king of the piano, was beating time with his head to a brilliant fantasia by Thalberg, played by Teresa Carreño.

Kindred geniuses saluted each other. The sun of midday, the sun rising in the east.

One second more and the word "bravo" escaped from the lips of Gottschalk. Concerted breathing, suddenly freed, echoed against

the walls of the *salón* covered with the portraits of the Knickerbockers.

Teresita was baptized in the font reserved for those famous in art.
Who ever had a greater godfather?

Gottschalk kissed her upon the forehead, and this kiss was the
seal of approval she had earned from the great maestro, and which
she still must win from the most commercial city of the Americas.

Somebody may think perhaps that I am painting for my own
pleasure an imaginary scene into which truth enters for very little.
I do not care to do so, but if anyone does not believe me, I have
the means of proving myself honest.

A delicate hint had sufficed to persuade Gottschalk to second
Teresita in an elaborate composition for four hands. Then at once,
moved by an irresistible impulse, the king, with all his inspired
enthusiasm, with all the feeling and fervor of which only passion
that has been stirred is capable, began to play himself. It was the
expression of gratitude which could not find outlet in words, and
which was much better understood in tone by this little angel, in
whom music was incarnate, and for whom harmonies had held
meaning before reason. When Gottschalk left the piano the blood
seemed to rush to Teresita's face, the beautiful black eyes grew
veiled as by a cloud, and all at once she fainted [but not without
first registering in her mind certain peculiarities of Gottschalk's
fingering and pedaling, according to her great-aunt Gertrudis].
Teresita for the first time had actually heard a genius play as she
had only imagined it should be done. Suddenly she experienced
that which she had thought impossible. The blow was too strong
for her childish constitution. Gottschalk's greatness had affected
her as if she were a lily bent double by a hurricane.

Her great friend, a Dr. B., warned the father: "Take care, great
care of this little girl, for she is a vial filled with more spirit than
it is naturally supposed to contain, and an explosion might result."

The trial by fire had proved the brilliant butterfly of the
Andes worthy. She had earned the right to try her wings in
larger space. Gottschalk himself urged it. Preparations began at
once for the private audition to which Manuel Antonio invited,
besides his own friends, every New Yorker prominent in music.

Irving Hall (now Irving Place theater) was the setting. It had
boxes and two balconies, seating 1,250 persons in all. L. F. Harrison lost no time. In making the contract he added a clause
that gave him exclusive right to engage Teresita for any future
performance in New York that season at $50 per concert. It
was not Manuel Antonio's intention that his daughter should
become a professional attraction at the age of eight. He was too
far-sighted to overlook the fact that Teresita needed schooling,
a far larger repertoire, and the teaching that Gottschalk had
promised her, whenever he should happen to be in New York.
He could afford to disregard that clause in the contract. To this
his brother, the lawyer, agreed. If there were another concert,
the $50 would be very welcome; if not, no harm was done.
Accordingly the date was set for the afternoon of November
7, 1862.

Then came the assembling of the program. Custom required
variety. In the case of a little child whose reaction to her first
large audience was not to be foretold, common sense, too,
advised it. The first choice as assisting artist was Theodore
Thomas, already a notable violinist in solo as well as ensemble,
and at the very outset of his career as conductor. The first time
Teresita had played for him—it had been the Chopin "Nocturne in E flat"—he had burst into tears. Teresita, uncompre-
hending, had turned to her father: "What is that man crying
for?" Years later, when she heard the young Josef Hofmann,
her question was answered. She too was moved in the same
way.

On the appointed afternoon the hall was well filled. Teresita's part of the program consisted of the "Souvenirs" from *Il
Trovatore* by Goria, "Grand Fantaisie" on *Norma* by Thalberg,
and the "Capriccio" on *Hernani* by Prudent, composers whose
flourishes have been outlived by the operas from which they
borrowed the most popular tunes. The success of the audition
was complete. Face to face with an unexplainable phenomenon,
the audience was enraptured. Teresita was in her element, es-

pecially when it came to Gottschalk's "Bananier," which she had just memorized in two days. The "Gottschalk Waltz" composed by her in his honor on the very day of their first meeting she also played at this matinée in four-hand arrangement with her father. It was at the end of this composition that the clapping had frightened her into taking shelter behind him.

At home for the moment calamity was forgotten in the happy confusion of Teresita's triumph. Even Clorinda, the undemonstrative, allowed the corners of her mouth to lift. She quite enjoyed holding court in reflected and silent glory among reporters, with whom she could converse only in the language of gesture and smile, and among friends who could give such effusive voice to their enthusiasm for the child she so quietly yet completely loved. It was the uncle who had to tell the gentlemen of the Press whatever they wanted to know, how much Teresita practiced a day, whether she were healthy, what she liked to eat, what her favorite playthings were.

Excitement rose to such a breath-taking pitch that Manuel Antonio was powerless to resist longer. He found himself falling in with L. F. Harrison's suggestion that Teresita give a public concert. The date was set for November 25. "I shall be an artist all my life," said Teresita. No more fervently did her great-uncle, Bolívar, take his oath on the *Monte Sacro*.

Ancestors may frown their darkest. Their part is played. On her inheritance Teresa Carreño y Toro is founding a truer, rarer aristocracy.

The momentum of the first concert produced a second and then a third, fourth, and fifth in close succession.

Gottschalk in Cincinnati wrote to L. F. Harrison:

I am really delighted that you are doing so well. Little Teresa seems according to what I see in the paper to be quite the furore now. I am very much pleased with it. She is not only a wonderful child, but a real genius. As soon as I am in New York, settled down and at leisure, I intend to devote myself to her musical instruction. She must be something great, and shall be.

There was another Irving Hall concert in which Teresita added the "Prayer" from *Moïse en Égypte* to her repertoire. This she supplemented with Mendelssohn's "Spring Song." More important and just as crowded was the one in the Academy of Music in Brooklyn, the Second Philharmonic Concert of that season. In it Theodore Thomas appeared as conductor of Beethoven's "First Symphony." Mme. Angri, soprano, and the Teutonic Choral Society assisted, Teresita of course being the prime attraction. It was nearly midnight when, obviously in need of sleep, she finally played Thalberg's "Variations on Home Sweet Home."

Another concert was a morning affair "attended by a large assemblage, many of whom were the young daughters of the best families not yet entered into society, and presenting an appearance fresh as spring flowers."

For a child and a novice, five concerts in three weeks were enough, decided the father. The insatiable Mr. Harrison thought otherwise. He conceived the master trick of his career. With his usual effrontery, he asked Manuel Antonio to give him a farewell concert on Teresita's ninth birthday, and to let him call it a benefit for her. Manuel Antonio, not realizing to what he was committing himself, politely consented. The elated manager outdid himself in propaganda, and so successfully that the Academy of Music, a hall seating more than 3,000 people, was filled to the last inch of standing room. Hundreds were turned away, everybody being very naturally under the impression that he was contributing his share to a handsome birthday present for the child who so lavishly squandered her gift of music.

The night of December 22 was cold and windy, the auditorium a bare and draughty place. To make it worse the heating system was out of order. From the beginning the temperature slowly began to sink to the freezing point. The first rows of chairs and the stage—the hall was designed for opera rather than for concert—were open to frigid air currents. A critic reports that two concerts were going on together, one consisting of the music on the stage, the other of coughs in the front rows. Teresita was the chief victim, and who but Teresita could have held for three hours the attention, enthusiasm, and applause of an audience martyred by cold? This child of the tropics dressed in gauze and tarlatan ignored the elements and actually raised the temperature by the fire of her playing, encouraging by her example Theodore Thomas and her other assistants to do the same. The only thing that mattered to her was that there were new pieces on the program that night. Gottschalk's "Last Hope" she had learned in a day, and a capriccio of her own was hurriedly dictated to her father that very morning. Again she played the "Gottschalk Waltz." The papers next morning declared that Teresita had never been in better form. But of the tremendous receipts of that evening's concert neither father nor daughter ever saw a penny. Even the birthday present that Mr. Harrison in a sheepish moment had promised Teresita was not forthcoming. Manuel Antonio's inconvenient pride kept him passive. At least artistically the success was unqualified. Teresita had won and kept her laurels. New York was hers. The way, in whichever direction she cared to travel, was paved.

AMONG her listeners in a New York recital had been Robert P. Haines of Boston. To him the stamp of New York's approval was not the final one. Boston was the musical Athens. New York might have a flair for the musically sensational; Boston knew what was musically right. It was due to his prodding that the reluctant father, who would have greatly appreciated a few months of Southern contemplation, was caught once more in the whirl of the land whose motto was: "Make hay while the sun shines." So, before the beginning of the new year Teresita with her father and her uncle, Juan de la Cruz, found themselves established in the comfortable Tremont Hotel of dignified tradition.

Their first disastrous experience with managers had taught them to be circumspect. George Danskin was very different from L. F. Harrison. He had a real liking for music, to the point of writing piano pieces now and then for his own pleasure. He knew his Boston and how to approach it. Here at last was the opportunity to add to the all-but-exhausted funds of the family. No time was lost. On January 2, 1863, little Teresita was ready for her second *"Bautismo de Gloria."*

At the first concert Boston had only a half-sized audience to offer her. *Norma, Trovatore,* "Home Sweet Home," the Doehler "Nocturne," and two Gottschalk compositions were on the program. A singer, Matilda Phillips, and the Germania Society's orchestra assisted. Most of the people who made up the audience were negatively prejudiced. Boston prided itself upon its appreciation of the classics, and therefore could well afford to look down with becoming superiority upon the virtuoso style rampant, which overflowed in obvious, florid cascades calling themselves *Souvenirs de—, Variations sur—,* and *Caprices sur* this and that. Here was a really formidable task for a prodigy's little hands.

The first surprise of the evening was to see running across the stage like any other child a real little girl, not a young lady dressed in memory of one. She looked scarcely taller than the

HAVANA 1863          BOSTON 1863

CINCINNATI 1864          NEW YORK 1864

*Teresita the Prodigy*

chairs she passed with a purposeful stride, and she still was obliged to mount her piano stool carefully, but evidently no longer needing a special platform for her feet. New York had already taught her to arrange her dress more symmetrically, and to improvise a prelude in elaborate imitation of the Gottschalk manner. That this child must be measured with the standards of grown artists Boston was quick to realize. In a hall, too large by far for a piano soloist, the noticeable flaw was lack of strength and security, mainly in octave passages. Playing without notes was then still something to exclaim about.

Rafael Pombo of the *Crónica,* a journal published in Spanish, tellingly described the Teresita of this time:

The most admirable in her execution is herself; the correctness of her taste; the inexplicable passion with which she plays; the use she makes of her physical means, of those tiny hands of a child of nine, without great visible effort and without disturbing, at least in expression, the look of serious and profound concentration which before the piano seems to submerge her in the moral depths of the composition; her electrical instinct for effect, the almost infallible clairvoyance with which she divines the secret intentions and feeling of a Mendelssohn, a Chopin, or a Gottschalk. She has an evident predilection for the simply touching and for the purely classic in form, and we have not heard her play badly, relatively, except a certain composition of mediocre value which did not enter into her choice. Genius has made her guess that violence is the force of weakness, and that there is nothing more poor than the merely spectacular music that seeks the strange and astonishing instead of the simple and the pure, and which sacrifices the idea to circumlocutory evasion of the point.

Pombo is here moved to quote Lamartine: *"L'homme n'enseigne pas ce qu'inspire le ciel."* And he goes on to describe her appearance more discriminatingly than anyone up to this time.

Physically Teresa Carreño is entirely beautiful, much more ample and robust than is usual in a child of nine, a most curious example of parallel development of the physical with the moral and intellectual, balsamic and eternal spring of the soil where she was born. Her head is large, and as an Englishman said, well equilibrated; the forehead notably undulated, prominent in the upper part, and with the arc of inspiration above the eyebrows; a straight, fine, and electrically mobile nose. A mouth of the most vivid scarlet reveals energy and at the same time allows a certain sweet and mournful expression to play. Her ear peeps out from the mass of ebony of her hair, large and gently inclined, just as the physiognomists could imagine that of a musician of vocation. The eyes are small in contour but enclose two large and very tender pupils of jet, reflections of moist light, which give the effect of a double brilliant point in each pupil. She has a delicate and graceful chin, a full and transparent looking face with that peachlike glow that seems as if it were inwardly lighted, a flexible neck, and admirable hands and arms. Away from the piano her expression is frolicsome, but as soon as she begins to play, the outline of her eyes seems to fill itself with shadows and tears as if the world of art and sadness pressed upon them.

A busy life began for the Carreños. Visiting cards with the picture of the prodigy in the corner had to be printed in haste to satisfy those who besieged Teresita at the hotel for autographs, or in her absence, just for a sight of the piano on which she practiced. Teresita was in her element. For once there were no school lessons. She could play as much as she liked, and in spite of the twenty concerts that followed each other in and near Boston, sometimes at the rate of two a day, she managed to add to her repertoire, and to compose a little besides. Her imagination was sometimes overstimulated. One night on entering a theater she was dreadfully frightened by a devil of her own invention. For the first time she and her father heard *Fidelio* together. During the intermission a group of friends were amused to hear her ask: "And tell me, Papa, those who are married in operas, do they stay married?"

Back in her hotel she read over a Chopin composition she had never before heard. In the delight of discovery she spread out her arms, drawing herself up to full height, as if to include the world. "From here to heaven, Papa," she shouted.

The second concert with an entire change of program had already taken place on January 8. Matilda Phillips again assisted, and Teresita played a nocturne by Ravinna, followed by one by Gottschalk for an encore; then Thalberg's *Moïse,* Prudent's *Hernani,* and the Chopin "Nocturne in E flat," which the papers called "really the gem of the evening."

It was Teresita's own idea to give a matinée for children. George Danskin too had imagination. He saw possibility in the interest children always take in their contemporaries. Such an event would be sensational, a good appetizer for the next big concert. He immediately addressed an open letter to the Chairman of the Public Schools.

Sirs: The kind reception accorded to Teresa Carreño in this city, and the unanimous approbation bestowed upon her performance at the Music Hall by the press and the public have been to her a source of much gratification. To mark her appreciation of so much kindness, and at the same time to demonstrate to children what a child may accomplish, I propose to give a matinée at the Music Hall on Saturday next, to which Teresa Carreño would be glad to invite the children of the public schools; apart from her love of music she is never so happy as when in the society of children. On receipt of your reply, should this meet your approbation, the requisite admissions will be provided for distribution as the teachers may direct.

The mayor of Boston, J. W. Lincoln, Jr., having given his sanction, Teresita presented the committee with 1,200 tickets for free distribution among the pupils selected from the Latin, English High, Girls High, Normal, and German Schools.

The concert was given two days later. Children sat in the balcony and overflowed onto the platform. Parents, friends, and spectators filled the orchestra seats. Teresita was the sole performer. "Last Hope," *Lucia,* and "Home Sweet Home" were the compositions listed. After each Mr. Lincoln stepped forward. "Will all those who wish to hear little Teresita play again please raise their hands!" And up went hands, fluttering handkerchiefs, and a whole chorus of cheers. Just before the last number a mite of seven presented Teresita with a basket of flowers as big as herself, and Teresita opened her arms wide to thank her with a warm kiss.

The next morning Mr. Danskin proudly flaunted a letter from Mayor Lincoln, which he took care to have published in all the papers of the city.

My dear Sir, I feel that Teresa Carreño and her guardians ought not to leave this city without a more permanent testimonial of her re- markable powers than I was able to present during a brief personal interview.

The concert was one of the most delightful musical entertain- ments ever given in our city. Music has recently become an im- portant branch of education in our public schools, and the example that this young pianist set before our children of her proficiency in the art, will, no doubt, have an inspiring influence. and excite them to greater exertions in their studies.

The winning simplicity of her manners, her apparent uncon- sciousness of her own merits—seeming only anxious to please oth- ers—adds a great charm to her musical performances; while the skill and artistic taste which she displays in execution, call forth the admiration of professional persons as well as every lover of art.

On the following Tuesday evening Teresita gave another solo recital in the more suitable setting of Chickering Hall. Although the price had been raised to a whole dollar a ticket, the place was crowded. For two hours Teresita played with but slight intermission, although there was a footnote on the program urging that no encores be demanded. The father had not feared fatigue for his daughter as much as the effect of an entire piano program on the audience. Teresita herself had no qualms. Lost in her music she played a barcarolle by Thal- berg, Goria's *Trovatore,* Mendelssohn's "Rondo Capriccioso," and Boston's favorite, the "Nocturne in E flat" of Chopin. To these she added *I Puritani* by Herz, and Doehler's inevitable "Nocturne." Of her own accord she appended a waltz of her own. Boston "gave way to the most boisterous and fantastic demonstration." Immaculate ladies left with bonnets awry and

gloves split open, forgetting umbrellas and purses. The Boston
*Herald* went so far as to say: "This little child has created more
excitement in musical circles, a more genuine furore than any
artiste who has been in Boston since the visit of Jenny Lind."

Other cities called for concerts by the pet of Boston—Providence, Cambridge, New Haven, and Salem among them. But
this did not prevent Teresita from incorporating Beethoven's
"Sonate Pathétique" in her repertoire, completely assimilating it
in less than a week. The Providence *Daily Post* grew romantic
like the rest over

the little sylph who comes upon the stage with wings of silk and in
drapery of white. Her venerable father is a musician, and has been
her tutor—Prospero and Miranda in the tempest of war and earthquakes among which they have lived! He has brought to us from
the mighty Orinoco and the shadows of the lofty Andes a spirit
as fascinating and beautiful as Ariel. If Church has ravished our
eyes by portraying their stupendous elevations, their boundless
sweep, their affluence of color and shape and cloud scenery in his
"The Heart of the Andes," la Carreño has taken captive our senses
by reflecting the diapason of nature as it bore upon her ears from
tornado and cataract . . . her notes are echoes of her native land.
A tourist in a fine extravagance has said: See Naples and then die.
But while dying he would now pray to hear Teresa Carreño. (Ra-
leigh)

Gilmore's Grand Band Concerts in Boston were the attraction for the many. Mass effects, stupendous variety, incongru-
ous mixtures, drew the crowds. This musical P. T. Barnum had
an unfailing instinct for box-office talent. He at once saw the
possibilities inherent in the combination of these monster performances and the most diminutive of pianists. Extremes were
his province. He succeeded through the lure of financial profit
too great to be refused in overcoming the scruples of Manuel
Antonio, and obligated Teresita for three closely fitting concerts. Two of them took place on Sundays, and were advertised in deference to Boston, the pious, as "sacred." At each
concert Teresita played only twice, two major works and some

encores. Mme. Anna Bishop sang, and several solo performers belonging to Mr. Gilmore's band took part. Teresita's "Polka-Caprice" appeared in these concerts for the first time. Band and orchestra combined their volume in potpourris and the "Julien Exhibition Quadrille." Teresita tactfully chose the most biblical compositions on her slate, Thalberg's "Prayer" and Gottschalk's "Jerusalem." In her encores she allowed herself to become more worldly. The Boston audience—these concerts were so popular that people had to be turned away—for once forgot its aversion to Sabbath applause and gave Teresita one of the heartiest of demonstrations, reaching a new height when she ended with her own arrangement of the "Star Spangled Banner."

There was one warning voice. Mr. Dwight of *Dwight's Musical Journal,* the most influential one of its day, admitted her genius but gave counsel: "May it only have wise training and not be early wasted before the public! It is too precious for continual exposure. Such gifts are of God, and should not be prostituted for mere gain."

NOBODY was prepared for the great climax of Teresita's Boston sojourn. One morning Mr. Danskin, purple and breathless, confronted Manuel Antonio with what he called the chance of a lifetime, the goal of ambition for the greatest virtuosi, the supreme of all coveted honors. It was not to be believed! Carl Zerrahn, Boston's beloved conductor, had offered Teresita an appearance in the Second Philharmonic Concert of the season. Manuel Antonio beamed.

"But he demands that she play Mendelssohn's 'Capriccio Brillante' with the orchestra," added Mr. Danskin.

Manuel Antonio's expression changed. "Impossible! She has never seen it, there are only ten days before the concert, and we have no copy of the music."

"At least permit me to get the music," countered Mr. Danskin. "If she is unable to learn it, she still can play her solos." And to this Manuel Antonio agreed. George Danskin dashed from place to place, but nobody in Boston appeared to possess the composition. In desperation he sent to New York. On the afternoon of Wednesday the music came, Friday was the day of the first rehearsal, and for Saturday the concert was irrevocably set. The only one who did not have a desperate case of nerves in the process was Teresita. Here was something fresh, something that fired her imagination. That nobody really thought she could do it put her on her mettle. And what fun to play with an orchestra of fifty musicians! She found that the martial theme memorized itself, that the passages lay comfortably for her fingers. The melodies she kept singing to herself, when she was not practicing them. Gradually, as they worked together, Manuel Antonio's fright gave way to hope, and then to confidence. The rehearsals went surprisingly well. Teresita at the piano, with or without orchestra, was as sure-footed as an eagle on his summit.

Again only Mr. Dwight voiced criticism. "Wonder children," he complained, "just now carry the day; and it is only those concerts in which little Miss Carreño plays that seem to pay; and for those there is a new name, to wit 'Musical Enterprise.'" Then he speaks of the "little magician who coins so many notes and dollars," and adds in complete desperation: "By the way another prodigy, Master Willie Barnsmore Pape, is coming."

The Boston *Transcript* went on with its encomiums regardless, backed by Carl Zerrahn himself: "The conductor begs leave to congratulate the Boston public upon the opportunity of witnessing this trial and triumph of the greatest prodigy which the world has known since the days of Mozart," it said. The advance notices of the program were headed: "Philharmonic Concerts. Carl Zerrahn has the honor to announce to his subscribers and the public that he will give his second Grand Philharmonic Concert at the Boston Music Hall Saturday evening, January 24th, 1863, assisted by Señorita Teresa Carreño and Mrs. Celia Houston Ford (pupil of Signor Bandelari) who will then make her first appearance in public."

The historic day was a busy one. For good measure Teresita had been allowed to send out cards for a reception to children in the Music Hall that very afternoon, the price of admission being twenty-five cents. The children of the Perkins Institute for the Blind came in a body, bringing her keepsakes of their own making. The program was short and not too taxing, Godefroid's "A Night in Spain," the "Last Hope," and the variations on "Home Sweet Home," followed by the "Star Spangled Banner" as amplified by Teresita. Far from tiring her, the foretaste inspired her for the more important performance on that evening.

The Music Hall was overcrowded, buzzing with conjecture. How could a little girl barely nine years old have the presumption to match her complete inexperience with the mature artists assisting her in a totally unfamiliar sort of ensemble? How could she with any understanding play a composition that four days before she had neither heard nor seen? Mr. Dwight slumped in his accustomed seat on the left side and expected the worst. "Musical Enterprise" was the right word for it.

Nobody paid much attention to the overture. When at last it was over, the orchestra had finished tuning, and Carl Zerrahn stood ready, Teresita entered the hall. As she mounted the stool before the piano, her friend, she gave Mr. Zerrahn a happy smile. With the dash and assurance of one too young to admit real difficulties, or to create imaginary ones, she began to relive the dramatic story of Mendelssohn's conceiving. She listened, blending with the orchestra, holding her own against its massive background, playfully letting the piano answer the liquid phrases of the flute, the winning melody of the violin in meaningful conversation. The orchestra and the pianist urged each other on to the final apotheosis. Then it was the turn of the audience to break in with uproarious applause, that, as for any keyboard veteran, no longer held terror for her. First shaking hands with Carl Zerrahn, she stood very still, while he spoke to the audience and then to her. She wondered what it was he was saying. Then he gave her a long scroll, and at last hung about her neck a heavy gold medal on the prettiest blue ribbon she had ever seen. For this her father had prepared her. He had told her to wait after her playing, to listen to Mr. Zerrahn, and should he give her a present, to say *"merci."* This she remembered to do before running off stage so fast that she caught and lost her heel on the steps of the green room, falling into the arms of her father, happily ready to receive her.

The strain of suddenly returning from the very stratosphere of music to the level of everyday excitement, the congratulations of overeffusive people, had been wearing after all. They would not leave her alone, even while Mrs. Ford was singing. Almost before she realized it, it was time for her solos, first a fantasia on *I due Foscari,* and then *Lucia.* The change from child to artist was too sudden. She had been playing for a time, when she awoke to the fact that she had lost her way. What should come next? There was a moment of hesitation. Manuel Antonio could feel the skin of his scalp contracting. "She is only a child of nine after all. Give her a present and she forgets her music," he thought. But Teresita was going on, not, to be sure, with the notes of the composition, but in a vein quite in keeping with it, until eventually she found her way back to the charted path. Manuel Antonio breathed again. He gave a quick glance at the redoubtable Mr. Dwight, who appeared not to have noticed the lapse. In a later intermission a prominent musician sought out Manuel Antonio, to ask whether Teresita had used a new edition. He had noticed an interesting variation not contained in others and, liking it especially, wished to acquire it himself.

Dwight again let his voice be heard. Although he goes on record to say that the child's face beams with intelligence and genius, and that those two qualities speak in a certain untaught life that there is in her playing, he once more gives advice: "The danger is lest her talent by such early exhibition and exposure should all run to waste in superficial, showy music. . . . Such a child needs a wise director, such as young Mozart found in his father." He suggests letting music lessons fade into the background for a year or two in order to give time for other training, physical as well as mental. It disturbs him that Teresita's arms seem to be unnaturally developed.

MANUEL ANTONIO must have taken these words to heart. How· ever for the moment there was no question of following their counsel. Boston was not yet willing to part with the prodigy. Her calendar was full. The Principal of the Elliott Grammar School invited Teresita to attend a gymnastic exhibition in her honor, for which she in turn gave thanks in music. She visited the Perkins Institute for the Blind. Invitations of a purely social kind poured in in unacceptable number. New *cartes de visite* had to be ordered, because for her farewell concert she wanted one for every lady in the audience. Teresita was not permitted to neglect her practice. Besides learning the "Sonate Pathétique" to please Boston, she meant to play some compositions in lighter vein by George Danskin in public as a surprise for him.

To Teresita the blue ribbon had meant more than the scroll signed by every member of the orchestra, which made her an honorary member of the Philharmonic Society. It pleased her more than the medal itself. Three inches in diameter this was engraved on the reverse side with a wreath enclosing a likeness of Teresita seated at the piano. The front bore the inscription: "Presented to Teresita Carreño, the child pianist, by the Philharmonic Society of Boston as a tribute of homage to her genius. January 24th, 1863."

Mr. Danskin at once acknowledged the tribute in a letter, also widely circulated by the Boston press. From Tremont House he wrote:

My dear Sir: In the name of Teresa Carreño, I have to thank you and your associates for the magnificent testimonial presented her this evening. It is the first public tribute she has received, and whatever may be her future artistic success, she will always with pride and gratitude remember the Philharmonic Concert at Boston Music Hall on Saturday evening, January twenty-fourth, 1863.

Inclosed you will be pleased to receive a note of thanks from the little girl. It is spontaneous on her part, the language in the simplicity of childhood; accept it in all its purity, it comes from the heart.

Teresita's letter was given in translation from the Spanish original:

Carl Zerrahn, esquire: You will pardon me if I cannot rightly express myself by word. When you gave me that pretty medal on Saturday night I did not know what it meant, thinking only it was a mere present to me; but when Mr. Danskin, the manager of my concerts, told me shortly after that the kind gentlemen who played with me presented it "as a tribute to my genius" I did know that you all feel kindly towards me and love me; that is all I hope for, for I do like to be loved and to be thought well of, and I shall always do my best to please, for my dear Papa and Mamma have always taught me to be good. With high consideration I am, Sir, your obedient servant, Teresa Carreño.

Everything Teresita did was of public interest, every detail of her life in Caracas. In imitation of her urbane father she had herself one day at the age of seven set up some maxims of her own. By chance they came to the attention of Mr. Danskin. He saw in them at once another angle of appeal. The next day they were published, reading:

1. Learn that you may teach.
2. Be not haughty, that you may be loved by others.
3. Take pity on the wicked, and endeavor not to be such.
4. Those children cannot be good, who do not respect their parents, and they are, moreover, considered as ill-bred. Children ought always to bear this in mind.
5. God says that he does not love those who are stubborn or speak falsehood. Children should therefore be good, and live in God, who is our Divine Providence.
6. Children should always be good and docile, and never allow themselves to be told things more than once. How much, then, they will be liked!
7. Avoid envy.
8. Children should always imitate a good example.

9. God ordains that we should protect old age when in want.
10. Never get angry, although you may have cause to be so.
11. The fear of the Lord ought to be the rule of our life.

From between the lines there emerges a little girl acknowledging the faults for which she had often been corrected, a little girl who would do anything for the sake of being loved by others, a little girl who dimly felt that hers was the responsibility of caring not only for her dolls but for her family.

It was time to take reluctant leave of Boston, and a veritable paradise it had been to Manuel Antonio. Here were human beings of his own kind, cultivated, tactful, and with proper reserve in their politeness! In New York he had disliked himself for this new state of mind, always on the defensive, this shell in which he could feel himself petrifying. At the earliest opportunity they must return to Boston, he decided. Perhaps later, since its tempo was congenial to them, they might even make a home there. Not the least of its charms was that Boston enabled them to return to Clorinda with the twin offerings of an artistic triumph beyond hopes and a heavy purse.

"One more concert," urged the impresario. It was set for January 27. To make a real climax of it, there had to be a special attraction. According to Teresita's wish, George Danskin promptly advertised that the *cartes de visite* were in process of printing, one for each lady in the audience as a gift, "and they will with such a subject produce gems of photographic art." He announced further that Teresita's selections were to be the choicest of her repertoire, and that not only would the "Sonate Pathétique" be among them, but also the "Capriccio Brillante" repeated with quintette accompaniment. It was Teresita's own idea to play a polka-mazurka, called "Rachel Adorée," in special tribute to its composer, Mr. Danskin, and her final encore was a waltz dedicated to the ladies of Boston by Teresita herself. Fittingly she called it "L'Addio." All agreed that the "Sonate" had been the high point of the evening.

A farewell it was not yet to be. The gentlemen did not wish

to be outdone by the ladies. A group of them asked to arrange a final testimonial concert by Teresita and for Teresita alone in Chickering Hall on the following evening. All the tickets were quickly sold at $1 each, the purse presented to Manuel Antonio containing $260. Again the "Capriccio Brillante," suitably accompanied by the Mendelssohn Quintette Club, appeared on the program, and this time a waltz by George Danskin. After the last encore a lady well known in musical circles hung another medal of gold around Teresita's neck. It was engraved with a harp, a drum, and other musical instruments, and with a dedication from the musical amateurs of Boston. The uncle responded for Teresita in a few graceful words of thanks.

Boston had adopted the Carreños. They were people more at home in a drawing room than in a box office, a gratifying contrast to ill-mannered prodigies, accompanied by vulgar parents with acquisitive eyes. Teresita's concerts, for a time the daily topic of conversation in Boston society, faded into memory more gradually than the smoke of the train that carried three happy people back to New York. Had Boston been given to more spontaneous expression, it might have echoed as a parting blessing the words of Felipe Larrazábal: "May Heaven grant that the sublime artist of Caracas shall always sing of pain not felt, torments and grief not suffered; and that like the bird that swings contentedly on the branch of the acacia, she may dissipate in magnificent chords the tempests of the heart that agitate and harm our miserable existence." And many there were who did not cease to wonder that one of those who brought comfort and forgetfulness in this time of conflict between brothers should be a little girl of nine from a country which stood for nothing if not for perpetual fratricidal war.

MANUEL ANTONIO would have been glad to follow Mr. Dwight's advice then and there. He had learned a great deal in Boston and was too wise not to realize that public taste was changing, that even now a program called for something more solid than empty arrangements of operatic airs. Before all Teresita needed a larger repertoire, assimilated in peaceful concentration. Again circumstances forced him to decide otherwise. One of his many Venezuelan friends in Cuba urged that Teresita be brought to Havana. He insisted upon immediate departure, lest the beginning of the heat wave make concerts unproductive. Gottschalk promised to throw the weight of his recommendation in the balance with letters to influential people. The managers made stupendous concessions, and altogether the knock of opportunity became too insistent to be disregarded. Secretly, also, Manuel Antonio longed to be once again his own interpreter, to speak his own language in a country that already knew him as the author of the *Urbanidad*. He decided to risk the journey.

Gottschalk himself announced his protégée to the journals of Havana:

Teresa Carreño does not belong to the kind of little prodigy that we have been judging for the last twenty-five years; Teresa is a genius, let us say it at once; she is only nine years old; she is a veritable child full of that indolent yet happy grace of her age. One need not have any fear for her; she never inspires a feeling of pity. On hearing her one sees, one feels at once that Teresa plays the piano as the bird sings, as the flower opens its petals. She is born to music, she has the instinct of the beautiful—she divines it! Her compositions reveal a sensitivity, a grace and an artistry like those that seem to be the exclusive privilege of work and maturity of age. I have only given her six or eight lessons, and nevertheless they were enough to conquer obstacles that for others would have been insuperable barriers. She belongs to the class of those privileged by Providence, and I have not the slightest doubt that she will be one of the greatest artists of our age. L. M. Gottschalk.

To his close friend, Espadero, he could write more fully and freely:

She is a genius—I have only been able to give her five or six lessons, and although she never had a teacher who knew anything (this is between ourselves) she already achieves a thousand miracles.—I wish you to do all you can to help her. She is a lovable, enchanting little girl. She understands everything good. Her father is an accomplished gentleman, distinguished, honored, and of good family. The child has tiny hands and nevertheless (you must take into account that she never heard anything in Caracas) does outstanding things; she has good musical ideas, and composes well by instinct. I would like to have you sing her praises in the newspapers. Look out for her.

Shortly before her departure from New York Teresita played once more at a private soirée in her own home. As always in the company of intimate friends she was happy and mischievously inclined. After she had played the "Prayer" from *Moïse,* she swung around upon her stool and said: "Now I will compose an opera for you." A journalist reported it thus:

A young girl stood in her window, and the count who was in love with her passed by and began to ask her to marry him; the young girl did not care for him, and retired from the window, the count to the corner. Just then a king passed, and he also asked the young girl to marry him; but the young girl would not admit him either. So the two lovers, meeting each other, began to fight, and the count was killed. The second act she played and explained at the same time. The king and the young girl were alone in the living-room; the king made love to the young girl. She rejected the crown, because she cared for one, who, in the form of a little mouse, by the power of a witch, had been able to introduce himself into the palace. With the avowal that she loved another, she cried that her resistance would be unconquerable. But a king does not resign himself to be disdained, and he began to struggle with the young girl, a struggle in which passion and jealousy were let loose, and he threatened to use his power to obtain the love of the young girl; but just then the lover discarded his humble disguise, and avenged with the death of the king the insults to which his loved one was subjected. The principal thought came opportunely as in the works of the great masters, and at the end predominated in the final duo, sung while the marriage was being celebrated, and while we heard the bells toll for the burial of the king. The auditors looked at one another without saying a word, while Teresita called for a dish of ice-cream in reward for her accomplishment.

WITH only few weeks at home for preparation, "Prospero and Miranda" set sail for their third adventure accompanied by Clorinda. Just as she was leaving, Teresita had the satisfaction of seeing her "Gottschalk Waltz" in print with her portrait in a favorite pose engraved upon the cover. Her chin rests on her hand, her elbow on the keyboard of the Chickering. She is wearing her medals in a row pinned to her concert dress. Three large editions were exhausted within a year.

Arrived in Havana late in March, the Carreños put up at the Hotel Inglaterra. It was found inadvisable to arrange a concert during Holy Week, so giving Teresita a welcome interim for rehearsal and practice.

As in New York, it was thought well to have critics and musicians hear Teresita before her first formal concert. The hotel was the right place for such an event. On the chosen day two large connecting rooms were thrown open to the élite of musical Havana. When Teresita appeared, unconcerned as if she were alone with her family, it was not of music that she spoke but of her beautiful New York doll. At her mother's suggestion she produced it, leaving it for her to hold, while she played and improvised upon the piano. One of those present at this hearing was a prominent lady of Havana whom mourning prevented from attending a more public affair. It touched her so deeply to see little Teresita run from her piano directly back to her great baby doll that on the next Sunday there arrived a large mahogany cradle, perfect as if for a real child, furnished with every necessary thing: sheets of batiste, a little mattress and down pillows, a coverlet of muslin embroidered in French roses, pillow cases trimmed with white lace and tied with pink satin ribbon, and finally curtains of finest cambric gathered together with three bows of pink satin. Teresita was in ecstasy. For this she would have given all her medals without a thought.

This musical introduction, together with the pressing letters of friends, created an atmosphere of adulation. The Cubans could be as extreme in their worship as in their hatred. A group of journalists outdid themselves in eulogies and exaggerations. Chopin and Mozart were overshadowed by Teresita Carreño; her little hands were said to be a conductor between the piano and Heaven; she was called "a miracle of instinct possessing the gift of divine prophecy." To one enthusiast it seemed that when the prodigious Venezuelan child plays it is not the piano nor any other instrument that we hear; it is a supernatural voice, a voice that does not articulate, yet that holds all shades of articulation, the voice of intelligence that sings without the organism, the voice of the heart that weeps without the aid of the eye. Teresita Carreño is the great mathematician of harmony. She is also the chemist, the metaphysician, the poet, and the orator of harmony, the universal queen of sound.

Within a group of the more independent critics Espadero was the most levelheaded. He had at once called upon the Carreños in order to judge for himself of Teresita's talent. Although he frankly admitted and admired her natural musical organization and her mechanical gifts, when Mozart and Chopin and other great musicians were belittled in comparison, that was too much. He felt it his duty to counterbalance the blind encomiums of the romantic Cubans. Like Mr. Dwight he wished to warn Teresita's parents that, before she could hope to measure herself with Camilla Pleyel or with Clara Schumann, she must have more serious education.

His remarks were met with derision, and even attributed to personal jealousy by Manuel Antonio, who was heard to remark to a friend that, when Espadero was about, he never dared to stir from Teresita's side for fear that she might be poisoned. But these were after all only minor flurries, and the day came for which everyone was waiting breathlessly, the Havana début of Teresita Carreño on April 8, 1863 in the hall of the Liceo, where Gottschalk, Ole Bull, and Jenny Lind had preceded her.

Cubans liked music, not for its deeper meaning as much as for its value as entertainment. Programs were hastily made up, adding ensembles of local talent to the offerings of the imported one. Teresita's was no exception. It opened with the "Theme and Variations" for flute and piano composed by the father of a Havana pianist. Then Teresita appeared. She presented herself with "enchanting gaucherie." So brilliantly gowned were the ladies, that the men were hardly noticed. One critic describes her as a "plump, funny child," and speaks of

her caressing glances, delicious arms roundly developed, and ending in model hands, chubby, perfectly shaped, the fingers neither short nor long, and of exquisite delicacy. . . . She wore white pantalettes trimmed with lace, a dress of knee length made of white gauze sprinkled with gold and scarlet dots that were almost unnoticeable. Around her waist she wore a very narrow ribbon of scarlet grosgrain fastened below the shoulder, and falling in long streamers over the skirt. The décolleté was somewhat pronounced, the sleeves very short, the arms bare. Around her neck she wore an extremely simple and fine gold chain, and over her breast on the left side hung two medals, a large one and another smaller one of gold in the shape of a star. Her short hair was trimmed to look almost like that of a boy. A little higher than the forehead she wore a band of narrow scarlet velvet ribbon very tastefully arranged, which enhanced even more the childlike beauty of the enchanting little girl. As an artist she resembles no one but herself. She touches the keys in a special manner with all the grace of a child, with all the sensitiveness of a woman, and at the same time with all the aplomb, all the energy and all the assurance of great professors.

Her contributions were the Doehler "Nocturne," the "Capriccio" of Mendelssohn accompanied by five musicians, and Gottschalk's "Last Hope." To this she added her "Saludo a Cuba" and the fantasia on *Il Trovatore*. Smothered under baskets and wreaths of flowers, with one of which she was crowned, this "colossal miniature of the garden of music" ended her first Havana triumph. Unanimously, even to Espadero himself, Havana agreed that "Teresita is the incredible become manifest."

The second concert warranted a larger hall. It took place in the Teatro Tacón, not quite filled, yet nevertheless holding an audience that was a compliment to the prodigy. After the overture to *Semiramis,* played by the Band of the Royal Engineers, Teresita entered on the arm of her father. She was immediately presented with a huge bouquet of pinks of all shades surrounding a lovely doll, dressed and decorated in the most perfect taste, and holding with both hands a golden ring enameled on the outside in blue with the name of Teresita Carreño. From the bouquet hung two streamers of red satin ribbon, one embroidered with her name and the other with that of the donor. In this larger place the Chickering lost much of its volume, but it pleased the audience that she played an impromptu of her own, dedicated to Espadero. After she had played her favorite nocturne of Chopin particularly well, a boy of her own age presented her with a wreath and bouquets of flowers. Half a century later it was this same little boy, become a famous oculist, who ministered to her again in Havana at the time of her final concert upon earth. With this little boy's father, Señor Desvernine, she played a fantasia by Pixis for four hands, then a "Jota de los Toreros" with her own father. After Prudent's *Lucia,* two assisting artists placed a wreath around Teresita's neck, and to honor her yet more the band finished with an arrangement of "Saludo a Cuba."

Before she was permitted to leave, the Liceo de la Habana, the most representative musical and literary organization of the island, stepped in to demand her appearance on April 25, 1863. Teresita reserved her most serious works for this occasion, the "Ballade in A flat" of Chopin and the "Sonate Pathétique." From the beginning the occasion was conducted with great ceremony. Don Pablo Miarteni, president of the Musical Section of the Liceo, was in charge. At his side on the platform sat Cristóbal Mendoza the poet, who read a long poem in Teresita's honor after the "Sonate." Then a wreath of roses with two streamers hanging from it was placed upon Teresita's head.

There was further praise in prose and verse, and in final culmination the vice-president of the Division of Literature read and presented her with a scroll which read:

The Department of Music of the Liceo of Havana bestows its membership upon Teresita Carreño, believing that there was not manifested sufficient proof of the enthusiasm she has inspired by her natural talents, and her extraordinary merit. Interpreting the wish of the Liceo, and of its numerous members, it extends this certificate, signed by the Board of Directors of the Society, in which is shown the favorable reception that this child artist has had on the different occasions when she has performed upon the piano. Her great youth, her undeniable genius, her spontaneous dexterity have been generally recognized and appreciated. Teresita Carreño by taking part in the exercises of the Liceo, April 25, has marked with the stamp of her Spanish-American genius the history of the artistic labors of this body, which prides itself that her name now appears in order among those of other members, and which, in honor of her genius, now takes this opportunity to place its certificate in her hands in the presence of this audience. Subscribed by the President, Director, and Secretary of the Division of Music of the Liceo of Havana, April 25, 1863.

A luncheon followed these exercises. On the way home Teresita, who had found it impossible to understand, or to attend to everything that was said, asked her father what it meant. He explained at length the significance of being made an honorary member in so exclusive a group. Teresita was not impressed. "I should have liked better to be named Secretary," she declared.

Immediately after this event the Carreños left for Matanzas. Time pressed. Rain, for a moment cooling the atmosphere, moistened the earth only to rise again as a steaming vapor. In Matanzas Teresita found time for play with little girls of her own age, while preparing, this time with orchestral background, for her concert in the hall of the artistic and literary Liceo of this city. The Doehler "Nocturne" opened the program. Then came a Gottschalk dance, "Dí que Sí," in four-hand form, probably with her father. As a tribute, the orchestra played a pretty little schottisch composed by Doña Pilár Ortiz and called "La Bienvenida a Teresita Carreño." When the concert proper was over, the entire Board of Directors of the Liceo de Matanzas, followed by Teresita on the arm of her father, gathered upon the platform, and as a tribute to real genius, two very delightful young ladies placed a wreath of gold upon her brow, a procedure to which Teresita was by this time well accustomed.

So the most outwardly rewarding of the three adventures ended on a note of triumph. In New York it was Teresita, the novelty; in Boston, Teresita, the musician; in Cuba, Teresita, wonder child of a sister nation, who drew the crowds. The concert season was everywhere at a close, and at last the Carreños could afford the luxury of returning to privacy at home. There was time to give thought to a much neglected little brother. Teresita had a maternal feeling about him, almost as if he were another doll of her responsibility. Meanwhile the family of Juan de la Cruz and Grandmother Gertrudis, the brave, were suffering from homesickness. A longer stay in New York could mean only futile expense and another problem for Manuel Antonio and Clorinda. One summer day they sailed back to Venezuela, Gertrudis to spend the last years of her life with her favorite daughter, María Teresa, living simply but happily in the surroundings to which she now was sure she belonged.

A VENEZUELAN to this day prefers to visit France rather than the United States. His children are sent there to be educated, he learns at least something of its language, and his wife imports her clothes from Paris. Common racial background makes each feel at home in the land of the other. Purely personal reasons kept Manuel Antonio from choosing this more usual course. The first year in North America had shown him that momentary success was not difficult of achievement there. Permanent success, however, could not be counted upon without the seal of European commendation. His original plan to develop rather than exploit Teresita's genius and to take her to Paris for that purpose, thanks to the income from the Boston and Havana tours, could now be carried out.

This time his own condition of health interfered. Manuel Antonio took life seriously. The conflicting problems of fatherhood, business, and art, in combination with the unfriendly climate of New York, had been to such a degree taxing that a complete rest of some months was the physician's ultimatum. So the life of the household on Second Avenue settled down to a routine like that of any average family. Teresita learned English quickly, but attended none too eagerly to her other lessons. She had tasted the power that being the breadwinner gave her, and after months of knowing herself the first person to be considered, she naturally found it hard to subordinate herself again as the obedient daughter. She knew that she had genius. Her father had wisely taught her that it was a quality to be respected, until it seemed to her something detached from herself, something to be dutifully venerated, almost like Mary, the Virgin. Occasionally it even became a nuisance. She found it irritating when other little girls treated her with diffidence and awe, not as they did each other. For her it was no harder to divorce the child from the artist than it had been for the lover in her opera to change from mouse to man, and no witch was needed to show her how.

In the fall of 1863—Teresita had continued to play here and there as occasion presented itself—there came a breath-taking invitation. President Lincoln wished to hear Teresita in the White House. Manuel Antonio forgot his ill health, Clorinda's needle shuttled in and out more busily than ever. So significant an honor warranted a new dress.

Although the letter from the White House stressed that Teresita would play quite informally for the family alone, it was of importance that every detail be perfect, especially the program, which Manuel Antonio planned and replanned until it suited him completely. He did not concur in Teresita's abject devotion to Gottschalk and his music. Secretly glad not to have his daughter exposed too often to the influence of this artist, his own taste leaned more and more strongly in the direction of the classics. Whatever suggestions he gave Teresita at this time rebounded from a mind negatively set. She refused to commit herself in advance to any particular compositions. Neither would she be moved to take the occasion seriously enough to practice for it. The more she felt her father's anxiety, the more nonchalant she appeared. On the way to the White House, even, she assumed complete indifference to his advice on proper deportment and procedure. He urged her to begin with a Bach "Invention," to which Teresita said nothing, having already made up her mind that nobody should dictate to her.

The formality of presentation went off without incident. The Lincolns were friendly and natural. Time came for the music. Teresita tried the piano stool; it squeaked and was unsteady. She ran her hands over the keys; the action was hard, and she frankly registered complaint. At a look from her parent she decided to begin. Bach, indeed! Striking a few introductory chords with a disagreeable clang that made her father jump, she plunged of all things into Gottschalk's "Marche de Nuit," then not giving her father even a second's chance to object, she modulated into the "Last Hope" and not inappropriately ended with his "Dying Poet." The President and his family found nothing amiss with her choice. Then abruptly she jumped from the stool, declaring that she would play no more on a piano so dreadfully out of tune. Her father but for his *Urbanidad* would have had a nervous breakdown on the spot. It was Mr. Lincoln who saved the situation. Very quietly and with his irresistible kindness he asked, "Teresita, do you know my favorite song, 'Listen to the Mocking Bird'?" Teresita nodded. "Would you play it for me? It would give me great pleasure." She condescended to announce the tune, and with that for a portal, suddenly inspired, she made her way through an endlessly winding path of improvised variations, stopping at last only from sheer exhaustion. Her father wiped his forehead. "What a fiasco!" He did not see that there were tears in Mr. Lincoln's eyes. Mrs. Lincoln too had swayed sympathetically to the familiar rhythm. Only Tad, the Harvard Senior, looking out of the window, was obviously bored. Manuel Antonio, impatient that the audience be terminated, at last bowed himself out of hearing with profuse apologies.

On her tenth birthday Teresita again found herself playing upon the familiar stage of the Music Hall in Boston. This time there was a rival attraction in the city, the "Sanitary Fair." In spite of it she was not forgotten. The announcement of her concert read: "Teresita Carreño's first Grand Concert, Tuesday evening, December 22nd, 1863, on which occasion she will be assisted by the eminent organist B. J. Lang, who will display the powers of the great organ." It was a new one, and a part of the returns from the concert was to be used to help pay for it. An organ "Prelude and Fugue" by Bach opened the performance. Teresita played the "Marche de Nuit" of miserable memory, and, after an organ version of the "Overture to Egmont," the paraphrase by Liszt of Verdi's *Rigoletto*. Another recent acquisition was played by Teresita, a grand caprice on "La Sonnambula" in transcription by Thalberg. After this she added several things of her own, a set of variations on Gottschalk dances among them. Mr. Dwight again registered a complaint:

The two things do not match in any way; the organ sounds purposeless, the piano feeble. [But he was compelled to concede:] She has gained much power, certainty in executing difficulties, intelligent conception, while her touch has a fine, vital, sympathetic quality. The most fresh and individual were the little compositions of her own which really show music to be the world she is most at home in.

[Other critics were more voluble:] Her figure has gained in fullness and strength, and there is no suggestion of overwork in her hearty laugh and hundred caprices. If her playing was before remarkable for a child, it would now be remarkable for a woman. She has acquired new command over the mechanism, and where there were formerly blurs and inconsistencies of reading, all is now clear and coherent. . . . The early maturity of her tropic blood manifests itself.

Teresita's birthday present from her father was a large book bound in bright red Morocco leather, hand-tooled, and inscribed in letters of gold, "Al Genio." The blank leaves were multicolored. In it Teresita's concerts from the beginning were to be recorded through criticisms and other clippings. It was carefully kept in Manuel Antonio's fine, neat handwriting until her years as a prodigy were over.

A private soirée had taken place before the concert in the Music Hall. After a Spanish dance of her own she had added a polka completed that morning. In it the reviewer finds her "as classical as the most classic." The Grand Concert was to be immediately followed by another in which every seat in the hall was to sell for fifty cents. A felon on one of her fingers interfered with the plan and threatened to incapacitate her for some time, putting an abrupt end to this Boston visit.

For three months Teresita had vanished completely from the professional horizon to appear again in the spring of 1864 at a private gathering of about a hundred people at the Carreño residence. A distinguished audience, including Major General Dix, was assembled to hear her. Teresita played a Beethoven sonata and Thalberg's "Les Huguenots." Following immediately upon this soirée a New York concert in Dodworth Hall on Broadway at Eleventh Street was so successful that it had to be repeated on April 18. Now it was Philadelphia's turn. Assisted by a company of brilliant vocalists, Teresita played on April 21 and 22 with Mason's "Silver Springs" as a now-popular newcomer on her repertoire.

In Baltimore Teresita remained for more than a week. The experiment of engaging the monumental Assembly Hall and of selling tickets at fifty cents each did not at first hearing produce the large audience expected, but Teresita appeared in her very prettiest dress and in her best form. As a new departure the program embodied an improvisation on modern airs. Teresita had suggested it herself and felt so much at home that she could be heard above the piano, singing along with it in her clear and shrill soprano. Wreaths and a first gold watch were her material souvenirs. Day after day she appeared in smaller public events, or in private entertainments, at last, most exclusive of all, within the silence of convent walls.

The strain of late hours, irregular meals, and social duties was beginning to tell on both father and daughter. The tempo of living had again been forced beyond natural limits, and signs of its unwholesome effect were noticeable in Teresita. She was disobedient, demanding, and generally difficult, nervous, much thinner, and growing too fast. It was time to call a halt. Manuel Antonio's own health needed the repairing influence of home and time, little Manuel the authority and discipline of a father, and both children, having advanced beyond Clorinda's powers of instruction, systematic schooling. Money was no longer the chief worry. Manuel Antonio now knew enough English to give music lessons even to monolingual Americans. So for more than a year, Teresita flourished in the impenetrable silence so tantalizing to the biographer. Meanwhile in Manuel Antonio the great objective of every Venezuelan, to see Paris, had time to crystallize.

TERESITA was in her twelfth year, but appeared older, giving promise of great beauty. She had lost the chubby appeal of childhood and its unself-conscious, demonstrative charm. Slender, with a nobility of carriage that made her look taller than her size, her curls tied back simply with a wide ribbon, she was the type of aristocratic Spanish girlhood. Liberal schooling in poverty and profession gave her the appearance of a person ready for emergency, with a will to conquer.

On March 31, 1866, the four Carreños braved the ocean, this time on the steamer *City of Washington*. Scarcely out of harbor the ship hit a sandbank, shivering with the force of impact. Only a few hours of delay and she was afloat again. Nobody was particularly apprehensive. Two days later a sudden report! The boiler had cracked. Caution should have dictated a return to the nearer port, but the captain preferred to trust to his invisible star. So on they went under sail. Passengers grew restless; the sky clouded; stormy weather blew up; high waves washed wildly over tipping decks. On the seventh day the rudder, weakened by the collision, broke off and was swept away. The *City of Washington* tossed about from wave to wave, drifting farther and farther out of the usual sea lane. Rescue appeared more and more improbable, then hopeless; food was becoming scarce. Among the passengers there was stark terror. The women, those who were not too ill to care, prayed and whimpered. The men, expecting to be drowned in each successive assault of the storm, preferred not to meet death in their senses, and drowned themselves prematurely in drink. The only stabilizing element in this chaos seems to have been a little girl. Quite calmly she tried to reassure her despairing mother.

"Don't cry, Mamacita, we shall arrive safely, I am sure."

Clorinda was silenced and amazed by her confidence.

"But how do you know, my child?" she asked.

Teresita replied unshaken, "I don't know it; I feel it."

This was an early instance of those rare flashes of intuition, almost clairvoyance, that accompanied Teresita throughout her life. Had she always followed their dictates later on, she would have made fewer mistakes.

Days later, true to Teresita's prophecy, there appeared upon the horizon the hulk of a large steamer, the *Propontis*. It was actually answering the distress signal of the *City of Washington* and approaching to her rescue. The passengers were transferred at infinite risk by being swung out over the angry ocean on pulleys in a barrel, one by one, and then lowered into the dancing lifeboats that served as go-between. Intermittent lightning and thunder added a lurid element of melodrama to the scene. A day and a half of heroic effort, and the 250 passengers were all safely carried over, taking with them only the clothes they wore. The *City of Washington* was left to dance until called for and was towed in weeks later. Quite in keeping with this hapless voyage, the *Propontis,* too, developed engine trouble and proceeded under sail. It was in no way equipped to supply a double set of passengers with food. Careful rationing had almost reached the bread-and-water level when Liverpool was sighted.

THE concert season in Paris was ending. The Carreño pocket-book desperately needed replenishing. A few recitals would be helpful. Manuel Antonio had counted upon them. Without a thought of rest the voyagers took the first opportunity to cross the Channel, arriving in France on May 3, 1866. After a month on the ocean, modest hotel rooms in Paris seemed Walhalla itself, and before the pavements felt quite solid under her feet Teresita was making new friends. Her French, with its amusing mixture of Yankee and Spanish-American tang, was passable, although on her tongue the gently curving line of French speech changed into brittle ups and downs, like the waves from which she had so recently escaped.

Teresita's first conquest was Mme. Érard, at whose house she met many musicians of quality. The story of the shipwreck was a potent introduction in itself, and when Teresita was quite able to arouse enthusiasm by her playing without making excuses for a pianoless month, Mme. Érard at once resolved to do all she could for the child. First of all a piano was sent to Teresita's hotel that she might practice. Next she arranged for a hearing before two competent pianists, M. Delcourt and M. Krüger, on May 5, just two days after Teresita's arrival. The success of this preliminary audition was such that Mme. Érard was moved to plan more important ones. On May 7 she presented her protégée to M. Quidant, well known as a composer, and to M. Vivier, the popular virtuoso of the horn. M. Quidant was stirred by Teresita's sympathetic interpretation of Chopin, but it was the "Marche Solennelle" of Gottschalk that won over M. Vivier. By happy coincidence this favorite of Paris society was about to stage his annual concert in the Salle Érard. It had not been his intention to number a piano soloist among the performers assisting him. After hearing the new prodigy he quickly changed his mind. A début under more favorable auspices could hardly be imagined. Besides offering promise of a fee to help bolster up family finances, Vivier's concerts were always well attended and by the right people.

Delighted with the playing of her first hand, and always mindful of the closing of the concert season, Mme. Érard promptly dealt another. It proved to be an even more lucky one for Teresita. On the evening of May 10 father and daughter were received by the aged Rossini himself in his ornate apartment, 2 rue de la Chaussée d'Antin. A spark of instant liking flared between the little foreigner and the maestro. To Teresita celebrities were just people like any others. Differences in years, she had also learned, were not necessarily a barrier to friendship and understanding. She for one was never more happy than in the company of those of another generation. At once completely at home in a setting pervaded by Rossini's geniality, Teresita took her seat at the piano, while Rossini as was his custom prepared to listen from an adjoining room. In compliment to her host, the composer, she chose the "Prayer" from *Moïse*. As the last note faded, Rossini crossed the room, applauding and shouting "Bravo, my child! You are a great artist!" Turning to Manuel Antonio who might well feel honored in his own right as a teacher, he analyzed his impressions more precisely: "I do not understand how this little girl plays as she does. The evenness and clearness of her arpeggios are as astonishing as the clarity with which she brings out the melody of the prayer." Spontaneously moved to be of practical use, he urged that Teresita be presented in London, volunteering to pave the way. Then at his request Teresita played the "Ballade" of her composing. Rossini applauded enraptured, insisting that she find a place for it on her first program. But this Teresita was too modest to do. Although visitors were expected to depart before ten o'clock, Rossini would not let his new friends leave before he had heard Clorinda's favorite, the "Fantaisie" on airs from *Norma*. In one evening the great artist had become the staunch ally of the prodigy. Through his influence many an obstacle was removed, many a door opened. As if he were her personal agent, he commandeered one after another of his acquaintances to the service of his "little colleague," as he liked to call her. *"Allez au concert de Vivier. Vous y entendrez*

1866

1867

1868

1870

1872

*Teresita in Paris and London*

*une véritable merveille."* With such a formidable protagonist
Teresita might well prepare for her Paris début with all eagerness.

Before this determining event another meeting, equally significant, was brought about, again by the consummate social
strategy of Mme. Érard. She had persuaded a somewhat reluctant Franz Liszt, in Paris visiting his daughter, Blandine Ollivier, to come to the Érard warerooms, rue du Mail, on the
morning of Vivier's concert, May 14, to hear Teresita.

With her father and mother she was the first to arrive.
Shortly after, the door of the private room opened to admit
the great master, on his arm, as usual, a beautiful young lady of
high aristocracy. Following him was a group of three men.
Teresita with her always ready eye for the ludicrous, noticed
that they were amusingly alike in height and air, but for the
fact that the one in the middle was as fat as the others were
thin. They were presented as three young pianists, with significant careers before them, Saint-Saëns, Jaëll, and Planté. But the
magnetism of the great Liszt completely overshadowed the
others, and for Teresita he alone continued to exist. After the
preliminary niceties were over, and Liszt had given strict order
not to permit anybody to enter the room, he patted Teresita,
whose timid look was misleading, on the shoulder. "Now, my
child, in order to make you feel quite at home with me, I am
going to play for you. Then you shall play for me." Beginning
with a few soft measures of anticipation he drifted into the
andante from one of Beethoven's "Sonates," playing as only he
could. It reminded Teresita of Gottschalk, yet reluctantly she
had to concede that her idol had more than met his match.
With childlike loyalty she decided on the spot to play one of his
compositions for Liszt. Her father had long ago learned that it
was wiser not to make suggestions. When Liszt led Teresita to
the piano, she began at once with the "Last Hope." Unintentionally it was a good choice. Liszt, knowing of Gottschalk by
hearsay, had never heard anything he had written. Coming
prepared to be politely bored for as short a time as possible, his

interest was arrested instead by this quiet little girl, who had the charm that he admired in women, and the common sense to bring him something new. But Teresita had not only succeeded in capturing his interest; she knew how to hold and intensify it. As she played Liszt stood up, slowly taking his place behind her. He listened to the end. Then, placing both hands upon her head, he said: "Little girl, God has given you the greatest of his gifts, genius. Work, develop your talents. Above all remain true to yourself, and in time you will be one of us!" This blessing engraved itself on her memory. Years later she could still at will feel those hands upon her head. This experience was to her "the proudest of my souvenirs."

Liszt spoke to Manuel Antonio: "If you will bring your gifted daughter to me in Rome, I shall gladly take charge of her further education." Then, turning away, he noticed that contrary to his express instructions the room was filling with curious people. Quickly taking up his hat, he bowed to each newcomer with elaborate, sardonic formality and left without another word.

Teresita was not permitted to follow Liszt to Rome, where he was to write that strange final chapter of his career. Manuel Antonio was poor, perhaps he could not afford the journey; he was proud, perhaps he was unwilling to accept favors, knowing that Liszt taught with no thought of remuneration. He, the father, was particular about the proprieties; perhaps Liszt's reputation made him hesitate to entrust his daughter to such an influence; or on the other hand perhaps he simply felt that Teresita needed more regular and methodical teaching than she would in all probability receive from Liszt. Whatever the reason, this first meeting was destined to be their last.

THE news that this engaging phenomenon of twelve had won the acclaim of a Rossini and a Liszt spread through musical Paris like a call to arms, with the result that the Salle Érard was crowded, not so much in honor of Vivier, but rather that curiosity might find satisfaction. The massive form of Rossini, surrounded by the devotees he had enlisted, was the focal point within the audience. Friendly applause greeted Teresita as she appeared upon the platform in her only concert gown of black silk, its severity relieved by a yoke of sheer black net. Her single ornament was a cross of gold upon a fine chain. Soft curls were allowed to fall becomingly at will.

Again the "Prayer" from *Moïse,* this time with Gottschalk's version of the "Miserere" from *Il Trovatore* as companion, was her offering of the evening. It aroused comment that Teresita played entirely without notes. From beginning to end she was transcendently successful. The criticisms were as extravagant as was for Paris the enthusiasm of an unusually attentive audience. They reached heights of description and comparison, but it must be said that her graces of person shared the columns devoted to her in the journals on equal terms with her accomplishments. "She is beautiful as Galatea emerging anew from the chisel of Pygmalion," said one; and another: "Her success is dizzying; she plays like Liszt; she is a star; she is an angel; she is a genius; she is a fairy." And more merrily he of *l'Évènement:* "There has just arrived in Paris a little girl—if she reads this she is going to be furious—I wish to say, a very young person, who is a pure wonder. She is a pianist with power that is really terrific, a Liszt in petticoats. I am told under oath that this little Spaniard is simply a star that is rising. Let me then record its first gleam." To an uninhibited enthusiast she has "the delicate feeling of Bellini, the dramatic energy of Verdi, the tender expression of Mendelssohn, and the facile improvisation of Beethoven!"

In spite of the critics who had complained about the number of musical events in this supersaturated season, over three hundred of them in all, there was no rest in sight for Teresita. Paris salons, weary of the empty sophisticated glitter of social life in the Second Empire, welcomed the freshness that a highbred young girl from strange lands brought into them, quite aside from the asset of her parentage and playing. On the very day after the Vivier concert Teresita played in the salon of Mme. la

Baronne de Romand before an audience allegedly of *le meilleur monde*. On this evening the gathering was not true to form. During Teresita's playing of the "Rigoletto" fantasia it is reported that almost every note was interrupted by applause.

Invitations to Rossini's famous "Saturdays" were more coveted than those to the salons of Napoleon III. In spite of the palatial dimensions of the apartment it was scarcely large enough for all the people that crowded the drawing room to the point of suffocation. Rossini was never more in his element. These soirées satisfied his craving for adulation and cost him very little. Friends saw to it that the larder and the wine cellar were always liberally stocked with all that was most delicate and rare, but nobody came for the refreshments. Only strangers failed to observe the unspoken rule that the food was to be seen, not eaten. Plates of fruit, silver, and porcelain retained their decorative integrity throughout the evening. On occasion a too inquisitive guest might discover that a certain especially luscious pear had never grown on a living tree. Madame Rossini, fittingly named Olympe, with her long Roman nose, and in a veritable armor of jewels, saw to it that decorum and thrift prevailed. Why did people beg for invitations to these evenings? There was after all sure to be good music, good conversation—and Rossini.

It was at such a gathering that Teresita first met Blandine Ollivier, sister of the more famous Cosima, who became the wife of Richard Wagner. This young hostess, herself a sensitive pianist only six years older than Teresita, felt sympathetically drawn to the child, and to further the acquaintance decided to take lessons of one so highly praised by Liszt. Once a week she climbed the long flights that led to Teresita's apartment for an hour of music, and since at one time or another everybody of consequence in Paris was sure to be seen in the Ollivier salon, it was natural that Teresita too should be drawn into that circle.

Manuel Antonio realized that to reap full benefit from this first appearance it should be followed up by a second, a concert in which Teresita must be the principal performer. Even

Pregiatissimo Collega

Permettete ch'io vi raccomandi Calduz
= mente La porgitrice di queste poche Linee M.me
Teresita Carreno Pianista digyà à Celebre e di
un Talento non ordinario, L'accompagnano La
madre e il Padre ( Persone distintissime ) Piacciarsi
Udire La Carissima Teresita ed' accordarle il vostro
valente appoggio, essa lo merita per tutti i Titoli.
Essa è L'allieva della Natura, che sarà ogno
-ra La madre delle Belle Arti, e perfezionata
dal Celebre Gottschalk. Siatele cortese e non
vi sia discaro il guadagnarvi un diritto alla
Riconoscenza del vostro Aminatore e Servo

Rossini

Parigi 6 Giugno
1866

Al S.r Arditi
Distinto Compositore di musica

P.l. Affettuosi Saluti ai Conjugi Mongini

Letter from Rossini introducing Teresita to Arditi, composer
and conductor

though the season was practically closed, a bona fide shipwreck was too heaven-sent a piece of propaganda to be deferred. Teresita accordingly announced a concert of her own in the Salle Érard for the evening of June 6, 1866. A singer, a violinist, and a dramatic reader were found willing to share in the program as minor satellites. This time Teresita had the courage to place her *Norma* "Fantaisie" on the program in company with *Lucia* and *Trovatore*. The "C sharp minor Sonate" of Beethoven, "the rock of mediocrities and child prodigies," represented the classics. One critic found in it nothing out of taste. "Only the finale was taken a little too furiously." All mentioned her vigorous and clear playing, her unbelievably casual ease in the midst of high-pressure difficulties, and the very one who had inveighed most loudly against the surfeit of concerts unbent enough to say "Teresita is not the kind of prodigy that makes us hold her parents in horror," and called her concert *le bouquet de la fin.*

ON the following day father and daughter were on their way to London carrying with them the promised letters from Rossini, one to Arditi, the composer and conductor, another to Mme. Puzzi, a teacher of singing whose salon was a musical center. It read:

Madame Puzzi:—

I begin by telling you that I am not in the habit of recommending mediocrity! The person who will present this letter, Teresita Carreño (who is endowed by nature with all her gifts) is a charming pianist, pupil of the celebrated Gottschalk. She is going to London, accompanied by her parents, very distinguished people, with the purpose of being heard, and, as she deserves, of being admired. Teresita has need of a powerful support in this city, and I ask for your all-powerful one in favor of this already celebrated artist, who, in spite of the deluge of pianists who pour in from all parts of the world, has excited great admiration in Paris. Be friendly to her, Madame Puzzi, and count upon the gratitude of your devoted servant.                        G. Rossini

Paris, June 6th, 1866
To Madame Puzzi, Artist

Madame Puzzi's drawing room determined the rise or fall of many a young pretender to the throne of art. In appearance she was anything but attractive. Teresita found her positively depressing, an effect that ugliness in any form had upon her. Yet there was magnetism in the personality of one whose superior intelligence had made her the power she was. As Rossini had wished, she took Teresita under her wing, saw that she met those who might be helpful, and found patronesses for the concert which she advised her to give.

Everywhere the "distinguished gentleman" and his radiant daughter met with cordial welcome, which seemed to justify the experiment of a matinée in St. James Minor Hall on July 23. The first appearance of a Venezuelan artist in London proved to be an honor to the land of her birth. There to her delight Teresita was not to be considered as a child prodigy, but as a musician among musicians. She rose to the challenge with *Norma* and *Il Trovatore* to which she added the "Ballade in A flat" by Chopin and the so-called "Moonlight Sonata." The artists who in plentiful number contributed to the program included two conductors. The reviewers credited Teresita with a proficiency "which would become an artist twice or thrice her age." Her execution was pronounced practically faultless. Many prominent musicians were included in the well-sized and fashionable audience. The only regret was that so fine a pianist should have introduced herself too late in the season to admit of closer acquaintance. Returning to Paris Manuel Antonio could feel satisfied that at least the ground had been broken and made ready for the planting of a future year.

GREATER than for gathering laurels was the need for making a living. Manuel Antonio's reputation gradually brought him a fairly large class of pupils. But not for one instant did he lose sight of the main reason for coming to Paris, Teresita's musical education. The Conservatoire of Paris was then as now the most direct line of approach to excellence in the art and the craft of music. M. Marmontel, its head, had heard Teresita play in her concert on June 6 and had been one of those to greet her enthusiastically in the intermission. There was no trouble in gaining a hearing. Teresita was examined in this school of long tradition—and refused. The objections were two-fold. Not only was she a foreigner, but the judges were obliged to admit that Teresita had already advanced beyond their requirements for graduation. M. Marmontel did invite her to appear in rehearsal with the orchestra of the Conservatoire, although their concerts were over for the season. Georges Matthias, pupil of Chopin, was ready to initiate Teresita into this master's ways of playing, and from now on Chopin became and remained a favorite composer in her repertoire. Lessons in harmony and counterpoint were given her by M. Bazin. Creatively speaking Teresita's most fruitful years were beginning.

While father and daughter were deep in their artistic pursuits, Clorinda was quietly exploiting her talents as a homemaker. With musical Paris away on summer vacation the Carreños lived frugally and busily, preparing for better things to come, happily unaware of the impending thunderbolt.

One day Teresita was composing while Manuel Antonio sat at the desk close by. Clorinda answered a knock at the door and admitted a boy carrying a number of beaded funeral wreaths, ordered on approval at the request of the daughter of a Venezuelan relative recently deceased. As her mother held one up to examine it closely, Teresita jumped from her seat. "Don't touch it, please, Mamacita!" she entreated. "What nonsense," her mother rebuked her. Not until Teresita became hysterical would she pay the slightest attention. The father understood better. "May I touch the wreath?" he asked quietly. "Yes, you may, but not mother!" A prophetic warning! Six weeks later Clorinda, whom Teresita loved more than she had ever been allowed to show her, lay dead of cholera in that same room. The blow was devastating. Little Manuel was sent away to school. New responsibility was placed on young shoulders already too weightily burdened. They did not give way beneath the load. The breaking of their common tie united father and daughter more closely than ever. Only where before it had been the daughter who depended upon the father, it was now the father who looked to his daughter for comfort. As for her great-uncle, Bolívar, adversity held within it for Teresita the concentrated essence of strength, and she learned to believe as he did that "happiness is the memory of sorrow that has been vanquished." In a heavy black silk dress, built higher at the neck, and nearer to the ground, Teresita, wearing her cross of gold and her cross of sorrow, reëntered the salons and the concert halls of Paris, where sympathy with her misfortune made her doubly welcome.

MANUEL ANTONIO longed for a change of scene, for his own people, his own language. Spain, the home of his ancestors and of Clorinda's, was within reach. For the moment life in Paris was unbearable. So in the middle of November the inseparable pair set out upon a new journey of conquest.

Arrived in Madrid the usual method of procedure was followed. The Spanish salons were hospitable, with the regrettable exception of the del Toros, Clorinda's proud relatives, who refused to forget that Clorinda's father had joined the Revolution in Venezuela, and that his daughter had married beneath her station. Their crested doors remained closed.

Teresita's first appearance was in the *salón* of Don Eugenio de Ochoa, the second in that of a celebrated oculist Don Francisco Delgado Jugo, who twice a month held musical gatherings, chiefly to display the talents of his gifted wife. Reviewing one of these, *La Época* of Madrid compared Teresita to "Goethe's Mignon, dreaming of the fragrant orange groves of her land."

Early in December, 1866, the time was ripe for the experiment of a large concert with the collaboration of an orchestra. It began the evening by playing the "Overture" to the *Black Domino* by Auber. Then came Teresita with *Rigoletto* paraphrased by Liszt. A polka by Lamotte served to introduce a violinist, whom Teresita accompanied in a fantasia on *William*

*Tell* by de Bériot and Osborne. Again the orchestra played a short waltz, and this in turn was followed by a Chopin group played by the star of the occasion. Another slice of orchestra in "Les Fiancés Tyroliens," and then for overflowing measure the Beethoven "C sharp minor Sonate," to which Teresita added one of her own waltzes as a fitting ending to a "musical motley" not easy to duplicate.

"She plays the piano as the fountain plays," wrote the critic of *El Español,* "as sings the nightingale, as sighs the zephyr. She lost her mother a few months ago, and the notes which she draws out of the piano in so masterly a way are tears that fall on the heart, sobs that move the soul. Some one will say that the mother inspired her from Heaven."

This same gentleman heard Teresita privately. Her father accompanied her in duets, and earned the comment: "Here too is a great artist." Before the beginning of the year 1867 she had played in the hall of the Conservatory, in the Teatro de Oriente. In every *salón* of importance, excepting always that of her relatives, people were battling with each other to present her.

Thereupon the pair left for Zaragoza, where the second concert, given under the auspices of the Liceo in Teresita's honor, was the most brilliant of the entire tour. The regimental band of Estremadura set a festive note with the "Overture" to *William Tell*. The Declamatory Department assisted with poems, the Department of Music with choruses, and sandwiched in between opera arias someone added a popular note with the playing of a bandurria. The length of the program is left to the imagination. Teresita contributed her "Ballade," Liszt's *Lucia,* Mason's "Silver Springs," and dances of her own. On her part she asked a gentleman to read a few grateful words of farewell in conclusion.

IN January, 1867, showered with laurels, with eulogies in prose and poetry, with medals and with money beyond expectation, father and daughter returned to Paris, taking residence in an apartment at 2 avenue Friedland. All doors opened as of themselves to welcome them back. Valuable indeed was the list of those for whose friendship she was indebted to one or the other of the salons of this city. To Mme. Ollivier she owed her conquest of Charles Gounod who, hearing her play her "Scherzo," affectionately exaggerated its worth by declaring publicly that Beethoven himself might have signed his name to it. It was Gounod also who sponsored an introduction to the salon of Princess Mathilde, cousin of Napoleon III. To be heard there was the ambition of every musical celebrity and aspirant. Musicians, painters, sculptors, and literary personalities crowded to listen within her doors and, says *Le Ménestrel,* "are the first to engage in conversation during the performance." One Sunday early in May Gounod accompanied Teresita to the palace of the Princess. He himself escorted her to the piano and to his surprise she began with Liszt's "Fantaisie" on airs from *Faust,* having just learned it in compliment to the composer of the opera. Enthusiasm rose to the height of the sensational. The newspapers gave due publicity. Princess Mathilde was a lovely and lovable lady, appealing to a romantic young girl before all as the offspring of the thoroughly unromantic marriage of Jerome Bonaparte and Catherine of Württemberg, familiarly known as the weeping princess. Mathilde had a sad look very becoming to her. Like everyone else she delighted in spoiling Teresita.

One of these evenings had been unusually gay. The princess had personally conducted Teresita through the palace, even into her own bedroom to show her the magnificent court robes she was accustomed to wear at the Tuileries. On the way down the broad stairway she was struck by the likeness between Teresita and the bust of Napoleon I upon the landing. The guests were called upon to compare the two profiles. There was a resemblance. The papers took up the suggestion and all but made Teresita out to be an illegitimate daughter of the great Bonaparte. "Perhaps," said Teresita after many years had passed, "it is because of my inborn hatred of politics that I was to be saddled with such an unwholesome connection." From this palace to the Tuileries would have been only a step. It was never taken. Very probably Manuel Antonio did not value the influence of court standards upon an adolescent daughter.

At the salon of the Princess Mathilde Teresita met Auber. The next afternoon he climbed the five flights to the Carreño apartment. How long they must have seemed to a man of eighty! There he played parts from the last opera he had composed, and forgot time in animated conversation, holding Teresita captive under the spell of his youthfulness of spirit. Princess Mathilde also introduced Teresita to Berlioz. His eyes, she remembered, were arresting, as if he could pierce through matter and beyond, especially when he sat motionless and absorbed while music was going on. Scarcely had she finished when he surprised her by asking that inevitable, stupid question: "My child, do you never feel nervous when you play?" Teresita replied simply: "Non, monsieur." But the father broke in quickly, perhaps more abruptly than the *Urbanidad* would have condoned: "My daughter is never nervous. She is too healthy to have nerves."

The most important of her new acquaintances proved to be M. Heugel, the music publisher and owner of *Le Ménestrel*. He gave Teresita a great forward thrust by finding her compositions worthy of publication just when she most needed fresh encouragement. It almost seemed for a time as if the creative urge might prove stronger than her desire to play in public. Up to this time her only printed composition in America had been the "Gottschalk Waltz." Although to her disappointment this was never performed by him, she now had the compensation of being able to advertise on the covers of her opus 2, the "Caprice-Polka," bristling with cadenzas, trills, and operatic difficulties, as well as on her waltz opus 9, "Corbeille de Fleurs," that these pieces had been publicly played by Gottschalk. Teresita's early compositions delighted in every conceivable intricacy. When she was interested in perfecting double-note passages, octave runs, dangerous jumps, and—always her favorite —the trill, her compositions reflected this preoccupation. Very naturally they also had flavor reminiscent of the works she happened to be studying, of the composer of the hour, be it Gounod, Chopin, or Liszt. "Le Ruisseau" bears a remarkable family resemblance to Henselt's "If I were a bird," and a Chopin "Scherzo" stood godfather beyond a doubt to the "Scherzo-Caprice" that Gounod so generously appreciated beyond its merits. Her "Reminiscences of *Norma*" were dedicated to the memory of her mother, and the "Ballade," a work of real merit, also à la Chopin, is full of the exuberance that often makes the works of youthful composers so refreshing.

More mature and more affecting are those of her compositions that grew out of her first contact with death. One, a prayer improvised during the last moments of a family friend, was never to be published. A "Marche Funèbre," true to the plan of its more famous pendant by Chopin, probably owed its origin to the death of this same person. There follow a number of "Élégies" and "Plaintes" touching in their simplicity. On the covers Teresita is unflatteringly portrayed, in a black dress of stiffly draped taffeta, holding a prayerbook. The tight bodice trimmed with black lace and beads has long and clumsy sleeves. A black velvet ribbon ties back curls grown longer.

Very soon she turned to a more familiar field, the *morceau de salon* and the opera transcription. Her dedications were chosen from among the names on her visiting list, Matthias, Marmontel, Mme. Ollivier, Sir Julius Benedict, and Mr. L. H. Beddington. "Un Rêve en Mer," "Le Printemps," and "Une Revue à Prague" made a brilliant trilogy. Whenever she became geographic, whether in her "Italian Sketches" or in "Highland, Souvenir d'Écosse," it is amusing to note a very winning, if unmotivated, harking back to the land of her origin, to the lilt of the Spanish serenade with its guitar accompaniment, and to the habanera. Of the somewhat later compositions she dedicated a "Berceuse," most beautiful of all, to her father. It has a delicacy worthy of comparison with Schumann's "Album for the Young" or with the "Songs without Words" of Mendelssohn. The last of her compositions to be bound together by her father in a book with gilt edges and an elaborate green cover was an étude called "La Fausse Note," a reminder of a composition of that name by Rubinstein.

At the home of the Heugels Teresita met the composer of "Mignon," Ambroise Thomas, a tall, gray-bearded man, as silent as Gounod was expansive. To him as to many of her special friends her only name was Bébé. However, by virtue of catastrophe rather than of years a *bébé* she no longer was.

Of all the people in Teresita's circle, the one she admired most was Adelina Patti. A first meeting at one of Rossini's soirées ripened into sisterly, if proverbially undemonstrative affection on the part of the prima donna, and into undisguised worship on the part of Teresita. There could be no greater joy than to accompany her idol's singing, no more precious secret than that there was a photograph of Patti behind that of her mother in the locket she wore. "If only I too could sing," thought Teresita. And very soon Rossini, always on the lookout to find potential interpreters for his operas, discovered that she had a pleasing voice of mezzo quality. The beginning of her training in this branch of art was under his instruction. He even encouraged her to think seriously of a career as a singer, seconded by the energetic prodding of Patti. There germinated a longing which accompanied her for many years, cropping out at odd intervals, filling more than a passing need.

Inwardly Teresita was restless. She wanted something as different as possible from daily routine. It lay near at hand that she might become an actress. The necessary qualifications, beauty, clear enunciation, vivacity, imagination, and a decided gift of mimicry were hers. Did she not use them daily for the delectation of one friend at the expense of another, yet always in wholesome good spirits for the fun of the thing? But woe to the one who tried to turn the tables by ridiculing her! During one of the soirées of Princess Mathilde a gentleman approached Teresita, in his hand a caricature which he had made off-hand as she played. It was unmistakably she, though by no means flattering. He had drawn her face framed in a towsled mop of curls and had given her a very beak of a nose. In high indignation she tore up the drawing, not caring that it was Gustave Doré who had perpetrated the insult, that she had impulsively destroyed a valuable work of art. Soon from the pen of Dwight of Boston the news spreads that "Teresita Carreño is studying singing and dramatic art with Delle Sedie of *Les Italiens.* . . . and with her face and figure we may expect a prima donna who will be a credit to art," he prophesies. (The piano had found a rival if not a substitute.) Teresita continued to give concerts, the more frequently because of the famous Exposition Universelle in Paris. The concert given in the Salle Érard on May 7, 1867, is reviewed by *Le Constitutionnel,* which says:

Large and maturely developed like the rapidly blooming flowers of her country, Teresa Carreño makes one think of the beautiful American virgins who came before Christopher Columbus, black eyes holding all the fire of the sun, their father and their god— Enthusiasm became charged with frenzy after the playing of a *Ballade* of her composition and a *Fantaisie* of extra difficulty composed by Liszt for the despair of his colleagues.—To appreciate her completely one must hear her intimately, be it in a Beethoven *Concerto* or in a delicious *Waltz* of Chopin—or in a *Lament* composed by her after a terrible family calamity, the mournful expression of which brings tears to all eyes.

And so life continued very lean and plain and workful in the little apartment, 2 avenue Friedland. Teresita remembered always her fifteenth birthday as one of the happiest, because in celebration she had butter on her bread for breakfast. Particularly to the liking of Teresita were the long excursions into the Bois de Boulogne, lively parties lasting from morning until night, which never lacked for variety of entertainment. Frequently they called for the inventiveness of the participants. On one such jaunt everyone was expected to improvise something.

In a melodramatic mood Teresita turned to poetry. Mounting a rock with exaggeration of the grand manner of the Théâtre Français, she chanted in measured imitation of French declamatory tradition:

> En franchissant les obstacles
> Que nous présente l'adversité
> Nous renversons les murailles
> Qui nous séparent de la Divinité.

She was to have ample chance to prove this true.

EARLY in May, 1868, on the day following her last Paris appearance of the season, Teresita and her father again crossed the Channel. There were promising signs that the protective ice of musical London was cracking under the heat of Venezuelan temperament. Paris was more unaccountable. It accepted each new artist with easy effusiveness, according to his entertainment value, and more or less soon replaced him as a later sensation presented itself. Coming late to concerts and then using the music as a soothing obbligato for choice bits of gossip was the accepted thing, and there was cause for public comment when the size of an audience did not dwindle toward the end of the evening. London's musical manners were far more courteous. Titled ladies lent their printed names as sponsors to Teresita's programs, and as she was able to draw upon more and more popular artists to assist her, these important beings began to appear at her concerts in person. Among her colleagues Teresita's friendliness and high spirits won quick understanding. It was one of them, the famous pianist Charles Hallé, who took occasion to present her himself to none other than the Princess of Wales.

This was an honor so exciting that it warranted a new dress, a dress with a train. Teresita's Irving Hall début had not been more thrilling than this, her official coming of age as a young lady appearing before royalty. It was not the music she was to play that concerned her. Far more necessary to practice an effective entrance, a deep curtsy before the long mirror in full, delicious consciousness of the swishing silk behind her. The evening arrived. Teresita managed very well during the introduction. But in spite of the quite obvious exaggeration of her motions, the Princess refused to pay proper attention to the train. This was annoying. The moment came to cross the polished parquetry floor that led to the piano, a final chance to make an impression. She meant to make the most of it. Throwing back her head, she chose a winding way to reach her destination, twisting and turning to make her train curve in and out like the tail of a salamander. One last completing fling! (Teresita failed to notice that it had displaced the light gilt chair intended for her) and she found herself seated with theatrical elegance—upon the floor! Not in her lifetime would she forget the mortification of that moment.

EARLY in July, 1868, Teresita gave a matinée of her own in the Hanover Square rooms. It stood out from the others not only because it was sponsored by the Duchess of Cleveland, Lady Duff Gordon, and others, not only because she was ably seconded by fine artists, not only because the concert was attended by all that was fashionable in London circles, but because one person, led by casual curiosity, happened to buy his ticket like any other mortal. Anton Rubinstein was in the audience. This marked the beginning of a friendship between two kindred spirits. On this afternoon Teresita was more than usually dazzling. Beauty, talent, temperament, all scintillated to their fullest. One of her own compositions headed the program. She took part in the Schumann "Quintette," and continued in classical vein with the C sharp minor "Sonate" of Beethoven, the Chopin "Polonaise" in the same key, and Mendelssohn's "Rondo Capriccioso." During the intermission Rubinstein made his way from his favorite seat at the rear of the left side to the artists' room. He shook Manuel Antonio's hand until it hurt, thanking him for the new genius he had brought to London. When he congratulated Teresita upon some of the best piano playing he had ever heard, he noticed even more than during the performance how similar in shape her hands were to his own. From this day on he became her mentor, the outstanding influence of her girlhood. That which Gottschalk had been for the prodigy, Rubinstein became for the unfolding artist. These two, so different in age and outlook, were irresistibly drawn to each other by a likeness in temperament as well as in the hands. To Teresita, though Rubinstein was not officially giving lessons and taught her only spasmodically when they happened to be

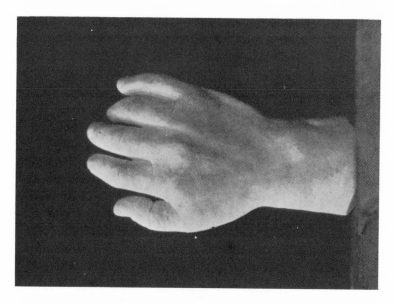

Cast of Rubinstein's Hand

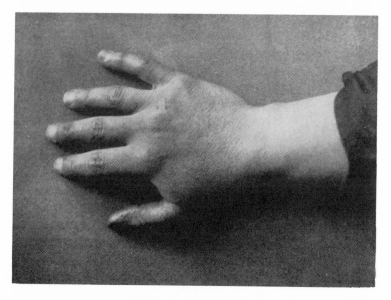

Hand of Carreño

in the same city, he was the greatest of all masters. She learned from him more than he was conscious of teaching her.

Rubinstein was anything but methodical. Running up and down as she played, fortified by a cigar that kept going out in his absorption, he did not hesitate to interrupt her abruptly in order to take her place at the piano. Teresita was used to Manuel Antonio's more tactful ways. There were stormy moments. She was no longer the child ready to accept the dictates even of an artist whom she adored. At one of these lessons Rubinstein, a musical autocrat if ever there was one, was laying down the law according to Rubinstein. Teresita presumed to question his reading of a certain passage, about which she too had conviction. "You must play this as I do," commanded the master. "Why must I?" countered Teresita. Rubinstein bristled. The moment had come to put her in her place. Angrily he drew himself up to his full height, made a widely curving gesture which ended by pointing at himself, and shouted in what was intended to be an annihilating tone: "I am Rubinstein."

Teresita was not cowed. She jumped from the piano stool, repeated the gesture in perfect caricature to the last detail, in which only the fury was her own, and mimicking Rubinstein's tone of voice to the life, she retorted, "And I am Carreño." For an instant two forces confronted each other in silent indignation, then exploded in a burst of merriment born of inner understanding. From now on Rubinstein might call her his adopted daughter, his sunshine, or even *bébé*. As an artist he must henceforth learn to regard her as an equal, concede to her the right of self-expression. The *enfant prodige,* as *La France* had so recently called her, was of the past.

*Es bildet ein Talent sich in der Stille,*
*Sich ein Charakter in dem Strom der Welt.*

GOETHE

# PART II

# TRIAL AND ERROR

I AM Carreño!" With this pronouncement she declared herself musically responsible. Conscious of unlimited power within, she had the drive, the will to draw into her own living only that which was acceptable to her as an individual, to discard that which she no longer truly was. Would she be able to manage her life as rightly as she did her keyboard? Or would she be satisfied with the triumphs already so generously hers by right of youth, beauty, and genius?

Genius is timeless. It exists ready-made, sound, and whole. It may reach out in one direction or another, momentarily changing its outline, yet keeping the weight of content intact, the periphery unbroken. The energy of genius, no matter how lavishly expended, how variously directed or misdirected, exists once and for all. The pattern changes, the balance shifts with the enrichment or erosion of time. Genius remains potentially the same, the inexhaustible spring of intuitive vision. It is taught only to find that it knows. It must because it can. Its essence is a quite unmoral passion for perfection, making a direct path from soul to soul, striking a spark instantaneous in its contact. It exists in fullness while demanding fulfillment. Events may encroach upon it, shape it, mold it into beauty or its opposite. Genius, uninhibited, remains elastic in expression, lightning-sure in its reactions. The faults of genius are never small, never mean; the fatality of genius is to be painted with an ample brush. Interference with its all-comprehensive stroke, even by intellect, the all-comprehending, is criminal subversion.

The London *Athenaeum* faced Teresita's problem simply: "Mademoiselle Carreño may have a brilliant future if she be not spoilt at the beginning of her career." It disregarded a significant fact. The threshold of one career already marked the close of another. To one completed chapter life had set its seal. From every angle it stood approved. When little Teresita promised herself: "I shall be an artist all my life," she instinctively knew that the reward she wished for lay within the art she tended. Adulation, flowers, riches, delightful as they might be, were in themselves unessential. Creating a thrilling world of imagination and revelation where others might not enter, yet which she knew how to share with all who would listen, that was what really mattered. Hers was a precious secret. All of it would never be revealed even to herself. She might give of it as lavishly as from the fullness of her affectionate nature she loved to give everything else she owned. The secret was hers alone, hers its lonely eminence, hers that inexhaustible spring from which she had the gift to draw at will that she might as freely give to others, according to their sensitivity, the hint of an existence where lesser things fall into just proportion. That was what Liszt meant when he charged her to be true to herself.

Teresa—with her musical coming of age she dropped the affectionate diminutive—did not always see the way so clearly before her. Daily living is full of clutter, disillusioning, sordid beneath the surface, and dull. Outwardly Teresa was the envied darling of Paris and London. Within the protection of safely grounded homes young girls would gladly have given all they cherished most to change places with her for a day, to bow so regally in rustling gowns of bright silk, to acknowledge applause with such proud courtesy. They guessed nothing of the careful planning on the part of both father and daughter to keep heads above water, to afford the dignity of a Paris apartment, to educate young Manuel fittingly in the hope that he would become a good soldier and later, perhaps, a good diplomat.

In time the annual trip across the Channel for the London season became for two people an unmanageable expense. Fortunately there was a Mrs. Bischoff, a friend with whom Teresa could safely live in London, while Manuel Antonio continued his teaching in Paris. He accepted this enforced separation with reluctance, foreseeing the change that it inevitably would mean in their relation to each other, the loosening of discipline and close companionship. Very naturally he mistrusted the influence of a franker, freer, Protestant England upon his daughter. It distressed him that she actually seemed to revel in the society of the would-be opera singers in the class of Delle Sedie, her singing teacher. To his thinking her manners had already suffered. He deplored the increasing loudness of her voice, her boisterous laughter at jokes that bordered on the indelicate. He would have wished her more discriminating in every way. Without deliberately going counter to his strict and static rules of conduct, Teresa no longer accepted his criticisms as final. She could not help observing how out of tune they were with life as it was lived in London and in Paris of the late Sixties. Her own spirit craved freedom. She felt more religious in fragrant forests than in churches, although in Paris she had observed the prescribed ecclesiastical routine meticulously. Stimulating though they were in many ways, she also began to resent the artificial atmosphere of the Paris salons. What labyrinths of convoluted being! Emerging from such a gathering, she felt like throwing her arms out wide and shouting aloud into the fresh, uncomplicated air. In England people were more themselves, more forthright. The Germans in London were particularly to her liking. Only few foreign virtuosos chose to settle in Paris, for then as now Paris preferred those of its own race and language. Teresa dreamed that some day she would go to Germany, learn its language, sing its songs, and as so often, she dreamed true.

Teresa Carreño was fifteen years old. *Le Ménestrel* had hinted in its columns that she would soon enter the teaching profession, predicting a large class of pupils. However, to entice them in sufficient number, it took a formal advertisment, which read:

> *Enseignement élémentaire et supérieur*
> *Cours et leçons de piano*
> *par*
> *M. Manuel Carreño et Mlle. Teresa Carreño*
> *Les mardis, jeudis, et samedis*
> *Leçons spéciales en anglais et en espagnol*
> *S'adresser chez M. et Mlle. Carreño, Ave. Friedland, 2.*

Manuel Antonio was undoubtedly the more dependable member of this pedagogic ensemble. It is unthinkable that a young girl of fifteen, busy with household and music, in which her enthusiasm for the operatic stage was for the time paramount, would regard teaching as anything but a chore. Madame Ollivier was the outstanding exception. Teresa's formal education had been short-lived and sketchy. Hers was the not unliberal education of travel and trouble. She, to whom the gift of knowing without being taught had been given, could not be expected to show tact and patience with those who were slow and clumsy. So the brunt of this coöperative undertaking fell upon the shoulders of Manuel Antonio, who, moreover, was planning to publish a treatise on the "Theory and Practice of Piano Technique." Using new and ingenious formulae based on strictly mathematical combinations, he had found the way of solving in principle the most arduous difficulties of rhythm and mechanics. This project was not to be realized, probably because Marmontel, who had been asked for his opinion, considered this work, carefully and cleverly conceived though he admitted it to be, merely another addition to the already overprolific literature on the subject. Or it may have been the Franco-Prussian War that entered an interfering wedge. To Manuel Antonio this must have been a major disappointment. He had counted upon this publication to give him distinction in his own right. Failing in this, his part in a world to whose outlook and standards he could no longer bend was played.

Teresa continued to appear successfully and unremuneratively in the most important and influential salons of Paris, those of Pierre Véron, the journalist, M. et Mme. Diémer, M. et Mme. Koechlin among them. The listeners were often as celebrated—sometimes as audible—as the performing artists. Her own concerts were still popular events. In the audience one might see "a quantity of superb toilettes generally not evident in concerts." Fashion attended and, wonder of wonders, stayed to the end. Coquelin himself, Sarasate, and Delle Sedie assisted at these functions. Blond, Nordic Christine Nilsson and dark, tropical Teresa Carreño offset each other effectively on more than one occasion. Decidedly Teresa had "arrived" in Paris. In that city there were no higher pinnacles for her scaling. She was no longer shy of putting her own compositions next to those of Gottschalk and Chopin on her programs, among them "Venice," dedicated to Mme. Ollivier, and "Le Ruisseau." But the accepted favorite was always the "Revue à Prague."

From the time that she was allowed to travel alone Teresa was more and more in demand as a member of concert groups on tour. Under the management of the famous impresario, Maurice Strakosch, she left home for weeks at a time, once to play in the cities of Holland assisting Minnie Hauck, the soprano. On another occasion, one of the pianists of a company formed to present the *Mass* of Rossini shortly after his death in November, 1868, Teresa visited the French provinces and later Belgium. A trip with the same artists in Germany was abandoned through fear of war, one through Switzerland being hastily substituted. For the time being Teresa was best known as the pianist of the Strakosch company.

Close upon her return she was again on her way to London. The Princess of Wales had not forgotten the little artist with the long, wayward train. Upon her own initiative she took Teresa's concert on June 21, 1869, under her particular patronage, an honor accorded only to two or three artists before her. But Teresa considered it a far greater one when she was asked to appear as piano soloist in one of Adelina Patti's "Grand Concerts." She was heard as well on the always select, always interminable programs that the popular conductor, Julius Benedict, had the custom of staging annually for his own benefit. On one of these occasions Sir Julius publicly advertised that he had restricted the duration of the concert to four hours only. "We wonder who had physical strength to test the accuracy of this promise," asks the *Athenaeum*.

DECLARATION of the Franco-Prussian War on July 19, 1870, found father and daughter on opposite sides of the Channel. Teresa remembered how thrilling it was to undo the notes brought to her by carrier-pigeon post, messages written on the thinnest of paper in her father's finely pointed handwriting and creased into accordionlike folds. Much as he disapproved of his daughter's prolonged stay in London, he was relieved to know her free from the deprivations he himself had to endure during the long siege of Paris. Lessons, salons, concerts dwindled, then stopped completely. One mouth less to feed in Paris! That was important, and Teresa by good fortune was able even from a distance to play the part most natural to her since the age of eight, that of breadwinner to her family. She rose to the occasion manfully. By force of pluck, perseverance, and personality, her reputation widened and heightened until she achieved a coveted engagement and financial security on a modest scale as one of the regular artists of M. Rivière's Promenade Concerts.

M. Rivière had for a time been known as conductor of the notorious Alhambra. When the license of this music hall was revoked, because Mlle. Finette, the cancan dancer, shocked and tickled the sensibilities of London, M. Rivière changed his tactics. He established the Promenade Concerts with a standing orchestra of one hundred pieces, supplemented by a large chorus, and on August 19, 1871, gave them the superb setting of Covent Garden Theater. In place of the white calico hangings relieved by red rosettes that his predecessors had thought suitable, he had devised ultramagnificent stage decorations. Ornamental framework gave the effect of a mammoth conservatory of flowers. What it lacked in restraint it achieved in brilliance. Against this setting a mixture of popular, semipopular, and classical music—each carefully sorted and consigned to its special evening—became so successful that an extra two weeks had to be added to the scheduled concerts of the first season. The purely classical ones took place on Wednesdays and were conducted by Arthur Sullivan. It was for these that Teresa was primarily engaged, although she did not consider it belittling to appear on those of lighter character, conducted by M. Rivière. For experience the training was excellent.

It meant not only a regular income, it also obliged her to add to her repertoire. In a Liverpool Philharmonic Concert under the direction of Sir Julius Benedict Teresa played the "G minor Concerto" of Mendelssohn for the first time. The *Athenaeum* takes notice that "the playing of this lady at the *Covent Garden Concerts* has been of a nature to attract more than ordinary attention."

Once having held her own in the tours of Maurice Strakosch, Teresa was booked far ahead for the spring of 1872 by his great rival, Colonel Mapleson, as a member of an operatic concert group traveling through the provinces of Great Britain. Colonel Mapleson was accustomed to do things on a grand scale. His own annual benefit concert in London was usually an all-day affair. It began with a matinée concert, to which celebrities contributed their talents gratis. In the evening there was an opera, followed by a ballet, and complemented by the playing of fountains and fireworks. Through these influential men, Teresa became professionally associated with the most highly valued, and paid, artists of London. In the exuberance of her new freedom, with her overflowing friendliness, her versatile genius, she made quick way to the affections of her colleagues, always ready to laugh at their jokes, to be a leader in their fun, to play their accompaniments, and to sympathize in their troubles, helping where she could. But Adelina Patti, coaching and encouraging her as she was able, saw to it that her "little sister" did not give up the idea of becoming a singer.

*Le Ménestrel* begins to complain that Teresa is making such a sensation in London that this city seems unwilling to return her to Paris—and Manuel Antonio, alone except for the visits of young Manuel on leave from military school, resigned himself *in absentia* to proud partnership in the triumphs of his daughter, and to the most mournful of all diminuendos, that of old age.

Tuesdays the Promenade Concerts were devoted to opera. In these Teresa was in her element, now playing the "Waltz" from *Faust* or another of her limitless fund of transcriptions, now taking part with a violinist in the duet on airs from *William Tell*. On one classical Wednesday she played the "Capriccio Brillante" in the concert devoted to Mendelssohn. When it was the turn of Beethoven, she took her part in the "Kreutzer Sonate."

Fresh from the Beethoven centenary at Bonn the critic of the *Athenaeum* writes: "If Mlle. Carreño had executed the Andante and Variations from the "Kreutzer Sonate" at Bonn, she would have elicited from the Teutonic amateurs greater enthusiasm than even she provoked at Covent Garden; her touch is indescribably charming, and her execution neat and finished."

At this time she was also heard for the first time in the great "E flat Concerto" by Beethoven which was later to become a highlight of her repertoire. According to the *Musical World* "the young lady's performance was heard with the greatest attention, and it is no small proof of her ability that, after being applauded at the close of each movement, she was finally recalled amid unanimous and hearty tokens of gratification." In this concert Mme. Rudersdorff, the singer who became even more famous as the mother of Richard Mansfield, also participated. This marked the beginning of a friendship that ripened significantly for Teresa in another land.

The Promenade Concerts proved to be a stepping stone to the really choice Monday Popular Concerts of Mr. Arthur Chappel. Playing on these programs meant association with artists such as Charles Hallé, Joseph Joachim, and Clara Schumann. In such company it was necessary to measure up to the highest standards. For her first appearance she chose Beethoven's "Sonate" in E flat, op. 27, no. 1, last given years before in these concerts by M. Hallé and Mme. Schumann.

To this appearance the *Athenaeum* completely capitulated, considering it worth while to consign one of its "original papers" to a review of the playing of this "Spanish American pianiste" on January 20, 1872.

Conventionalists and Puritans must have been terribly shocked at the laissez-aller style of playing Beethoven adopted by a young lady, Mlle. Carreño, at the Monday Popular Concerts on the 15th inst.! Disregarding all precedents and tradition, selecting her own tempi, and giving a reading altogether novel and unprecedented to the Sonate in E flat Op. 27, No. 1—the newcomer created a sensation as pronounced as has been excited by any exhibition of the more experienced style of Madame Schumann, and of the more exact and refined school of Madame Arabella Goddard. It is difficult to convey a notion of the abandon and charm of Mlle. C's execution. She has a nimble finger and can master all difficulties, and has, moreover, prodigious power, considering that the hands are feminine and almost juvenile. The effect upon the auditory was much the same as that produced on the public of the Princess's Theatre when M. Fechter gave a version of Hamlet so different from the stiff and stilted reading of English actors who have appeared as the Danish Prince. The severe judges and critical connoisseurs astounded at first by the verve and vigour of the Venezuelan artiste, were at last carried away, and found themselves endorsing the verdict of the masses in St. James Hall, that an original and exceptional artist had appeared who dared to take her own course defiant of pedantic ruling. The Sonata itself seemed peculiarly adapted to develop her specialties. It is full of breaks and surprises; it alternates in the expression of profound pathos and of the deepest despair—the former exemplified in accents of affliction and the latter evinced in paroxysms of forcible passages. The themes were well contrasted by Mlle. Carreño and it is useless to challenge the interpretation because it was not traditional. We must accept artists with their peculiar idiosyncracies, and we are too glad to be emancipated from dryness, formality, and from the commonplace, to argue against conceptions which are so impulsive and energetic. The Sonata has been rarely attacked by pianists; it was some twelve years since it has been heard at the Monday Popular Concerts; and a vote of thanks is due Mlle. Carreño for her introduction of what Beethoven called "Sonata quasi una fantasia" and for her poetic and spirited playing of it.

By way of warning, it may be permitted to suggest that the vigour of the left hand might be forced down advantageously. After a rapturous recall Mlle. C. gave Herr Rubinstein's picturesque transcription of Beethoven's Turkish March from the "Ruins of Athens" which she executed with due observance of the gradations of sound; now the march being heard fortissimo and then dying off in the distance to the softest pianissimo. Mlle. C. also took the pianoforte part in Mozart's quartet in g-minor (1785) having as colleagues Mme. Norman Neruda, Herr Straus and Signor Piatti; but the composition, replete with melody, requires no executive skill out of the common order. The addition of Mlle. C. to the classical chamber school of playing must be emphatically welcomed; her previous performances in London were at miscellaneous concerts, at which she indulged in the Fantasia; at the recent Covent Garden Promenade Concerts of M. Rivière, Mlle. C. Performed Concertos; now she has taken a new ground, and the Director of the Monday Popular Concerts is to be congratulated on his valuable acquisition.

The *Musical Times* concedes that she found great favor and commends her emphatic style, her strongly marked accent, and vigorous expression. But it criticizes her adversely because, "instead of repeating the finale of the *Sonate,* she added as encore Herr Rubinstein's transcription of Beethoven's *March from the Ruins of Athens.*" This was somewhat out of place, according to the *Times,* "in a concert devoted to classical music, and which it is moreover hardly wise for any other pianist than Herr Rubinstein to attempt in public."

The *Musical Times* was not the only voice ready to jack up Teresa when her taste was in danger of sagging. There was always Rubinstein. At one of her concerts Teresa had chosen to play the first movement only of the Mendelssohn "Concerto in G minor." As she left the stage the master confronted her: "Teresita, you are now my adopted daughter; but if you ever again play a single movement of a Concerto without the others that belong to it, I shall disown you," he bellowed for all to hear. Teresa remembered and obeyed.

WHILE M. Heugel was publishing one of her compositions after another, the Scotch "Highland" with the Spanish twist, "La Fausse Note" reminiscent of Rubinstein's étude of the same name, and the delicate "Berceuse," the only piece dedicated to her father, the early spring of 1872 found Teresa traveling as piano soloist on the concert tour of the provinces for which she had been obligated long before by Colonel Mapleson. Among the operatic stars in the company Therese Tietjens was that of first magnitude.

Teresa's engagement ended in Edinburgh. Dovetailing with it Mapleson had organized a series of operatic performances. The gala event, with Tietjens taking the part of Valentine in *Les Huguenots,* a recent revival in the repertoire of Her Majesty's Theatre, was scheduled for March 12.

Meanwhile for the moment Teresa found herself foot-loose. Completely carefree days were rare dispensations, and she meant to make the most of them. What could be more soul-satisfying than to stay where she was in the company of light-hearted friends, to sit in elegant prominence in Colonel Mapleson's box, and to relive night after night tales of horror and romance, intensified by the aura added by music. She could take full advantage of her holiday in no better way and prepared to relish every instant. So she did, if not quite as she had intended.

On the morning after the last concert Teresa and Therese in the gayest of moods set out to see the sights of the city. In the sunshine of the moment Teresa could afford to brush aside the caustic comment of the Edinburgh *Courant's* critic regarding her concerts. It had annoyed her slightly to read:

There was also a lady pianiste, Mlle. Carreño, who attempted Chopin's *Grande Polonaise in A flat;* and though displaying a good memory, and giving some passages with the left hand very cleverly, the general idea of Chopin's fine composition was lost entirely in a series of wild crashes, indistinct runs, and chords which would have greatly surprised the nervous Pole. In a fantasia on airs from "Trovatore," the lady played occasionally with considerable success, and was applauded at the close of the piece; but her style of touching the instrument is contrary to that which we are accustomed to in Edinburgh. The lady also appeared as vocalist in the closing quartette, in which the two basses were too powerful for the soprano and tenor.

The critic was probably not far wrong. Neither the members of the concert company nor Colonel Mapleson himself took these provincial concerts seriously, the important thing being to have as hilarious a time as possible en route. Sir Frederic Cowen in his reminiscences recalls a typical incident of this tour of 1872. The troupe arrived in Newcastle one morning with a free day ahead. Spirits were at high pitch, imagination ready to run riot in almost any direction that held promise of fun. Someone suggested a three-piano ensemble as a novelty for the program of the evening. The three pianists of the concert company, Teresa Carreño, Tito Mattei, and young Frederic Cowen put their heads together, swallowed their breakfast whole, and hurried to the music store. Finding three instruments in tolerable tune they set to work. That there was no music at hand for such a combination lent zest to their determination to give their fellow artists the surprise of their lives. *Rigoletto* was chosen as their victim. Around the most popular themes of that much abused opera they wove a fantasia of fire and fury in a three-cornered game of musical tennis, Teresa first serving a melody which her colleagues returned with variants and elaborations of their own. After a few hours of this composite improvising, their plan of action was clearly defined. According to Sir Frederic the audience found nothing amiss with the noisy medley, while backstage a delighted band of colleagues with difficulty were persuaded to wait until the final note before exploding in mirth. The performance served its purpose, but it seems not to have called for repetition.

As Teresa walked along on this morning with Tietjens by her side she hummed aloud for the joy of living. Turning a corner they came upon Colonel Mapleson, apparently in a frantic state. Without waiting for an answering "good morning" to his perfunctory one, he stormed:

What do you think? That woman, that Colombo, has left me high and dry. The cheek of her! She says she is ill and expects me to find someone to take her place. Does she think singers grow on trees like apples for the picking? I have tried everywhere. There is no one willing to sing the Queen in *Les Huguenots*. To blazes with these ungrateful creatures. I work myself sick to make them famous, and at the critical moment they fail me. I am a madman to order my life according to caprices of irresponsible females, to tiptoe over the quicksands of their shifting temper, to take measurements from stars that turn out to be meteors. What a life for a man! Why do I go on with it?

Suddenly his attention focused upon Teresa who, while looking appropriately sympathetic, was enjoying the fireworks and continuing her humming. A flash of inspiration cleared away his frown. "I have it," he whispered. "You shall sing the Queen, Bébé."

Teresa was in the right humor to respond to a good joke, and this was one of the best. She threw back her head, opened her mouth wide, and laughed until the tears came. The Colonel, keenly appraising, looked her up and down, then took her by the shoulders to make her listen.

"I mean it. There is no other way. You must not fail me." Teresa was reduced from amazement to silence. Could it be that he was in earnest?

Up went her left eyebrow, a danger signal: "That is ridiculous," she answered. "I am not a singer. I have never acted upon a stage in my life, I don't know the part, and I do not intend to make a fool of myself."

"Nonsense," growled the Colonel. "You have four days. What more do you want? You have a voice, you have studied singing, you are musical. There is not a moment during the day when you are not acting, whether you know it or not. You shall have plenty of rehearsals. You are made for the part. If worse comes to worst you can always fall back upon your looks."

Teresa exploded with a square-cut: "Indeed not!" These two words were and remained one of the *Leitmotifs* of her vocabulary. There was no doubt that the subject was definitively closed.

Tietjens had been biding her time. She knew her Teresa and how best to handle her. Turning to Mapleson quite casually she

said: "Teresa is absolutely right. It is much too difficult a thing
to expect of her."

A slight shrug of the shoulders was Teresa's response. It
seemed to say: "Let her think so if she wants to. I could do it if
I liked. But I don't wish to."

Unmindful that she was playing "Monsieur le Corbeau" to
Tietjens' "Monsieur le Renard," she began to reconsider. After
all, the matter had something to be said in its favor. Looking
Colonel Mapleson straight in the eye, her eyes narrowed, she
assumed the air of a shrewd business woman about to drive a
hard bargain. "I will sing the Queen, but under one condition.
You must let me have all the artists I choose to assist me at my
London concert."

"Agreed," said the Colonel. "You have only to name them."

Teresa had her weaknesses, but modesty was not numbered
among them. Brazenly, beginning with Tietjens herself, she
made a considerable list of other popular singers on the roster
of Her Majesty's Theatre. Mapleson gasped, mainly with admiration for a quality he recognized as kindred to himself. This
was not the time to count the cost. He prepared to make the inevitable sacrifice.

Having committed herself, Teresa was overcome with fright.
What if she should make a complete fiasco? For safety's sake
she stipulated also that the name of the artist she was displacing
be left on the program.

Once having undertaken the part, she went at it with all the
heat of her dynamic energy. The operatic transcriptions, the
improvised operas of her childhood had helped inadvertently to
pave the way for this, her first appearance in a real opera. Singing, acting, what fun it was! And what might not come of it!
Overnight she imagined herself a great singer, perhaps to travel
with the adored Patti in her private car of whose luxury she
had heard so much. She too might lead a fabulous, merry life in
a world as thrilling as it was unreal! She must not fail! Nor
did she. Even under her own name she could have taken pride
in her performance. The critics were mildly benevolent:

The *Margherita* of Mlle. Colombo showed cultivation in the finish of the runs and shakes, especially in "A questa voce sola"; but her intonation in the air in which she apostrophises Touraine, in the garden of France, was not quite perfect in intonation. Her duets with Raoul when he is brought in blindfolded went very well.

She did not, however, become famous overnight, and her feat was soon forgotten. Nobody encouraged her, all too youthful for the career of a singer as she was, to change from a profession in which she already excelled to one of unpredictable future. Perhaps later! With this in reserve, she turned back to her piano, and when in the Monday Pops she and Joachim played the "Kreutzer Sonate" together, she was in no doubt that this was the instrument with which she felt most herself.

In May of 1872 Teresa gave her own matinée in the Hanover Square rooms. Tietjens was prevented from singing by indisposition so convenient to vocalists. Otherwise it was a gratifying success, and the *Athenaeum* notes that "Mlle. Carreño has not only taken a place in the front ranks of lady pianists, but she is also an accomplished vocalist." With young Frederic Cowen she was heard in Schumann's "Andante and Variations" for two pianos, unconscious that life was about to write an even more startling variant for her.

MAURICE STRAKOSCH'S experience with Teresa on tour made him know that he could count upon her. More valuable still she had the gift of surrounding herself with an aura of cheerful, harmless camaraderie that was positively infectious. Jealousy and intrigue did not long survive in an atmosphere dominated by her wholesome outlook. With the keenness developed by years of familiar association with artists in their more difficult moments, Strakosch saw what a personal as well as box-office asset Teresa would be with the group he was selecting to travel in the United States during the coming winter. When he named the other artists, Teresa needed no persuasion to join them. Carlotta Patti, Adelina's less famous sister, offered herself as chaperon, the aging Mario, who had already given several farewell concerts in England, took the place of a father, and one at least was close to her in age, the young violinist Émile Sauret. Preliminary rehearsals soon made them friends. He was appealing to Teresa from the straight and long-cut hair that framed a thin and mournful face to his sensitive fingers. "He probably hasn't enough to eat," worried Teresa, and all that was maternal within her awoke to take him under her wing. "Amongst the departures for New York last week," says the *Athenaeum* on September 1, "were Madame Paulina Lucca, Mlle. Kellogg, Mlle. Carreño, Miss Clara Doria, Col. Liebhart, Signor Mario, and Herr Rubinstein, the pianist." It must have been a gay crossing.

The company made its début at Steinway Hall on October 4, 1872. Says this same journal:

It was fortunate for the once great tenor that he had as colleague Signora Carlotta Patti, who compensated for the decay of the voice of her comrade. Señora Teresa Carreño, the pianist, who created such a sensation last season at the Monday Popular Concerts, has delighted the American amateurs who were also pleased with the execution of the young Sauret.

The tour began in New York, where the Strakosch Company established itself in the Clarendon Hotel on Union Square. One evening Teresa sat eating her dinner at the long common table.

PARIS 1873

*Manuel Antonio Carreño with his Son*
*and Daughter*

*With the Patti-Mario Troupe in 1872*

ÉMILE SAURET                    MARIO

CARLOTTA PATTI

TERESA CARREÑO

Absorbed in thought she failed to notice that the vacant chair at her right was empty no longer. All at once her eye was attracted by a hand beside hers, an unmistakable hand. It could belong only to Rubinstein! It did. He embarrassed her to confusion by throwing his arms around her without regard for the other guests, giving her a hearty kiss for good measure. In the course of conversation he inquired: "Have you a nice room for practicing, Teresita?"

"Yes, indeed I have," was the answer.

"Then you are luckier than I. My room is on the court, small and dark, and the only view I have is of a pretty girl in the window opposite. Even that does me no good. Whenever she sees me looking in that direction, down goes the shade, and there is nothing left to stare at but the blank wall, which is not very inspiring. Do you suppose I might practice in your room when you are not there?"

Nothing could have been more to Teresa's liking. Every day from two to four, the time, she pretended, when it was her habit to walk in the park, her room was his. Although she respected Rubinstein's desire to be undisturbed while working, yet here was a chance she could not neglect to learn something precious. Teresa laid her plans. Promptly at two she put on hat and coat, taking elaborate leave of the Master as he entered, only to slip quietly into a connecting room whose other door gave on the hall. There she listened intently, until Rubinstein had finished his practicing and began to improvise at random. That was the signal for her to return from her alleged walk more refreshed than she would have been had she actually taken the brisk exercise she so graphically described. And now it was her turn to play, while Rubinstein became the teacher, until both were too tired to go on. The tour could not have begun better for either one of them.

Teresa was the first to leave New York. A reporter, come for an interview just after the farewell, was disturbed to find Rubinstein running his fingers through his hair and wailing: "I have lost her; I have lost my Sunshine!"

Journeying through Canada Teresa became more and more aware that her "Sunshine" was Émile rather than Rubinstein. His constant coughing worried her. From Charlie, her official duenna, she learned that his clothes were not suited to the severe climate, that his underwear needed mending, his buttons attaching. To take upon herself the rehabilitating of this young gentleman's wardrobe was not different from doing it for her dolls of long ago, only infinitely more rewarding. Émile Sauret accepted her solicitude with endearing helplessness. But better than that there was a spontaneous understanding in their musical give and take. Teresa felt in it a sign of more far-reaching oneness still. For the first time the mother and the musician within her felt fused. She was completely happy. Even her clothes showed it. In England she could never be as colorful as she liked. Now she gave her tropical soul free play, let her dressmaker run riot with ribbons and bright decoration. If Boston thought her "loud," and Tietjens called her somewhat *"schlampig,"* why should she care? She was gay at heart. With Émile Sauret she felt translated, set apart together, doubly herself. These two could electrify audiences, each one in his own right. In ensemble a spark kindled between them that heightened their magnetic effect. Before all their playing of the variations in Beethoven's "Kreutzer Sonate" was moving, no more to their listeners than to themselves.

There was something Teresa wanted to learn, how to curtsy as grandly as large-bosomed Carlotta knew how to do in spite of a slight lameness which had prevented her from engaging in an operatic career. She would give anything to sink so deeply to the floor, burying her head in semblance of modest gratitude in the folds of the gown billowing around her, then as gradually rising to her full height, proud and commanding. Teresa spent hours practicing before the mirror, while Carlotta Patti patiently did her best to make her mistress of the art. At last came the evening on which Teresa was to try out her accomplishment in public. In her excitement she made unpermissible mistakes in her playing, which the audience applauded noisily regardless. As she made ready to sink slowly down, Teresa felt Carlotta watching from the wings. Attacked by unaccustomed stage fright Teresa miscalculated, lost her balance, and sat heavily upon the floor to rise as best she could. People tittered, and worse than that, Carlotta was shaking with laughter, she knew. Tears came to Teresa's eyes. Never again did she attempt to impress an audience in that particular way.

Not long after this she found herself once more upon the stage of the Music Hall in Boston, playing the "G minor Concerto" of Mendelssohn, then Liszt's *Faust* "Fantasie," Mendelssohn's "Rondo Capriccioso," and the "A flat Ballade" of Chopin. The very favorable criticism mentioned as one of the sensations of the evening the masterly playing of young Sauret. Mr. Dwight recalled that Teresa has not played in Boston since her tenth birthday, "and now comes back a tall and beautiful young lady and accomplished artist." He remarked upon "the Spanish fire and impatience of manner which somewhat disturbs the pure impression of her classical interpretation," but he was stirred by her brilliance in bravura passages. "Sauret played Spohr's *Eighth Concerto* like a master. There were soulful tenderness and purity in his rendering of poetic pieces."

Then there came a trip southward. In Charleston's Music Hall Teresa and Sauret were heard in the fantasia on themes from *William Tell*. Soon after Mrs. O'Leary's cow had upset the fatal bucket the Patti-Mario troupe appeared in the stricken city of Chicago, playing in the only available place large enough that had been spared by the fire, a church. Then they turned back to the East. In March the Springfield *Republican* testifies that Carreño redeems in her opening womanhood the promise she gave as a prodigy. "She owns the celestial spark of genius. Miss Carreño's playing (the favorite pronunciation of her name was a nasal Treesa Creeno) is luxuriant, glowing, passionate to a degree not remotely approached since Gottschalk's death, and not equalled by that artist."

On the whole for all but Teresa and Émile it had been a dull tour. In late spring the company returned to England at least pecuniarily content. As for Teresa, she lost no time in visiting her father, bubbling over with stories of America, in which the name of Émile Sauret loomed ominously. Manuel Antonio was quick to sense serious implications. "'If you feel sorry for this young man's neglected condition by all means sew on his buttons, mend his clothes, buy his food even, but don't on that account marry him," he pleaded, throwing all the weight of influence in the balance against a union he feared. With foreboding of a greater separation than that of space he saw her off for England, hoping against hope that his child would not take the irrevocable step with Sauret, spoiled, weak, and selfish as he felt him essentially to be.

Teresa was conscious only of the deliciousness of a first love. At the beginning of June the journals hint that Mlle. Carreño is about to become Mme. Sauret, and on July 13, 1873, *Le Ménestrel* announces the union as a fact. Her name is listed as Mme. Teresa Carreño-Sauret in the programs of the London Philharmonic Society. This was another step upward, although according to the *Musical Times* "Mendelssohn's Rondo in B Minor was dashed off with a brilliancy of touch and energy by Madame Carreño-Sauret which pleased the general audience more than the judicious few."

The young Saurets took residence at 16, Clifton Villas, Maida Hill, West. Concerts, lessons, and happiness made the time pass quickly. Teresa played as before in the Monday Popular Concerts. On March 23, 1874, her first child, Emilita, was born.

Three months later she and her husband for the first time staged a joint concert. It was announced as a "morning concert," taking place on Thursday afternoon, June 11, in the Queen's Concert Rooms, Hanover Square. Sofa stalls sold for a half guinea and unreserved seats for five shillings and a half. They dispensed with patronesses, but the number of assisting colleagues, singers, and instrumentalists was large, including three conductors, Herr Ganz, Signor Campana, and Mr. F. H. Cowen to make it thoroughly cosmopolitan. Mendelssohn's

"Piano Quartette" in G minor opened the concert. Teresa collaborated with Sauret in playing the "Sonate in G," op. 30, of Beethoven. One of the women's voices in the trio from *Il Matrimonio Segreto* by Cimarosa was Teresa's own. The life of a singer was still exerting the pressure of its appeal. The piano solos were children of her own imagination, "Highland" and "La Fausse Note." The concert closed, reminiscently for Teresa, with a "Grand Duo" on themes from the *Huguenots* played by the Saurets.

For Manuel Antonio life held no further meaning. Teresa's marriage was his death warrant. To be estranged from her who was so peculiarly his, to be supplanted, no longer her sole confidant! Alone he felt himself unequal to the difficult task of guiding flighty Manuel into the ways of responsibility. Father and daughter still met as often as possible but never again on the same intimate footing. Shortly after Emilita's birth, the three Carreño's had their pictures taken together, at first glance a photograph of three unhappy people. Teresa was brokenhearted to find her father feeble and failing. For the first time she knew what it was to have to choose between two affections, two duties, each drawing her with equal pull. A new American tour was pending. When Teresa left her father that summer, both must have realized that they were facing a final separation.

At the end of August, 1874, Manuel Antonio was buried in Paris with quiet ceremony. *Le Ménestrel* writes:

Last Sunday the funeral service of a one time minister of finance of Venezuela was celebrated, one who became through political misadventures one of our best professors of piano, notably of his daughter Teresa Carreño. M. Antonio Carreño, who had studied music with passion in prosperous days, called his favorite art to his aid and comfort against misfortune. Moreover, a man of science and numbers, he transformed the mechanism of the piano into the art of mathematics, and according to his method he made of his young daughter one of the greatest virtuosos of modern times. He also taught her harmony as he had himself learned it, through reflective study of good music, and it is known that the compositions of Teresa Carreño are as highly esteemed in France as in England where for the last few years lives the beautiful young artist, married to the skillful violinist, Émile Sauret.

DEEPLY affected by her father's death, the more so because she felt that it had been hastened by her own doing, Teresa welcomed the distraction of another journey across the Atlantic. She felt herself adrift without anchor. Sauret, she soon had come to realize, would have to be considered a problem, not a support. The rivalry between home and art was becoming a harrowing reality. With a doubly heavy heart she was obliged to leave her baby in the safekeeping of Mrs. Bischoff, while she set sail, again under Strakosch's management, with a company of which Ilma di Murska was the prima donna, and Sauret the violinist.

The tour was to begin in the East, reaching to the far West with plans for an extension as far as Australia. In Boston, where Teresa's friend, Mme. Rudersdorff, had established herself as a singing teacher, Mr. Dwight still wrote trenchant reviews. In his journal of October 3 he had declared that M. Sauret never made so excellent an impression, that Mme. Sauret was left unhappily to play three solos at the end of a program that, like most, lasted much too long. He liked best the "Andante in F" of Beethoven, and mentioned the "Spring Song" and the "March" from the *Ruins of Athens* favorably. In these concerts the composition most likely to be saved for the end, because of its wide, if musically unwarranted popularity, was Braga's "Angel's Serenade" in trio form with Teresa presiding at the piano and the composer himself playing the cello, while di Murska sang the part of the heaven-hungry daughter.

When artists were to be added or substituted, it was Teresa who was entrusted with their choice. One of these young aspirants was a tenor, Nathaniel Cohen, who in his diary described life with this troupe. At their first meeting Teresa by her natural friendliness at once put him at ease. He forgot to be nervous when she quietly sat down at the piano to play the accompaniments for the songs he had brought for the audition. Teresa praised the quality of his voice, as always unstinting in her enthusiasm. For six weeks he became a regular member of the company. After a week of rehearsal the first concert took place in Los Angeles. Since the railroad was not yet completed, they traveled by boat to disembark at San Pedro where Teresa recovered from her seasickness in the Pico House. The Saurets had taken a great liking to their new colleague. He ate his supper with them over fine Bass ale, and found Teresa, especially, talkative and in high spirits. It was a relief to find in her a woman who did not always have to talk about music, and he had not yet become aware that Teresa's emotional barometer could register extreme ups and downs. Personal unhappiness she had learned to hide under the protective cloak of merriment. It was not that she had ceased to mourn for her father, or to long for her child; but she had recuperative powers so elastic that she could on the instant ignore a profound attack of melancholy to infect a whole gathering with joyousness she had only assumed. At the end she herself was capable of forgetting that it was not real.

In Los Angeles the audience was responsive, being largely German and so, music-loving. Four performances in which Teresa and Émile were singly and together the favorites followed each other closely. Between concerts there was time for drives to the seashore—Teresa appreciated its grandeur best with her own feet on terra firma—and for a side trip to play in Anaheim, a German wine-growing settlement. In the presence of raw nature in any form Teresa felt herself expanding. The ocean had her respect, but it was the mountain scenery she could love. On the way from San Luis Obispo to Santa Barbara she reveled in the magnificent, precarious precipices the stagecoach just managed to avoid, as it swung around curves that made the others cover their eyes. This was living! While Sauret cowered inside, Teresa and Nathaniel mounted to the driver's seat, one on each side of him, rivaling one another in telling minstrel jokes and singing Negro songs for his amusement. They counted thousands of ground squirrels, and were not at all anxious to arrive in time for the concert that evening. It was followed, as was customary there, by a very informal reception for the performers. In the same jolly way as before they again entertained the driver on the way to San Bene Ventura, where the house was nearly sold out. It was a rare thing for known artists to come to so small a place.

Backstage all was peaceful on this particular night; that is, until the Saurets were to play together. Émile was apparently out of patience, perhaps with his wife. That was becoming less and less uncommon. Inadvertently or not, with the first note of their duo his foot began an insistent tapping. Teresa, enraged at this implied criticism of her tempo, answered with chords that should by their increasingly bitter tang have given warning. Tap, tap went the foot. Teresa boiled. She tried by playing fortissimo to· drown out the sound of this unwelcome metronome. Sauret went on playing and tapping. Nathaniel Cohen in the dressing room next to theirs heard the music stop. Suddenly there was a crash! A tirade in angry French pitched higher and higher. Nathaniel rushed to see. There stood Teresa, an avenging fury, eyes flashing, adjectives rolling avalanchelike down upon her husband. "I am enough of an artist to count without your assistance," she shrieked, flinging herself out of the room. Sauret's temper had exploded more destructively. On the floor, where in his rage he had thrown it, lay his precious violin, broken beyond repair. At breakfast next morning this marital ensemble was by mutual agreement not on speaking terms. It was Nathaniel's part to play the embarrassing role of placating go-between.

There was one last stage ride to Soledad, the railway terminal —harmony was at last reëstablished—and then to San Francisco, where the artists were to be redistributed. Nathaniel was chosen to accompany the Saurets to Virginia City for a week of concerts. Valerga, the soprano, had just resigned. What would become of the duets? Teresa offered to sing them with Nathaniel, succeeding so ·charmingly that he wondered at her doing it so rarely. Later she confided to him that she meant to sing in opera upon her return to Europe.

The troupe finally disbanded in Carson City, a mining town

in which every other building was either a saloon or a gambling den and musical hall. The Opera House was sold out for both nights. It might not be a godly city, but it was music-minded. Teresa sang and was herself pleased with the sound, as with the warm response of her disreputable audience. She had never been in better form or in better humor. Prophetically with the strains of the "Last Hope" the tour ended.

THE two Saurets were at odds. That was no secret to anybody but perhaps themselves. Scenes were nothing unusual, and they themselves did not take them ultraseriously. But Teresa's exuberant vitality was too much for the self-contained Émile. It overpowered him, and she too became irritable. Touring from town to town, where anything she played was acceptable, no matter how badly she did it, left her nothing to live up to. Her nature required difficulties to conquer. More than that she wanted and needed her home.

There was to be another baby soon. Teresa decided to await its birth in New York. As for Émile, to be tied down as father of another child that he did not want was not to his mind. In his irritation he flaunted his temper at the least provocation. Everything upset him from the mustiness of the boardinghouse to the emptiness of his purse. Suddenly he was overwhelmed by homesickness for England, and one morning he entered Teresa's room to announce abruptly, "I am leaving." Teresa was dumbfounded. Cold-blooded though he was, she had not thought him capable of this. He should see that she was not one to be downed. Reaching under her pillow, she took what remained of their capital, seventy dollars in all, divided it into two equal parts, and taking a certain pride in making a last gesture, she gave him one half. Then pointing melodramatically to the door she said: "Go! But remember this, if you leave me now, I shall never receive you again as long as I live." The door closed behind him.

Teresa was alone. The shock was too great. The baby did not survive. Disillusioned, ill, and penniless—even Manuel was far away in Africa with the foreign legion—she, the always self-sufficient, had to depend upon a few loyal friends and Mrs. Bischoff. Two things were certain. She could not in her humiliation return to England to be pitied, and she and Sauret were separated forever. As soon as possible she must find occupation, earn enough to bring Emilita to America. For the present there was no thought of such a thing. Teresa was slow in recovering, the summer season musically nonexistent.

A letter from Mrs. Bischoff, to whom alone she had written the details of her unhappiness, was usually a comfort. Thank God, her child was well, cared for, and cherished! One morning there arrived a letter which contained more than the usual words of commiseration and reassurance. "Preposterous, revolting; never so long as I live!" That was the first reaction. Again and again she read it through. Mrs. Bischoff wanted to adopt Emilita, her baby! She had come to love the child as her own, she said, and could offer her the security of home, provide her with every luxury, educate her well, eventually make her heir to the family fortune. There was one stipulation only. Teresa must give up all thought of seeing Emilita again, must promise to make no attempt to communicate with her ever. "Her little baby!" Instant angry refusal was at the tip of her pen. While putting her feelings on paper, maternal protectiveness had time to assert itself. What after all could she, a wandering musician, offer her child? Poverty, insecurity, fatherlessness. The love of a mother seemed to weigh light in the balance. She was still young to sound the spiritual depths of resignation, even though at the age of eight her music had expressed that quality. Against all her instincts Teresa made the decision. In favor of the rights of her daughter to lead a carefree, sheltered life, she signed her name to the abdication of the privilege she cherished most, that of motherhood.

TERESA's world of the moment was a vacuum, the next step not worth the taking. Self-preservation supported by pride forced her to muster her resources. The thought of staying in

New York sickened her. Instead she resolved to make a fresh start in Boston.

Once there she turned to Mme. Rudersdorff. Here was one who would give practical advice without being too openly sympathetic. In this Teresa made no mistake. It happened that Mme. Rudersdorff needed an accompanist for her classes and for her concerts. In exchange she offered a modest salary. Teresa found herself at once in a congenial atmosphere to whose lighthearted camaraderie she could not long remain unresponsive. Appreciating the therapeutic value of a new interest, Mme. Rudersdorff tactfully chose the right moment to suggest that Teresa join her class of singers. Once more encouraged to enter the realm of fictitious tragedy, this time to offset her own too real distress, she began to prepare for the opera stage in earnest. Occasionally she was reminded that she was a pianist, and accepted an engagement to play here and there in the neighborhood. It helped in meeting expenses. Her repertoire lay dormant. She felt no urge to increase it.

When Mme. Rudersdorff appeared in public, Teresa was invariably at the piano and the other students in the audience. To invent some prank at the expense of their teacher was tempting because of a certain element of danger connected with it. On one particular evening Mme. Rudersdorff was singing not far from Boston for a charitable purpose. The students attended en masse. Dressed in black touched with the scarlet she loved—her nature like Teresa's delighted in the colorful—she stood superbly still in the curve of the piano, waiting for Teresa's improvising before the beginning of the aria, while the audience was composing itself. Suddenly she stiffened. What was she hearing? Teresa, unconcerned except for a twinkling eye, was preludizing on a certain nose exercise known to every Rudersdorff pupil. Tittering and nudging in the front rows suggested that there were those who were thoroughly enjoying themselves at the expense of their teacher. Mme. Rudersdorff turned slightly and as unnoticeably as possible hissed through closed teeth: "Stop that, you little devil." Teresa took her own good time in finding a modulation suitable to the key and the spirit of the aria. The concert continued without further obstruction, this episode indicating that Teresa's emotional barometer was rising once more to fair.

A frequent guest in the house of Mme. Rudersdorff during the season of 1876 was the great conductor and pianist, Hans von Bülow. It was there that Teresa's playing and her beauty first came to his notice. He was less impressed with Boston itself as a musical center, much preferring Philadelphia.

The cosmopolitan setting of the Rudersdorff circle was unaffected by the frostbitten provincialism of Boston. In the summer Teresa accompanied the Rudersdorff colony to Berlin, Massachusetts, where Mme. Rudersdorff had rented a farm. There, in the quiet she loved, Teresa made preparations to appear, this time under her own name, in opera. The role decided upon for her début was that of Zerlina in *Don Giovanni*. The uncomplicated clarity of Mozart's music was grateful to her own confused state of mind. Mme. Rudersdorff had chosen wisely.

Teresa's good friend, Maurice Strakosch, happened to be in America with his opera company, which included Tietjens and the two baritones Brignoli and Giovanni Tagliapietra. Brignoli's huge size and manner invariably caused laughter. But Tag, as he was familiarly called, was, according to M. Rivière, "perhaps the handsomest and most dashing baritone that ever appeared in Grand Opera." Strakosch was found willing to engage Teresa for a performance of *Don Giovanni* in the Academy of Music of New York, where years before she had succeeded and frozen in her so-called benefit performance on her ninth birthday. Teresa was in the habit of making a success of everything she undertook artistically. Her fiascos were registered in other fields. And so it was again. The papers acknowledged her gift and found her capable, without however giving vent to extreme enthusiasm. The New York *Daily Tribune* of February 26, 1876, wrote:

Mlle. Tietjens reappeared at the Academy of Music last evening, singing for the first time here the part of Donna Anna in *Don Giovanni*.

Her success was as great as on former occasions and she was received with delight by an immense audience. Miss Beaumont, though new to the stage, rendered the difficult part of Elvira in a most acceptable manner. The trio at the close of the first act by Mlle. Tietjens, Miss Beaumont, and Brignoli was given admirably, and was enthusiastically encored. The débutante of the evening, Mme. Carreño-Sauret, in the part of Zerlina was warmly greeted by the audience and made a pleasant impression. Her singing shows careful study and excellent method. In the second act she seemed to gain confidence and sang the solo in a creditable manner.

This review is complemented by one in *Dwight's Journal* of March 18, 1876. The company was made up in Boston on short notice in order to give Tietjens, already attacked by her fatal illness, a hearing in the medium for which she was most famous. This single performance of *Don Giovanni* took place in the first half of March. The critic wrote of Carreño:

The debutante of the evening, the beautiful Mme. Carreño-Sauret, in the part of Zerlina acted with grace and spirit, and in spite of the indulgence asked for her on the ground of health, sang most of the music well, showing herself possessor of a clear, rich, telling voice which seems to promise a career.

AFTER these experimental excursions into a neighboring field Teresa took stock of her assets as a singer. In all honesty she was obliged to admit that her voice, powerful as it was, lacked a certain roundness and richness. Perfection would be hard to acquire and harder to maintain. Her piano playing was natural, effortless, relaxed. In singing self-consciousness entered in, and she could not help fearing and tightening. And even if she did succeed in achieving a relative degree of fame, how short the life of a voice! Besides, it would be difficult for her to follow unquestioningly the dictates of an opera director. She had ventured far enough in this direction. It had served its purpose in

BOSTON 1876

*Teresa as Zerlina in Don Giovanni*

restoring her balance, in showing her once again clearly that, whatever the byways she might be tempted to explore, the piano was her instrument.

Mr. Weber, owner of the Weber Piano Company, was of the same opinion. Teresa had played his pianos now and then, and under her fingers they sounded superbly their best. He decided to engage her to represent his interests in concert at a modest but fixed salary. For fourteen years she played under Weber contract. Her daily needs were provided for. It was no longer advisable to live in Boston. New York was the far more convenient point of departure for a pianist, and there again she took up residence in the fall of 1876.

Young James Huneker heard Teresa in one of the first of her performances after she had freed herself from the operatic urge. Time after time he was impelled to propose to her. Together with Adelaide Nielson and Mme. Scott-Siddons he considered her one of the three most beautiful women then before the public, and he remembered her on one hot night wearing a scarlet dress as fiery as her playing. "I close my eyes," said Mr. Huneker, "and then, as if I were surrounded by a scarlet cloud, I see her and I hear her. . . . Even her manner of playing for me has always seemed scarlet, as Rubinstein's was golden, and Joseffy's silver."

A person immediate in reaction is never long in making friends. A casual invitation from Juan Buitrago, a South American violinist who had accompanied the Carreños on their first voyage to Philadelphia in 1862, to hear his talented young piano pupil, Eddie MacDowell, play, was for Teresa the beginning of a lifelong and intimate friendship with the MacDowell family. Fanny MacDowell, Eddie's mother, was associated with a Conservatory of Music in an administrative capacity. Her genial husband Thomas owned a not-too-prospering milk circuit. Although Fanny was not herself a musician, she liked to surround herself with young artists. One of these was Buitrago, adopted as a member of her household in return for the instruction he gave to young Edward. Teresa recognized at first hearing the extraordinary talent of this boy of fourteen, and was immediately attracted to his parents, who encouraged her to confide to them the story of her unhappiness. Taken captive by Teresa's charm and beauty, their sympathies were enlisted in her behalf. In their simple home on East Nineteenth Street, Teresa could rely upon finding unwavering affection and practical advice. There was the understanding family life she longed for, there was a friend with whom she could share a joke, for their sense of the ridiculous was fundamentally alike. Soon it was "my dearest girl" and "your devoted Fanny." Interrupted by temporary misunderstandings their close intimacy lasted through life, largely because Fanny MacDowell, sixteen years her senior, had the common sense to respect Teresa's independence, while exerting a decidedly leveling influence. On her part Teresa brought color and radiance to enliven the work-a-day world of the MacDowells.

Teresa Carreño's importance in the musical development of Edward MacDowell in his formative years was determining and constructive. As she went freely in and out of his house, playing on his piano when the spirit moved her, he must have learned much merely by listening. More than that she occasionally practiced with him, taking his part against the majority opinion that music was no profession for a boy, that it was bound to make him a "sissy," the worst that then as now could befall any male. Edward's father was disturbed, his mother secretly delighted at the thought of having a musician in the family. It worried her that under the able instruction of Señor Desvernine as of Señor Buitrago, Eddie was not as attentive, as patient, or as skillful as she would have wished him. Teresa offered to try out her own methods. He did not, she discovered, have naturally good coördination. His fingers, if willing, were clumsy and stiff. When Teresa was at the end of her resources, she would sit down at the piano herself. "Look at me, Eddie! Do it the way I do." To which Eddie conclusively protested, "Yes, but that's you, not me."

Musically imaginative as he was, there were times when he

was, like most normal boys, actually lazy. One afternoon the composition in question was Chopin's "B flat minor Scherzo." Teresa herself had never added it to her repertoire, and Edward to her distraction was dawdling over it. The time had come to do something drastic. "I shall make a bet with you, Eddie," she suggested. "Tonight, I promise to play the whole *Scherzo* for you correctly from memory. It is easy enough. If I have not learned it, I will give you a nice present. If I do it without mistakes—you shall give me a kiss." Eddie curious and unafraid—it could not be done in a few hours—easily agreed. After supper Teresa reappeared and without hesitation played the piece from beginning to end, then turned around for Eddie's approval. But he had vanished. There he stood on the landing! Teresa followed him in a heated chase, which she at least thoroughly enjoyed, upstairs and down, until she cornered her victim, breathless, in the cellar. She managed to kiss him soundly, and left him rubbing off the indignity with his handkerchief. "It did not, however, wipe away the lesson," said Teresa.

TERESA's operatic interlude had one far-reaching result. She had found a personable, amusing, and warmhearted colleague in Giovanni Tagliapietra. They appeared together in the Emma Abbott troupe at the Philadelphia Centennial in 1876 and increasingly often later on. He sang like an angel and was as fun-loving as a mischievous child. Teresa loved to hear him tell how he, a young student of naval architecture, one dark night in Italy had jumped from the window of his dormitory to join the forces of Garibaldi in 1866 and had followed his idol for three thrilling years. Teresa believed every tale, even the wildest, to the last word. Here was a real man, her equal in temperament, who could understand her better than that cold-blooded fish Sauret. He needed no protection—except perhaps from those silly girls that so blatantly adored him—and he was strong enough to care for her, to fight her battles. Home and such a husband! What more could she ask of life?

For Tag falling in love was as undiscriminating and daily a pastime in life as on the stage. But that Teresa failed to notice. When he brought her flowers, sang to her accompaniments, made love to her, nothing else existed.

Once, hidden behind a huge bouquet of roses, he met her train at the end of a tour, to the despair of young Walter Damrosch, for whose interests—it was his first concert experience as accompanist—Teresa had appointed herself protector-in-chief. She saw to it that the number of rehearsals granted the novice was adequate. She even on occasion took his place. In return she earned temporary adoration and lasting friendship.

At this time paradise to Teresa seemed nothing more far away than a suburb of New York City. Forgetting her lack of judgment in the choice of a first husband, Teresa unthinkingly surrendered to her impulses for a second time. In short order Teresa and Tag were established together in a small house of their own renting in New Rochelle. The garden extended behind it in terraces down to the water where they were in the habit of rowing, and for Teresa living in this countrylike place

*1878*      *As Valentine in Faust*

*Giovanni Tagliapietra*

came close to the ideal. How she had hated living alone! To plan, to cook for two, even to scrub floors, became a rite. It made home more dearly hers. Disguised in apron and turban she sang as she worked. Sitting proud and straight in her phaeton, Billy the horse prancing before, she had the pleasure of feeling herself noticed and envied, as she drove her handsome husband to the station mornings, or called for him at night. In the evenings people stopped before the open windows to listen to their blended music. How could anyone say that there was no such thing as perfect happiness! Tag's good spirits matched her own, his devotion seemed to leave nothing to be desired. This was living!

There had as yet been no official release from the marriage ties that bound Carreño to Sauret. Teresa was undisturbed by the equivocal situation in which she found herself. As a child she had often felt smothered by the social and religious conventions she was obliged to observe overpunctiliously. As soon as she had her independence, she asserted her right to do as she chose, to be accountable to herself alone, and she actively resented whatever interfered with this right. Not that she was irreligious, although for years she did not enter a church except to be uplifted by its architecture! But half fatalist, half pagan, she worshiped a God whom she acknowledged as an all-directing, inescapable father. She was not free from superstitions. It was a good precaution, for instance, to make the sign against the evil eye every time a priest approached. With better logic she disregarded the man-made decrees that set store rather upon the letter than upon the spirit of matrimony. Marriage to her was nonetheless sacred because it lacked the sanction of civil and religious ceremony. She knew that she meant to do her part to make the relation a lasting one. Of her husband she expected no less than of herself. A common-law marriage, which was at this time legal in New York State, seemed to Teresa as dignified as any other. She did not require that her conservative friends agree with her and took little notice if they did not. It might even serve a purpose in showing which friends she could depend upon to stand the test. Among these were the MacDowells. Their affection was not deflected by an interpretation of marriage that could not but shock them. As for Tag himself, he lived, like the improvident cricket, in the present. What was marriage to him, the gambler incarnate, but the greatest lottery of all. He gladly left it to Teresa, busy as any ant with homemaking, to plan for the future.

A music correspondent remembers a concert given by the pair at the old Park Theater at Twenty-third Street and Broadway. It was in the early days of their companionship. Teresa played solos and did not consider it beneath her then to accompany Tag's songs. The eyes of all the men were for the beautiful Teresa, of all the girls for handsome Tag. His colleagues of the opera began by being amused at his new infatuation, then became amazed that it apparently was going to last. Even a game of poker or his favorite bottle could not keep him from catching the train for New Rochelle on time. Teresa and Billy would not, he knew, fail to meet him. And later, over a steaming plate of spaghetti that Teresa learned to prepare according to perfect Italian tradition, she would dramatize for his benefit the most humdrum details of the day that was closing.

Concerts took subordinate place for Teresa at this time. Reluctantly she accepted an occasional engagement. The most important one of the year 1877 was with the New York Philharmonic Orchestra, her medium being Mendelssohn's "G minor Concerto." This was, she felt, where she belonged. Why could not she too be allowed to play only good music, to live always up to her best? If more were demanded of her, she felt the power within her of rising to unexplored heights. Her wings were strong to carry her to Andean altitudes of unimagined splendor. Was there in the world no audience that could follow her, urge her on? Did fate mean to condemn her to life at second best? She returned to the accustomed routine, discontented with the artist that she was, unresigned to audiences as she found them.

Her great satisfaction was her home, before all when on March 1, 1878, she became the guardian of a new life, another daughter providentially sent to fill the emptiness left by the sacrifice she had made, but never ceased to feel. For a time the duties of motherhood and housekeeping completely absorbed her. Not until the end of the year would she consider a longer tour.

Then Mr. Weber offered Tag and Teresa together a journey with Wilhelmy the violinist, and di Murska the singer, a combination much superior to the usual ones. Early January, 1879, found the troupe in Boston. Together Carreño and Wilhelmy played the "Kreutzer Variations" says the surfeited Mr. Dwight,

"as if possessed by one spirit, both moved by a higher power invisible. It was one of those inspired moments which now and then occur to relieve the tedium of too many concerts. The beautiful pianist whose face and movements had until then worn an expression of impatience and almost disgust at being repeatedly recalled after flashy virtuoso pieces (Gottschalks) now evidently felt at home and happy in good music; her cooperation was perfect, and her face poetic and inspired. Why cannot artists always have artistic tasks to do?

And then he mentions Signor Tagliapietra "one of the most artistic and refined of baritones." It was Carl Zerrahn who conducted the improvised orchestra in the Music Hall of happy memory.

The tour continued with the pull of home and profession always in opposite directions. Besides, a disturbing cloud threatened storm. Teresa was beginning to see in Tag qualities that she had not in her trustfulness investigated. Carefree and moneyfree she had from the first known him to be. On that account both agreed that she should be the one to administer the family purse. She had inherited from her father an interest in the practical side of life, from him also a sense of pride that admitted of being in debt to no one. Necessity had educated her to rigid economy. Tag's income and hers together should have sufficed for pleasant living on a modest scale. For a time

Tag entered into this planning as into a new game. Then his extravagant instincts, his love of taking a chance, came to the front. Gradually Teresa realized that she must not count upon her husband's earnings. Over the poker table they might vanish in a night. More and more often Billy trotted disconsolately back from the station with one disappointed passenger. Subjects of disagreement became frequent, and led to scenes in which amiability changed to violence on the instant. The explosion of two high-pressure temperaments in conflict were audible outside. It was spare, white-haired Hughsie, the real treasure of a factotum, who discreetly closed the windows. Tag jealous and bored by turns sought for more peaceable companionship among his all-too-willing friends of both sexes, then sheepishly returned to the uncertain weather of a fireside he still needed and periodically cherished. When the two appeared in public together the frank admiration accorded to his wife became irksome to Tag, and Teresa purposely did nothing to calm his jealousy. It did not occur to her to leave him. He was still in his contrite, appeasing moments dear to her. Above all he was the father of little Lulu. For her sake this marriage must be made to last. But if Teresa had to pay the bills she meant to hold the reins of the household. There was no meekness in her makeup. She disliked this trait in others, as much as stupidity, with which in servants or in students she had no patience whatsoever.

Of the latter she had a number whom she taught more or less as she felt inclined. They served in giving ear to her troubles, and when they were too unyielding to her erratic methods of instruction, she would, instead of correcting their mistakes, play for them herself by the hour. Her own practicing at this time was desultory. After a passage had misfired in public a number of times she might spend a tearful morning ironing out the difficulty. Her standing repertoire sufficed to fill the needs of a country at the very bottom level of musical taste.

At the insistent prodding of Teresa young Edward Mac-Dowell in the interim had been taken by his mother to study music in Paris. His unabated confidence in Teresa's artistic judgment led him to send her a bundle of his early compositions in manuscript, among them his first "Suite," "Erzählung," and "Barcarolle." In an accompanying letter he asked her to examine them. If she approved, he promised to increase his efforts; otherwise, should she find them worthless, he begged her, with characteristic self-depreciation, to destroy them. He would then write no more. Teresa at once replied from the equally characteristic fullness of her enthusiasm, urging him to continue at full steam and above all to consign not a scrap to the wastebasket. She made up her mind then and there that her fingers and no others should be first to introduce Edward MacDowell to the public. America may well be grateful to Teresa Carreño for her enlightened encouragement of Edward MacDowell's gift, and for her propaganda in the face of obstacles presented by audiences that were as unreceptive as they were unprepared. It is to her unselfish efforts that MacDowell's early popularity was in great measure due.

TOURING the United States and Canada in the Seventies and Eighties must have been a doubtful pleasure for one who looked upon music as an art. The companies were carelessly thrown together and ill-assorted, often a fading stellar magnitude giving its name to a group of lesser satellites. The programs were a jumble of light music for the many, and more classical music for the few, making up in length for what they lacked in depth. They followed Goethe's dictum: "He who brings much, will bring something to each." Concerts were listed with circuses and prize fights under the heading of "amusements," and were criticized rather for the personal appeal of the performer, for mannerisms, for accidents in the performance, than for the quality inherent in the music. Fifty cents was considered a high price to pay for a ticket of admission. Accommodations in small towns were meager, trains unreliable and uncomfortable, meals irregular and poor, and audiences disheartening. People came and went, conversed or slept at pleasure during the concerts. At the opening of the Queen's Hall, Montreal, in January, 1880, says the Montreal *Star:* "Carreño played at a disadvantage, coming directly from the train," and goes on to say: "It seems to us that a great deal of unnecessary fuss was shown in the frequent moving of the piano by three men." Later in the year, in the same city, the *Gazette* passes favorably upon the new departure of keeping doors closed during the performance. "The length of the programme and the demand for encores made the concert longer than usual, not more than half the audience being present at the conclusion."

Chicago, where Teresa found genuine stimulus, had a fore-sighted critic, who remarked, "Carreño had so much improved of late that one would scarcely recognize the passionate but somewhat reckless pianiste of days gone by. Certainly the fire of genuine ambition has touched her gift of genius, and she now adds to her talent a scholarly thought and method which will undoubtedly send her to the front of the first rank of pianists." That would not have been noticed in the small town of Ilion, New York, where Teresa's co-artist was Mr. Archibald Forbes of London, famous English correspondent, who lectured, framed by Carreño's solos, on "Royal people I have met." It must have been a genuine relief to return to more usual colleagues such as Reményi the violinist, and Kate Thayer, the singer, with whom she toured in the South.

January, 1881, saw Teresa in Baltimore, contributing a group of Norwegian scenes of folk life by Grieg to a program devoted to Russian and Norse music. February took her from Montreal, where she shared the honors with her husband, to Chicago and southward to Knoxville.

Here under the name of the Carreño Concert Company a new procedure was followed. One half of the evening was devoted to the usual concert program, the second to opera in concert form. All began well. "Madame was led to her seat, her pretty face wreathed in smiles." Next it was Tag's turn. He sang a few bars, then stopped. "I am ill, very ill," he explained and left the stage. Somewhat later he reappeared, apparently quite restored, to sing the part of the Count de Luna to Teresa's Leonore in *Il Trovatore*. Her encore was "Home Sweet Home." She must have sung it with fervor. On the following Monday selections from *La Favorita, Marta,* and *Faust* divided honors with the piano in the "Waltz" from *Faust,* "La Campanella," and "The Last Rose of Summer." Speaking of Teresa as a singer the Knoxville paper effervesces: "Carreño rose to the height of a musical medium, and carried her audience into the spell of opera's profundity without the aid of English words." And Signor Tagliapietra's voice was pronounced "the finest in all respects on this side of the Atlantic."

After a concert in Philadelphia on April 27, 1881, in which Teresa accompanied the "Double Concerto" of Bach for the two Gärtners, father and son, both violinists, there is suddenly a hiatus. No more mention of concerts. Lulu, the one who mattered most in her affections, fell ill. The best available doctors did what they could. On the sixteenth of May, 1881, a little over three years old, she died. Teresa was crushed. Tag too loved his child, precociously intelligent for her years. Temporarily grief brought the two parents once more closely together.

Fanny MacDowell was a very practical consolation, and Teresa also found relief in the friendship of one of her pupils, a Southern girl of eighteen, Caroline Keating by name. When Teresa found herself attacked by gloom, it was Carrie to whom she telephoned to make an appointment for theater or vaudeville. Afterwards, her spirits restored, she would review the whole performance in caricature, leaving Carrie convulsed with laughter. Not only their likes were similar. According to Brignoli they actually looked like sisters.

In September, 1881, after a summer engagement at Manhattan Beach a new group formed, which called itself the Carreño-Donaldi Operatic Gem Company. It included Mme. Teresa Carreño, the greatest living Lady Pianiste—Mr. Dwight would not have agreed. His list of the three greatest so-called "petticoat pianists" comprised Sophie Menter, Clara Schumann, and Arabella Goddard—Mme. Emma Donaldi, grand Italian prima donna, Signor Ferranti, King of Buffos, also Signor Stantini, a tenor, for whom nobody seemed to have a kind word. By common consent Mme. Carreño was declared to be "strong enough to carry the whole party." Signor Ferranti's time for being funny had evidently forever passed. Yet his sunny Italian good humor won him friends in spite of it. Mme. Donaldi had lost whatever public appeal she once possessed. When her criticisms became too painfully bad, she withdrew on the plea of illness which did not fool the reviewers. Buffalo was one of the places in which she defaulted, and on short notice a duet between Carreño and Stantini was substituted. At this time Teresa's singing earned so much commendation that it became a regular part of the programs.

In Chicago Teresa was from the first a favorite. Nowhere was she more appreciated. This was due in no small part to the insight of the best and most discriminating of all her friends, Mrs. Regina Watson. First of all Mrs. Watson was a thorough musician, a good pianist, to whom matrimonial happiness chanced to mean more than a concert career. At her home in East Indiana Street she had established a school for the "Higher Art of Piano Playing." Chicago society gave her its friendship and sent her its most gifted children. She became a strong influence in many single lives, and in the musical development of Chicago she was a driving force for good.

Teresa and "Ginka," as her intimates called her, were drawn together by their likemindedness. They respected and admired each other. Teresa as a performer was the impersonation of Ginka's ideals. Her vitality, her power, her directness as an artist and as a human being alike found echo within her. So she would have dreamed of playing herself. To Teresa Ginka was the embodiment of frank friendship and of honest devotion to a calling. She was not blind to the faults of Teresa's impulsive nature, nor slow in confronting her with them, when she was in danger of making a major mistake. Besides, Ginka had achieved that in which she had herself failed, the combination of a successful profession and equally successful home life. With Ginka and Lewis, her husband, Teresa found her intellectual and spiritual level—both Dr. and Mrs. Watson held dominating positions in their respective fields of medicine and music—found sane counsel, and the peace of well-being in a household that ran smoothly yet without ostentation. So Teresa would have dreamed her own home. As long as they lived there was never a serious misunderstanding between them. To Mrs. Watson's lasting credit be it said that she was the one who paved the way that finally was to release Teresa from the depressing routine of the concert player on tour in the United States of the Eighties. For the time being, however, it continued in its dull and devious ways.

Electric light had been newly installed in the Chicago warerooms of Weber and Company. To celebrate the occasion Teresa on February 2 played Schumann's "Symphonische Etuden," and the "Staccato Étude" by Rubinstein, also his "Waltz in A." "Where is Donaldi?" asks the critic. The week before she had claimed to be ill, and now suddenly she had departed for New York. Her absence was more mystifying than deplorable. The tour went on very well without her. Saint Paul gave the group only a small audience on February 13, 1882. A paper found it pertinent to compare Mme. Rivé-King and Carreño, because in close succession they played the same piano and some of the same works there. "Carreño is the greater genius, Rivé-King the better artist. Carreño enters with a quick, girlish step. The manager had to adjust Rivé-King's chair. Carreño adjusted hers herself, even moving the immense Weber Grand into position as easily as if it were a chair." Teresa and Ferranti sang together in a duet representing a night patrol.

In Des Moines a hot local political fight and a competing lecture were enough to reduce the size of the audience to a minimum. The Burlington *Hawk-eye* admits that Burlington is not generally enthusiastic over piano playing, "and when it recalls a pianist twice in an evening there must be reason for this extraordinary behavior." It endows Carreño's playing with

Wieck's *drei Kleinigkeiten:* 1. *das Zarteste Gehör.* 2. *der feinste Geschmack.* 3. *das tiefste Gefühl.* In Joliet a new music critic devotes his first effort to Carreño thus:

"The celebration opened on time with a measly small audience" and "a very pert looking damsel with snappy black eyes, round features, chubby lips, a carefully chiseled nose, a No. 2 shoe, weighing 185 pounds, was led out by the accompanist. She sat down at the piano, and immediately picked a quarrel with it. She kept it up until the umpire decided the battle a draw. . . .

June, 1882, brought Tag and Teresa together again for a concert in Oil City, Pennsylvania.

A series of appearances by the Carreño Concert Company at Narragansett Pier in the hall of the Mathewson House was something of a vacation. It was noted that "during the stay at the hotel the elegant manners and excellent English of Mme. Carreño and her husband Tagliapietra have won them many delightful friends." One of these was Colonel Sidam of New York. While Teresa was resting on the piazza one evening after a concert, he introduced himself as the one who had presented the little Teresita with her famous crying doll at her Irving Hall début.

Teresa looked back upon the season just ended. Outwardly it had been successful enough, but inwardly discouraging. Was this the best of which she was capable? "In Germany," Mrs. Watson had said, "people comprehend music in all its dignity. There you must go to be understood. There you will learn what music can really mean to an audience, and it will inspire you to explore its depths." In America the appeal of the "greatest lady pianist" and the "greatest lady lion-tamer" were not essentially different in kind. But how could she earn the money to go? What would become of Tag?

In September, 1882, another tour with Lizzie Arbuckle and the Weber Male Quartette took her again to Chicago to play for the benefit of the Norfolk Light Artillery Blues Armory

Fund. Here she saw her old friend Maurice Strakosch who graced the concert in the role of accompanist. Everywhere Teresa reaped the laurels. Miss Arbuckle failed to please, and the Weber quartette in its *a capella* singing would have been more effective with an accompanist to hold them to pitch.

BREAKING off her tour just a month before giving birth to another daughter, Teresa faced everything but the peace she needed at home. Tag was becoming more and more objectionable. If he came home at all at night it was sure to be in the worst of humors. Drink, he knew, was beginning to affect his singing. Of late he was meriting the reputation of being vocally unreliable, so that some of the choice engagements went to others. That his wife's popularity was on the upgrade helped to aggravate the situation. Tag was not one to tolerate shining by reflection or having his demands for money refused. The atmosphere at home was electrically charged. Scenes multiplied in frequency and violence until Teresa grew to fear her husband's return more than she had before worried over his absence. She could not shut her eyes to the fact that she was no longer first lady to Tag. His philanderings were open scandal.

The climax came one night in December. After an unusually heated altercation Tag entered the living room, and drawing out a sharp knife in perfect Sparafucilean manner, slowly rolled up his sleeve. In a voice that would have given any opera audience "zero at the bone" he hissed: "I am going to kill you." Ordinarily Teresa would have trusted to the cowardice always inherent in generous measure in all of Tag's accesses of brutality. This time she had double reason to be afraid and stood petrified, unable to move or cry out, certain that today he meant to put an end to her and to the child soon to be born. Tag, accustomed to act murder without actually committing it, was satisfied with the effect he had produced. Was he not still a great artist to be able after all these years to fool his own wife? He slammed the front door exhilarated by his triumph.

As each chug of the train drew him closer and closer to his companions of the poker table, he felt sure that luck would be with him that night.

Under such auspices a dark-eyed little girl was born to Teresa on Christmas Eve, 1882. Tag, in one of his rebounding moments of devotion and tenderness, insisted that she be called Teresita. A beautiful, delicate, oversensitive child she became, but as she outgrew babyhood there was one habit of which she could not be cured by ridicule or punishment. Invariably she insisted on rolling up her sleeves, a gesture which her mother could never see without a reminiscent shiver.

The year 1883 was to bring Teresa somewhat greater satisfaction. Late in January she was again on tour playing concerts arranged and conducted by Mr. Heimendahl, a versatile and painstaking musician of Chicago, whose too meticulous earnestness kept him from reaching to the hearts of his less particular listeners, as well as to the heart of the excellent music he played. He did notwithstanding help to raise the standard of program building considerably. To be asked to play as visiting artist with his orchestra meant recognition as an artist of worth. The *Inter-Ocean* took pains to commend Teresa's "pretty preludes and interludes," and called her "the most finished interpreter of Chopin in the world." But the *Times* struck a jangling note, complaining: "One could only regret that her eye for harmony of colors in dress does not seem to equal her ear for harmony of sound."

Less flattering, but too remunerative to be refused, was the invitation of Rudolph Aronson that Teresa take part in the concerts of the Casino of New York City. Her reappearance on the concert platforms of this metropolis under such auspices after an absence of over a year was not likely to increase her prestige as an artist. She would have preferred being heard under the baton of Theodore Thomas, whose neglect to engage her was a puzzle and a worry. But she needed the money and, whatever the setting, never refused an opportunity to play with orchestra. Especially just now she was eager to test before the public a concerto she had added to her repertoire, one that suited her entirely, that of a modern Norwegian called Grieg. Her disappointment was great when this had to be abandoned on account of insufficient time for rehearsal. Had she dreamed that one day Grieg himself would hear her and approve his work under her fingers, she might have been less impatient with this mischance. Meanwhile there were signs of better things in store.

REALLY challenging artistically was the offer of a long tour with Leopold Damrosch and his orchestra in the spring of 1883. After all, it was good that the Grieg Concerto had been saved for this, and Teresa at once set about refurbishing all the other orchestral works in her experience. Next to Theodore Thomas there was no conductor more to be respected as man and musician than Leopold Damrosch. From the first he and Teresa understood each other well, meeting on the common ground of reverence for the best in music. The Damrosch concerts remained among the happy memories of these shadowed years.

A much-quoted incident occurred on this tour. It was no secret that Leopold Damrosch had not a kind thought for women composers. Teresa, too, was well aware of the fact, it being understood that nothing of her own might appear on his programs. One day in a city of the Middle West they were trying out pianos for a concert. In answer to a request that she play something Teresa began with a stern, marchlike melody accompanied by massive chords. "That's a good piece. Who wrote it?" inquired the maestro. Using the gesture she had once so effectively copied from Rubinstein, Teresa pointed at herself, eloquently saying nothing. This happened to be the "Hymn to Bolívar" that the Venezuelan Government had asked her to set to music for his centennial, the performance of which did not however, for an unknown reason, take place at the intended time.

It was probably in New Haven on the platform of Carll's

Opera House that Teresa actually first played the Grieg Concerto, and, being new, it met with varying degrees of favor. All agreed that it was well performed. Concerts followed each other in close succession throughout the East, sometimes at the rate of two a day. In Springfield the stage was too small to allow the instruments, uncomfortably huddled together, to play freely, so that the quick last movement suffered in consequence, but "the performance of Mme. Carreño showed the same marvellous memory and justified confidence that are her traits. It was a great task to play the Grieg 'Concerto' as she did without notes, and with such power, spirit, and proportion as to lead without disparting the piano from the orchestra." "She is a remarkable performer and ought to be a great artist," says a discerning voice that felt in Teresa's playing greater potentiality even than present achievement. Not so right-minded is the judgment of another critic of Providence, Rhode Island. Speaking again of the Grieg "Concerto" he grants that "Mme. Teresa Carreño exhibited an easy grace and massive strength as a pianist quite phenomenal, and a more attractive piece would have made them better appreciated by the audience."

Sandwiched in between the concerts of the Damrosch tour, Teresa appeared with Brignoli, Scalchi, and others in a mixed operatic concert which took place under Arditi's leadership in the Academy of Music of New York. In retrospect Teresa became once more the little Teresita of those first years in England. On the part of the reporters there was dissatisfaction because the printed program was not adhered to and the cornetist had defaulted at the last moment. In Montreal Teresa, already an old friend of musicians in that city, appeared as co-soloist with Mme. Albani, sharing honors with that diva.

"She is," says a journalist, "the only pianist who comes to Montreal two or three times a year," and it concludes in words too pertinent and musical to bear translation: *"Elle ne cherche son succès que dans son intelligence, son cœur et son travail. Elle aime et respecte son art par-dessus tout."*

The acclaim accorded Damrosch in other cities the conductor

did not succeed in harvesting in Chicago. The *Tribune* remarks, "lack of snap, superabundance of sentiment on the part of the leader, shown in dragging tempi," although he was obliged to admit that his readings were, if not always interesting, at least always accurate. Teresa in her own right received a royal welcome, but the *Herald* deplores "a tendency of the orchestra to keep one note behind" in the Grieg concerto.

The Damrosch group halted in Denver for a number of concerts, for which Teresa took time to prepare the Weber "Konzertstück." To the irritation of the veteran Damrosch the Denver audience was out of tune with the strictly classical types of program offered it, and, except for a constantly decreasing minority, preferred to stay at home. This called forth an announcement in one of the more capricious columns of a Denver paper. It was ironically conceived by a musician much disturbed by the artistically negative attitude of this city. It reads:

It is not hard to guess why the Damrosch season in Denver has not been a financial success. Our public is fond of the higher style of music, and is ill-satisfied with everything short of it. Beethoven and Chopin and Wagner and Liszt are good enough in their way, but every school-girl in Denver plays Beethoven and Chopin and Wagner and Liszt, and our people did not care to hear all the familiar symphonies and Etudes and Sonates thumbed over again. If Mr. Damrosch had announced an opus from "Brittle Silver" the Denver public would have thronged to hear it—were it in C minor and H major. The truth is that, having been educated up to the "Brittle Silver" standard, our Denver folks are chary of descending to the level of Beethoven and the other seed-bread and Lager-beer fellows.

The article continues:

According to the general wish Damrosch gives a popular program:
    Golden Robin Polka    Smith
    Overture "Brittle Silver"    Wood
    Old Folks at Home    Mlle. Martinez
    Grand March "Mulligan Guards"    Braham
    Overture Pirates of Pensance    Sullivan
    Symphonic Poem "Shells of the Ocean"    Jones

Il Baccio (with oboe obbligato)     Anon.
Potpourris of National Airs     Gilmore
Maiden's Prayer     Anon.
Mocking Bird with variations     J. Brown
                Mme. Carreño

Inasmuch as the music will be of a light and lively character ladies must not hesitate to bring their children, who will be admitted at the usual price.

Damrosch left Denver with a light purse. What audience there was Mlle. Martinez and Teresa took by storm. She was declared an artist for the people, before all in Liszt's "Hungarian Fantasia," also a recent addition. The Middle West had proved to be unfertile ground for music of this kind. In Kansas City, on the way back to more productive fields of effort, empty seats stared at empty seats, and the scattered applause awoke echoes. Indignantly the *Journal* cries out: "Thus we receive the great leader; thus we welcome Carreño, grand interpreter of symphonies and tender harmonies. Shall we ever wipe out from our escutcheon so heinous a stain?" It speaks of Teresa's power, coming from the very shoulder, of the slight backward inclination of the head, of the fervor in her eyes, and, like so many others, the critic compares her favorably with that other popular pianist, Rivé-King, who in a recent concert had also played the "Hungarian Fantasia" in Kansas City. Teresa was glad to return again to familiar New York and, exhausted as she was, she rounded off the season with another Casino Concert, mediocre in every respect save in Teresa's solos.

RATHER earlier than customary in the fall of 1883, Carreño entered upon a round of concerts beginning in Toronto. The hall was not filled in spite of the fact that the vice-regal party honored the event with its presence in all formality, disregarding the weather which kept those of lesser degree away. As the Marquis of Lorne and Princess Louise made their entrance under guard of the Queen's Own Rifles, who took their seats around the royal box, the band of Royal Engineers broke stirringly into the national anthem. Brignoli sang his deepest, Josef Adamowski played the violin, very much unnerved because the dampness caused two strings to break during his part of the performance, and Teresa carried off the honors.

After this she joined Clara Louise Kellogg, the singer, and a numerous sustaining company on a westward-faring journey. From Rochester to Kansas City critics agreed that Miss Kellogg, no longer in her most effective years, had grown large, very large, that her toilettes were superb, her jewelry breath-taking to the ladies. But Chicago finds that "even if her voice is rejuvenated—which is a matter of doubt—her manners are possibly a thought worse than they used to be. She howled roulades in the ante-room, and guyed the other performers so vigorously as to be heard in all parts of the auditorium. Her voice was never pure nor refined. It is less so than ever." Besides, she was accused of more often singing below or above than on pitch. Audiences in the Middle West received her warmly as a friend of many years' standing. They liked her, rough and good-natured as she was, wept over her touching ballads, and gaped with amazement at her famous trill, her scale so free of the *Gersterslide*. Not so most of the critics. One caustic gentleman of Kansas City remarks that "she had taken the *Times'* advice, and had this time brought her voice with her." With the equally even-tempered Ferranti critics dealt more harshly yet. The Detroit *Evening News* goes beyond the limit of decency and of its province by saying: "He is a gibbering monstrosity; but then what could be expected of a man who wears a gold ring on his thumb?" Mrs. Alta Pease was reported to have "enunciation of the hot potato order" and altogether failed to "catch on," at least in Detroit. Mr. Rhodes, the eighteen-year-old violinist of the company, was encouraged, as "promising." Carreño, the only one in artistic prime, was the lost star in this constellation. In Chicago, as always, "Carreño appeared to be in extraordinarily good spirits, and it did not require a very sensitive musical ear to understand that it was a pleasure for her to play, and that she gave vent to her happiness on the keys of the piano." On almost all of her programs at this time there appear the "Norwegian Folk-Scenes" of Grieg.

In the Cleveland Tabernacle concert the immense audience came as a surprise. Chicago's *Inter-Ocean* pays her a great compliment: "Carreño never fails or disappoints as an artist." But occasionally she loved to astonish her listeners, or to play a joke on them, as she safely could in Chicago. In one of her recitals at Weber Hall she had played the "Kreutzer Variations" with Mr. Heimendahl. The atmosphere was dull. It needed something to enliven it. In answer to rather weak applause she returned to the stage, improvised a little, and then to the delight of an audience now thoroughly awake, threw back her head and sang Gounod's "Sing, Smile, Slumber" to her own accompaniment. In February, 1884, after the Christmas interim Teresa was once more on the road. A New York appearance with Emma Juch was followed in March by a more important week in Chicago.

Teresa played under the auspices of the Beethoven Society and the patronage of the great Chicago magnates of industry, N. K. Fairbank, Cyrus McCormick, and J. V. Farwell among them. The Schumann "Concerto" and Weber's "Polacca Brillante" were her medium. "An audience of creditable dimensions, but of rather less than the average endurance" attended, although for the *Tribune* it was "the best playing of this kind of music ever given in Chicago." "Strictly speaking," says another critic, "there were no interpretations except those of Madame Carreño." The Beethoven "Overture" and all the others were "decently and hopefully played." Mr. Heimendahl, it added, in one of the compositions had performed exactly like a returned missionary.

Teresa's concert in Chicago on March 8, 1884, enhanced by the songs of Charles A. Knorr, is the one of all these years of exploration most worthy of record. It marks the coming alive of the "Second Suite Moderne" of Edward MacDowell in the United States. The program states that it is played "for the first time in America." Holding the place of honor in the center of the program, interpreted by his friend and teacher in a city that, of all others, was ready to receive a newcomer open-mindedly, his work stood with the "Appassionata," Mendelssohn's "E minor Prelude and Fugue," and other smaller classics in appropriate neighborliness. Edward MacDowell in Germany must have welcomed an introduction so representative. The papers were cordial, if not at once completely won over, and acknowledged the promise of this, the first American composer to be seriously considered on a par with his European colleagues.

Less altogether satisfying was a second recital on March 12. Mr. W. C. E. Seeboeck, playing the Chopin "Concerto in E minor," showed himself a most exasperating missing link at the second piano. "But," said W. S. B. Matthews in *Music and Drama,* it was perhaps "the most astonishing exhibition of musical genius I have heard in this city. Carreño's performance of the *Concerto* was masterly. Poetically and artistically considered it was beautiful." While pronouncing her one of the greatest artists of the time, Mr. Matthews, one of Teresa's close personal friends, realized that she had not yet reached her climax, "for it is only in the last three years of her twenty years before the public that she has really begun to do hard study," but he added: "I would rather hear her play than any other pianist I know of." Evidently in high spirits, Teresa again sprang the surprise of singing her final encore. Mr. Matthews, who knew his music, could but admit that "it is fair to say that the artist is in reality a fine singer, who could easily become famous as a vocalist alone." Said the *News,* "The large audience almost unanimously sat out a recital that lasted three hours and a half."

Encouraged by its cordial reception, Teresa placed the Mac-Dowell "Suite" upon her program again in a concert given at the Detroit Conservatory. It interested only mildly. Farther west and eastward again continued the journey, then southward. A layman's reaction to one of Teresa's concerts was rhapsodically given by an old man of Titusville, Louisiana. It welled from the depth of his untutored feeling.

I did not see much in it when it first began. There was a good deal of noise and running up and down the piano, but all at once it seemed to me a morning on the farm years and years ago. The dew was sparkling on the grass; the perfume of a thousand flowers was in the air, and over the hill the first beams of the sun were streaming in all their golden splendor. Suddenly it faded into eventide. The wind rose soft and low, and whispered in the pines; the clouds came up and the rain pattered on the roof; the storm grew louder, the thunder rolled, the lightning flashed, and the music of the storm in all its glory was upon me. But as I listened the storm cleared away, and there came before me once again the stirring sound of mothers and wives weeping for very joy. And this passed too, and in its place came the cradle song of long years ago, and as I listened there came a grand crash of sweet melodies, and I looked only to see the piano quivering still, but the musician gone.

And gone she is for a time from the biographer's horizon. It is plausible to assume that Teresa spent as much time as possible with little Teresita, growing to look more like her mother every day, and with that awesome look of babyhood not yet acclimated to earth. Would this baby too be only lent to her for temporary comfort? Tenderly the mother watched over her, played with her, and dressed her as if, rejuvenating, another doll had been brought to her to tend.

It is not hard to imagine that Teresa had come back with fresh purpose and energy to the preparing of new programs, in the shaping of which Mrs. Watson's exacting German standards must have counted for a great deal. She was not among those that applauded Teresa for singing her encores. Neither would she tolerate anything that savored of salon music. About this Teresa and Ginka were not entirely in accord. Teresa knew what the average audience wanted, and was willing to compromise in order to give pleasure, while Ginka insisted upon offering only that which was artistically superior. Like any

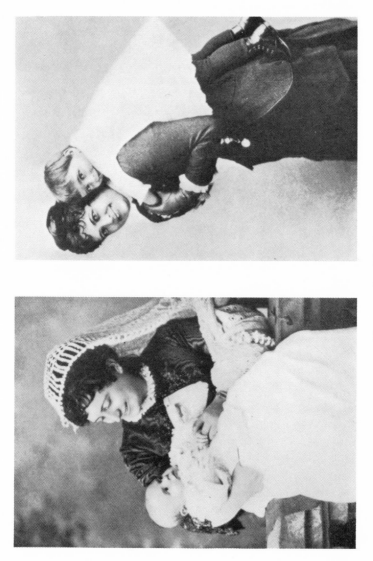

*Teresa the Mother*

good German autocrat she believed that what people should like, they could be made to like. Discussions on this subject were known to last the night through. But admittedly or not Teresa was influenced to choose her new repertoire more thoughtfully than before. Perhaps also to compensate for the vacillating devotion of Tag, she began to concentrate earnestly upon the refining of her playing technically, reviewing her readings in the light of her changing ideals, adding to her list the "Hexentanz" of MacDowell as well as his "Erzählung."

One day as she watched Teresita, scarcely able to walk, improvising a little dance to amuse herself, the composer within her awakened, and she wrote down the melody of the "Teresita Waltz," the encore without which none of her later concerts was allowed to end. She herself referred to it disparagingly as a "mere bagatelle." But the ingratiating habanera lilt, and the wistful charm with which she invested it, remain a treasure if a modest one, like a spider web of early morning outlined in drops of dew. *"Auch kleine Dinge können uns entzücken."*

On January 7, 1885, Tag and Teresa welcomed a son. It seemed only fair to call him Giovanni. Wishing to take advantage of their momentarily improved relationship, Teresa decided to arrange for a joint tour. Printed circulars were distributed, announcing that Mme. Carreño and Signor Tagliapietra might be engaged for the season 1885–86 either for a fixed sum or on percentage basis. A sample program was appended. Neither one suspected that far more romantic adventure lay ahead.

While a new pattern was in the weaving, the mother once more entered upon her nomadic life. Early in March she had the pleasure of again sharing honors with Camilla Urso in Philadelphia. Again the Sunday Casino Concerts claimed her. The "Suite Moderne" had its first hearing for New York on March 21, 1885, at Chickering Hall in one of Mr. Frederick Archer's Monday organ matinées, Teresa giving it the central place on the program. In Toronto, the "Hexentanz" by MacDowell, called "one of her pupils," appeared prominently. For

Señor Buitrago, Teresa on this occasion was not too proud to play the orchestral part of the Mendelssohn violin concerto in accompaniment.

The Teresa of this time is more matronly in appearance and much heavier. Her favorite concert dress of stiff black moire antique en train is trimmed elaborately with lace, the sleeves also of lace, and the corsage half décolleté.

Sometimes there was rough sledding. In a chamber-music concert shortly following upon her Chicago recital a cellist had to be substituted at the last moment. There was no time to rehearse the Schumann Quintette. "That cellist can thank his stars that the lady was able to render her own part and read his also," said a critic.

Teresa had not been entirely out of touch with her relatives in Venezuela, chiefly because Manuel was now holding his own in a subordinate post in Caracas. As captivating as he was unstable, Manuel had been responsible for many of her moments of depression since the death of Manuel Antonio. To know him safe within the circle of his native mountains, of family friends—what true Venezuelan would ever disown an intimate one?—was a distinct relief.

Young Manuel Antonio with his dapper beard, square-tailored and not too long, never walked unnoticed in the streets. Young girls, framed becomingly in their parental windows, tried their best to attract the attention of this straight, handsome young man, whose six feet of height stood out among his shorter compatriots. With all his dignity Manuel had a provocative smile. It held promise of fun and romance. Wisely the parents of eligible daughters held themselves aloof. It was no secret that the little money he earned flowed stream-like through his hands, that he contracted debts and took his time to repay them. Manuel's place, they rightly thought, was not as head of a family but as head of a procession. No parade was quite complete without him. Although well educated and an excellent linguist, Manuel was not intelligent enough to discount the doubtful currency of vanity, gambling, and general irresponsible living at its depreciating value. Why should he worry as long as he had a sister to get him out of debt, or scrapes of any kind? It surprised nobody but her, when, while visiting Teresa in search of employment, he followed one of his inconsequential impulses and on the spur of the moment married the daughter of a small merchant in New York's lower East Side. There was no doubt that she was a very pretty, happy-spirited young person, nor that her background and his were as different as a glass prism and the Kohinoor. And yet this helter-skelter marriage proved to be the one lucky move in Manuel's game of life. In Rosie he found a gaiety which matched his own, and far transcending it, staunch character

and devotion, pluckily facing the strain of moving in an unaccustomed stratum of society. Rugged independence and te-
nacity were as much a part of her as the unquenchable good
humor and optimism that steeled her against social disparage-
ment. Fortunately she was not oversensitive. That the coarse
and the fine were incongruously interwoven within her was her
salvation. The New York butcher's daughter and the diplomat's wife were alike ready to find life an exciting adventure.

Teresa greeted the news of the marriage with disapproval.
Altogether she and Rosie agreed as well as it might be expected
that a del Toro, grandniece of Bolívar, the perfect cavalier, could
agree with Madame Sans-Gêne resurrected.

*"Du bist Orplied, mein Land."* Not more fervently did the
poet and the composer sing their worship of the land of their
imagination than Teresa felt it alive within her for the land
of her remembrance, of that childhood which had lasted only
for eight years in all. Caracas appeared to her a golden city of
fairy-tale splendor, not to be entered until the trail had been
blazed with many deeds of valor, a sun-dusted city, seen elu-
sively through the gossamer tissue time had let down between
it and her. Was she ever to see it again? Instead, here she was
in New Rochelle, preparing without particular anticipation for
the concerts she and Tag were planning together for the coming winter, resting from a too strenuous season, and thoroughly
delighting in one thing only, the care of her babies.

One morning out of the blinding blue of midsummer, there
came that which threw the Tagliapietra household into a tornado of excitement and activity. An official-looking document
from Venezuela was in itself enough to arouse some curiosity.
It came from the President's office. Only after several readings
did Teresa grasp the full import of the communication. In the
name of the Government of Venezuela, its President formally
invited her, Teresita Carreño, to visit Caracas, there to give a
series of concerts in the coming fall. The offer was not only
flattering, but generous, promising assured and triumphant success. She might again see the scenes of other years, redefine the

blurred outlines of memory. Neither Tag nor Teresa was apt to receive negatively any suggestion that added variety and adventure to the flattening panorama of their lives. Tag saw the possibility of greater personal success than he was finding in the United States, and Teresa thought it salutary that her husband learn to appreciate his wife as one who counted in the life of a whole nation. Might it not improve their loosening relationship, establish it upon a surer foundation? From every angle the invitation was not to be ignored. Besides, foreign horizons meant greater future prestige at home. To overcome any possible reluctance there came word from Manuel, urging acceptance, promising to do his part in paving the way for their coming, and also from her aunt, María Teresa Carreño, asking them with all Venezuelan cordiality to be her house guests during their stay. A favorable reply was on its way to Caracas by return mail. Preparations were set in motion at once.

Teresa did not know or care that Venezuela had just been passing through a period of depression so severe that it had earned the title of "fatal biennial." Politics in any form, because they had never affected her personally, she did not even try to understand. Neither the Civil- nor the Franco-Prussian War had kept her from playing successfully in spite of them. She would have been the first to ridicule the suspicion that reasons of state might play a part in the invitation extended to her now. Yet many believed that, because the Crespo administration was tottering, any measure that would substitute a common enthusiasm for virulent antagonism should be encouraged, such as the coming of Venezuela's greatest living genius, Teresa Carreño. When they at last set sail, it did not worry them in the least that coincident with their proposed arrival in Venezuela hotly contested elections were to take place. In Puerto Cabello high-powered dispute had ended in rioting and violence. Seven persons were wounded; one was killed. The opposition used the incident to its own advantage by putting the blame on the government incumbent. All over Venezuela feeling on both sides rose to the seething point.

Such were the internal storms amid which on a cloudless after-noon of mid-October, 1885, the steamer *Caracas* docked at the port of La Guaira, its houses looking as if made of pastel-tinted cardboard plastered in tiers against the rocks. With inexpressible happiness Teresa set foot upon native soil. A special car stood waiting at the station of the railroad which had been inaugurated two years before as a part of the celebration in honor of Bolívar's centenary. As the train climbed from one lonely eminence to the next, drawing her into cooler heights of mountain and forest, as she watched the turquoise ocean disappearing behind her, and felt the transcendent grandeur of virgin nature once more familiarly about her, she saw herself again as that eager-eyed little girl who more slowly and primitively had driven down the rocky roads to meet her unknown destiny. How different the Teresita of today, hardened at thirty-two by trouble and by many bitter mistakes. How would she be received, and what would she have to say to her countrymen? "It is in me to do more than I have yet accomplished. I must go upwards relentlessly, like this train. I feel that I must," she thought. On wheezed the locomotive. Tag, the unheroic, was distinctly relieved when the last precipice had been skirted. He was the first to hear a band playing in the distance, rousing Teresa from her absorption to listen. To the strains of "Gloria al bravo pueblo" the train came to rest at the platform, thronged with a dizzying mass that resolved itself into unfamiliar faces, young and old, shading from black to white. All were waving handkerchiefs, throwing flowers, and shouting. Could all this be for her?

The answer came from a group of gentlemen, young gentlemen in their most formal dress, waiting stiffly at attention to receive her. One of them, Señor Gonzales Picón Fébres, after a few words of welcome, presented her with a bouquet tied with streamers of bright blue silk inscribed in gold letters: "A Teresa Carreño Sus Compatriotas." Teresita—in Venezuela she is to this day known by no other name than that—was unprepared for any such demonstration. Everything, from the sound of her mother tongue to the unbridled enthusiasm that now welcomed her home, touched her. To the remarks of Señor Fébres she just managed to reply in an uncertain voice: "These tears which come from the heart speak for me. I do not deserve so much." Once seated in the waiting carriage drawn by the most beautiful pair of horses in all Caracas she quickly regained her composure. Meanwhile the dedicatory verses of a rising young poet, Alirio Diaz Guerra, printed as leaflets, were being scattered among the people. At last, escorted by twenty equipages filled with all that was most distinguished in society, Teresa was permitted to proceed at snail's pace down the Avenida Central toward the home of her aunt, who with her one-year-old baby had in 1862 braved a foreign land for the sake of Teresita, the prodigy.

Caracas was thoroughly enjoying itself. The narrow sidewalks were jammed. From every window handkerchiefs were waving and loud were the shouts of *"Viva Teresita."* Her carriage, the target for flowers that finally covered her like a blanket, moved on in stately measure. As she bowed and waved acknowledgment every man became her potential slave at sight; every woman measured her as a possible rival. This was indeed a homecoming. The matron of New Rochelle, proud mother of two delectable babies, so reluctantly left behind, for the moment did not exist. Instead here was a queen, returned from exile of many years to the country where she again might reign over devoted subjects. She played the part with gusto, unconscious that Tag found the role of Prince Consort less to his liking. Nobody seemed to take notice of him, and he was the only one glad to have the triumphal *corso* end at 45 Avenida Norte. His frankly rude impatience made an unbecoming background for Teresita as she took long and effusive leave of her followers, and feeling himself at further disadvantage with relatives he had trouble in understanding, a clairvoyant thought came to him. It would have been better far had he stayed at home.

As usual, when things went wrong with him, Tag made

Teresa suffer for it. Once in the privacy of the house he became sulky, abusive, and ceased to care what might be the impression he made upon his hosts. For Teresita Tag's tantrums were daily diet in New Rochelle. There she could ignore them. In Venezuela they offended her pride deeply because her standing as something above the mortal was at stake. Husbands in Caracas treated their wives with punctilious respect, above all in public. Tag's explosions, likely to occur anywhere at any time, would not only belittle him but her in the eyes of her countrymen. She felt the danger and began to regret as he did that she had urged him to accompany her.

The day was not to end without another demonstration in Teresita's honor. After dinner quiet had descended upon the house that was her shelter. The patio, fragrant with odors that poignantly reawakened memory, lay in grateful silence. Suddenly came the tramp of many feet and the confusion of laughing voices! The entire Club Bolívar, most exclusive of its kind, had come to serenade their famous compatriot. C. V. Landaeta, its spokesman, congratulated Teresita in poetic words upon her safe arrival in the land of her birth, presenting her with a sumptuous bouquet of flowers. A country where orchids grow wild could afford to be lavish. There was singing by the tenor, Señor Molina, accompanied by young Tomás Michelena, the festivity lasting far into the night.

Teresita, rejuvenated, took the deepest satisfaction in all these tributes, and lost no time in making public a letter of appreciation in the *Opinión Nacional,* the organ of the Government. It read:

On touching the shores of the land of my birth, I have been honored in receiving from my compatriots splendid proof of their cordiality towards my humble self; I do not deserve so much.

I am grateful, very grateful for the kind expressions of friendship and consideration with which I have been welcomed in this city, after long absence in foreign countries; and I take this occasion to declare with all my heart the thankfulness I feel for so much kindness, which I shall know how to return.

My greetings to the illustrious Press of Caracas, to the Reception Committee, to the members of the Club Bolívar, and other persons from whom I have received unmistakable signs of esteem, and, very particularly, to the worthy President of the Republic, the highly honorable General Joaquín Crespo.

Daily distinctions were conferred upon Teresita. The freedom of Caracas and the keys to the city were hers, and a deputation formally sent by the Government one morning presented her with the *Busto de Bolívar,* a medal given only to outstanding citizens or to an occasional foreigner for distinguished service rendered to Venezuela. In return, piloted by Manuel, Teresita and Tag one morning called upon the President to ask, as was polite procedure, that he accept the dedication of her first concert scheduled to take place on October 29, 1885.

Preparations began in earnest. The Teatro Guzman Blanco was placed at her disposal as the only fitting hall for so sensational an event. The first complications arose with the assembling of the program in which national and social politics made demands. First of all, since the concert was to take place on the eve of the name day of the *Libertador,* it was deemed suitable that his grandniece dedicate this, her first appearance, to his memory, as well as to him who now occupied the presidential chair. That Señor Molina, in return for taking part in the serenade of the Club Bolívar, should be asked to contribute some tenor solos, was a natural courtesy. Then, as background for the Chopin "Concerto in E minor," which Teresita had chosen because it could most easily dispense with full orchestral accompaniment, Teresita had to gather and blend together a string quintette and a pianist. This called for frequent rehearsing, and time passed busily for all but Tag. Left to his own vagabonding he soon found congenial company, and his bellowing voice and laugh became familiar sounds reëchoing from wall to wall in the streets by day. At night he had soon tapped most of the gambling resources of Caracas, finding them inexhaustible wells of diversion. Venezuela, he found, had its points after all, and Tag was almost glad that he had come. A more amiable mood made him quite ready to appear in the first concert.

In its final form it was framed at each end by orchestral *sinfonías*. Each of the assisting soloists appeared twice upon the program which fell into two parts. In the first Teresita played the "Concerto." The second began with her "Himno a Bolívar" for chorus and orchestra, now to be heard for the first time publicly in Caracas. Henselt's "If I Were a Bird," Gottschalk's "Tremolo," and her own "Saludo a Caracas" made up a group of piano solos. Liszt's "Sixth Rhapsodie" in brilliant conclusion called for the "Teresita Waltz" as encore.

The freshly redecorated Teatro Guzman Blanco was completely filled. Fashionable society attended *in toto*. Conjecture and gossip ran high. The atmosphere which Teresita would need to penetrate was surcharged with an unblending mixture of admiration, envy, disapproval, and curiosity. Many would have welcomed a good fiasco rather than a good concert. The minority were drawn by the music itself. To most it meant the best show of the season, one that would refreshingly break conversational drought.

Notably excepting the field of opera, musical taste in Venezuela had been at a standstill for years. Caracas, taught by an annual season of French and Italian opera finally considered indispensable, was a better judge of good and bad singing and acting than of piano playing. Beyond that it was content with sentimental songs and dance music. The Chopin "Concerto," heard for the first time in Caracas, at least with anything but second piano accompaniment, must have lured many of the audience beyond their musical depth, without, however, impeding their enjoyment of this ovation to Venezuela's glorious daughter. It began uproariously as soon as Teresita, elegantly clad in unrelieved black, the arms bare, the décolleté severe and low, crossed the stage with her famous stride, so purposeful and elastic that it made the boards vibrate beneath her feet. Unembarrassed as one equally at home in the salons of the world and in its cottages she sat immovable a moment before beginning.

One of the really absorbed listeners, just recovered from a serious illness, closed his eyes so as not to be diverted from the music of the artist by the beauty of the woman, now in the perfection of maturity more appealing to him than the freshness of youth. His annoying neighbor insisted upon telling him what it was she was playing, while all he wished was to listen uninformed and undisturbed. At the beginning the music had seemed to him a perfect imitation of the frantic applause which had greeted her entrance. Then it became vague and melancholy like the dream of an unhappy poet. The doctor had forbidden his staying for the whole concert. But that night he could not sleep for thinking of *"esa bella Americana."* The critics were unanimously taken captive. She not only honored herself but Venezuela, they said. Chopin himself would have thanked her for making his composition greater even than he had conceived it. "She not only interprets, she exalts." Difficulties they declared nonexistent, and her legato, her shading, her phrasing, and her delicacy, all were alike found admirable, beyond praise.

Teresa stood among the bouquets, wreaths, and garlands heaped about her, bowing regally, only with more personal graciousness than usual. If there was a flaw, it was the absence of Crespo, probably prevented by duties of state, and of her cousin, Guzman Blanco, still in exile. It was an open secret that Guzman Blanco was slated to be Crespo's successor, that he was in fact already the power behind the throne, and that it was Guzman Blanco who had used the pressure of his influence to assure Teresa's homecoming.

The papers, flaming with eulogies, asked for more concerts. One even hoped for a plan to repatriate Teresita in her own land, and gladly the *Opinión Nacional* spread the good news: "Our great pianist is preparing another concert. Everything in this concert will be surprising and new." This time Teresita chose to dedicate it "To the refined and illustrious Society of Caracas."

Teresita dared to entrust the "Capriccio Brillante" of Mendelssohn and the "Polonaise" of Weber-Liszt to Señor Pineda and the orchestra for accompaniment. Señor Pedro J. Izquierdo sang a number of arias, after which Señor Guillermo Smith sounded a jubilant note upon his cornet. Teresa's personal part closed with Beethoven's "Andante in F" and Kullak's famous "Octave Study." The orchestra again framed the whole. Tag did not appear.

Artistically and financially Teresa had cause to be gratified. Such playing Caracas was not likely to hear again. But what of the "refined and illustrious Society of Caracas"? As day after day passed, and not a single lady from among those to whom Teresa had dedicated her second concert came to call upon her, much less to invite her, she became aware that something was amiss. Whatever attention she received was from gentlemen—attention often too glowing for comfort—or from an occasional family closely connected with the existing government. It was a source of acute embarrassment, especially to Teresa's aunt, that her own friends completely withdrew at this time, the more because she guessed the reason. Teresa found herself with more than enough time on her hands to practice undisturbed. Effusive public ovation had not prepared her in any way for this private fiasco. She felt profoundly wounded. As so often she called pride to the rescue. A letter written to Caroline Keating Reed in a rosy moment gives no inkling of cloudy horizons.

February 1st, 1886

We have been here since the 15th of October, and upon my arrival in this city the whole city went to meet me, with a band of music, speeches etc., etc., and all the demonstrations of affection from my countrymen. I will not enter into details for it will be all you want to know, the result of it all. To you and quite in confidence (for anyone else not knowing me might think me vain and ridiculous) I will tell you that I have been treated as a queen. My entrance to the city was such a general rejoicing that the streets through which my carriage was to pass from the station to the house, were crowded with people who cheered me as I passed and waved hats and handkerchiefs and treated me really as if I had been the queen entering her city. Since the ovations, flowers, speeches, serenades, decorations, medals, in fact all sorts of sweet and honorific demonstrations have been poured upon my head, and I have felt all the time as if I did not deserve anything and were worth very little in comparison to the honor I was receiving. The government presented me with the *Busto* of Bolívar, which is the highest honor they can bestow on anyone, and Tag also was presented with it after the first concert at which he sang, which was on January 10th. The most touching of all to my heart has been a beautiful golden medal which the press of Caracas presented me with, and a Diploma containing so many highly flattering things that I hardly know myself after reading it. We stayed here in Caracas one month after the 15th of October, and then we travelled to Puerto Cabello, Valencia and Ciudad de Cura and then returned here on December 28th, and since then have given two more concerts here. Now we are en route to Ciudad Bolívar and Trinidad and from there to Maracaibo. After Maracaibo we return here and probably we will after a short season here return home! The very word home thrills me all over! Just think what a long separaparation from my two darlings, from all that my heart longs for day and night! You who so well know how my heart is wrapped up in those children can imagine how cruel this separation is to me, how great the sacrifice, but as it is for their sake that I am doing all this, I must pick up my courage and try to bear it. Tag is almost entirely like himself again, and the climate has restored him to health again, which if nothing else had been obtained from our trip out here, this would be quite sufficient. You will be surprised to see how much longer we have stayed here than we first intended, but as business turned out so well, we determined to remain about these parts for the rest of the season. . . .

Outwardly Teresa continued to appear unmoved, serene, all-conquering. She only regretted that in those first, overjoyous days she had, chameleonlike, shed the protective skin of aloofness to show the warmth of her sincere affection to those one-time family friends whose endearing demonstrations were only half meant. She had forgotten how colonial, how more than puritanical Caracas still was, with its tightly corseted standards in which her freedom-hungry spirit could no longer be confined. Bad enough, thought Caracas, that a del Toro had become a public performer, even publicly singing in opera. Since she had real genius, that might have been overlooked. But it was unforgivable that she had gone counter to her religion, no longer even attended mass, that she had been divorced and had married again, moreover, according to so-called common law unrecognized in orthodox Caracas, and that she had now brought with her this unmannerly, objectionable person, her quasi-husband. Had Teresa left him at home, instead of flaunting him publicly in Caracas, her own wholesomeness and charm might have lifted the barriers. More and more Tag's behavior was becoming scandalous. First it was only hinted, but soon established as a fact, that Giovanni Tagliapietra had treated his wife with such violence that she was obliged for a time to change her residence, that Manuel had to keep him away from Teresa at the point of a pistol. Scenes of disagreement and reconciliation were clearly audible upon the listening street. Their quarrels became teacup gossip. Women declared themselves unwilling to trust their children to such a siren. Rumor with her distorting and magnifying glasses made matters worse. She had, so it said, found more than normal favor in the eyes of Guzman Blanco, her second cousin on the maternal side.

Teresa was ready to leave Caracas to its scandal-savoring parties, and to take Tag away to more healthful cities of Venezuela, where together they might gather new laurels in spots less hampered by tradition. She realized that he would not have resorted to making such an exhibition of himself if he had had something else to do. After an extended tour through the provinces she decided upon giving a farewell concert in Caracas, which, on account of its success, had to be repeated. The first was called a gala function and was listed as being under the auspices of the youth of Caracas. It took place on January 10, 1886. At the head of a long program in which the two artists were supported by the orchestra, Teresa expressed her gratitude in print—was there a sarcasm in the words?

As the greatest proof of my devotion to my compatriots of beloved Venezuela, I have returned to its arms to offer it my farewells in a last concert. It is with that alone that I am able to return so many evidences of affection; and my husband, also delighted, has agreed to take part in it, showing in this way his love for those who have showered me so often with delicate attention. Wherever fate may take me, there will always gratefully beat my heart for this piece of earth which I so dearly cherish.

This concert, which the youth of Caracas commemorated with a medal of gold presented to Teresita, offered the novelty of a duet from *Il Trovatore* sung at the close by Teresita and Tag together. Finally, by general request, another farewell concert took place on February 24. It was given in honor of the Ministers of the Cabinet for the benefit of the Caracas Hospitals, and again terminated with a joint duet, this time from *Lucia*. The Chopin "Concerto," on this occasion accompanied by full orchestra, was repeated, and a "Tarantella" by Gottschalk, also with the orchestra assisting, evidently had its first hearing and probably its last. Definitely and finally to leave Caracas on this charitable note was Teresita's firm intention. On neither side was there unbearable sorrow at parting. Caracas was offended that Teresita would not tailor her life to its fixed measurements; Teresita found it intolerable to be drawn into close and narrow perspective by the myopically guided pencil of provincial prejudice. Had not someone been reported as having said that many young girls of Caracas played as well as she? Ridiculous as such a criticism was, it rankled.

Once more the pair started upon a trip that led them as far as Trinidad. Everywhere they shared the program together, everywhere a triumphant reception, if not always a full house, awaited them. The unprejudiced cordiality of the provinces did much to reëstablish a happy state of mind within and between themselves. Teresita could again enjoy to the full the parties given for her. Because it helped to keep domestic peace it pleased her that Tag was well received. To sit through endless literary festivities staged in her honor, to hear poem after poem of which she was invariably the subject, all this did not seem to tire her. If only she had left Caracas on the same note of triumph on which she had entered it! Flowers and presents did not allow her to forget that minor ending.

Meanwhile Guzman Blanco was again in office. One of his first acts was to urge Teresita to revisit Caracas. Beside the fact that it would have been rudeness to refuse the new President, here was the chance to strike that compensating major chord.

During her absence public opinion had not changed in Teresita's favor. The very fact that Guzman Blanco stood as her sponsor did not increase her popularity. The new Government was holding its own with characteristic difficulty. Guzman Blanco was known to be vain and personally ambitious. Nothing was more important to him than a statue in his honor. Even the genius of his cousin he considered just another feather with which to adorn his already well-trimmed cap. Her fire, her wit, her charm were enough to turn the head of the most resistant man, and Blanco was not one of these.

A literary festival was prepared to celebrate his return to power in formal fashion. Prize-winning sonnets were read in his honor. José Antonio Calcaño read one of his poems, commemorating the last hours of Bolívar's life. An intimate interlude warmed the atmosphere. Seated in the presidential box, Guzman Blanco noticed his predecessor close by. With gentlemanly tact he invited General Crespo to join him, while Señora Blanco took her seat with Señora Crespo. Enthusiasm needed only this to flare up wildly. Applause came from the heart, now for the President, now for the artists, the lion's share always being reserved for Teresita Carreño. Politics, literature, and music melted into inseparable homage.

After this it seemed only natural for Teresa to give a "grand gala concert herself in honor of the illustrious American, Guzman Blanco, and of his most respected Señora," to congratulate them upon their happy return. It took place early in September, 1886. Knowing that nothing could please him more Teresita quickly composed a "Hymn to Guzman Blanco." The solo part against a background of chorus and full orchestra fell to the lot of Tag. Under the baton of Señor Pineda Teresita played the "Hungarian Fantasia" of Liszt and the Weber-Liszt "Polonaise." Tag chose some of his old favorites from his rather limited concert repertoire. Teresa the composer, the pianist, and the wife had reason to look with pride upon the success of the evening. The stage was festive with the gaily colored flag of Venezuela draped around an oil painting of the new President. Former disappointments faded into insignificance. This was the major ending. To add another farewell concert after this seemed like tempting Providence. There is record that such a one was planned. The reason for its sudden recall is not given, the responsibility resting upon "unforeseen circumstance." It is highly probable that a new project made hasty departure imperative.

THE enthusiasm Teresita had aroused in Guzman Blanco surpassed the reasonable. Her return to Venezuela must at any price be assured and that speedily. Congress had just voted the annual appropriation of 100,000 bolivars to finance the season of opera which was to begin early in the new year. Could anything be more timely than to entrust Teresita, who had herself sung in opera, with this enterprise? The idea was a brilliant one, thought Guzman Blanco, not stopping to consider that the qualities that make a great artist and a good manager are in their essence of different kind. Tag needed no persuasion to second the plan, and if Teresita had any qualms, they were soon overcome by the confidence of the other two. Without delay it was decided; Tag must go to Italy, Teresa to New York, to assemble the company, both to meet in Caracas in early January. Tag, in his element as future manager of the Teresa Carreño Grand Opera Company, immediately set off. Teresita, scarcely stopping for the most necessary farewells, embarked

for New York, where with every fiber of her being she longed
to be. Not the opera company, but her two children were the
magnet that drew her home. Never would she set sail again
without them.

Fall was at its loveliest when she once more greeted the New
York skyline. This was the country of her habit, more really
hers than the country where she was born. But once more with
those friends whose trustworthiness she had missed, she gave
no hint that the glittering brilliance of that glorious tour had
had its obscuring shadows. In every sense her success and Tag's
had been phenomenal, unprecedented. Teresa talked even herself into believing that it must have been so.

If Teresa missed Tag at all, it was with relief that she could
have her children to herself. On entering her home she felt
peaceful and contented, as so rarely when Tag was near. Hearing and engaging singers for her opera company was a diverting by-product among her other activities, one that she found
herself unable to take very seriously. That time was short and
few good singers left unemployed at the height of the season,
would have caused Teresa more worry had she rated the musical taste of Caracas more highly. In this she miscalculated.

Time and distance did not make it possible to keep in close
touch with Tag's procedure. In the way of the genius, expecting nothing less of others than their very best, Teresa trusted
that smooth emulsion would result from this miscellany of
talent assembled without the binder of common experience and
common drill. In January there was still time for a few concerts reaching from Boston, where Teresa shone in "the fifth
grand concert of the Ideal Music Course of the Boston Symphony Orchestral Club," to Cincinnati, where three recitals followed each other closely.

Finally on Friday, February 25, 1886, Teresa with her French
maid, Josephine de Paul, two children, and thirty-two people
of the operatic ensemble left the ship *Valencia* at La Guaira.
The inevitable intimacy of life on shipboard had given Teresa

more than a hint of what might be in store for her with a group so unevenly tempered, and often she had occasion to wish that the ship might be turned back to safer harbor. It took all her cheerfulness, tact, and personality to adjust differences, and to reassure the none-too-brave company whom a rousing storm had reduced to unaccustomed prayer. Fortunately there remained five days after landing before Tag's arrival presented a further problem. Teresita was already established in an apartment she had rented near the Panteón when he appeared in all his importance as "Director and Administrator" of the company, for which Teresa was officially responsible, and to which she lent her more famous name. "Let us prepare to enjoy the ineffable pleasures which the present season of Italian opera will offer us," welcomingly and hopefully writes the *Opinión Nacional*.

The published list of artists included singers by their own admission famous in all the principal theaters of Europe and the United States, a complete *corps de ballet* with a *prima ballerina,* and an orchestra of thirty professors of whom five came from Europe. The conductor was Fernando Rachelle. The roster promised three operas new to Caracas, *The Huguenots, Mignon,* and *Carmen,* also *Ruy Blas, Lucia, Rigoletto, Un Ballo in Maschera, Faust, Norma, Lucrezia, Aïda, Roberto il Diavolo, L'Africana, La Sonnambula, Il Barbiere de Sevilla,* etc., etc. Each subscription series gave admission to ten different performances, the prices ranging from $10 to $13, boxes for six persons selling at $120. *Un Ballo in Maschera* was chosen to introduce the company. Seats sold quickly. The city buzzed. A representative of the press who was invited to hear the dress rehearsal reported that all who had the privilege of being guests at this performance were delighted with its quality. He then devoted equal space and eulogy to the freshly redecorated walls and the woodwork, and left it to the public to judge of the merits of the individual artists, merely taking the opportunity to felicitate Señora Carreño for her cleverness in choosing so admirable a troupe, and Caracas for having in its walls a company "that will make it forget its natural troubles and enjoy countless delights."

Dr. Manuel Revenga, to whose courteous pen fell the difficult duty of writing the criticism of the first public performance, expressed himself with kindly appreciation, but, for a Venezuelan, with marked reserve. He stressed disproportionately the difficulties Carreño must have encountered in bringing together a group of artists at such a short notice just when the most and the best were already under contract elsewhere. Considering this handicap the management, according to Señor Revenga, could only be said to have done well. The two elements that spoke most loudly for the success of the enterprise he found in the quality of the voices, almost all conceded to be admirable, and in the fact that it was sponsored by Teresita Carreño. Quite incredible he found the ridiculous rumor that there existed in Caracas a spirit of hostility toward this great artist, and consequently to the undertaking to which she lent her name. Carreño, he asserted, in no way deserved such an attitude, nor was it in keeping with Venezuelan courtesy. It would be unthinkable for people as deferential and just as his countrymen were known to be to harbor a grudge against a Venezuelan, all the more so because she happened to be one of her daughters. Wishing to waste no more words upon such bagatelles, he turned to the description of the glittering audience, distinguished by the presence of the President and his illustrious family. With the exception of the tenor who obviously was suffering from acute stage fright, and so left his audience cold, Señor Revenga had nothing unfavorable to say of the entire company.

The second series opened with *Lucia,* more genuinely successful for the appearance in the title role of Señora Linda Brambilla, who fired the critic to extravagant words of praise. This, however, did not suffice to keep the attendance from falling off noticeably from then on night after night. In spite of reviews that gave hint of the ominous undercurrent of general dissatisfaction, in spite of the apparently good impression made by Tag as Valentine in *Faust,* there could soon be no hiding of the fact that animosity was gaining momentum, fanned to heat by the opposition party on the alert to make the most of any governmental *faux pas.* *La Campana,* a short-lived journal, whose reason for being was to run counter to whatever happened to be in favor with the Government, however praiseworthy, jumped at the chance to make this operatic venture a point of political contention, the opera house its battleground. *"Don Fiasco continua in alza,"* cries *La Campana.*

No wonder that similar unrest was felt behind the scenes. Strange were the things that happened there. During rehearsal one morning a bottle containing a nasty liquid suddenly broke at the feet of Teresita. Nor could a stone that grazed her head have been a mere accident. Added to the customary interludes of intrigue and rivalry within the company, fear of danger from without spread its disorganizing influence. Abusive articles appeared; threatening letters fed the already overstimulated imagination with dread and terror. Even from the audience came audible hisses and whistles of disapproval, while an egg splashing upon the stage not infrequently added its spurt to the legitimate sound of song and orchestra, an occurrence which the performers learned to take philosophically. It did not, however, help to improve the ensemble, which was undeniably bad. Teresa was too busy to take in the full meaning of the controversy of which the opera company was the unhappy focus, and which the politicians and their agents so thoroughly exploited. The opposition needed a target for its venom, for which it chose the deplorable Tag. Generally disliked, he was the logical one to attack. One morning an anonymous letter threatened him with a volley of ripe tomatoes, should he reappear upon the stage as *Rigoletto.* Rather than brave the insult Tag chose the safer course, and published a letter in which he took reluctant leave of his audience, also making public the one which caused him to take the step. The amusement with which this abdication must have been greeted may well be imagined. At his expense the city rang with ridicule and anecdote. Only one brave voice was heard to urge his return to the stage.

Even this new humiliation did not down Teresa. She was made of tough, resilient fiber. If failure were once again to turn to success some drastic measure alone could do it. Meanwhile Holy Week gave breathing space. Teresa, ever inventive in a crisis, had time to map out new tactics. There was still her popularity as a pianist left to turn to account. When it was announced that at the next performance of *Rigoletto* she would play the "Polonaise" of Weber-Liszt between the second and third acts the public was forced to admire her resourcefulness. There was at once a marked increase in the size and the cordiality of the audience.

Signor Rachelle, his nerves on edge from the strain of overwork and the miscarriage of all his best intentions, came to the limit of endurance caused by rumors of a plot to blow up the opera house during the next performance. That he could not face. So, feigning illness he left the company to the mercy of bombs that never exploded. Another conductor lasted only for a night. Teresa on this occasion again tried to save the day by playing the "Sixth Rhapsodie" of Liszt during the intermission, proudly ignoring danger. Two of her young admirers were clapping to the point of paralysis. One of them, too exhausted to continue, jokingly suggested to the other: "And now that we have applauded the artist, let us recall her again, and as cordially hiss the impresario."

The opera must continue. That was all that mattered to Teresa now. But, try as she might, nobody was found willing to step into the vacancy. This put Teresa on her mettle. One of her beliefs was that the impossible exists only to be proved possible by the strong-hearted. The papers announced one morning: "Teresa Carreño herself will conduct the orchestra in *La Favorita* and *La Sonnambula*." Admiration once more flamed for the intrepid amazon, worthy indeed to be named with the great Bolívar. And she who had never before conducted was able

CARACAS 1885

Teresa the Impresario

BOSTON 1888

Teresa before her departure for Germany

as well as any man to hold orchestra, soloists, and chorus together. Moreover, she rather enjoyed the experience. The exhilaration of feeling within her unplumbed depths of power rising to the surface at her call uplifted her spiritually, although, overfatigued by this unaccustomed exercise, her arms ached through the night in spite of the efforts of a devoted masseuse by day. But what did that matter if the season could be brought to its close without further mischance? Indications were hopeful. The journals praised Teresa's conducting; whenever La Brambilla sang the house was well filled.

The greatest lack of all was in the quality of the tenor. Caracas knew its arias, and refused to be satisfied with a voice whose long, high notes were barren of all sweetness, growing thinner and duller only to break off at the end for lack of control. Even La Brambilla could not make up for that. Again, in addition to the conducting, Teresa appeared between acts as pianist. Her pluck might have saved the day had it not been for the sudden real or assumed indisposition of La Brambilla herself. This was the *coup-de-grâce*. *Il Trovatore* and *Lucia* had a hearing each under Teresa's baton. Then even she had to concede that "Don Fiasco" had won the day, and that the opera season must end a week before its time.

As for La Brambilla, miraculously restored to health, she found herself able to give a recital on May 1, the very day that was to have marked the triumphant farewell of the Carreño Opera Company. Other concerts by the prima donna followed, whose success was the more flamboyant for the background of failure against which they were silhouetted. Teresa made hasty preparation for leaving. As a last act of generosity the Government bought the properties of the disbanded opera company for 20,000 bolivars, finally also the concert grand piano especially designed for Teresa by the Weber Company. That same piano may still be standing as it did in 1935, turned upon its side, in a dark corner of the Teatro Municipal, ruined by dampness and the all-penetrating *comajen*. The old janitor still remembers that ill-fated opera season in which there was nothing luminous but Teresa herself in all her beauty, her genius, and her courage.

For a person like Teresa Carreño, who had achieved the unachievable since childhood, to whom intuition had pointed the way, it was natural to believe that, Teresa being Teresa, obstacles would overcome themselves, that no matter how uncharted the jungle paths upon which she chose to enter, they would inevitably lead to the chosen destination. In coming to Venezuela she made two fatal mistakes. She chose both the wrong time and the wrong method. Far from binding her to the country of her origin, it estranged her from it. This mutual misunderstanding, for which both sides may be held responsible, was not to be entirely dispelled during her lifetime. As advancing years brought perspective and more lucid understanding, a longing to revisit her country was born. She had made plans to revisit it in 1917, plans which were foiled by her death. Had this visit become a fact she would have found an understanding welcome by a musical generation more ready to receive her message and by a society less overcritical of the external and trivial, more open to sincerity and greatness of heart. Teresa would have felt at home in the Venezuela of today.

Many instances in her later life gave evidence of this perhaps unconscious nostalgia. There was one glittering day in the Swiss Alps. Carreño and a number of others were together in the little funicular train that puffs its way from the Scheidegg to Grindelwald, the seat of Carreño's summer colony of 1912. Suddenly Carreño's attention was caught by two people in front of her. They had not spoken a word. Turning to her husband, she said: "Those people, I am sure, are from my country. I am going to speak to them." She was right. For the rest of the trip she talked only with them. Rarely had she been so elated, so absorbed.

Not alone were the roots of her being embedded in the fruitful tropical soil that clung to them. There it was also that the tender shoots sprouted that foreordained the line and tempo of her growing as person, as artist. The tree developed into magnificent prime of stature and of flowering. Then, blessed by the glow of sunset, its leaves carpeted adopted earth with scarlet and gold. But whether the sap coursed violently or quietly, whether it became thinned or enriched by frequent transplanting, there remained that which in its essence was of Venezuela.

TERESA returned to New York under the disappointment of thwarted affection. It had flowed strongly, ready to expend itself upon anyone who approached her with simple friendliness. There had been few of those. Instead she had felt herself shut out, set apart, ostracized. As she reviewed the season in the perspective she realized that she had been shortsighted, that she herself was largely to blame for the outcome. "I have been stupid, unforgivably stupid," she admitted to herself. Pride again did not permit her to share this secret with her friends at home. For them she jotted down only the happy hours, until they firmly believed that the brilliant success of the first visit was only surpassed by that of the second. Covering the original canvas of drab misadventures with the gayest colors on the palette of her imagination, Teresa herself soon felt better. Only in Venezuela some still remember the underlying painting, without caring to expose it.

And soon came the cheerful distraction of moving into a new home. Teresa, suddenly feeling the need of being closer to her friends, the MacDowells, chose 207 East Eighteenth Street. The mentally relaxing activity of making the house livable suited her mood. The furniture she bought was to be paid for little by little. In time her home should be entirely hers. Tag was consulted only in second intention.

The routine of concert life soon caught her in its automatically spinning wheel, as if there had been no interlude. Hughsie and Josephine were there to take care of the children. Teresita began to show signs of uncommon gift for the piano. For the entertainment of friends she played the Bach "Prelude" to the appliqué of Gounod's "Ave Maria," sung by her father. Piano her mother taught her according to Manuel Antonio's method. When practicing was finished, Teresita was eager to go on with inventions of her own. "And now may I do my nonsense?" she would ask. It consisted in transposing whatever struck her fancy from one key to another.

Often little Giovanni sat quietly by her side. If someone in-

terrupted, he reprimanded them curtly: "Sh! Dada is playing
Bach!" Next to that the greatest thrill of his babyhood was the
room that displayed his father's operatic wardrobe. Each separate costume was a living person with whom, hardly able to
speak intelligibly, he held long conversation.

In Teresa's eyes nothing remained of the perfect lover she
had once seen in Tag. Strangely enough, just at this time the
announcement sent out more than a year ago had borne fruit,
the two were more often heard in concert together than before.

Meanwhile Ginka Watson, whose nature could not bear to
see things going wrong without doing her part to right them,
kept on urging a separation. "It is in Germany you should take
refuge from that creature, your husband," she tirelessly repeated. And Teresa just as regularly countered: "Where shall I
get the money?" There the matter rested. She would never
again leave the United States without her children. The idea,
however, germinated, and Ginka, the practical, was cogitating.

In March, 1888, Teresa opened the door of her house one morning to a dapper, blond Italian, fresh from the stormy Atlantic,
which had behaved more uproariously than usual that winter
of the famous blizzard. He radiated sunshine and kindness, to
which Teresa instantly responded, and announced himself as
Arturo, her brother-in-law. He had come, so he said, in search
of the good fortune he had failed to find as a soldier in Italy.
There was nothing remarkable about him except that he was
entirely uncomplicated and still at sea as to his plans and ex-
pectations. His gifts were the modest but dependable ones of
honesty, industry, and pride, leavened by a detached and humorous slant he threw even upon his misfortunes. Helplessness
was always provocative for Teresa. She at once made it her
duty to see that he was properly clothed and introduced.

It did not take Arturo long to feel the disharmony existing
in his brother's household, nor to become aware of its cause.
That anyone could wish to maltreat a person as ravishing as his
sister-in-law was beyond his comprehension. He in his turn ap-

pointed himself Teresa's protector-in-chief, and wedged himself in, a willing buffer, to lessen the shock of domestic controversy from whichever side it might originate.

In nearly every crisis he found himself on Teresa's side, and at last he came to agree with Mrs. Watson that the only hope for peace lay in separation once and for all, preferably with an ocean between. He played with the children, who adored him, and he was daily in and out of the house, for Teresa took comfort in his presence, sympathizing with his predicaments. No matter how earnestly he tried, Arturo, hampered by a strange language, by different habits of life, and by the fact that he had never been trained for anything in particular, was not able to find work that was either interesting or remunerative. He went along his slow, laborious way patiently and uncomplainingly, earning little beyond a living wage, keeping his simple room with artistic economy as neat as a convent. To live frugally was no special deprivation to Arturo. He was as vain as any other young Italian soldier of fortune, but he did not indulge his vanity at any expense but his own. He was more inclined, when he had saved a little, to buy a toy for the children or a bunch of flowers for the mother just returned from a concert journey.

After the Venezuelan interlude Teresa seemed possessed by the drive to practice hours upon end. To her friends her playing had never sounded better. MacDowell appeared more and more often upon her programs—he had been introduced even to Venezuela by way of the "Hexentanz"—and the D minor concerto still in manuscript was taking shape under her fingers.

Shortly after their marriage in 1884 the young MacDowells visited London, primarily to attend every possible performance in which Henry Irving and Ellen Terry took part. On account of Marian MacDowell's poor eyesight they were obliged to sit in the most expensive seats, their one great extravagance. Out of this experience there evolved a composition written in homage to Henry Irving, meant as a musical character sketch of Ellen Terry, an airy scherzo for piano duet. Lacking courage to approach Henry Irving, MacDowell let this work lie dormant until, later on in Germany, it became the Scherzo of the "Concerto in D minor," dedicated to Carreño. It was eminently right that she should be the first to play it publicly. A double joy was in store.

Theodore Thomas, who rarely admitted soloists to his Summer Night Concerts in Chicago, made an exception in favor of Teresa, inviting her to play the MacDowell "Concerto" under his baton on July 5, 1888. That her friend of long ago had not thought her worthy of taking part in any of his concerts since her return to America had given Teresa many unhappy hours. This at last was ample compensation. Not only was she to be his assisting artist, but she was to collaborate with him in bringing out, for the first time anywhere, the "Concerto" which was already peculiarly her own. How much this appearance meant to her is clearly shown in her letter of thanks, published in the biography of Rose Fay Thomas. She wrote timidly, humbly.

Chicago, July 6, 1888

Dear Mr. Thomas:

It would have given me the greatest pleasure to come to see you this morning instead of writing, but knowing how pressed for time you are, I deprived myself of this pleasure, thinking that you would feel thankful that I did not come to take away your valuable time from your numerous occupations.

I only wish to thank you from all my heart once more for the kindness and consideration with which you treated me yesterday, and to tell you how proud and happy I feel that once again I have been allowed the pleasure and privilege of playing under your masterly baton.

Let me also thank you in Edward MacDowell's name, who feels highly honored that his composition should have come under your notice, and that it should have been brought before the public under your leadership.

I sincerely hope that I may have the pleasure of seeing you again, and if I may I will come and knock at your door when you are in

New York, and hope that you will always look upon me as the same little girl whose tottering footsteps in her profession you, with your powerful hand, were the first to guide and support.

Yours very sincerely,

Teresa Carreño

Besides making Teresa newly conscious of her powers, this occasion crystallized the determination in Ginka Watson's mind that something must be done at once to free her friend from an impossible situation at home, and to send her to Germany, where under Tapsig she herself had studied.

In the winter season of 1888 Teresa for the first time joined the Redpath Lyceum Circuit, the oldest of its kind in the United States, and toured through the Middle West together with her old associates, Emma Juch, Hope Glenn, and Lichtenberg, the violinist, using her usual repertoire and meeting with her usual success. The announcements stated that "the extent of her popularity makes her a public educator, and that she computes to have averaged more than 150 concerts a year, making about 1650 concerts in eleven years." Though this may safely be considered a manager's gross exaggeration, it is true that Teresa's record was unbroken by a single year of relaxation from concert routine, and in spite of the birth of many children, it exceeded in all probability that of any pianist, male or female, of that decade in the United States.

AMONG Ginka's students was Helen, daughter of N. K. Fairbank. Both father and daughter were fervent admirers of Teresa's playing, and so it was to Helen that Mrs. Watson decided to confide her hopes for Teresa's future. She agreed that Teresa could not find true appreciation as an artist in the United States as long as she was a member of Lyceum Circuits and other such combinations, that her home life was intolerable, that the emergency called for immediate action. Helen made up her mind to ask her genial father for help. It was not the first time that he had been approached in the interest of a musician in distress. When his daughter told him that it was imperative for

Teresa to have $5,000 at once, and that he must be the one to lend it to her, he laughed aloud.

"It is against my principles to lend money to an artist. As far as I am concerned I might as well throw it outright into Lake Michigan. Never yet has any one of them returned a cent of any loan I made him." His daughter's hopes crumbled at this abrupt dismissal. "But I happen to like this woman, and I want her to succeed. She shall have the money," he concluded. Together the two friends drew up the message that spelled freedom for Teresa.

In New York Arturo happened to be with Teresa when the telegram came. It was he who was immediately aflame with enthusiasm. "Teresita, you must go. Never will such an opportunity come a second time. Make up your mind at once while Giovanni is away." Teresa was unconvinced. Her last adventure had turned out badly. What reason had she to expect a better outcome for this. She heard herself saying, "How could I ever hope to repay such a sum?" "No need to worry about that," urged Arturo. "There will be no difficulty once you are known in Germany. Think of your children! For them alone you must accept, whatever the risk. I shall not leave this room until you do." Before he had finished Teresa knew what her decision would be. "May the dear Father in Heaven help me," she said, as she signed her name, less boldly than usual, to the ending of another chapter. Arturo triumphantly departed with the telegram. His step was elated and light. The sense that her departure would spell inevitable personal loss was not yet upon him. Teresa, left alone, was overcome with dread. Her respect for everything that Germany meant in music reached the point of veneration. Could she hope to measure up to its standards as an artist? German criticism was often devastating, she knew. Could she consider herself ready to face it confidently? She must have time for preparation. And yet on Tag's account, if on no other, there must be no delay. Arturo agreed that a few months in Paris with Manuel, now risen to the dignity of Secretary of the Venezuelan legation, would be advisable. Tag

returned to a *fait accompli,* and, not suspecting that the separation was meant to be final, was persuaded to consent without
difficulty. He begged to be taken. But that was a mistake Teresa
would never make again.

Friends did their utmost to hasten the departure for fear that
something might happen to prevent it. When one day in early
July of 1889 Teresa found herself standing on the deck of the
steamer *Gallia,* bound for England, Mrs. MacDowell and her
husband comfortingly by her side as fellow passengers, it was
as if she had been catapulted there by a force outside herself.
Tag, hidden behind a huge bouquet of flowers, seemed as unreal as the country of her destination. Until the last moment
little Giovanni, in tears, had to be kept from running back to
his father. Arturo held his breath until connection with land
was completely severed. Not until then did he take time to
think of himself. As the ship took its measured way and disappeared, he became poignantly aware that the day had darkened.
Tag returned to his house, to the emptiness that Teresa had so
overflowingly filled, quickly shook off his lonesomeness, and
set off in his usual manner to make the most of his unshackled
leisure.

Then more than now an ocean journey was the chance of all
others to take spiritual inventory. The long, placid days in the
steamer chair made Teresa for the first time conscious of herself as an entity. No longer was she Teresita to be adopted or
discarded at will, nor Teresa to be bullied or protected. "I am
Carreño," came the echo of a happier, younger voice, and she
said it again with firmer assurance, with better understanding.
She would shape her own destiny, live her own life, however
buffeted, undisturbed and unafraid. In her mirror she took the
lines of her face under scrutiny. Disenchantment had straightened them, pointed them, deepened them, hardened them. Determination should keep them so. That she was still lavishly
beautiful she scarcely noticed. It had never added to her happiness.

Arrived in London on July 13, 1889, she deposited her money

and in bold strokes signed her name simply "Teresa Carreño," in official abdication of marital ties. Life in an English hotel of the most conservative type soon made it apparent that her children's manners left much to be desired. Giovanni, when left unattended, took delight in investigating all the mechanisms new to him, even to pulling the chains of the toilets. It was quite as embarrassing to have the young tornadoes burst upon the quiet of the dining room, shrieking with wild excitement. The disapproving eyes of all England seemed focused upon her as they were sent from the room in disgrace.

ONCE in Paris bitter memories reawakened. Teresa was little tempted to renew old ties. She meant to build a new life, but not on the ashes of another. Only one simple duty was kept uppermost in all her planning, that of preparing with all concentration for her Berlin début in the fall. Her six long hours of daily practice were of a more thorough searching kind than any she had known before. She meant to discover what her best really was. For she must knock at the gate of the world's strongest musical citadel, armed with no less a weapon. Only by this arduous road could she earn her way to that new independence through which she would be able to bring up her children in peace. And how delicious to be for the first time in her life really free, free to use the ample sums lying in London to her credit, accountable to no other person. Best of all, with the country of her destination she would have not a single connection, not even that of language. She saw herself a diver standing on a cliff, giving a last glance far down at the still surface that in a moment would be shaken into flowing motion. Who could foretell the shape or the direction of those wave patterns? How far might they not reach!

On July 22 Carreño rented an apartment in the Avenue Mac-Mahon. Manuel lived in the same house. For the furnished *entresol* and first *étage* she payed 750 francs a month. While she practiced and Josephine did the cooking, the children were most often to be found with Rosie. Carreño felt the sting of jealousy. On one occasion, when the children had returned late from a thrilling visit above, Carreño could be heard from Manuel's apartment scolding in her penetrating mezzo: "If you like it better with your aunt, you might just as well pack your bags, and move up there altogether."

There were drives through the Bois de Boulogne. Once, poor as she was, she had walked as a celebrity along the very ways where now she rode forgotten. There were fascinating mornings of shopping for hats and dresses and corsets. Mme.

Mulot-Larchevêque, 23 Boulevard des Capucines, designed two concert gowns, one of mother-of-pearl velvet, the other of embroidered creamy yellow silk. Each made her the poorer by 850 francs, but the new Carreño must be suitably gowned. This was as justifiable as the expense of having photographs taken of Teresita and Giovanni, separately and together.

Of these months of adjustment Teresa's letter to her friend, Carrie Keating, gives the most valid résumé. It is dated October 4, 1889.

As I presume you would like to know what I have done since the 3rd of July, I will tell you. We had a beautiful trip across, and (wonderful to relate!) I was hardly seasick at all. It is true that Mrs. MacDowell was so courageous and did so well, that I could not very well do less than follow her example. We arrived in London on the 13th of July, and remained there nine days. We did London pretty thoroughly and it gave me the greatest pleasure to see all the old familiar places of my childhood and girlhood again after so many years. Mrs. MacDowell and I went to visit the different places at which I lived and my heart ached again for the old times when my poor father was by my side.

We reached here on the 22nd of July, found Emanuel and his wife waiting most impatiently for us with arms opened. You have no idea what a surprise I gave them, for they had no idea of my coming here until they received a telegram which I sent from London the day after we reached there. Emanuel looks better than ever; he has grown very much stouter and looks all the better for it, and is the same dear good boy, now with all the qualities of a good man and all the boyishness left behind. His wife is a most lovely girl, and when I think of the outrageous things that were told me about her I feel like going home and cutting the tongues of the *knaves* who said them. She is one of the best and dearest girls you ever heard of, and I am anxious for you to know her. They are as happy together as the day is long, and it does my heart good to see them so. Manuel's position here is very nice, and they enjoy themselves immensely as of course, Emanuel being Secretary of the Legation, this gives them many an opportunity of enjoying themselves.

I have been here ever since. First I had an apartment in the same house with Emanuel, 3 Avenue MacMahon, close to this one, and now have taken this one until Nov. 1st when I go to Berlin. Of music I have heard little. In London I heard Verdi's Otello given exactly as it was given when first produced in Milan, all with the exception of the prima donna who was very fair. Tamagno's voice is magnificent, specially in the upper notes, and Maurel's Iago histrionically is worthy of Salvini. His voice is no longer what it was, but he is such a great artist that he makes you forget that. As to the Orchestra and Chorus I never heard the like. The Orchestra specially fairly took me off my seat.

Here there is nothing but the "Exposition," and specially the "Eiffel Tower." People dream of it, eat on it, speak of nothing else and wear it in every way conceivable, until at last you seem to be surrounded by a lot of maniacs. In all justice we must say that all this fun is well deserved, for it is a most marvelous piece of engineering, but you get a little tired of hearing so much about it.

Mr. and Mrs. MacDowell, my sister-in-law and I went one day to the very top, and the sight was grand. The Exhibition itself is very interesting, but I have not been able to see as much of it as I should have liked. I shall go again before it closes and see some more.

My first appearance will take place in Berlin at my own Concert, assisted by the Philharmonic Orchestra, on the 18th of November. The friends of the family are requested to pray for the occasion! How I wish you were here with me then, and now and ever! Do you think you'll come over next summer? If I stay, I hope you will come, but to tell you the truth, Carrie dearest, I am so dreadfully awfully homesick that I hope next summer, if I live, will see me in America, for there is no land to me like the United States, no people like the Americans. God bless them! They have no idea how much I love them. I paid a visit to my dear old friend Gounod, and you have no idea how cordially, how affectionately he received me. He played for me his last composition "mon dernier enfant" as he called it, a most beautiful orchestral composition, and made me play for him on his Steinway grand of which he is awfully proud, and told me I was the first person he had ever allowed to play on his piano besides himself. Wasn't that flattering, and wasn't it good of him? He is not only a great man but he is a great good man! I can't tell you how much true pleasure I derived from this visit which lasted two hours for he would not let me go sooner. . . .

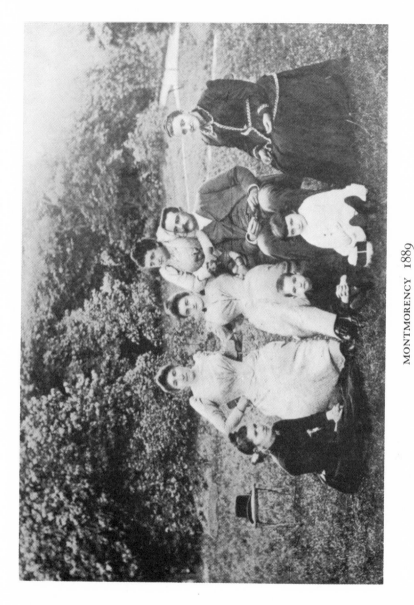

MONTMORENCY 1889

*From left to right: Josephine de Paul, Mlle. Pénache, Rosie Carreño, Teresa Carreño, Manuel Carreño, Mlle. Degrouel, Giovanni, Teresita*

Another letter, a copy of which Teresa kept in her business files, was addressed to her friend of Boston days, Hans von Bülow. It read:

Cher Maître:—Je ne me doutais guère que la prochaine fois que j'aurais le plaisir de vous écrire ce serait de Paris, c'est à dire que je me trouverais en Europe si près de vous. Comme vous voyez je me trouve à Paris et je ne veux que vous le sachiez par personne d'autre que par moi-même, et je viens par ces lignes vous envoyer mes bons souhaits. Je suis venue en Europe pour me faire entendre et, si je peux, faire quelques engagements de concert. Le 18 du mois prochain je donne mon premier concert à Berlin, et j'ose espérer que j'aurais le plaisir de vous voir à Berlin pendant mon séjour. Je vous prie de continuer cette bonté et amitié que vous m'avez toujours témoignées et qui m'honorent tant, et je me mets sous votre aile protectrice!

Veuillez présenter à Madame von Bülow mes meilleurs souvenirs et, agréez, je vous prie, l'assurance de mes meilleurs sentiments d'amitié et d'admiration.

Teresa decided to confront Berlin unattended, which meant finding a place where the children could safely board with Josephine and be given their first schooling besides. In Montmorency at the highly respectable Institution de Demoiselles, directed by two maiden ladies, Mlles. Pénache and Degrouel, the ideal place was found. Carreño was already in touch with Berlin's foremost impresario, Hermann Wolff, whom she found to her relief as much at home in French as in German, and quite able to advise her about anything from concert halls and programs to a suitable *pied-à-terre*.

ONE evening in late October Teresa Carreño descended from her train into the jumble of sounds and odors that was Germany. Somehow she managed to reach the Askanischer Hof safely, if in a daze. Herr Wolff had chosen well. It was a place frequented mainly by those of artistic profession, adequate and moderate in price. On the top floor, the one where she could best practice without disturbing others, there was a room large enough to accommodate an upright piano on the side of the house facing the court. From Paris she had brought an annoying cold which increased her loneliness. There was no use in trying to make an impression upon her German impresario in that state. She would use the time of her isolation in learning German. Mornings while her room was being put in order she made a habit of reciting German phrases aloud, interspersed with penetrating sneezes, as she paced up and down in the unheated corridor. Her neighbors were mystified to hear a voice repeating with insistent determination: *"Ich bezahle meine Rechnung nicht. Ich bezahle meine Rechnung nicht!—Hap-chi, Hap-chi, Hap-chi!!!"*

In the front room across the hall lived Frau Koch and her daughter Emma. The mother was a typical German Hausfrau, whose outlook accommodated itself easily to the limits of her four walls. Her daughter Emma had a wider horizon. She had studied under the Master Liszt, and had made occasional excursions into the concert field, in which she acquitted herself creditably, even accompanying Joachim on one memorable tour. Now she had settled down to the more sedate and profitable life of a music teacher à la Liszt, chaperoned by her ultra-conservative mother, whose views on most subjects she shared.

*"Hap-chi! Ich bezahle meine Rechnung nicht,"* insisted the decidedly foreign and forceful voice. There was no doubt that she meant it, whoever it was. Frau Koch's curiosity was aroused. She opened her door. Carreño, believing that she had unwittingly made herself objectionable, apologized, bad German mixed with bad cold. At least she could offer this peculiar person temporary warmth in a room cozily heated by the efficient tile stove. Undoubtedly she would then discover why it was that the lady so loudly refused to pay her bill. Frau Koch had not expected to find her guest so sympathetic. Both laughed heartily over the misunderstanding, and Carreño was delighted to be able to drop into accustomed French. As the days passed, the cold vanished under the care of her neighbors, and the concert loomed closer, this acquaintance ripened into intimacy. Carreño took pains to consult the Kochs about the thousands

of details connected with her concert. But in the end she meant
to do as she herself pleased.

Hermann Wolff and Louise, his wife, whose caustic wit
made many within the musical fraternity uncomfortable, were
not slow in falling under the spell of a personality so refreshingly different from the ones that usually met in their drawing
room. Wolff, in spite of his easy-going joviality, was an astute
manager. Teresa was impressed. The two together played the
intricate game of artist versus impresario with friendly and
skillful rivalry. They crossed verbal swords in sharp thrust and
parry, thoroughly enjoying their differences and readjustments,
and remained close friends for life in spite or because of them.
Hermann Wolff was a businessman with the soul of an artist,
Carreño an artist trained by hard experience to count the cost.
Now more than ever, in order to meet her obligation to Mr.
Fairbank, she must hold her own financially. She must not let
herself be flattered or fooled. The two close antagonists respected the qualities that each represented, and avoided dangerous misunderstanding on the common ground of humorous
give and take. Their letters are full of witty badinage.

Nobody knew better than Hermann Wolff how to promote
interest in a new artist and how to direct gossip in spinning her
magic web. From Louise's day-at-home there emanated rumors
of a full-blooded South American Creole, whose romantic epi-
sodes were the talk of the United States. Hints of this kind insinuated themselves even into the apartment of the Kochs.
Could it be true that there was an unlovely, sordid background
in the life of this beautiful woman whose manners were so
naturally distinguished? They decided to withhold judgment
until after the concert. This did not keep Emma from feeling
acutely embarrassed when in a public place Teresa, with the
familiarity to which close association under the roof of the
Askanischer Hof entitled her, took Emma's arm to walk up
and down during the intermission.

Carreño chose the Singakademie for its intimate atmosphere,
and for its great tradition. There Rubinstein and Clara Schu-

mann had appeared before her. It was with such as these that she wished to be compared. The custom of having only one soloist in a concert was strange but to her liking. Wolff recommended a début with full orchestral background as the most effective introduction, and together they decided upon the Grieg "Concerto" with the accompaniment of the Philharmonic Orchestra under the baton of its standing conductor, Herr Kogel. Nobody as yet had heard Carreño. Wolff had insisted upon that and wondered. Could a person who had never had training or experience in Germany succeed with a German audience? He doubted it. But after all the risk was hers alone, and personally he liked her enough to do all he could to create a proper setting. From the United States came letters in her behalf, the Venezuelan colony reserved seats in a block, and to the surprise of Herr Wolff tickets were actually selling in fair number.

Among the few letters of introduction Teresa had found time to present was one to Emil Breslauer, editor of *Der Klavierlehrer*. He chose the night before her concert to call upon her, and Carreño, increasingly nervous as time shortened, felt that she needed the encouragement of a neutral colleague. She offered to play for him, and he listened intently, silently. There was no doubt that he was stirred, he himself did not know whether with pleasure or pain. Very different, very absorbing he admitted it to be. Then the pedantic pedagogue raised his voice. "But your technique is so unusual. We in Germany have a more controlled style, do not let ourselves go so extremely!" And he proceeded to show Carreño how the conservative German virtuoso was accustomed to play upon the stage. When the little man had gone Carreño was in a worse state than before. She had never given much thought to method and technique, had just played as was most convenient, as it brought out most easily what she meant to say. In America nobody had complained. But perhaps there was something to be said for Breslauer's point of view. Once more she sat down at the piano, trying her best to work out a passage according to his suggestions. The effect failed to satisfy her. "There's no use," she thought, as she gave it up after several hours of effort. How could she change her way of doing overnight, even if she knew exactly what she wanted! Her dreams, when she finally fell asleep, were disquieted by a procession of gnomes who hooted her off the stage because she had the wrong method.

It had never been Carreño's habit to practice to any extent on the day of an important concert. A walk in the Tiergarten and good news of the children from Josephine lifted her sagging spirits. It was a spiritless day. The one rehearsal accorded her had gone satisfactorily. Herr Kogel had seconded her well, and the orchestra at the end had made noises of approval. The last movement of the "Concerto" she must remember to take at a more moderate pace. The orchestra had been left breathlessly behind. There was no further faltering. The grandniece of Bolívar would cross her Andes too. As eagerly, though not so happily, as on the day of her début in Irving Hall she watched the sinking of the day that would pass upon her worth as an artist. No candidate ever visualized the implications of success or failure more clearly. The thought of her yellow Paris gown of crepe de Chine cheered her. Would she look more beautiful in it than in the simple dress of white her mother had once made? Was this the same little girl of long ago? Then her world had been filled by her piano and her dolls. Life with her piano and her children still was all she asked for. Then she had felt within her that she would play her best; now she knew that she must play her best, for the sake of the children that needed her, for the sake of the friends who believed in her, for the sake of her own inner peace. As she turned from the window against which her imagination heard the rain prickling as in that far-off twilight of November, 1862, she seemed again to hear a voice: "It is time to be dressed now, Teresita."

*In der Mässigung zeigt sich der Meister.*
Goethe

# PART III

# ARTIST

I AM Carreño!" The Philharmonic Orchestra gave the concert its official and perfunctory opening with Mendelssohn's "Overture" to *Die Schöne Melusine,* while in her cell backstage Carreño strode up and down, clearly aware that she was facing the ultimate test. In a moment she must be able to bring Latin and Teuton into common understanding, or return to the untenable life of yesterday. Three short weeks had convinced her that musically this was her country, that personally she wanted to know these Germans and their intricate language. She felt that here idealism, mental thoroughness, and orderly economy lived together in helpful harmony. There was much for her to learn. She must not fail tonight. How long since she had felt ill at ease and humble before a concert as she did now! The Bechstein seemed a foreign instrument, unapproachable and menacing. The cigarette in her hand trembled.

Hermann Wolff looked in to assure his new protégée that there was a fair audience, and himself that all was well. Too sensitive to the reactions of artists to do the wrong thing at a crucial moment, he said a few meaningless words that succeeded in drawing forth an unexpectedly robust and healthy laugh and as tactfully disappeared. This exotic beauty had aroused his liking. He wished her well, not for his own sake alone; but he was too experienced to count upon anything *ante festum.* What he had heard at Carreño's hands had impressed him, but what of her nerves, what of the critics? *"Das verdammte Temperament,"* he growled taking his seat next to his wife. Although he was fond of music and of people, first of all he was a businessman. In passing he took in his audience. The members of foreign diplomatic circles stood festively out from the underfed and carelessly assembled music students, who, taking their passes as a right, felt themselves privileged to criticize with double severity and to leave at the first tingle of ennui.

The overture was finished. Carreño stood with nerves quiver-

CONCERTDIRECTION
HERMANN WOLFF.

Montag, den 18. November 1889,

Abends 7¹/₂ Uhr präcise:

**Im Saal der Singakademie**

# CONCERT

von

# Teresa Carreño

mit dem

## Berliner Philharmonischen Orchester

unter Leitung des

## Herrn Kapellmeister **Gustav F. Kogel.**

## PROGRAMM.

1. **Ouverture** zum „Märchen von der schönen
Melusine", op. 32 . . . . . . . . . F. Mendelssohn.

2. **Concert** für Klavier mit Begleitung des Orchesters A-moll, op. 16 . . . . . . Ed. Grieg.
    Allegro molto moderato. — Adagio. —
    Allegro moderato molto e marcato quasi Presto.

3. **Zwölf symphonische Etüden**, op. 13 . . R. Schumann.

4. **Andante** für Streichquartett . . . . . P. Tschaikowsky.

5. **Polonaise brillante** f. Klavier mit Begleitung
des Orchesters . . . . . . . . . . Weber-Liszt.

## Concertflügel: Bechstein.

**Während der Musik bleiben die Saalthüren geschlossen.**

**Billets** à 5, 3 und 2 Mark sind in der Hof-Musikhandlung der Herren
**Ed. Bote & G. Bock,** Leipziger Str. 37, sowie Abends an der Kasse zu haben.

Buchdruckerei der „Volks-Zeitung", Akt.-Ges. in Berlin, Lützowstr. 105.

*Berlin Début Program*

ing for the touch of the keys. Barely giving Herr Kogel time
to take his stand before the orchestra, head thrown back, tight-
lipped, she crossed the stage of the Singakademie, upon which
Mendelssohn had so often made the great Bach live again.
From the middle of the platform she measured her adversaries
with a glance that radiated force, warmth, and magnetism.
With one of her famous bows, all-inclusive like a searchlight,
traveling down, across, and up again in slow and regal acknowledgment of the applause that welcomed her, tamely at
first, then with rising intensity, Carreño won over many an
unbeliever before playing a single note.

Silence! An angry rumble of the kettledrums and Carreño
was off to the attack. Mightily the opening cadenza of the
Grieg "Concerto" thundered and reverberated in this hall of
classic aura, like cannon roaring out of quiet. Backs stiffened,
eyes sought each other for information, for confirmation. Could
this be a woman? Some goddess might have played an Olym-
pian piano like this. Geographically the music unfolded itself
in jagged Nordic vistas. Fir-dotted cliffs disappeared palisade-
like in dark waters. Caves that made a perfect setting for the
frolic of elves and trolls undermined stark mountains. Wherever Venezuelan imagination led, this composite person, the
audience, helplessly followed. Whatever the eye saw, that the
ear heard; in such perfect harmony meaning and motion
blended. One deaf to sound might have caught the flavor of the
music by watching the changing play of expression that edited
each mood and idea as Carreño dreamed, danced, and drove
her way to the climax. Attention was held taut until the final
smashing chord, which was still vibrating when the audience
let go in frantic applause of hand and foot, punctuated by
bravos. In spite of themselves the critics were hypnotized to
join in. Under their very noses a new Lorelei was luring Berlin
to fearful depths. By some illegitimate magic—what Bechstein
had ever been subjected to such treatment—she was upsetting
some of the most cherished tenets of German musical faith,
transcending standards of accepted good taste. In the last

*maestoso,* leaving the few who were already familiar with Grieg's score openmouthed, did she not have the audacity to change the master's own arpeggios to saber-rattling octaves? A dangerous person, the more so for her incontestable beauty!

Again in her cell, now become her sanctuary, Carreño flung a shawl about her shoulders. Why did every room in Germany have to have a different temperature from its neighbor? America could teach this country much about the comforts of life. Shivering, partly from cold, partly from excitement, Carreño began to take inventory. She had played very nearly her best; that she knew. Her audience had been affected strongly; that she sensed. Could it be that they were making fun of her?

She was still thinking this over when the door opened slightly to admit the head of a very subdued Herr Breslauer. *"Liebe Gnädige Frau Carreño,"* he wailed. *"Ich war ein Esel, ein E-s-e-l! Es war groszartig, noch nie dagewesen groszartig!"* The ever-watchful Herr Wolff cut short the flow of compliment with a curt: *"À plus tard, Monsieur, Madame doit se reposer,"* escorting him firmly into the buzzing hall. Hardly had they taken their places when Carreño, not stopping for even a glance at the mirror, stepped out before her judges once again to face her hardest task unseconded, the "Symphonische Etuden" of Germany's own Schumann. Still ringing in their ears must be the authentic interpretation that the divine Clara had given them, or the more robust reading of Sophie Menter. Berlin knew beyond a doubt how these variations, exploding with difficulties, should sound. It was temerity indeed to attempt to brave the enemy in the heart of his own fortress! The drawbridge was at an angle, the moat wide and deep.

Carreño began. She announced the theme slowly, drily. Impeccably correct it was, like an exercise. Some who secretly regarded this as one of Schumann's least grateful works began to dread the lengths that stretched before. Was this superwoman going to commit the unforgivable sin of boring her listeners? Not so! Still holding temperament in check, she kept her hearers alert with biting, sarcastic accentuation and relentless rhythm, little by little abandoning her reserve, building up her effects with the assurance only he can have who recognizes space and time as servants of that which exists timeless, spaceless, a unit. She tossed off, laughed off, prodigious difficulties. At times her hands moved so swiftly from her stocky wrists that they appeared as a blur. Impulsive change of tempo there was in plenty and notes that jangled as they oversprang the power of the Bechstein, but no mind was allowed to wander in the process. Let the sensitive jump, let the pedant be shocked from his ruts. Follow he must through the pungent pages to the very end. With the sharpness of steel Carreño stabbed the most stolid listener alive. Soothing gentleness, eerie loveliness, that she did not find or bring this night. It was Carreño fighting for freedom. The ending march piled climax upon climax until with a last accelerando victory was hers, leaving exhausted upon the scene all but the pianist herself. The critics, usually so voluble, sat speechless.

Excitement during the intermission reached the decibels of a stock exchange in session, which would not be suppressed even after the orchestral interlude until Carreño was again seated before the piano. No more concessions, no more restraint! The Weber "Polonaise," doubled in hazards by Liszt, was her war horse. She rode it with all the fire and fury of her tempestuous being. The sparkle of her runs was so dazzling that some instinctively closed their eyes. Before the end all were her slaves. She held them breathless, as she made an incredibly even, swift, and surging trill shiver down to the vanishing point at her own excess of leisure. Then one rocketlike, multicolored flame of sound, and it was finished.

Aloofly she accepted the homage of flowers, bowing in a comprehensive sweep, as if condescending to acknowledge herself the unchallenged superior of her captives. Returning time after time in response to demonstrations that grew more and more hysterical, she wondered again, "Are they making fun of me?" Seeing people crowded around the stage, waving their handkerchiefs, standing on the seats, stamping on the floor, they reminded her of a mob of Venezuelans in revolution. It took all the vocabulary of Herr Wolff to convince her that she was, indeed, a success. In the *Garderobe* after the janitor had dimmed the hall lights, and later on in the streets, that miraculous trill was still the universal topic.

In the cool of night the critics found time for more dispassionate reflection. They were one and all obliged to grant that here was a pianist to be reckoned with, at least potentially one of the first water. They marveled, if not without reservation, at her endurance, her daring individuality. What of it, if her tone lacked richness and delicacy, if her tempi were too erratic, if she dealt in extremes beyond the measure called for by tradition! They called her the "lioness of the keyboard," "Brünnhilde, the Walküre," a name that accompanied her through life. Typical was the review of the *Allgemeine Musikzeitung*.

. . . It is long since I have heard a pianiste who has attracted me as completely as Frau Carreño. Here at last comes an independent personality, standing out from among so much mediocre talent, which, neatly combed and brushed, pervades the wide avenues of prevailing pianism. With complete and blinding technical virtuosity, with strength sufficient for two pianists, and with an uncommonly and strongly sculptured sense of rhythm, Frau Carreño combines spiritual freedom and independence of interpretation, which lifts her far above mere pianism into the realm of true art. Everything about this woman, speaking from an artistic point of view, is tailored to extraordinary measure, and therefore I understand that many of her listeners are repelled by the power of this presence, which has nothing feminine, and yet again nothing unbeautiful, or unnatural in its artistic expression. Comparing Frau Carreño with the average pianiste, she stands out as a Brünnhilde against one of the "flappers" of our time, and if this Apollonic Wishmaiden upsets our comfortable Philistinism somewhat with the crackling flame of her passionate nature, a call for help may be in order on the part of endangered conventionality, but it will not affect the victorious and compelling art of this tower of strength. I do not doubt that the guild of critics may dwell upon certain unevennesses, but I confess openly that it is repugnant to me, still under the impression of the brilliant achievement attained by Frau Carreño in the Grieg "Concerto in A minor," the "Symphonic Studies" of Schumann, and the *Polacca* of Weber in E, arranged by Liszt, to weigh with academic coolness the pros and cons of some individual tempi, or of a possible excess of force. Instead I am delighted once again at last to have chanced upon a pianiste in whose soul something unusual is happening, which materialized musically in its own special way. The Philharmonic Orchestra under the direction of Herr Kogel accompanied the Grieg "Concerto" very well. In the "Polonaise," it did not follow the rhythmic nuances with which the soloist enhanced it, sympathetically enough. I hope that after the stormy and endearing applause tendered her, Frau Carreño will allow herself to be heard more frequently before the Berlin public.

Hans von Bülow, who had done her the honor of attending the début, was heard to say: "She is undoubtedly the most interesting pianiste of the present," and that in spite of the fact that he had little use for women as musicians. A letter to Wolff expresses his feelings on this subject: "Do I need more of the 'Eternal feminine' for my concerts? Ask yourself about the drawing power (to the box office). I for my own part miss rustling garments on the platform with delight."

On the morning after the concert Hermann Wolff interrupted Carreño's breakfast in order to translate for her the mountain of criticisms into French. On the strength of these he insisted that she follow up her success immediately with a solo recital unassisted. Carreño, still dazed and somewhat skeptical, consented.

On the evening of November 30 she found herself once more at the same Bechstein in the same hall, this time completely sold out, due, some said, to the miracle of a single trill.

A stately figure in softly trailing velvet, Carreño crossed the stage accompanied by acclaim as spontaneously from the heart as her own playing. This was not an audience to be conquered, but a crowd of followers eager to be led wherever she chose. Berlin had adopted "Die Carreño" after a single hearing. Before the first note of the "Appassionata" sounded she felt that she belonged.

As in the "Symphonische Etuden" the week before she began with extreme deliberation, reticently, severely. Those who looked for tenderness and charm in the "Andante" were disappointed. It stood in naked simplicity, classic in architecture. Had they been mistaken after all, wondered the critics? Suddenly she hammered them to acute tension with disagreeable reiteration of those arid diminished sevenths that usher in the "Finale." Something momentous was about to happen. Visibly, as a body, the audience was drawn forward. What a tempo, what fierceness of rhythm! Could she possibly hold it through? She could, and she did. Rejoicing tirelessly and disdainfully in every difficulty, Carreño made vivid and vocal the terrific passion inherent in Beethoven's music, and led it with inexorable inner logic to its wild, intoxicating close. The Titan of Bonn stood revealed, as Klinger has revealed him in marble, untamed, unpolished, unresigned. Even those who disagreed with Carreño's convictions most loudly during the intermission, had to admit that they were held in complete subjection. They felt that here was beauty of soul both simple and great, seeking not its own. That she saw her truths in superlatives did not in essence detract. Is not genius itself an exaggeration? What if she played the left hand before the right, dragged out her melodies, or pounded the all-too-responsive Bechstein at times without mercy! That which she said had the rightness and persuasiveness of truth itself. "She plays like Rubinstein on one of his good days," whispered the critic of the *Norddeutsche Allgemeine Zeitung*. Conversation buzzed excitedly, yet in undertones as if under the impression of an aurora borealis. The gentle Herr Breslauer complained in his journal: "It is impossible to evaluate her. Even the most coolheaded are caught in the rapids. But"—here the piano pedant raises his head—"from the German point of view much should be different." The Chopin group, although more temperate, drew forth decided pros and cons. Again it was in the music that approached the virtually impossible that Carreño was most completely at home on this night.

The Paganini-Liszt "Campanella" was one of her affinities of long standing. Nearing the famous trill, Carreño became conscious of two in the front row busily conversing, evidently with minds far removed from music. Lifting her left eyebrow, which should have warned them, she began the trill. It rose lightly as Ariel, growing in speed and force until there was not enough strength in the fingers of one hand alone to admit of further power. (The two in the front row, she noticed, were still deep in their own affairs.) Carreño trilled on, using both hands to hammer out a vibrating quiver, breath-taking in its crescendo. (Could it be that they were still unaffected?) The trill from its incredible height dwindled into nothing. (Aha! They talked no more.) Again it soared to peaks where human beings no longer may breathe. Not until she had the satisfaction of seeing two faces upturned to her own in speechless amazement did she let it sink into silence. Decidedly, in the sacred name of good taste this was too much. Marvelous as it was, such things should not happen in Germany. "Probably," said a critic, "the words of the German poet: 'In moderation the master shows himself,' have not yet been translated into Spanish."

The octaves of Liszt's "Sixth Rhapsodie" closed the concert proper with their blaring fanfare. A music-hungry mob crowded forward for its quota of encores. Carreño, to whom the concert had seemed one of the shortest, played on until by order of the management the hall was darkened. The temper of the press in general was typified by the *Volkszeitung*.

Grandiose as the effect of her playing are also its faults, but I would be a Philistine indeed for this reason to indict our guest before the forum of the academicians. The style of her offerings still needs schooling; yet with all her exaggerations we welcome her as a sounding protest against that affected lifelessness, of which today even virtuosos of the first rank make themselves guilty.

Back in her hotel Carreño poured out her joys and her hopes to her friends across the hall. Now she could soon have her children with her, pay her obligations, and find the permanent home for which she had longed. She was still at her liveliest when she noticed that Emma was yawning and that Frau Koch had fallen asleep. Another day was at the dawn.

She awoke, her determination fixed to go to the children for the holidays. To this a reluctant manager was obliged to consent, but not until he had exacted a promise that she return by the middle of January as his prize exclusively on the same terms customary with artists like Eugen d'Albert. In the interim he would lose no time in making her name known wherever his influence counted. Engagements began to trickle, then to pour in. Hans von Bülow himself asked for a repetition of the Grieg "Concerto" under his baton in the Berlin Philharmonic Concert of January 31, an honor accorded few newcomers. In her 3-by-4 diary of Russia leather adorned with a four-leaf clover Carreño enters on the day of the public rehearsal, "great success," on the day of the concert, *"great* success." This appearance was to cement a lifelong friendship, occasionally spiced with misunderstandings, between two whose temperatures registered at the thermometric antipodes, the cold, meticulous scholar and the hot-blooded, impulsive Amazon.

Three days after this concert, Hans von Bülow wrote: "Carreño is a phenomenon, an exotic one, a young Kundry. I call her *benedicta in nomine Apollonis,* for she sweeps the floor clean of all piano paraders, who after her coming, must take themselves elsewhere. Wherever she is heard she is engaged for a second, yes, even a third time—I recommend to you this enrichment in new sensations." More practical witness to her triumph, Carreño could enter an income for January of 3,450 marks.

On February 13 Carreño gave her third concert, this time again with orchestral accompaniment, playing three concerti, one of which was that of MacDowell.

IN the midst of ovations such as Germany usually reserved for its own acknowledged great, one wish, suppressed during many years, rose to the surface with such frequent recurrence that it would no longer be denied. Carreño had never forgotten her first child, the one she had been forced to abandon to the care of another. For fourteen years there had been no word of her. Not to be able to imagine one's own daughter! See her she must! For one whole morning Carreño composed draft after draft of a letter that, she hoped, would speak to the heart of her old-time friend. She wrote laboriously in German:

Dear Mrs. Bischoff:—On the 21st instant I go to Wiesbaden to fulfill a concert engagement, and I come most earnestly to beg of you to allow me to see my daughter for a few minutes.

I think that in all these years of a silence so painful, to me, in which I have longed oh! with such a heavy heart to hear something of my child without in any way causing her or you any pain, I have sufficiently proved to you how thoroughly I wished you to keep all my rights over her, (for this was the promise I made to myself) that she should grow loving you with all her heart and undisturbed by the thought of her unfortunate and unhappy mother. I still intend to keep this promise, for more than ever I am convinced that for the child's own sake I acted right, and if she does not know who I am, and what my relation to her is, I will never tell her, for her own sake; but I cannot come so near, longing as I do for one look at her and not see her. In the name of the love you bear that child who after all is my child—and I gave her to your keeping that she might in a measure with her child-love compensate you for the love and kindness which I owed you, and though lawfully having the right to claim her, I have never attempted to do so, nor will I as long as you live—in the remembrance of the love you once bore me I appeal to your heart to let me have the comfort of seeing her when I come to Wiesbaden. What I ask you is very little for you, and it will be so much for me.

The next day after the concert I shall call at your house and hope that you will grant my request.

With the deepest feelings of gratitude for all you have been to my daughter, and for all you were to me in days gone by, I remain,
                              Yours faithfully, Teresa Carreño.

Mrs. Bischoff chose not to receive Carreño. Emilita knew of her real parentage, but in a way calculated to make her feel ashamed of it. Carreño was, so Emilita had been told, a light-minded woman of the prevalently objectionable artist type, more addicted to luxury and jewels, of which she owned trunkfuls, than of taking responsibility. That this wall of fiction might some day be dynamited was her ever-present dread. It was a menace in itself that Teresa had come to Germany and had taken it by storm. With all the intensity of a jealous woman's nature, she meant to stay alone in the affections of this young girl upon whom she had lavished the care and comforts due an only daughter. She replied through her lawyer two days after the meeting was to have taken place.

February 24, 1890

Mrs. Bischoff asks me to answer your letter written to her from Berlin and to say that she in no wise can acknowledge the legal rights to the little daughter of Mr. Sauret which you stress in it. As matters stand, it is incontestable that the child stands under the control of her father, and that the father alone has the right to decide about her care, upbringing and education. You will admit yourself that by Frau Bischoff she is being treated in such an outstandingly affectionate, sensible and actually motherly manner, that interference with these conditions could not but be harmful for the mental and moral development of the child.

Under these circumstances my honored client is obliged to deny herself in her own interest as well as that of the child any kind of intercourse with you, personal or otherwise, and asks you to give up any further attempts to intrude upon her, to which under existing law you have no rights. This will be all the less painful to you, because since your divorce from your husband you have never in the slightest degree concerned yourself about the child, and have even expressed the wish at one time that henceforth you desired not to exist for her.

Carreño turned from the inhospitable door to her work for comfort. A full schedule of concerts stretched ahead.

To the army of music students who hopefully flocked to Germany in the Nineties Carreño became the embodiment of their ultimate ideal for themselves. She was the superlative pianist,

the incomparable, the most complete, the most splendid, and
as a natural corollary she must be of course the happiest mortal
on earth. Inhabiting her own private utopia, at whose glamorous
perfection they could only guess, they gave Carreño a place
aloof, too high for belittling envy. They saw her embowered
among flowers of perennial freshness, surrounded by a rainbow
aura of their own youthful, extravagant imaginings. She grew
to be their musical gold standard. Secretly each one thought
herself a potential Carreño. Perhaps some day they too, through
the magic effect emanating, so people had said, from the Berlin
musical atmosphere, would hold court against a fragrant floral
background, while silks and satins beyond dreams and counting
hung idly in wardrobes, like those of Carreño. Jewels like
hers, too many of them, defying choice, filled chest upon chest
of their imagination. They endowed her with a geyser of a bank
account, that miraculously took care of itself, with friends of
high degree who would never fail or disappoint her, always
appear when needed, yet never outstay their welcome, devoted
servants who would not so much as allow her to pin on a hat
or button a shoe. And like Carreño they would play, and play,
and play for hours upon end, living perpetually on that high
level of ecstasy to which she lifted her hearers. So her life must
always have been, must ever be! How thrilling just to pick up the
handkerchief she carelessly dropped on the stage, to see her set
her ample, generously rounded signature to one of her programs for an album of memories, to feel the glance of piercing
velvet that seemed to read and comprehend them at once and
wholly! Oh! to be a Carreño!

Carreño sat in the twilight, wearing a plain woolen wrapper
that had warmed her for many years. Cigarettes had punctured
it in places. But Carreño, watching the soothing smoke rings
thinning into nothing, liked it all the better for the holes. She
was not one to cast old friends, even inanimate ones, lightly
aside. Her mood today was one of extreme melancholy. What
curse had been laid upon her that she, like the Flying Dutch-
man, must travel eternally from place to place without a

home, far from her country, her children! Why had life denied her the rights, the security given ordinary mothers, safely protected by their husbands? She should have shown more sense in choosing hers. How could she hope to sift out a few true friends from the flatterers that surrounded her to the exclusion of any real privacy? How could she answer all these unimportant letters, thank people for their flowers, sign her name endlessly for silly young things, while her dresses needed mending, and she should be going over her accounts. No manager must be allowed to take advantage of her. Indeed not! What would Tag say to the letter that told him definitely that between him and her all was ended? How long would it take her at the rate of her present prospects to repay the loan of Mr. Fairbank? Could she afford to have Teresita and Giovanni with her now? No! They were better off in Montmorency. The daily news of them which she required indicated that they were well and happy. Teresita was already speaking French very nicely and Giovanni, the darling, had written her an undecipherable scrawl that she carried in her bag wherever she went. She would see them on her way to England, God willing! That alone was worth living and working for. Tomorrow she must be off again for another city she would learn to know only through its hotels and its concert halls. In Dresden she had not even had time to see the "Sistine Madonna." Instead she was obliged to receive the boring, perfunctory calls of official dignitaries. Thank fortune, her trunk at least was packed.

Far below sounded the even tramp of soldiers, a military band suddenly breaking into one of those marches that give spring to tired feet. It reminded her that the piano was awaiting her pleasure. Although she did not feel well—her nerves, she supposed—and not at all like practicing, from the very first note she responded to the healing power of the art to which she had committed herself. Troubles receded. She became as young Germany dreamed her, the empress of the piano. Slowly, painstakingly as any student, she sought for new and deeper meaning in the compositions already so intimately hers, demanded more than she had yet given. She studied self-forget-fully, time-forgetfully, until a knocking upon the wall re-minded her that to her neighbors sleep was more necessary than music. Suddenly she felt tired and hungry. She put more briquettes into the friendly tile stove—that institution which for warmth and economy still seeks its equal—and quickly brewed a cup of tea on her spirit burner to make more palatable the open sandwich of blackbread, butter, and cold meat of which her daily supper consisted. Oh! to be with her children!

THE first tour extended from Holland to Prague and back to include Belgium. Everywhere Carreño appeared as a revelation. She was delared to be the only one who could boast of a "full house in this overcrowded season." No pianist since Tausig and Rubinstein had been so royally welcomed. None could compete with her unless it were the formidable d'Albert, now on tour in America. Carreño made mental note that here was one rival who must be heard. A critic from Antwerp's *Le Précurseur* called her a Venezuelan capable of thawing the North Pole; the Prague *Politik* invented the term "Keyboard-millionairess" in her honor.

Carreño had been called upon to play the Grieg "Concerto" in Leipzig on March 29, 1890. The Centralhalle was its setting. In one of the front rows of the Gewandhaus Saal sat two men, one a Leipzig music publisher, Herr Fritzsch, the other a man of undersized figure capped by an enormous head, from which two points of light flashed searchingly. He was seen to listen in rapt attention, punctuating a passage here and there with a whispered *"enorm, groszartig, gewaltig."* He was first to applaud at the end, first to greet Carreño in the artists' room after the "Concerto" was finished. Doubling in a precise bow he introduced himself: *"Mein Name ist Grieg."* Carreño's heart missed a beat. There jumped to her mind all the liberties she had taken with the last pages of the master's work, the octaves she had substituted for the arpeggios in the score. For once she found no words, stood like a schoolgirl waiting for a just reprimand. "Madame," said Grieg, "I did not know that my concerto was so beautiful." The photograph he gave her on this day is inscribed, not too grammatically, in his hand: *"Die ausgezeichnete Meisterin mit Dank und Verehrung Edvard Grieg."* From that day on they were fast friends, he one of her frankest critics.

That he was not always in agreement with her a letter from Grieg to Andreas Winding clearly shows:

Frau Carreño played Chopin's "E minor Concerto" and Liszt's "Hungarian Fantasia" with orchestra excellently. But the devil is in these virtuosos who always want to improve on everything. In the first measures she pleased to play more slowly in the passages, so that the tempo went *Heidi!* And in the Finale she suddenly took the second theme much more slowly. There should be a penalty for such things. And on top of it she acted so proud; that was the worst of it. But thereupon I gave her a piece of my mind and added: "Well, Chopin is dead, he doesn't hear it! What Weingartner says of the *tempo rubato conductor* is true also for the performing artist. They all suffer from virtuoso or importance mania.

In Paris on a passing visit with her children Carreño was laid low by a violent attack of quinsy, or *angine* as the French doctor more poetically called it, not making it less painful on that account. She suffered acutely, a high fever which lasted for days leaving her so weak that she did not care to start for England without Manuel in attendance.

On the opposite side of their compartment, as the train sped toward London, there happened to sit a stolid-looking German reading his paper. Carreño, in reckless spirits matched by a brother in a holiday mood, was up and down, packing and re-packing her bags, commenting in strident soprano upon everything that passed through her mind or before her eyes. Soon the farther window was the object of her attraction. She crossed over, jostling the phlegmatic stranger without apology, then trumpeted back to Manuel in Spanish: "Our portly friend will think that I wish to make love to him, but I only wish to admire the scenery." So boisterously they enjoyed themselves at his expense, like two thoughtless children. Arrived at the station, hardly had the train whistled itself to a standstill when another whistle caught her ear. Did she imagine that she was hearing the Siegfried motif? No, there upon the platform stood a group of jovial young men evidently expecting someone. Suddenly the "portly friend" pushed forward, his lips framing the same motif in reply. The group rushed to greet him. Who could this man be, so musically awaited, on such intimate terms with Wagner? It came to her like a stunning blow. The great Hans Richter himself! Carreño, like every pianist worth the name, had hoped one day to play under his baton. She moaned in self-abasement. "How could I be so rude, so mad." How ironically the maestro had bowed himself out of the compartment. "What a fool I was"—and there was nothing she despised more—"what a damn fool," she repeated. No great harm was done, however. On November 9 and often thereafter she was to play a concerto conducted by Richter. The incident was never mentioned between them.

Musical London which had once meant home to Carreño, and which she came to capture anew in the late May of 1890, had changed in twenty years. It received her cautiously, finding her too spectacular, her programs too unconservative. The London *Times* disliked "the trick of appending little final flourishes to almost every work played," and talked condescendingly of the "beauty in pink cashmere and silk brocade." Carreño was not disheartened. "If London refuses to be taken in a concert or two, I shall simply have to convert it," she decided. It was important to be accepted in England, a country loyal beyond all others to the artists of her adoption, and she meant to return until she too was numbered among them. Socially at least she was a success.

Back again in Paris Carreño faced problems other than musical ones. She was too much a Venezuelan to leave her earnings lying stagnant in a vault. She had an urge to join the jugglers of the stock market, tempered by the experience of one acquainted with poverty. Fortunately there was among her friends a man who taught her how to handle investments wisely. When her gambler's instincts threatened to prevail against the calculations of the business woman, she reminded herself of the $5,000 owing her benefactor in Chicago. Yet in her purse—a slight harking back to atavistic longings—there was almost always sure to be found a lottery ticket. That was one of her few harmless indulgences, returning to her in pleasure what the fates denied in coin.

Waiting for her in Paris Carreño found the much dreaded letter from Tag postmarked Toronto, May 22, 1890. He wrote in placating, operatic Italian, trying to touch her in the spot he knew to be most vulnerable, the welfare of their children:

Dear Teresita:

I received your letter which gave me pleasure and displeasure. I spent two wakeful nights asking God for the grace of giving me the idea of an answer, and finally He dictated this one, and I thank Him a thousand times for the decisions which He Himself placed in my heart.

Hear therefore what I shall tell you, and I call God to witness that what I say will be rigidly carried out. God told me this: "Teresita, you are a good and honest woman, and furthermore an even better mother, and that is why I love you more (if that is possible) than I loved you in the days when I first met you. I do not know whether you have the same affection for me, but you cannot deny that after twelve years of life together you must have some feeling for the father of your children. And now it is precisely on account of the love that we both bear them that I speak. We have these two little angels, so good and so lovely, and we must be proud of them and make their life as little unhappy as possible, strewing roses, not thorns upon the path they must tread. . . . Let us leave the past behind us—let us think of the future—my errors towards you were provoked by my love. . . .

Teresita, I wish to make you happy, and I swear that you will become so. Only love me a little and you will be happy with your children and your old Nanno. We are at an age when illusions no longer exist. Give me your hand and you will see what Nanno is able to do after so many years of unfortunate experience. . . .

I want to make you my queen, love you, respect you and do all within my power to make you forget the unfortunate past.

Think well before answering, for upon your reply depends your future and mine and that of our children. In any case I have to tell you that I can no longer live without seeing them, and should you decide not to see me, I still would come to embrace them without embracing their mother. Write me soon. Kiss the children for me. And as for you, who sent no kiss to me, receive one from your Nanno, who always loves you and will still make you happy.

I have insured my life for $10,000, so that if I should die tomorrow, you can have the money for the children. I did this yesterday, Mutual Life Insurance, N.Y. Therefore, I still have $2000 which I saved, after having settled everything. Now I am on the way to earn much money.

Dr. Anderson in Detroit gave me a wonderful pin with six lovely diamonds for Teresita, and I had bought two very beautiful earrings with diamonds for you, which I have here. I also bought for you two Japanese kimonos as a surprise, one for summer and the other for winter, immense shawls and lots of small things that would have given you pleasure.—Another kiss from Nanno.

P.S. After my firm decision, all now depends upon you, to make a good person, a good father, and a good husband of me.

Your Nanno

All debts are paid, I have about $2000 left, but I am giving up the house. Write me to Steinway Hall, since I do not yet know where I shall live.

Carreño was not tempted, neither for herself nor for Teresita and Giovanni. She laid aside the letter with distaste. Not even a ripple of longing was left to see again this man she had known too well, too long. That subject was closed. It was easy to brush aside the past, the more because she had already out-lived it, and because summer, a long summer of happiness, was close at hand.

With Manuel, Rosie, the children, and Josephine she took a cottage at Berck-sur-Mer on the Normandy coast to "rest and pick up." There were woods on one side, the sea on the other, and the place was as healthful as it was cheap. Proudly she writes of Teresita and Giovanni: "They have grown so much, and, forgive the vanity, so pretty too." It pleases her that Teresita reads music well. From villa Pauline, chalet Number 8, she writes to Carrie Keating urging her to come. "You are over-worked and (as I have done) have borrowed too much on your capital of vitality! But, never mind, darling, you and I are made of the stuff that never says die, and we wouldn't." She apologizes for not being able to ask her to live in her house. The two teachers of the children were to be there: "They were so good to my babies that I want to do what I can to show them my appreciation of their behaviour, and they are two very charming girls." Even here the responsibilities of her profession are ever present: "The only thing which will interfere with our visit together will be my work, for I have to work very hard this summer on account of having so many engagements to fulfill next winter, and having to get new things ready for my concerts."

Carrie arrived, was met at the station and nearly smothered under the great black cape, as Carreño threw her arms about her. Berck-sur-Mer was the meeting place of the Venezuelan colony of Paris. Carreño joined in with them, even playing an occasional game of tennis or watching the shooting matches in which Rosie excelled. She found that this, indeed, was the ideal place for relaxing tired nerves, regaining strength—and losing weight. Autumn too soon crept in upon her happiness, and the day of parting from the children approached. She had counted upon making a new home for them in Berlin. Wolff had sternly objected. Engagements, really important ones, were coming in. She must not be distracted. This season, he said, would set the pace for all future ones, solidify her position. He predicted for her more engagements in Germany "than all the pianists together," trusting that she would be well disposed toward "a very fatiguing season which promises good returns in marks, florins, rubels, francs, and crowns," and himself, incidentally, equally good ones in ten-per cent commissions.

Wolff's snappy letters were meant, and seldom failed, to make Carreño smile even in her gloomiest moments. He had a genius for understanding artists. To brave their stormy temperament was refreshing as the driving wind after listless summer heat. He could hardly wait to have it lash his face again. At the end of September he wrote:

Chère amie: J'ignore s'il vous intéresse, mais je dois vous le dire: je suis de retour. Berlin commence donc à être complet et n'attend que votre arrivée pour être complètement complet. Très bien dit, n'est-ce pas? Ma femme est encore à Grossgmein avec ses enfants (et les miens). . . . Quant aux affairs, je trouve Scheveningen, comme

M. Fernow vous le propose, parfaitement acceptable. Vous vivrez pendant une huitaine comme une "déesse en Hollande," vous aurez succès, *très beaucoup bon,* nous en ferons une jolie petite réclame pour les autres pays et villes qui auront plus tard l'honneur de vous entendre et payer, et tout finira aussi bien qu'il commence.

He might have noted, as she did in her diary, that this would give her the opportunity of trying out the Saint-Saëns "Concerto in C minor" on a European audience with the promise of 1,000 francs to add to her bank account.

On October 9 the strenuous season began. With few intermissions Carreño played daily, traveled almost daily, grateful only that Herr Wolff knew how to plan the routes with a view to proximity, economy, and the least possible discomfort. In one of her first concerts on October 13 she was to play the Saint-Saëns "Concerto" under von Bülow in Berlin. In a letter to Wolff he writes:

Saint-Saëns ist doch ein famoser Musiker! Sein viertes Klavier-konzert kann einen von dem Ekel an Musik curiren, den man sich in Ihrem (daran unschuldigen) Bureau zuzieht durch Einblick in die allerhand Parti (tor) turen, denen Sie—Gottlob—eine nur flüchtige Gastfreundschaft gewähren. Welche Sardousche Technik und Eleganz! Wie hat Alles Hand und Fusz, wie gehen feinsinnige Originalität, Logik, und Anmuth harmonisch mit einander! Hoffentlich spielt Teresa (Carreño) das Werk correkt!

If ever a man knew the meaning of that last word it was Hans von Bülow. He himself was its living embodiment. Carreño respected him for it and learned. There was no need to worry on this occasion. Again he wrote to Wolff after her Leipzig concert—"Die Señora (Carreño) war pyramidal—Sie leistete wahrhaft Staunenswürdiges, nach meinem Dafürhalten in jeder Hinsicht noch Vollendeteres als in Berlin—Publikum war ganz *aus dem Häuschen,* raste förmlich."

Speaking of this second concert the *Allgemeine Musikzeitung* hears a new note in her playing: "Frau Carreño," it says, "enchanted her audience through her apparently more ethereal and yet fiery and brilliant piano playing completely. The artist seems to have become more and more accustomed to her Bechstein, which used to sound harsh now and then under her powerful touch, but now has developed the greatest beauty of tone in spite of all the fullness of volume which the fingers of no German pianist have ever surpassed."

In Dortmund she played the "G minor Fantasia and Fugue" of Bach-Liszt. This collaboration suited her perfectly at the time, Bach as a tribute to German taste, Liszt for her own gratification. To be a true interpreter of Bach unadulterated, Carreño at this time lacked objectivity and perspective. On the other hand the Grieg "Concerto" and its *fidus Achates,* the Weber-Liszt "Polacca," were heard in the majority of her orchestral concerts, giving way occasionally to the Saint-Saëns "C minor Concerto" and the "Hungarian Fantasia" of Liszt, an old friend resurrected.

The "Second Concerto" of MacDowell also had another hearing in Dresden on October 28, 1890. As Wolff had feared, the press with few exceptions called it a superficial work empty of thought. The public received it in a more friendly spirit. Encouraged by this she dared to propose it for a first hearing before the ultraconservative Gewandhaus audience of Leipzig. Von Bülow at first rebelled. A laconic telegram caused·him to change his mind. It read: "No MacDowell, no Carreño."

Until the end of November Germany claimed her, a congested tour of the large cities of Switzerland followed, often two concerts in the same city, and more concerts in Germany nearly up to Christmas. Important musicians found that she was somebody to cultivate. Max Reger enthused: "Last Friday I heard Teresa Carreño, the newest star, decidedly the best among the pianists of today." And, not least of her satisfactions, the income for 1890 totaled the sum of 34,134 marks.

THE entrance of 1891 deserved a new diary, again of red leather gilt-edged, embossed with four-leaf clovers. The first entry as usual is a prayer: *Que le bon Dieu soit avec nous et garde nos enfants en bonne santé.* On that same day Carreño, who had spent Christmas in Montmorency with the "babies," left for Austria.

Hermann Wolff meanwhile is relentlessly training his new star to be as reliable in business as in profession. When she side-steps her obligations or procrastinates in their fulfillment he severely calls her to task: "Chère amie, pensez un peu à l'avenir. Vous n'avez pas l'intention de délaisser la musique. Mes sociétés sont habituées à vos promptes réponses—nous ferons bien de n'y rien changer. Je vous prie donc de me répondre le plus vite possible à toutes mes questions."

It was to be a memorable year in that it marked her first visit to Russia. On January 28 in St. Petersburg Carreño's diary, in general kept for her itinerary and her expenses exclusively, records: "Saw Rubinstein for the first time after twenty years." During her brief stay she dined at his house on every free night.

The Russian tour, lasting well into February, was not either critically or financially successful. Carreño was as always popular with her audiences, less so with the critics. The St. Petersburg *Herald* finds that she too often goes beyond the measure of the beautiful and the noble, that a Chopin Nocturne can't stand a forte like the Schubert-Tausig, March, and states that the "Romance" of Tschaikowsky could scarcely be recognized, so changed and exaggerated was its interpretation. "Great excitement was created by a trill which lasted about half an hour, more beautiful pianistically than musically." Among Carreño's complaints not the least was that in default of a Bechstein she was obliged to play a piano of second grade.

Came a short and in comparison heavenly interlude of concerts in Germany. March again called her away, this time to Scandinavia where in April the King of Sweden conferred upon her in person the gold medal *"Litteris et Artibus."* Then at last she might return to the place that such as it was meant home to her, the Askanischer Hof.

It was foreordained that the most talked-of pianists of the day, both under the same management, in the course of time must meet. On April 10, 1891, a date she would never forget, Carreño sat gossiping over the teacups, taking unofficial lessons in the ways of the musical world from Louise Wolff, the one best qualified to give them. A caller was announced and greeted with the enthusiasm Frau Wolff reserved for old friends. Before the formula of introduction had blurred first impressions, intuition had registered a warning which was to haunt Carreño in retrospect. Such might have been the effect upon her if a snake had suddenly crossed her path. Eyes seconded the shock of repulsion. She thoroughly disliked this gnomelike person who, careless in dress with stringy hair cut long and a straggly mustache, reminded her of nothing so much as of a tree that badly needed pruning. She resented his high voice minor in inflection, the sinister look of his eyes peering through narrow slits, eyes that saw too much and revealed nothing. His hand felt flabby in her own hearty grasp. So this was he with whom she had so often been compared! So this was the great Eugen d'Albert!

Carreño mentally added this encounter to the list of her disenchantments. She listened distantly as he complimented her with effusion upon a recent performance of the Grieg "Concerto." Unflattered she used her usual stencil in reply: "You are very kind," and then fell silent. Not his new Gronberger dog, not his recent visit to the United States, not the villa he had just bought in the suburb Lichterfelde, not even the fact that it was his birthday roused her interest. She soon invented an excuse to leave. Thus on a deceptive cadence, this first meeting ended. D'Albert on his part was both musically and personally impressed. Carreño's indifference nettled him. Women generally capitulated at sight.

Louise Wolff knew that nothing would give him greater pleasure than to see Carreño in one of his concerts. Diplomat that she was, she succeeded in bringing her to the managerial box on the occasion of a public rehearsal of the Sternsche Gesang Verein. D'Albert was to be heard in Beethoven's "G major Concerto."

On that day the Philharmonie was sold out as for her own concerts. But the box in which she sat was to her satisfaction the focus of every opera glass. At last the lights were lowered. D'Albert looking more gnomelike than ever came pattering across the stage escorted by wild applause. He made a jerky bow that ludicrously threw a lock of hair into his eye. Carreño settled down to the prospect of a half hour with a concerto she did not care for and an artist she positively disliked.

Then serenely as if from the upper air there unveiled itself that most touching of introductions with all the simplicity of childhood, all the philosophy of ageless wisdom. Carreño felt a catch in her throat. She had not realized how lovely it was. Leaning forward she waited for the next entrance of the piano as for a revelation, and a revelation it was. What did it matter, how he looked, how he talked. That man could play with a purity beyond imagination. Not since Rubinstein had a pianist given her such affecting happiness. Never had she found such depths of beauty in that all-too-short slow movement, such impertinence in the rondo. A thousand beguiling little devils seemed to be dancing with harmlessly pointed pitchforks. She laughed aloud. When the "Concerto" was finished, Carreño insisted upon being taken backstage, shining with the thrill of hearing herself outplayed, much to the amusement of Louise Wolff, who did not hesitate to throw in her "I-told-you-so." Here indeed was true greatness. It scarcely bothered her that d'Albert was basking in the idolatry of his adorers, that they knelt on the stage and kissed his hands, for now she could understand. Before her very eyes, through the magic of Beethoven, the dwarf had been transformed into a giant. She could not resist the temptation to dine that evening at the house of a mere acquaintance, because the invitation was baited with the promise that d'Albert would be there.

On his part the approval of Carreño affected d'Albert

strangely. Her innate generosity of spirit enfolded him completely. Her compelling power was full of a magnetism to which he strongly responded. In her warming presence what might he not become! D'Albert felt it important to see her again. The season now ending had been a crowded one for both. Hermann Wolff had seen to that. Now their paths intentionally or not crossed more often. Occasional absence added its spicy tang to their meetings. They were seen together at concerts. Each played at the meeting of the Tonkünstler-Verein at the end of May and in turn applauded the other. D'Albert had chosen the Martucci "Concerto," Carreño, as usual under protest, the MacDowell "Concerto." The audience received her well to the extent of demanding a repetition of its prickling Scherzo. MacDowell had a harder stand against the ultraconservative body of critics. One reviewer used his imagination: "It was as if little figurines on a what-not began to dance, the only humorous touch being that a whole orchestra had to play for them, much ado about nothing the final outcome." He admitted that it merited the encore given it, adding however that the rest of the "Concerto" was not worth mentioning, and that "after the passionate pianist had left the stage, a large part of the audience also fled from the hall before the Bruckner 'Te Deum.' " The Börsen Courier noted a momentary loss of memory on Carreño's part in the Presto, one for which d'Albert might easily be held responsible. The Vossische Zeitung on the other hand found the "Concerto" full of imagination, grateful for the pianist though lacking in clarity of form in the last movement, and the applause and profusion of flowers with which the pianist was overwhelmed noteworthy.

The outcome of the season surpassed expectation, and Wolff, the secondary beneficiary, had every right to gloat over it and to count upon an even-more-glowing future. In the highest of spirits he writes: "Ne vous fâchez pas de la différence de vos cachets de l'ancienne époque '89–91 et de ceux de l'avenir, procurez-vous une poche de cuire plus grande que celle que je connais et qui ne suffira plus pour ces cachets."

On June 2, but added in retrospect later, stands a startling entry in Carreño's diary: "Went with my Liebchen to hear his *Quartette* played by Joachim's Quartette at the Singakademie." The day following holds another revealing sentence: "Told my whole history to my Liebchen." For privacy they took the train to Ludwigsfelde one day in June, walking for hours through the country they both loved and picnicking in a grove where only the sunbeams found entrance and thrushes sang their obbligato. On this particular day there was so much to be said, so much to be confided, that the last train for Berlin had left before they thought about so practical a detail. Both d'Albert and Carreño perpetuated this day in her diary, she simply with the words: "Went to Ludwigsfelde with Liebchen." He more specifically in German: "Alone together in Ludwigsfelde. Rode to Berlin on a freight train. Arrived at two in the morning. It was very nice, as always when we are together."

Musical Berlin wagged its tongue and looked tolerantly on. For d'Albert, eleven years Carreño's junior, new vistas of delight were opening. The more experienced Carreño, who had so resolutely cut herself off from the past she had outgrown, found life again worth living, not for the sake of her children alone, but for its own radiant self. Then for the moment happiness was clouded by separation. After dinner together at Wolff's one evening Carreño left for Paris, d'Albert for Switzerland.

As if from another world, another century, Tag wrote once more, not believing in a final break. Carreño gave answer with categorical, conclusive brevity.

SHE was intent upon making the most of her unscheduled summer. One week in Berlin had proved that their happiness, d'Albert's as well as hers, depended upon being together. More and more he needed the lift her abounding vitality gave him, and she in turn a deeper insight into a nature that revealed itself so divinely to her in sound. Music and pity had drawn her to misadventure with Émile Sauret, music and loneliness had led her to seek refuge with Giovanni Tagliapietra. Music and true love now at last pointed with compelling finger to Eugen d'Albert.

An intuitive person easily becomes a fatalist. Carreño was no exception. This was their destiny. Two weeks in Montmorency were enough to assure her that the children were in perfect health. The longing to be with d'Albert became irresistible. On June 21 her diary tells the tale: "Left for Wiesbaden to go and meet Liebchen." Five enthralling days together in Neuchâtel did not suffice. Neither could she be separated from her "babies." Together she and d'Albert made a vital decision. The entire summer should be theirs. While Carreño returned to Montmorency to prepare her children for the journey, d'Albert found the ideal place for their companionate holiday in Chaumont. There Carreño joined him on July 9. D'Albert's piano arrived before him at the Grand Hotel. Carreño took a chalet for herself, the children, and Josephine.

Overworked and overtired as she was, life in this remote paradise, secluded with those she loved about her, brought the refreshment born of untouchable happiness. On long mountain walks she discovered that both she and d'Albert liked to live without pretension, preferably in the country, that they longed equally for peaceful home surroundings, that they both loved children. Seeing Carreño with hers d'Albert wished that his son, Wolfgang, might have had such a mother instead of the flighty, if charming, actress he had married at the age of twenty and was in the process of divorcing on grounds of extravagance and weak-minded flirtations. "With the constant inspiration of Teresa's presence, what might I not compose," thought d'Albert. "With him beside me, how might I not play," sang Carreño in her heart. To him she was the guardian of that sacred fire which he needed to enflame his own creative urge; to her he meant the renewal of youth. That this perfect vacation was an inviolate secret even from Wolff himself—so they believed—made it all the more enchanting, and it was understandable that they wished it to endure as long as possible.

In order to put off that inevitable first concert of autumn, Carreño invented excuses, feigned illness. At first Wolff in a letter full of his old banter is unsuspecting and hopes that she is feeling better. He writes:

Mme. Louise Wolff épouse du sousigné, mère personelle de tous ses enfants (connus) est encore à Kufstein. Elle reviendra lundi prochain poussée par une impatience très naturelle, quand on a un époux tel que votre ami Wolff. . . . Mon baiser directoral et amical vole vers vous, chère amie, je vous bénis en vous serrant la main de tremolo. Votre ravissant Wolff.

In September Wolff is still in equable mood. "Vous renoncez à Braunschweig; Riedel [the conductor] en pleurera," he writes and hopes that she is well disposed after so long a vacation. Toward the end of the month he becomes restive, demands to know what her plans are, whether he can still reach her at Chaumont. He takes her to task for being slow in sending programs, for refusing engagements in October, and begs her urgently to begin her tour with Hanover in early November.

MEANWHILE Carreño had left Chaumont on September 26 to settle her affairs in Paris alone. Her diary speaks tersely and eloquently.

1 Oct. Had telegram from Liebchen saying he had bought house.
4 Oct. Left for Dresden.
5 Oct. Arrived Dresden at midnight. Liebchen met me on the way. Babies will thank God.
6 Oct. Dresden Hotel Kaiserhof [where she had registered under the name of Josephine de Paul].
7 Oct. Went to see our house for the first time. Found it beautiful.
12 Oct. Went into our lovely home at Coswig. Slept there for the first time.
13 Oct. Home with all my darlings. Thank God!

Villa Palstring, in Coswig on the Elbe between Dresden and Meissen, was rechristened "Villa Teresa" and became the setting for their idyll. Its walls of gray stone offered the space and seclusion they craved. Feverishly working against time Teresa ordered furniture, china, curtains, and at last food supplies. She

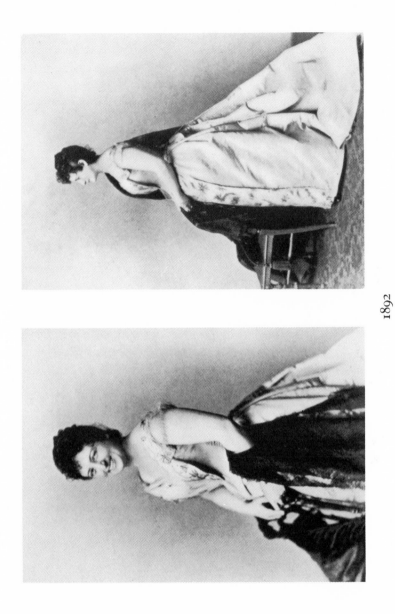

1892

*Teresa Carreño-d'Albert*

directed painters, plumbers, and carpenters, thoroughly reveling in the confusion, while two Bechstein grands lay mutely, accusingly on their sides in the Coswig station, where upon some pretext Carreño and d'Albert had separately required them to be delivered. What did concerts matter when she was preparing a home for her children, for her husband, the first home she had really ever owned!

Wolff grows more and more impatient. Carreño's erratic changing of her programs makes him nervous. It is more than probable that he knows her secret, yet does not feel free to speak of it except in innuendos. On November 3 he grumbles:

J'ai été deux fois à la gare croyant que vous arriveriez pour repartir pour Eberswalde. Probablement vous êtes arrivée avant hier soir déjà. Enfin je vois que vous évitez de me voir. Je ne connais pas vos motifs —mais je ne peux pas m'empêcher d'être très étonné. Jusqu'ici vous aviez toujours cru bon, avant le commencement de vos voyages, de venir causer *de tout!* Enfin je me courbe!

A few days after he finds more cause for dissatisfaction. Carreño must either have failed to arrive in time for the rehearsal in Hanover or have forgotten to bring the score of the concerto. For what other reason could it have been that she played only solos.

Carreño did not take these admonitions too much to heart. She was thoroughly absorbed, happy and busy. Besides, there was no time to lose. D'Albert was committed to a tour in the United States, beginning in March. Every day counted. November saw them practically installed, the pianos set up in opposite wings. Laughingly they thumbed their noses at the public they had, so they believed, successfully fooled. A concert journey for either one or the other was a disagreeable interruption, a return to earth from a heaven all their own.

Carreño's diary reads:

4 Nov.  Greifswald. Liebchen in Parchim.
5 Nov.  Home! Liebchen zu Hause so Gott will!
7 Nov.  Start for Hanover.
8 Nov.  Hanover.

13 Nov.   Elberfeld 450m. Liebchen came to stay over Sunday with me.

19 Nov.   Wiesbaden at 6 p.m. Liebchen came to meet me. Stayed at Biebrich.

22 Nov.   Berlin Askanischer Hof.

24 Nov.   Returned home by the 8 a.m. train. Found babies well, thank God.

7 Dec.   Liebchen in Wien.

9 Dec.   Liebchen in Budapest.

10 Dec.   Liebchen in Wien.

11 Dec.   Liebchen in Graz.

12 Dec.   Liebchen in Wien.

13 Dec.   So Gott will Liebchen zu Haus.

15 Dec.   [Carreño once more enters her own concert laconically] Königsberg 700 M.

22 Dec.   Erster Tag [in d'Albert's hand. It was Carreño's birthday].

Carreño as well as d'Albert had forgotten that the two most photographed pianists could not hope to live long incognito. One morning the *Signale* brought the paragraph: "A strange bit of news from the realm of art comes to us by way of Dresden. Eugen d'Albert and Frau Teresa Carreño are said to be married. The pair has bought itself a house in Coswig." Paradise was invaded. D'Albert, true to his conventional background, had long urged official marriage. Carreño, equally true to her philosophy, thought it simpler to evade that issue, but from now on signs herself Teresa Carreño-d'Albert. The upheaval in musical circles that had for a long time gossiped about something of this kind can be left to the imagination. Since it was sure to influence the box office favorably on the principle that any kind of publicity is better than none, Wolff could afford to resign himself to the inevitable. On the eighth of December he writes: "Il est possible que dimanche matin je serai à Coswig pour vous voir et votre mari." And so with the unalterable fact brought to light excitement gradually quieted down. "Artists are that way" was as good a conclusion as any, and following upon it the unanimous prophecy: "It cannot last."

In the sanctuary outlined by the high walls of their garden the two artists were attempting to prove the contrary, turning with new zest to their profession. D'Albert resented every concert that took him away from the opera he was composing. Carreño went back to her piano, and learned from the husband of her admiration to bring a new sense of measure to her interpretations. The Tschaikowsky "Concerto in B flat minor" was added to her list. Humbly Carreño one day asked Bülow, under whose direction she was to play this work, to give her a lesson in its reading. "I don't give lessons," growled the master. Carreño smoothly replied: "Indeed you do. Every time you conduct, whenever you play, you give a lesson to me." So tactful a compliment unruffled even a Hans von Bülow.

A quarrelsome friendship was theirs, but one elastic enough to stand the strain, kept so by common admiration. Bülow always stood up for the masculine in music. So he writes in true form: "Stupendous, flabbergasting, but for the most time inartistically, Teresa played like an acrobat." Then he voices the hope that musically d'Albert's better nature will triumph over Teresa's. From its beginning the Tschaikowsky "Concerto" was particularly Carreño's own. Who could forget the excitement of those smashing introductory chords, thrown with effortless freedom into the keys, turning into sound so rich and powerful that many an orchestra had difficulty in holding its own against them?

D'Albert and Carreño had many friends in common. One of those most treasured was Johannes Brahms. At a dinner party he was inveighing against the women pianists who insisted upon cluttering the concert season with their weak-minded music. Carreño accepted the challenge. "You forget, *Meister,* that I am here, and I am a woman," she good-naturedly reminded him. "You are not a pianiste, you are a pianist," answered Brahms, who was not noted for making pretty speeches.

One day in Vienna he and d'Albert were conversing together over beer glasses, the subject being matrimony. "Why have you never married, *Meister?*" asked d'Albert.

"That is quite simple; because I have never found a wife like yours," he answered.

LOVE is the great lubricant; it reaches the most strangely assembled parts, and keeps the machine running with no apparent friction. It is the great stabilizer which can hold two personalities as divergent as London is from Caracas in harmonious balance. Carreño and d'Albert had much to learn from each other. Of the two Carreño in spite of her maturity was the more teachable. Under his influence her taste developed. She gradually discarded the flashy works with which her programs had once bristled. Vogrich, Gottschalk, and even Rubinstein disappeared. That MacDowell suffered the same fate was due to d'Albert's prejudice against him both personally and as a musician—he had once been obliged to officiate at the second piano, when MacDowell had played his "First Concerto" for Liszt in Weimar—a prejudice in which jealousy was probably not an inconsiderable factor.

Constructively d'Albert was without doubt responsible for a new control, a new inner unity in her readings. Carreño more seldom let herself go to wild extremes of length and height for the mere joy of being able to do so. Her tone took on subtle shades. As never before she studied to find deeper values in music and appreciably enlarged her repertoire.

Being the wife of d'Albert involved more than musical give and take. For a young man of twenty-six he was already set in his ways. At sixteen he had clearly realized that he was too easily influenced, and had tried his best to steel himself against this failing. Once in the land of his idolatry, the Germany he loved with the same passion he brought to his hatred of England, he became intoxicated by too sudden and phenomenal success, allowing himself to succumb to the pampering and flattery of women. This was his besetting curse, until one or another became indispensable to his happiness and—so he thought—to his creative unfolding. Until his death women were made to play a contributing but a subordinate part. Inasmuch as they gave his musical imagination wing he valued them. When it sagged, as sooner or later it must, their usefulness automatically ceased. The one who was willing, as selflessly as a Senta, to drown herself in the task of creating the conditions under which d'Albert's music could flourish uninhibited, was the one apt to hold him longest.

His first wife, Louise Salingré, suited the boy of twenty very well at the beginning. She laughed at his peculiarities, made light conversation when he felt taciturn, protected him even from his mother-in-law. Patiently she had followed him through the labyrinth of his eccentricities, even to the point of taking part in spiritualistic séances that bored her as much as they fascinated him. The crisis in their marital relations came because of a basic conflict in their natures. Louise refused to conform to d'Albert's standards of penurious carefulness verging on the stingy. That, rather than the love affairs which d'Albert used as a pretext for divorce, brought about the crisis. He insisted upon the custody of their son Wolfgang, for whom as for all children he felt real affection.

Considering her past Carreño entered upon her third marriage with surprising optimism. Nomadic life had accentuated domestic leanings. There could be no more thrilling adventure than that of building a home, organizing it on the ample scale consistent with her income—d'Albert had bought the house; she would keep it in running order and pay the bills—and in general playing the part of the perfect German *Hausfrau* à la d'Albert whenever she did not have to be the *Meisterin* of the platform. This meant not only submitting herself and her children to the wearing of the Jaeger woolens prescribed by Dr. Lahmann of Dresden's famous Weisser Hirsch, but even taking part in the daily exercises upon which d'Albert insisted. Feet bare, hair flying, clad in flapping wrappers they followed their leader. These early morning rites in the garden must have provided amusement for many a passer-by. It meant cold-water treatments and the supplanting of the conventional doctor by exponents of *Naturheilkunde*. For milk they grew to depend largely upon the two goats in their stable. Wholeheartedly Carreño adopted his theories for her own, even to the education of children, although in this field his experience was much more limited than hers.

This might easily have become the source of many a misunderstanding, but it was sidetracked as an issue by the departure of d'Albert for America. Carreño had resisted the impulse to accompany him on the tour in which her husband was to appear in thirty concerts with Nikisch and his orchestra. Before sailing he writes in nostalgic German: "And yet this, if God will, only short separation is dreadful too!"—and farther on, the first cloud in the blue, he accuses himself: "Why do I ever make you sad?" On February 22, 1892, Carreño tells her diary: "My darling left for America via London at 7:22 P. M. May God take him safely across and bring him safely back and help me to bear this awful separation." And on March 4: "Liebchen arrived safely in New York. The Lord be millions of times thanked for the great mercy."

Barely in New York he takes up his pen again in homesick vein: "—I am so happy you are still in Coswig, in our house, our home—I feel so much quieter knowing you there." And he goes on: "All about us and me was in the paper today. The people here are much more inquisitive than in Europe."

In the middle of March he expresses himself more fully in his finely pinched writing:

—And how loving, how sweet you write, my beloved.—Your letters are a great, great consolation to me, and I live on them, and they give me strength to bear this dreadful separation. My love, I was so sad that in addition to everything you had that anxiety about Mrs. Mac-Dowell [Edward's mother]; she is pretty well now, and it is no wonder that she was ill, the way she and all the people here live. Think of this drinking ice-water, coffee, and eating two meat courses at eight o'clock in the evening *with the children*—in a room that has certainly 18 Réaumur. That the people live at all is a wonder. That we live as we do and that I am as pedantic as I am often makes you laugh, my darling, but it is a great safe-guard to us, and knowing that you live so too always makes me a little quieter. All the people in America live like lunatics, as it is impossible by this method of living not to be sick sooner or later. My beloved, I don't drink much water, and never out of faucets— And how these artists live! Zum Beispiel—I told you I arrived with Nikisch Sunday evening eleven o'clock; instead of going to bed as I did, I hear he sat up with others playing poker until six o'clock in the morning! And then Paderewski

—he seems never to have gone to bed before eight or nine o'clock in the morning. And then when they are ill or nervous they blame America!

Altogether in a bad humor he complains that Mrs. MacDowell constantly reminds him of the fact that he is number three, that she keeps wanting him to do something for Giovanni and Arturo, and continues: "Never have two human beings needed each other more than we." He sees "the whole world in black," but "as a light in all this darkness is my really great success."

The following day sees him in Baltimore. He speaks of a long walk through the streets of Washington:

"My picture sitting at the Knabe piano is in every shop window," he finds worth reporting, also that he stopped for a shave, and he apologizes: "My beloved, I can't do it myself. I tried, and wanted to do it, as you bought the razor for me, and I know it pleases you,— but I scratched myself awfully, and my face hurt long afterwards in spite of my taking a new knife; I am not up to it!"—Then he goes on in German: "I played the Berceuse as encore and played exquisitely. . . . If only Terry had heard it . . ."—and then adds: "It is my sole, my only joy to write to you, to pour out my heart to you, my only good, adored wife." Later a postscript: "A propos of Fr. S.: I believe if I had not told her that I must practice, she would still sit here. I find all the people so lacking in sensitivity. Why does she speak with me about Sauret and Tagliapietra? Does she think she is giving me great pleasure thereby?"

The next day, back again in the Hotel Normandie, New York, he continues at length:

"Of all places I like best to be here, because it is a little—only a few hours nearer to you. They would not cease recalling me after the Concerto (Chopin) which I really played very, very well, my beloved Darling; I wish you had heard me! You never heard me play the Chopin Concerto, and it is the piece I certainly play best. I wished and longed that you had been there! I imagined how nice, how sweet it would be, if you were sitting in the gallery, and how you would appreciate and love every point, everything I did well!" [he never sees himself in the audience listening to Carreño however] "I played (as I always do) as if *You* heard me! The solo pieces I did not play so well.—I can't play the Impromptu of Schubert any more. I have already played it so much. It is a piece that requires inspiration and then—it is the piece Terry loved to hear me play, and I can't play it any more without her being there, and it seems to me to be sacrilege! In the *Valse Impromptu* of Liszt I thought so much of you my darling —I was quite away in my thoughts and didn't think about the piece at all—then all of a sudden I didn't know where I was and fumbled about a little—that I know how to do very well!—I don't think that anyone noticed it."

Again he is amazed that someone wanted to talk about New Rochelle to him "with the usual delicacy of the world." In Germany nobody bothers Carreño about his number one, he comments:

My love, my darling [he continues] now I am going to tell you something that seems nearly supernatural! The same night (I have reckoned back) that you dreamt that I had come back because of those Italians [meaning Giovanni and Arturo], I passed a sleepless one in which I took the resolution to leave everything in the lurch and go back to you because of the excitement I had through those beasts. Isn't that funny?

[Once more he complains of one of her friends] Her artistic judgment doesn't go very far and her ideal is Huneker of whom she speaks every minute. That does not upset me at all, but I don't think she understands me,—otherwise she would never have told me that it was stupid of you to marry an artist again and cited a paper which said you were at least true to art in your choice of husbands. I felt it like an insult and would have given anything not to be an artist, as the comparison with those pigs is too much for my pride.

[And growing more cheerful he concludes] My own sweet pet, how you are an angel to do everything just as I like it! How you tell me everything! How you knew that I should like you to stay in Coswig! My darling, you are too good to me! I don't deserve it. I should tell you what I wear?—darling, do you do that? Do you ever tell me what stockings you wore in Dresden or anything? Don't you know that I love to hear it?

COSWIG 1893
*Carreño and d'Albert*

For Carreño as well as d'Albert the three months of separation crawled slowly, busily away. Outside of her close-knit concert trips she gave her attention to her household and her garden. D'Albert must find it in full bloom for his homecoming. She planted pinks, mignonettes, begonias, petunias, daisies, and marigolds. When her husband finally returned he found her literally ill with joy.

D'Albert had long wanted a legal marriage. Now, for his sake and for that of their child-to-be, Carreño consented. The servants were sent off for a vacation, and, taking the children with them, they left for a week in Folkstone, England. The marriage took place on July 27, 1892, so the diary reveals: "The Good Lord has granted our prayer!! . . . London at 1 p.m."

D'Albert was impatient to be at his composing. On August 1 Carreño writes: "Home thank God." The trip must have been a wearing one, for on September 27 there is the next entry: "My precious baby girl Eugenia born at 1/4 before 3 p.m. May the Lord bless and keep her!"

There began a period of tireless work. D'Albert's opera, *Der Rubin,* a string quartette, and his second "Piano Concerto in E major," a gift for Teresa, were the result. He had never worked with more ease, with more success, with more privacy. Only an occasional pupil, or an invited friend invaded the sanctuary.

Carreño had served her marital apprenticeship. It was unthinkable that one of her individuality should for any length of time be submerged by a husband however great he might be. Their ideas about the education of children differed. Carreño was not as willing as at first to defer to her husband in this. The rights of motherhood were at issue. This was a subject of controversy, at first smoothed over with tact by one or the other, but showing symptoms of trouble ahead. Carreño was free of debt. Mr. Fairbank had been fully repaid. She was sure of as many well-paid engagements as she cared to accept, could feel at liberty to spend lavishly, to patronize Bertha Pechstein, the most expensive of designers in Berlin, for her concert dresses, to buy luxuries for the children, for her house. The staff of servants matched the family in size. This worried the thrifty d'Albert as much as the noise the high-strung children could not help making. Differences of opinion grew into quarrels out of proportion to their importance. Carreño's strident volleys of temper were countered more subtly by d'Albert's sarcastic digs. They hurt each other only to be the more charmingly reconciled. Absence of greater or less duration did its part to keep the rift from spreading.

The first year of matrimony was nearing its end. The public and the always gossip-hungry musicians had to admit defeat and turned to other subjects for more nourishing food. Apparently these two unblendable instruments were still managing to intone a melody in consonance. Carreño worked with fervor to make the most of her husband's "Concerto." Was it not her very own, written with her and their baby in mind? The *Neue Musik-Zeitung* concedes that the first hearing with d'Albert as soloist in Bremen and Braunschweig earned "great success." Hanslick adds his comment. "D'Albert is a lucky man. He can either play his own Concerto, or let it be played for him by his wife."

Carreño's first appearance under the baton of her husband in Berlin on the eighth and ninth of January, 1893, was for her another great personal triumph. Modestly the diary says: "Great success for my Toto's composition." But the "Concerto" fared less well at the hands of the critics. "She did," they admitted, "do the utmost with a dull, colorless composition," playing it with "complete masterliness." It would have taken a less selfish, less jealous nature than d'Albert's to overlook the fact that it was the performer, not the composition, that was drawing the applause. Although his name—as usual in man-worshiping Germany—stood first on the program, there was a sting in a combined triumph which gave Carreño precedence, and d'Albert could not bring himself to laugh at the *bon mot* which traced its source to this concert. "Frau Carreño," it was said, "yesterday played for the first time the second concerto of her third husband in the fourth Philharmonic Concert."

The *Tägliche Rundschau* was unduly sarcastic: "The little Swabian town of Weinsberg, famous for the fidelity of its women, will now be able to help giving honorary citizenship to Carreño for saving the work of her husband, at least for that evening. The hot-blooded Mexican," it continues, "shows peculiar and pleasing changes in her playing; it is softer, the whole interpretation more feminine, so that one looks forward to her playing of some real music very soon." The critic becomes positively venomous when he dismisses d'Albert with what seems to be personal animosity: "He remains that which he is in fact, a cosmopolitan nomad, who has no home, no nationality, no pedigree." If d'Albert read this paragraph—and there is little hope that it escaped his eye—he cannot be blamed for beginning the year in a bad temper. Although Carreño writes on January 19, "My Toto concert 1500 m. The public fanatic with his *wonderful playing*. God bless him. Played his sonata for the first time!" he would have been more generous than he was to delight that his Majesty, King of Saxony, had honored his wife with the title of *Königliche Kammermusikerin* in March, 1893, and had announced his intention of attending Carreño's Dresden recital in person. Loyally Carreño—she after all was the one who really appreciated it, though she could not call it either great or grateful—took the d'Albert "Concerto" from city to city, introduced it to conductor after conductor. For that year it was the mainstay of her appearances with orchestra. Better accepted was the first "Suite" of d'Albert, often found on her recital programs, wholly or in part, where the MacDowell "Suite" had formerly held its place.

The year 1893 marked a period of depression for the concert world. Carreño would like to have given up playing entirely for the spring season, but Hermann Wolff held her to her contracts. In his usual vein he wrote on February 10:

Chère Amie: J'ai encore à vous répondre à votre aimable invitation d'assister à votre concert de Dresde. Nous serions venus, ma femme et moi, mais le même jour nous avons le VIIIᵉ Concert Philharmonique. Donc nous ne pouvons pas, ce que nous regrettons d'autant plus, que dans des concerts qui ne sont pas pleins, nous le sommes—de "Galgenhumor" [Gibbethumor]. Certes avec mes nombreux mains (j'y compte mes pieds aussi) j'aurais fait un tapage inoui, enfin un tapage digne de votre succès. Que voulez-vous rien ne marche cette année. Cependant votre concert à Berlin ne sera pas mauvais. C'est toujours ce cher petit Maurice [Rosenthal] qui attire les "savants" et "savantes." Le reste ne vaut rien. J'appartiens au reste!

That something infinitely precious had been acquired through d'Albert's influence is attested by the *Signale* following this same Dresden recital: "To her hot temperament, her orchestral touch there has been added a third companion, a wonderful clarification." A new sense of musical values had come to her, in no wise interfering with her sparkling spontaneity. Her music was herself. It was bound to change as she changed. No static art was hers eventually to be outmoded. Very truly she wrote years later in answer to a questionnaire, asking for a résumé of her musical schooling: "I learned from everything, from everybody—and I am still learning."

On February 21 d'Albert had returned from a tour of three weeks in Russia with 16,000 marks in his pocket. From then their journeys took them in rarely interlocking directions, but on April 12 Carreño came to Berlin to hear Joachim's group play her husband's second "Quartette" for the first time in that city.

Since d'Albert was frequently called upon to conduct his own "Concerto," it seemed natural and pleasant for Carreño to go with him to cities where he was giving solo recitals in between, and a major mistake it proved to be. Carreño did not know how to play the part of a concert artist's wife with proper abnegation and tact. She was very apt to steal his thunder even in the green room. Jealousy raised green fingers. D'Albert, quite openly preferring to go off with groups of friends without her, became embarrassingly disagreeable when she objected to sharing him with others.

Finally the season with its higher ups and lower downs ended brilliantly enough. The Beethoven festival in Bonn, upon the roster of whose performing artists the names of d'Albert and Carreño both appeared, was a fitting climax, because it proved that she was no longer a star apart, but a musician among musicians, definitely one of Germany's own.

A WORKFUL summer lay ahead for both. Carreño was absorbed in making additions to her repertoire, for example, the "E flat Concerto" of Beethoven, and the "Chromatic Fantasia and Fugue" as von Bülow had edited it. D'Albert, deep in his opera, *Der Rubin,* took time off to teach little Teresita, or "Dada," as she was called, piano, taking a fatherly interest in her unfolding gifts. Pupils in considerable number were clamoring for lessons at Coswig gates, and were often taught interchangeably by one or the other of the artists. D'Albert's sarcasm reduced many a young aspirant to tears that his wife was called to dry.

The holiday was not to end without its rubs. Pupils brought restlessness to the quiet town and to Villa Teresa. The growing confusion and complication of life were irritating to edgy nerves that needed soothing not stimulus. From the servants' quarters came rumbles of disagreement. D'Albert would have preferred to live more economically, to see the helpers reduced by two, including Fräulein Knauth with whom he was on cordial terms of mutual dislike. Although d'Albert's son, Wolfgang, was received by Carreño with genuine affection, discipline and right education were more than ever a subject of heated controversy. His coming gave rise to the most quoted of all the Carreño-d'Albert anecdotes. One morning d'Albert abruptly interrupted Carreño's practice: "Come quickly! Your children and my children are quarreling with our children." To be possible it should have been diminished to read: "Your child and my child are quarreling with our child." But true or false it makes an amusing story, stranger to the ears of 1893 than to those of this day.

Fortunately the fall season opened with a strenuous list of concerts for both, whose climax was the first performance in Karlsruhe of d'Albert's opera, *Der Rubin.* "Great success. Thank God!!" says Carreño who had gone with her husband. Then she was called to Holland and Denmark, leaving Germany to d'Albert, where they met again three weeks later in Berlin. One of his letters gives a picture of his state of mind during their separation and of their more and more precarious relation to each other.

Oh my love, what will become of us? Your dear letter of yesterday was so sweet, but you suffer as I do, and that is dreadful to me. Yes, let us think of the money, but we can earn money, and still we do not have to be separated for so long. I have written it to Wolff: Russia with you, or not at all! He was completely flabbergasted that I wished to give concerts there with you—why? My darling, this longing is dreadful. I need you as I need the air (even more). Oh darling, we must plan to be happy, and not to quarrel any more, mustn't we? I know it is always my fault, but I will be different, I promise you. Oh Totty, it is not true that I like to be with people, or else how is it that when we are separated I see nobody, and avoid all parties?

—Oh love, our differences always grow out of the house. Think of the time until we came home in the spring. Was it not glorious? But at home you have many cares, and that makes you touchy. . . . Angel, Beloved, to travel with you is the greatest joy of my life. When people ask me where you are I always say Kopenhagen. The other cities are too far away. I understand that you don't care to go to the theatre without me—neither can I—without you I could not play in Leipzig. Only you give me peace.

. . . I am sorry that you have to play those stupid charity concerts on the twenty-third and twenty-fourth. Wolff wrote: "Charity concerts bring returns," and it is true.

He complains that Joachim changes his program every minute. "I am angry that I play with him." If all goes well he thinks it would be nice to take a trip to Italy together and do nothing at all, and again speaks of the household expenses as the source of all their troubles, ending with the promise: "It shall be the work of my life to show you my gratitude." Again Carreño comes to Berlin on November 30 to hear d'Albert play with Joachim. Clearly the two could not be happy apart; neither could they be completely happy together at home.

At the end of summer they had come upon an idea that prom-

ised to solve some of the difficulties. Why not give concerts together on two pianos? They would be quasi-pioneers in this
field. Their coöperation should give further proof of their conjugal oneness, and provide welcome refreshment for the press
surfeited with the unchanging repertoire of the artists they were
paid to hear. D'Albert discovered that Friedemann Bach was at
his best in the "Sonate in F," and by the end of October he had
memorized the Sinding "Variation." The Christmas interlude
gave time for practice together. For a closing number on these
programs they decided upon Liszt's "Concerto Pathétique," adding a group of solos each to fill out the concert. The plan had
the sanction of Wolff. This marital give and take temporarily
brought new zest into their relations and, best of all, there was
no longer time to quarrel about matters of less moment.

In Amsterdam on December 28, 1893, they had occasion to try
out the Sinding "Variations" at the same time with the d'Albert
"Concerto" played by Carreño under the composer's direction.
That it brought a fee of 1,500 marks augured well for the future
of the ensemble. Carreño now professionally called herself Teresa d'Albert-Carreño instead of Teresa Carreño-d'Albert as in
previous seasons. It better accented her individuality. Their début
was received with the enthusiasm worthy of it. It must have been
amusing to see Carreño striding majestically before—acknowledging as important the presence of her audience, while little
d'Albert tripped behind, taking his seat with a perfunctory bow
for the crowd he regarded less highly. Musically the effect of
their playing was so electrifying, its inner unity so compelling,
that even today there are those who speak of these *Doppelkon-
zerte* as a unique experience. For once the critics could join in
the unfeigned admiration of the public. They called it an amazing feat, "an ideally perfect ensemble," and throughout the
spring these concerts were in great demand. Financially the result was less favorable. The receipts were not much more than
each might have harvested alone, generally 1,000 marks per concert. For Carreño the season came to an early close. There was
to be another child.

T̲ɪ̲ʀ̲ᴇ̲ᴅ̲ after a strenuous winter the pair returned to Coswig under tension, which took every occasion to discharge itself. D'Albert, with or without provocation, was irritable, mean-spirited; Carreño joyful, melancholy, or hysterical by turns. Explosions of anger grew more frequent, more violent, and more public, the interludes of silence longer and foreboding. D'Albert began to seek solace in flirtations that he knew would enrage Carreño. To make things easier the children were sent to the seashore in August where after a series of scenes at home d'Albert joined them. This for the moment brought the pair to their senses, and on September 16, 1894, Carreño on the rebound is able to write to her friend Carrie Keating Reed, only recently married, with her habitual exuberance, perhaps to reassure herself in a rare moment.

I can only tell you that the word happiness, which seemed to me to exist only in the dictionary, the good Lord has shown me that it exists also on earth, and that it exists in fact, and not only in words or dreams. My husband combines all that is great in *genius* and *heart,* and I spend my life wondering how it is possible that so much greatness and goodness should be combined in only one human being . . . Teresita and Hans—we call him so now, as I could not bear his name otherwise; it brought too many horrible recollections with it!—have at last found a Father who is all love, tenderness, and goodness to them. Our house is a sort of mutual worshipping admiration society.

Carreño was not aware that the chasm between her and her husband had widened to irreparable dimension. The birth of a daughter Hertha on September 26 gave a final month of peace. Then the concert season once more took the artists their separate ways. On the plea that there was insufficient time for practice together the two-piano concerts were by common consent abandoned. D'Albert was often at home when Carreño was not. Restless in her absence, he sought other distraction. Carreño's appearance was the signal for explosions of temper, threats only half intended, for illness born of unhappiness. On October 17 the diary becomes Carreño's confidant: "The most unhappy day of my life. Had I not lived to see it and hear what my husband said to me!!! May God help me to bear my suffering! Only God knows what I suffer!!!"

Just then with deeper understanding of a weakness she detested she writes to Teresita.

How can you tell me that you are jealous of Herr K— [the tutor]? My own Dadachen! Have I not talked with you a long time about this ugly feeling some time ago when you told me that you were jealous of Alice? My precious own girl! You must do *all you can* to overcome this horrid feeling, or you will be a very unhappy girl in your life. As I told you before, the person who is jealous acknowledges his (or her own) inferiority, and our pride must teach us not to be jealous. Now, think well over what I say, and give me the joy to overcome your nasty, ugly jealousy. . . .

Your sweet letter gave me so much joy, my darling! Write me very often and tell Fräulein to pay for the stamps, and I will return her the money when I return home. Tell me all that happens in the house, every little detail is dear to me, as I want to go on in my thoughts living with you all from one minute to another. Has Fräulein P. had a lesson from Papa yet? How did she play, if she did have a lesson? How are you practising? Good and very regularly? Tell me all!

And Teresita does, even in poetry. She pictures her mother sitting proudly on horseback, "hoch zu Ross" with sword in hand, and, knowing it would please her mother, or only imagining the splendors of a concert career, she writes: "Oh, if I could only play in public!! This wish is so great!"

All this was the lull before the cyclone. Upon release from duty Carreño found her husband at home. The unbelievable happened. D'Albert's philanderings had reached proportions too serious to be ignored. He found it beyond bearing that he was treated with contempt for what he considered unimportant incidents. He expected his wife to minister to his wants, to cater to his self-respect, and to shut her eyes to his shortcomings. Carreño, who now openly belittled him, no longer fulfilled these requirements. In a fit of temper he left home, with his way mapped clearly before him. This time there would be no coming back. D'Albert and Carreño would never spend another Christmas together.

His attitude can best be clarified by his own explanation, making the break final. Carreño was less analytical, but her silence is quite as revealing as his words. On December 17 he writes from Amsterdam in German:

My dear good Teresita:

It is infinitely hard to be frank, and not to wound. But how does one give proof of confidence and respect, through courage to tell the truth or by pasting over conditions with deceitful lies?

I must pour out my heart to you, tell you how I feel, how I am affected, what I wish for the future in the interest of all of us and for the good of my art. Fräulein Knauth told you that I only wished for *your* happiness. That is very true, for you always said that my happiness was yours, and that is why I write about my happiness, or rather unhappiness, and about what must happen to reconstruct a quiet, bearable happiness. On that account your happiness is the chief thing. Before all I must once and for all deny that H. G. and M. V. are responsible for my change of heart. I value myself after all too highly to allow either the one or the other to have any influence over my life. Those were only outward circumstances: The real reason for my change of soul, and so for all of this uproar, lies *much deeper*. Its development has gone on unnoticeably but inevitably for two years in a psychologically perfectly defensible way. You noticed it less than I, because this kind of sensitivity, the expression of a constantly pondering state of mind, is entirely German, and therefore must be entirely foreign to the understanding of one who comes from Southern lands. Forgive that I say this to you!—You said the other day that we had always lived so happily.—You perhaps, but not I. There were scarcely four days without some disturbance, differences of opinion, or scenes, and every disturbance left a wound in my heart, and brought sadness to the inner tenderness of affection that I offered you in such abundance. I am not equal to these disturbances, to you they are element of life, necessity. How often did I not tell you that you would go too far, that sometime I might become an entirely different person! You did not think it possible. The disturbances did not excite you half as much as me. You say many things that you do not mean at all—and I always believed everything. This continuous irritation almost made an end of us. This inner revolution of my soul is understandable, natural, and I can justify it before God. You must not forget that I am still young enough to reconstruct my inner man, to change and recreate myself completely, and you no longer can, and so do no longer understand me. The chief part of your life is behind you—I, so God wills, have only reached half of it. Added to that is your amazingly vivacious temperament as against my more quiet and simple nature.—No wonder that we could not get along together. For the foundation of marriage more is necessary than merely love. We were only happy when we were constantly being considerate of each other. You always said so, but I was the one who was the most considerate, and so you often thought we were happy when I, at least, was not. For two years I have never been completely happy within. That is the reason why I composed so well—I concentrated upon my work with iron perseverance, and found redemption in it.

Of your perpetual contempt of all that is German I will not speak—that was only a bagatelle. . . . I often tried to reveal my inner self to you. You never understood it. How often I told you, nobody else would have stood it with you. You answered, you would have sent him to the Devil,—now you can send me there.

What do I wish? You would long ago have asked. I wish that we both shall agree that we can no longer live together as before, and shall have to arrange our life accordingly. I wish for no divorce! You wanted that, but I want peace and quiet and that is not possible with females. I have lost my belief in everything, want to be alone, live alone. In this opinion Brahms—with whom I contracted intimate friendship in Vienna—reinforced me. It is much better it happens now than later, before we spend more money, before we become more unhappy still, before the children grow older. Dada has considered a life apart as the only right course for me for a long time. Children and fools speak the truth.—

I send you many kisses, and ask you again to receive my words with composure.

Eugen.

He follows this tirade up with a laconic note, congratulating Carreño upon her birthday, accompanied by two vases for appeasement.

D'Albert's letter, although it contained some fundamental truths, was hardly one to bring the happiness that he so ardently seemed to wish for her. No wife likes to be reminded that she is only important as a background for his more weighty concerns, that his philanderings are outward circumstances, that, after three years of adaptation to the life he liked, she, the Venezuelan, is incapable of understanding him, the German. (Carreño was not the only one who found d'Albert's Germanophile fanaticism puzzling. Hanslick ironically commented upon it when he wrote: "D'Albert emphasizes his unadulterated Germanism, which one is occasionally inclined to doubt in view of his French name and English birth.") Most cutting of all was the reminder that Brahms and her own little daughter had been enlisted on his side and that the sooner they separate—the cheaper it would be.

It was fortunate for Carreño that she had the capacity of losing herself in Christmas·preparations for the children, and also that she was not one to grieve in silence. It did her good to unburden herself to the only too sympathetic Fräulein Knauth. As usual in moments of crisis her reaction was instantaneous. No half measures, no compromise for her! She would insist upon divorce upon her own terms. The way to strike d'Albert the most telling blow would always be by way of his pocket-book, and she did not mind at all dealing it.

*"Dios sea conmigo y mis hijos y perdona a Eugenio,"* says the first page of the diary of 1895. She prepared to steel herself to go on as if nothing had happened. Like Bolívar she would build happiness upon the pedestal of sorrow vanquished. Carreño threw her head back, and as she had advised Dada, called pride to her aid. By one of the thousand channels that make the private lives of artists public property the unhappy secret began to filter out. "I told you so," smugly said some; "here endeth the third lesson," commented others. Sympathy was in general with Carreño. Whether for this or more objective reasons the critics had never praised her more glowingly. It took courage to put herself again at the service of the d'Albert "Concerto" under the direc-

tion of Felix Mottl, and it could not have hurt her feelings very much that the critics called it "a washed-out piano story in four unprepossessing movements," while lauding her to the skies for accomplishing "wonders unthinkable since Rubinstein."

The most trying ordeal, one they both would have given much to avoid, faced them when they found themselves obliged to play in another concert together. D'Albert conducted his "Concerto." "In the hands of the excellent pianist the work achieved signal success." And fittingly, sadly, their ensemble faded out in the strains of the "Concerto Pathétique."

CARREÑO waited for word from d'Albert's lawyer, one that would clarify their future. Finally on February 27 she addresses d'Albert himself in desperation.

My present situation must end. I must at last know how I have to arrange my life.

You said to our friends: that you could not breathe the same air with me, which, after the way you behaved towards me, I can well comprehend. I have written you before: you have a conscience.

So I ask you to write me quite in detail what your wishes are, and what way of life you wish that we shall follow, so that I may know what is to happen to me, and what I have to do with the servants, etc.

Farewell! Teresita.

D'Albert evades the issue. On March 5 Carreño writes again, wisely leaving the decision to him.

Since I go to Spain next month, and, as you know, my tour lasts five or six weeks, our two children Eugenia and Hertha cannot possibly stay alone in the house with Emma and just one other servant.

I hear that you are going to Italy and these poor children would remain unprotected without father or mother. That I cannot allow, and I would rather give up my trip at once. If you agree I shall take them with Emma to Dr. Lahmann until my return, and so the house can remain closed until I come back, unless you decide that we are to live somewhere else. Farewell! Teresita.

The trip to Spain was abandoned, probably due to the illness of Hans. There was no lack of engagements waiting for her in

Germany. While Carreño was reaching pinnacles undared before d'Albert was pianistically in partial eclipse. A new star had already begun to kindle a responsive flame before the other had paled. Although the peace and quiet he needed "was not possible with females" he never as long as he lived was without one or the other of them for any length of time. Hermine Fink, the ascendant star, was the one who held him longest, for a span of ten years. She had sung the principal soprano part in d'Albert's opera *Der Rubin* in one of its early performances and so had consciously come into his life for the first time in February, 1895. This had been Carreño's own opera, the one composed under her inspiration. She had attended the Première in Karlsruhe the preceding October, and afterwards, thrilled by the success of the husband she adored, she had felt moved to play until late into the night for the group of people celebrating the event in the house of the "Generalintendant," unaware happily that she and the next Frau d'Albert were in the same room.

In order to avoid a meeting d'Albert asked that Carreño stay away from Coswig until he had seen to his packing, had paid off the servants. He himself put the little girls in care of the mother of Fräulein Knauth in Liebstadt. The convalescent Hans was sent to a sanitarium for children, Teresita to a private school in Dresden. When Carreño returned to all there was left of the home she had loved, she found it bare, everything in boxes, with only two servants in attendance.

Even Fräulein Knauth had gone. In an affectionate letter to Carreño she told of her engagement, adding that what she had seen of married life in Coswig had so prejudiced her against it that she had almost decided not to try it for herself, especially since Carreño had warned her in a moment of bitterness that "one can never marry too late or be divorced too soon."

At the end of the month d'Albert finally made up his mind. He accepted a call as *Kapellmeister* to the Court of Weimar where Carreño had played for the Grand Duchess only a month before, taking Wolfgang with him. Carreño, completely unnerved, sought the seclusion of Tyrol for a needed vacation.

Good businesswoman that she was, Carreño insisted upon a divorce on her own terms. D'Albert, duly informed, was horrified. This must not happen. He must be the first to file suit. His "always pondering German mind" hit upon several plausible grounds that he might magnify and use for his own ends. First he did his worst to have his wife declared insane, have her safely buried in an asylum. That plea had been helpful in ending his first marriage. Her nervous tension, her hysterics, her extravagance, were these not clear signs of a disordered mind? This first assault failed completely.

RESOLUTELY turning away from her troubles Carreño decided to make a new home for herself and her four children in Berlin. She found one that suited her and, more difficult a problem, one in which she might practice day or night without restriction, on the top floor of Kurfürstendamm 28. She entered it on May 19. A broad staircase carpeted in deep-piled red led up story upon story. On each landing windows of colored glass shed a religious light, the one uppermost representing a bird of Paradise with a malevolent glint in his eye.

The apartment itself was dignified, airy and spacious, its L shape typical of Berlin. To the right of the dark hall was a small reception room or study, to the left the formal salon, its furniture decorated elaborately in rose brocade upon ornate gilt frames. At one end behind the inevitable table stood the even more inevitable sofa, the seat reserved for the most distinguished visitor. Opening out of the salon was Carreño's studio. Even when empty it was full of her personality and became the real living room of the apartment. Two concert Bechstein grands, standing end to end on layers of carpet to deaden the sound and generally covered for the same reason, held the center of the room as they should. The music rack, placed on top of the closed piano to further spare the ears of those beneath, was never without its attendant ash tray. Carreño was so inveterate a smoker that she taught herself not to let her cigarettes interfere with her playing. She could dispose of the ashes at any tempo without break of continuity even in the most florid cadenza. Near the balcony which gave on the Kurfürstendamm stood the writing desk with its many cubbyholes bulging. The ebony music case made to Carreño's order practically filled one side of the room. Near the glass-paneled dining-room door stood a couch, a table, more chairs, and the tile stove. The walls were closely hung with pictures, photographs of Carreño's parents, of the children, of musicians, Brahms, Beethoven, Liszt, and of dear friends. The dining room, high ceilinged as the others, was the typical *Berliner Zimmer,* one corner pierced by a court window usually intended to give light for the sewing table of the Hausfrau. Only through this room as a passage could the bedrooms be reached. The kitchen lay far behind in inconvenient distance.

It was a different woman who took up life in her new apartment. For d'Albert the last three years had meant an exciting episode. Whether Carreño admitted it to herself or not, he was the love of her life. That he still had the power to make her miserable and often used it with satisfaction was one of the stings of her later days. Carreño never fully recovered from this divorce. She had been Teresa d'Albert, Teresa Carreño-d'Albert, Teresa d'Albert-Carreño, to become again Teresa Carreño. She faced it frankly: "I am growing old."

Meanwhile, not downed by a first reverse, d'Albert hit upon an idea that he thought approached genius. There had never been a legal divorce ending Carreño's common-law marriage to Giovanni Tagliapietra. Therefore they must still be considered married, and accordingly what was there to prevent a suit for bigamy from being filed against her? (This is the man who claims through his biographer that he had, though perfectly innocent, shouldered all the blame and all the costs of divorce in order not to cause annoyance to Carreño.) It did not appear to matter that, were he upheld, his own children would no longer be considered legitimate. This attack too rebounded against the assailant. Giovanni Tagliapietra's letters were brought in as proof, and a good friend in New York gave his affidavit that there had been no formal marriage. The suit was reluctantly withdrawn, leaving Carreño victor on a sorry battlefield.

One of the attending casualties, which also had its element of tragedy, was that it meant a definite break for life with Manuel, her brother. At this critical time he had refused to side with his sister, preferring to disown her instead. Had he forgotten the many times she had saved him from the consequences of his unworthy escapades, selling the few jewels she owned to pay his debts? The poorer for yet another illusion lost, Carreño filed the application for divorce. She no longer had a husband, no longer a brother. There remained the children. But for this there were times when she would have ended it all. As she took her lonely walks by the Canal its water exerted temptation. It would have been easy to yield herself to its smooth depths.

On October 2, 1895, a divorce was granted Carreño on the grounds of willful desertion. D'Albert was instructed to take out a life-insurance policy in favor of his children, to provide them until the age of independence with a liberal allowance for maintenance and education. D'Albert heard the decree with indifference (less than a month later he married Hermine Fink). Carreño burst into tears.

From the courtroom she drove to her friends, the Kochs. Still red-eyed but smiling she burst in upon them. Again her natural resilience was her ally. "Well, it's all over," she announced. "Have you anything to eat? *J'ai une faim canine.*" Then once more she broke down and unburdened her soul at length, managing however to eat a good luncheon between sobs—while the *Droschke* waited below forgotten.

WORK, the universal comforter, proved to be the best counter-weight to trouble. She lost herself in it, and even turned once more to composition, abandoned since childhood. At home she led two full and often conflicting lives, that of the artist, and that of the mother. Either one could have absorbed her completely. After an early breakfast there were the usual household details to be adjusted. The rest of the morning belonged to music, practicing, teaching, or reading over manuscripts sent by hopeful young composers who banked upon her to make them known. After lunch—Carreño always prepared the salad dressing of oil and lemon at the table—she found a game of solitaire restful before the siesta. Then perhaps another lesson, an hour with the masseur, or more work at the desk before tea. There were bills to be paid, dates to be accepted or refused, notes to be written, programs to be sent. Wolff must be reminded not to be neglectful, to keep her fees high, her concerts in close and logical sequence, to find engagements that were increasingly important. In this year, particularly, Carreño was not easy to satisfy. From now on she would be nobody's fool.

Very elastic was the number of those who used to gather around Carreño's long dining-room table over the teacups and the cookie jar. Carreño presided at the head of the table and brewed the tea which she herself liked very strong and black. Conversation was gay or serious according to her predominating mood. If the day had been a peaceful one this was the time for the children to ask favors. Later the twilight hour was most suitable for the daily walk. Dinner was generally an intimate affair, occasionally shared by a few guests. Family conferences, letters to the children away at school, and another game of solitaire brought the day to a close. The to and fro of concert trips often interrupted this schedule, bringing attendant confusion to the household. The children were made to understand from early childhood that it was by their mother's coming and going, her happiness or depression, that their own lives must be regulated. Meeting the train that brought the artist back from glories they could only imagine to become their mother once more was the high spot of childish memory.

Even before the divorce had become final Carreño decided that for reasons of health the summers must not be spent in Berlin. By happy chance she found in Pertisau on the Achensee in the Bavarian highlands a peaceful spot in which to plan her new life. During many years it became her *Sommerfrische*. The mountain air had an invigorating lift, woods and lake quieted her nerves. There she could live the simple life that pleased her, take long walks in heavy boots and comfortable old clothes. Housekeeping was confined to the essentials. As a buffer between Carreño and intrusion there was always *"die gute* Krahl,"* a lady by virtue of character and education, who could take Carreño's place in many ways, and with whom she could safely leave her children. No less important, she had a talent for keeping down expenses and for making herself tactfully invisible. Never had they lived so well and so cheaply as under her management. There was time for practice, for rest, and for the children, even with a dozen students about hovering for their turn to have a lesson. Primarily undertaken for financial reasons—lessons at 40 marks each did help to meet expenses—Carreño found that, tiring as it was, she liked to be surrounded by young people, finding real satisfaction in being helpful to them at the outset of their careers. Some were to be teachers, others had visions of a more dramatic future behind the footlights. She received them all with the same outgoing friendliness and anticipation. Those that proved to be unworthy of her interest soon disappeared, and a very few were admitted to the inner sanctum of her affection to become her adopted "Berlin sons and daughters," she their "Berlin mother."

Turning the current of misdirected affection back into the channel of motherhood, since childhood art's only lasting competitor, Carreño determined that henceforth she would live for her children alone, redouble her efforts only for their sakes.

She faced the fact sorrowfully. Inheritance and the unfortu-

nate circumstances of their birth had handicapped her two
elder children. Giovanni had the handsome presence of a Spanish hidalgo offset by a willful nature and lack of ambition.
Teresita with all her promise of great beauty was nervous and
seldom completely well. How to guide these children to successful maturity was an ever-present worry. While the divorce
was pending Giovanni managed to get along fairly well in a
school in Dresden. Teresita, also in a private school of that city,
was far more of a problem. Many of Carreño's headaches were
caused by these two undeniably gifted Tagliapietras.

The one of all others to whom Carreño could turn for advice in a domestic quandary was her friend of old, Fanny Mac-
Dowell. She would not have believed in progressive education
had she known of such a thing. Her rules of conduct for children were contained in three simple words: "Love, honor, and
obey," the latter to be enforced with stern discipline. For most
of Carreño's difficulties with her children Fanny conveniently
blamed d'Albert.

Do you not think [she wrote] that you may have been a little unwise,
a little too extreme in newfangled notions imbibed from that scala-
wag d'Albert in the feeding and the general management of your
little flock? See how strong and well you are! How sturdy as a child!
You were not brought up as you are bringing up your own darlings.
I know you do it because you believe it is for their good, but why
try experiments with your children? Do you think Jaegers and vegetables and peculiar bathing are all to combine to make a healthy
family? Even you, strong as you were before you met that little
monster, fell ill with the kind of diet you conformed to at his wish.
Oh, Teresita dear, cast off all the chains that gnome bound you with,
be your own beautiful self, and let common sense drive out all the
fads that you have adopted.

Occasionally she took up the cudgel in defense of her son.
When Edward failed to receive even a word of congratulation
from Carreño upon the Chair established for him at Columbia
University, she complained: "I hope the day will come when
you will think differently of him and his work—you who were

one of the very first to appreciate and make known his talent. I don't know what he thinks of your silence—you cannot deny that you started it by your own enthusiastic rendering of his works." Again she attributes Carreño's change of heart to d'Albert. It was he who had revolutionized her attitude toward Edward's music, who had even succeeded in turning her against America. It would have been better, she thought, not without prejudice, if Carreño had remained in the United States, even at the expense of living with Giovanni Tagliapietra. Would she not by this time have owned her house, which had risen in value enormously since then? She asked for the assurance that "you will hereafter not have any pity, or love, or whatever you may choose to call it, for men." In contrast there was invariably kind mention of Tag's brother, Arturo. "He colored, when I gave him your message. He lives separately from Tag, is industrious, and tries to get along. He speaks excellent English and through thick and thin he has stood up for you."

Carreño was a slave to her concert schedule. Outside of that she did as she pleased. Before any member of the household made plans for the day himself, it was well to consider how Carreño was feeling that morning. It was for her to dictate, for them to conform.

To her children Carreño was a dual being. She was a goddess living apart in a splendid world, one which they could imagine but which she did not share with them. From this she now and then returned laden with flowers, her bag full of presents for those who deserved them. She spoiled and scolded almost in the same breath as impulse moved. They must be careful in addressing her. Any contradiction was stopped with a curt: "How dare you speak to your mother in that way." That was the goddess, not their mother. But every stormy reprimand had its reaction in demonstrative forgiveness. Then she became the real mother who loved them and hugged them, who worried over their clothes, their health, and their manners.

It was in times of illness that she was most truly theirs. Often she sat at the bedside of a sick child the night through, instinctively doing the right thing, radiating curative magnetism. She used to say herself that if art had failed her she would have become a nurse. "And I would have been a good one," she added.

The first Christmas in the Berlin home, in spite of sad memories, was gratefully peaceful. What freedom to be alone with the children, not to be obliged to consider anybody's temperament but her own! The tree in the corner was decorated by Carreño with the help of Krahl. Standing in the corner of the studio, the presents in profusion arranged on separate tables around it for family and servants alike, it made the apartment take on the essence of home.

There had been no dearth of concerts ahead that fall. Carreño needed them as an outlet and attacked her crowded, neatly welded schedule with all energy. Fees too were becoming generous once more. The majority of engagements was in the upper brackets from 600 to 1,000 marks. More than any other pianist of her sex Carreño was in demand for concerts with orchestra. At twilight one day after rehearsal she happened to be watching the fading sunset from one of the bridges that span the Elbe in Dresden. A young man, finding her profile alluring, stopped beside her, inquiring if he might accompany her. "Mein Herr," she replied with that sharpening of the voice which commanded instant respect, "I have just been accompanied by seventy gentlemen. One is not enough for me," and strode away unmolested.

The musical critics, not unlike the critics of today, were apt to see their artists from widely differing angles. *Die Neue Zeitschrift für Musik* does not find that the Carreño of early 1896 has basically changed since her first appearance in Germany. To him

Frau Carreño belongs to those volcanoes that are still in full eruption. She feels constrained in pedantic fetters like a bird in cage. She loves freedom, loves to jump and tear around without rein like the horse of the prairies. Instead of exhausting itself in the course of the evening her power progressively increases. She grows constantly wilder, more passionate. Above all at the end, when the real program is finished, when others in her place would let themselves sink into a comfortable chair, she just finds her stride; then she rages with untamable fire. Her eyes sparkle with a weird light. It is then that this beautiful woman is surpassingly beautiful. It is then that her playing reaches its climax.

His colleague on the same journal comes to an opposite conclusion a little later on. À propos of the Seventh Philharmonic Concert in which for the first time in Berlin Carreño was heard in the "Emperor Concerto" of Beethoven under the conductor Artur Nikisch, he feels that she must be warned not to go to the other extreme.

She gave the "E flat Concerto" of Beethoven and the "Hungarian Fantasia" of Liszt with impeccable technique and understanding, but we missed her usually overflowing temperament. This highly imaginative artist must not let herself be frightened by pedantic school teachers. Her fire, her passionateness are the very traits that differentiate her from the numberless hordes of pianists of both sexes who are technically capable but who do not stand out with any particular artistic individuality. She should not take the trouble to repress these qualities, or else she will be robbed of her most beautiful jewel, her own personality.

It is easy to comprehend why Carreño preferred to file away her criticisms without reading them.

If d'Albert had not found her a worthy wife, she was determined that he should learn to esteem her from now on a formidable rival. It must have displeased her to read in reference to this same concert a review of Otto Lessmann in the *Allgemeine Musikzeitung*. He would have her be on the one hand more true to the tradition that was so truly d'Albert's in the reading of the "Concerto," on the other hand more true to herself and her gifts.

Another gentleman of Leipzig steers a middle course.

On seeing her [he rhapsodizes] many a person must have silently sighed with me: "Einst ging sie zu zwein, Jetzt geht sie allein" in free modification of one of the most meaningful songs of Robert Franz. But before the all conquering power of her art, the sympathy that one would so gladly offer her in this hard test of life recedes.

In the "E minor Concerto" of Chopin and the "Hungarian Fantasia" of Liszt, after having been received with cries of joy at the outset, she scored a resounding triumph. Through constant purification she has abandoned the amazonlike fury with which she used to pounce upon the greatest tasks of virtuosity as if upon an ironfast cohort of enemies, and that without loss of glowing fullness of expression and freshness of temperament.

From now on the critics were more and more divided into two camps, those that wished her to keep forever the fire of youth, and those who welcomed the note of contemplation that with advancing years more truly expressed her changing self. As regards the E flat concerto, as soon as it had become more thoroughly her own through time, the great assimilator, all were agreed that it was one of her masterpieces.

In the season 1895–96 Carreño gave no less than seventy concerts. They took her from Germany to Great Britain and back again before the coming of the new year; February, 1896, saw her on a tour through Scandinavia where great success was a foregone conclusion;—it is curious that in Italy and France, countries racially allied to her own, the public was less responsive, the critics less cordial, than in Nordic lands—March was spent mainly in Switzerland, April again in Norway and Sweden. When it came time to join the children in Pertisau, Carreño was exhausted. The pupils who had assembled from far and near held their breath for fear that a lesson might be canceled. But even this so-called vacation was interrupted by a concert engagement in Lucerne, too lucrative to be refused. Carreño made a holiday of it, used it to show Teresita the wonders of Switzerland.

Aside from this trip Carreño found diversion in polishing the string quartette she had composed during the past year, the child of her unhappiness. In the sensitive hands of the Klingler Quartet it came to life under ideal conditions in the Leipzig Gewandhaus on September 29, 1896. Among the quantities of flowers presented to her lay a silver wreath from her pupils. The critics were friendly if, as habitually where a woman was creatively concerned, somewhat condescending, and the "Quartette" was in due time accepted for publication by Fritzsch in Leipzig. Carreño had made the acquaintance of Herr and Frau Fritzsch during her first days in Germany and had become so grateful for friendship in difficult hours that she presented the publisher with all the German rights to her "Teresita Waltz," not realizing at the time what a costly gift it was she was making. Another composition, a serenade for string orchestra, remained in manuscript and was probably never performed.

After this preliminary introduction to the fall season it was time to organize the household for the coming winter. Giovanni, in spite of lack of application which kept his school grades chronically in the danger zone, got on fairly well in Schnepfenthal, one of the best and most expensive of German schools. Teresita was the real problem. Fräulein Kretzschmar in Dresden, whose school Teresita had entered the year before, understood her charge well, and analyzed her difficulties with lucidity.

Life in a *Pension* does not agree with Teresita, and yet there is nothing definite to be cured. Against threatening anaemia exercise would be a remedy, but her foot will not allow that. Wine and iron liqueur are forbidden by her former way of living at home. The last cold was without doubt due to the open window.—She is desperate because she may not do what she considers salutary and open windows do not belong to this category. . . . She needs a special governess for herself alone, because she is in many ways unreasonable. When she is supposed to do needlework her eyes hurt her, and yet she reads as much as possible. If she is supposed to go for a walk her foot hurts her, and still she writes on the same day to Krahl that she will call for her to go to a concert. And so she practically lives in constant contradiction. She said at first that she must eat fruit, but she won't touch it. She should eat vegetables, but she refuses them. Since she eats only little meat she really does not get enough nourishment. You can't achieve anything with her by force. She has a certain passive— shall we say suffering—resistance. The only thing to be done is to give her a tutor who will look after her entirely. Only in this way can she hope to finish the year tolerably well.

A subsequent experiment of keeping Teresita at home under private instruction was also unsatisfactory. Carreño felt that after all a school would be more capable of coping with her daughter's difficulties. The Breymannsches Institut was situated, as it is today, in the unspoiled country near Wolfenbüttel. The setting was as congenial to Carreño's taste as the simple, homelike atmosphere of the place. Founded by the niece of Friedrich Fröbel, it breathed his spirit and clung to his ideals for the education of children. The accepted academic subjects, the household arts, music—and the weekly bath found their place upon the schedule in close fraternity. Plain living was enlivened by teas, parties, plays, and excursions into the near Harz mountains. The standards of instruction and conduct were high and enforced with gentle firmness. Good manners were encouraged, not for outward adornment, but as the expression of character and kind thoughts. Carreño had good cause to be glad of her choice.

Teresita was not so easily pleased. She finds the girls uncongenial and stupid. She complains of her eyes, of headaches, of the food, then upon remonstrance she writes that she has "learned to suffer without complaining," an accomplishment which in the course of a few weeks is again forgotten. She accuses herself of making her mother constantly unhappy, blames herself for never satisfying her, and admits that she suffers greatly. She worries about Carreño's projected trip to the United States, and fears that her life will be endangered by "that awful man I am obliged to call father." But it does please Teresita that the English teacher asked her to play for the school, and when she did so they all acted as if she had presented a valuable present. "I never had so grateful an audience," she concludes. A special grand piano had been sent for her use during the school year. No dog ever guarded a bone more jealously. Even on the day of formal student recitals hers was the only hand allowed to touch its keys. The other performers were obliged to content themselves with an ·upright instrument.

To return to America had often been a temptation to Carreño. She had not been justly valued there. Now with the background of great European success her reception should be very different. Of a number of offers that were tentatively made her she finally accepted the most profitable. A foolproof contract, drawn up with the help of the canny Wolff, finally lay signed in her desk. Rudolph Aronson, her former impresario of the Casino Concerts, backed by the Knabe Piano Company, was to manage the tour. The agreement called for forty concerts at $400 each, transportation and living expenses for two people to be paid by the manager. As her traveling companion Carreño chose Henriette Orbaan, a pupil sent to her under the patronage of the Dutch Government.

In the interim there was a heavily booked tour awaiting her through Russia and the Scandinavian peninsula. Everywhere Carreño's success continued to be sensational. In Helsingfors she was obliged to give four concerts, two recitals, one concert with orchestra, and one concert at popular prices. After the third a large laurel wreath was presented to her with great ceremony, and the students could hardly be restrained from unharnessing the horses of the carriage to draw her home themselves. At her final appearance the audience became positively unmanageable. There were some who kept calling for "the hand, the hand," insisting upon kissing it, upon touching her dress. Carreño to quiet them at last stepped to the edge of the platform, pausing for silence: "Jag kommer tillbaka" (I shall come back) she promised in her best Swedish. Enthusiasm became fanatical. The critics broke their record for superlatives. Hardly ever had there been such a triumph. It followed her even to the train, where several hundred people were gathered to bid her farewell. Women and children nearly suffocated her with flowers, while a chorus roared loudly in competition with the cheers of the mob. Tired and well content Carreño at last sank back into the seat of her compartment and spread out her cards for a game of solitaire. As her nerves ceased to tingle she began to feel low in her mind. This year Christmas could not be spent with her children. Instead she would be on the ocean, probably seasick in a storm.

It was on the eve of the new year, 1897, that the *Aller* docked in New York. Rudolph Aronson greeted Carreño at the pier and escorted her to her apartment in the Hotel Netherland on upper Fifth Avenue at Fifty-ninth Street, her American *pied-à-terre* for many years to come. That her first appearance was to be with the New York Philharmonic Orchestra promised well for the tour and challenged Carreño to do her best. She chose the "D minor Concerto" of Rubinstein for this ordeal. As she crossed the platform, her friends noticed the now-predominating shades of gray in her hair, simply arranged on top of her head, falling becomingly in natural waves that softened the etching of her profile. Her black velvet dress was richly decorated but simple in line. Frau Pechstein was an artist who knew how to create the illusion of height. Before the preliminaries were over, before a note had been played, Carreño could feel that her audience was ready to play follow-the-leader over whatever hurdles she would take them. She was free to forget them, to relive once more, in memory of her great mentor who had died in 1894, the romantic themes that she loved. In this thrilling setting the "Concerto" became new and fresh. The audience listened in excitement that, as one reviewer commented, would have interrupted her opening cadenza with applause "had it been a less refined audience." Not since Rubinstein had played this concerto in New York himself had it been so beautifully interpreted. W. J. Henderson, a critic to be respected, notes that her technique has become more sure, more smooth, that her style has broadened, and James Huneker adds: "Carreño is more than able to pilot her vessel with all the ease of a trusty and experienced piano-mariner."

To the critic of the New York *Advertiser* she appeals from a different side. He probably had not heard her in her wilder days. "She is a strong woman, playing her instrument strongly. —She either stands revealed in the glare of midday, or you hear her clear cry in the tropical jungle at midnight, while near-by two burning points tell of something lurking and feline." Under the caption, "The Lioness of the Piano," one which aroused Carreño's anger more than any other, the critic of the New York *World* hears in her playing the bitterness of disillusionment with life.

She has lost the feminine tenderness, the poetic feeling, the suavity, which were once elements in her playing. She has become purely a bravura player—almost brutal. She seems to have been completely influenced by the methods of her late husband. She was once magnetic, but she has lost that quality in spite of the still potent charms of beauty and grace.

Pooling the various conflicting verdicts the consensus nevertheless is that the prodigy's return entitles her in her artistic maturity to a place among the first of her contemporaries, that in whatever way she may assert herself she does so with the legitimate authority of genius polished in the school of hard work, and harder experience.

CARREÑO came back to the United States prepared to make amends for her neglect of the composer she once had so actively championed. A telegram sent to her in Louisville on April 21, 1897, sounds as if the slight of former days were not yet forgotten. It ran: "Have just seen Saturday program of course appreciate compliment but dislike Hexentanz and Concert-Study would consider personal favor if you left me out this being only occasion you play MacDowell this season would prefer not having my weakest piano work beside Brahms best [Variations on a theme of Händel] no need reprinting program why not simply omit number. E. S. MacDowell."

Whether Carreño complied with the request is not known. But as soon as the "MacDowell Concerto" reappeared in her repertoire the temporary estrangement was entirely put to rights. A grateful, whimsical, if slightly formal letter, dated December 18, 1897, helped to reëstablish the friendship in all its former heartiness.

My dear Teresita: You must have thought me very indifferent—to say the least—to your tremendous successes with our Concerto. I have meant to write every day—and if today had not been my birthday; consequently a holiday—I might have put it off again until tomorrow. The day I heard of your first playing it I myself was playing in Boston with Paur. I tried to imagine how you played it and did my best with my rough hands, and I really think it helped, for they gave me a laurel wreath. Truly I have been driven nearly crazy with work these last weeks so I beg you to pardon my delay in expressing thanks which are none the less sincere for being tardy. I go for a month's Western recitals in two weeks and have only just begun to practice for them—have not had time before. Added to all this poor Marian is have a wretched time, as one of our Boston friends, a lady—whose family all live in Kentucky, has just arrived in New York all alone and hopelessly insane. I telegraphed to her family and two doctors and nurses have full charge, still the shock to Marian was not the best thing in the world— So you see we have been in a state of confusion to say the least, and this late acknowledgement of your choosing my concerto for one of your many triumphs has some excuse. And the Concert Study!—Well, I can't help it—I detest the thing, though I have now to "ochs" on it myself. The concert tuner agrees with me. He says it is the only thing in my recitals that gives him work.(!) It's like beating carpets. Again pardon the delay—and levity of

Truly your<br>Edward MacDowell

Wolff immediately prepared to draw profit for coming European tours by publishing abroad news of Carreño's success in the United States. Jubilantly he wrote:

Avant tout laissez-moi vous dire, combien nous avons été heureux que la mer était une assez bonne mère pour vous de sorte que vous pouviez me télégrafier "right." Puis j'ai appris avec un profond contentement votre premier succès. Il parait qu'il a été le plus "très beaucoup," que l'on puisse avoir, et comme un tel premier succès décide tout, il est certain que votre tournée sera une suite de triomphes. . . . Je suis curieux d'apprendre comment la vie en Amerique vous plait maintenant. J'espère que pas trop bien—car nous vous considé-

Dec. 18. 1897

My dear Teresita

You must have thought me very indifferent - to say the least - as your tremendous success with our concerto - I have meant to write every day - and if today had not been my birthday; consequently a holiday - I might have even put it off again until "tomorrow". The day I heard of your first playing it - I myself was playing in Boston with Paur. I tried to imagine how you played it and did my best with my rough hands, and I really think it helped, for they gave me a laurel wreath. Truly - I have been driven nearly crazy with work these last weeks so I beg you to pardon my delay in expressing thanks which are none the less sincere for being tardy. I go for a months' Western recitals in two weeks and have only just began to practice for them - have had no time before - Added to all this poor Marian is having a wretched time, as one of our Boston friends, a lady - whose family all live in Kentucky, has just arrived in New York all alone and hopelessly insane - I telegraphed to her family, and two doctors and nurses have full charge; still the shock to Marian was not the best thing in the world - So you see, we have been in a state of confusion to say the least, and this late acknowledgement of your choosing my concerto for one of your many triumphs has some excuse. — And the Concert Study! — Well I can't help it - I detest the thing, though I have now to "ochs" on it myself — the Concert tuner agrees with me. He says it is the only thing in my recitals that gives him work (!) - It's like beating carpets - Again pardon the delay - and levity of

Yours E. W. A. MacDowell

*Letter from Edward MacDowell to Carreño*

rons comme citoyenne européenne maintenant, qui a seulement le droit de ramasser de temps en temps beaucoup de dollars en Amérique.

And he was right. Carreño could now look at America from a different perspective. Standing on the foundation built of her established success across the Atlantic she now towered in honored relief. No more traveling in uncomfortable, dirty day coaches in the company of pseudo-artists that seconded her only feebly, no more second-rate hotels and low fees, no more sitting up late after a concert to wash underwear and mend concert dresses that had been worn too often. Was she much happier now, she wondered, as she looked out upon the Avenue? She used to be so strong, so well. Now there were headaches and twinges of rheumatism to plague her. The doctors were not helpful, their unanimous advice a season of complete rest. Rest indeed! She thought of her children in their expensive schools, of her apartment at 2,500 m. a year, of Bertha Pechstein's last bill of 7,000 m., of Fräulein Krahl, Josephine, and the two other servants. Carreño laughed. It struck her ears disagreeably, and she cut it abruptly short, reaching instead for the Russian cigarette, which helped to make life tolerable.

Then, quickly she turned from her own troubles to those of others. How might she help poor, pathetic, patient Arturo!— her eyes glowed with a gentler light. And dear Mrs. Watson who, gifted as she was, really should be playing in public instead of teaching day after day. She must find her a good manager. When Henriette knocked at the door, Carreño's spirits were so far restored that she volunteered to give her a lesson next morning and suggested a shopping expedition.

Almost immediately after its promising beginning Carreño sensed that all was not well with the tour. Aronson had written her that he had contracts for more than thirty engagements. When she arrived there were only twenty-three. Moreover, he had scheduled her first recital in the hall of the Waldorf Hotel where major concerts, such as she was contracted to give, did not habitually take place. That in itself was contrary to the bargain. When after a concert the fee was not forthcoming, dissatisfaction reached the breaking point. Evidently Aronson, if overflowing with good intention, had insufficient capital. Knowing that the Knabe Piano Company had guaranteed the contract, she did not hesitate to make this firm responsible. Another impresario must be appointed.

Acting for R. E. Johnston, J. W. Cochran now became the personal representative of Carreño's tour. He was a young man not without experience in the managerial field. His genial nature and sense of humor appealed to Carreño as much as the fact that he idolized her. So without too much apparent confusion the concerts went on as planned.

In Boston, still the arbiter of all things musical, the *Herald* writes: "She returns to us more stately of presence, more imposing of manner, than when she was here last, and at the same time a more deep, serious, and matured artist, ranking with the best in her art." To the Boston *Gazette* "Madame Carreño has reached a position where criticism is superfluity. In the matter of technique, in the largeness of style, adaptation of means to end, fine taste, and self reserve, she is the finished artist." The Boston *Times* gives the final vote of confidence: "Among the few virtuosal triumphs which this generation is likely to remember might be cited the first concerts given here by Rubinstein, Bülow, d'Albert, and Paderewski. To this short list it is now our pleasure to add Teresa Carreño." The Philadelphia *North American* agrees:

Every promise of her earlier years has been more than fulfilled. No such piano playing has been heard in Philadelphia for years, without forgetting the wonderful performance of Adele aus der Ohe upon the occasion of Tschaikowsky's visit to this city, when she played that composer's first Concerto from manuscript, and broke her health in the effort which it cost her. As for that gentle genius, I. Paderewski, he is in quite another class.

Chicago had every right to claim a major part in making Carreño famous, and it was there that the greatest ovation of the entire tour awaited her. The criticism of the *Chronicle* sounds like one of 1863:

The audience shouted like politicians at a political convention. The women's shrill sopranos sounded above the hoarse roars of their escorts' approval, and they split their gloves and blistered their hands in the wildness of their enthusiasm. When from sheer exhaustion they could applaud no more, the tumult even increased by the stamping of feet, and hundreds of white handkerchiefs fluttered from balcony and parquet. The Campanella trill was the event of the evening. At the close the people mounted the stage, hugged and kissed her, and someone proposed three cheers for Carreño which were given with a will. Then two hundred people started in procession for the green-room to obtain souvenirs.

Aside from the exigencies of a performing artist's daily life, aside even from the longing for her two little girls ill at home with the measles, there was another ever-stalking dread. It had lurked in hiding during the days of happiness with d'Albert, and finally came to light in print before the final break in 1895:

One of the husbands of the pianistic bird of brilliant plumage, Teresa Carreño-Sauret-Tagliapietra-d'Albert, is on the war-path after his fickle spouse. The enraged baritone declares he will go to Europe and, if need be, take by force his two children from the custody of their beautiful mother, who, rumor asserts, is fonder of her present husband, Eugen d'Albert, than of any predecessors. Tagliapietra, called Tag popularly, is not an amiable person when aroused, and it looks as if there were a storm brewing for the Carreño household when the opera baritone's operatic season is ended.

The storm had been temporarily sidetracked, but during Carreño's visit to the United States it again gathered force. Tag's special grievance was that Carreño had left him with several months of rent and of installments on their furniture unpaid. Hardly landed in America she was subjected to the annoyance of letter after letter asking for the $1,000 which he believed to be his due, although it was Carreño who had always paid all their common expenses. He refused to take part in an interview in the presence of a lawyer, but gradually the letters strike a threatening note, and his demands increase to $2,000 for founding a "Singing Conservatory." Again he appeals to her sympathy: "With you rests the balance of my old age, just as you had the youth of my life," he declares theatrically. "I would come personally to see you, but I am so poorly clothed that I would feel humiliated." When he proposed serving her with a summons, it was time to take precautionary measures. A detective was engaged as a protection from possible attack, and the time of Carreño's sailing for Europe was kept secret. Even the elder MacDowells and Juan Buitrago, who were to spend the summer in Berlin and Pertisau, took passage with her on the *Saale* under assumed names, sailing May 18, 1897. In September comes the final echo of a long-surmounted past. Tagliapietra's demands have diminished:

In my life with you, you were always ready to help strange people. I don't understand why you should not help a man who has lived fifteen years with you, a man from whom you had three children, a man who only claims what he has spent for you, at last, a man who, outside of family quarrels, has treated you with respect and consideration. I only ask you for $1500 to be able to open a Conservatory, and make my living.

It is no longer affection he allegedly seeks, but money to prevent suicide. This constant persecution might have gone on for years had he not found another solution for his difficulties.

Half a year later he married Margaret Townsend, daughter of a once wealthy lawyer, and passes out of the picture as far as Carreño is concerned. Such artists as Joseffy and Edwin Booth frequented the Sunday evening salons of the Townsends which, in the eyes of conservative New York society, were a shocking desecration of the Sabbath. The house at 343 West Thirty-fourth Street gradually lost caste as business crept up, and as the Townsend fortune dwindled took on a shabby, forlorn look. After the death of Mr. Townsend it was sold as a boarding house in which Tag and his wife continued to share a back bedroom downstairs. It was their little dog "Frolic" who on April 12, 1921, announced in low moaning howls that the once-so-colorful career of his master had ended.

BERLIN 1897

*Teresa Carreño with her Children Giovanni and Teresita
Tagliapietra, Eugenia and Hertha d'Albert*

In every way this highly important season had fulfilled its purpose for Carreño, who might well feel gratified that she had won in the United States the right to be compared only with the greatest of her field, irrespective of sex. Nevertheless, she was not reluctant to abandon it for the atmosphere of Germany more congenial to the artist. Still something of a Yankee at heart, she loved America, but no longer wished to live there. This trip had settled that question definitely.

On the way back Carreño had time to reread the weekly letters that Teresita wrote from school. One brought the tears to her eyes:

Do you remember how lovely Coswig looked in summer? Once, the time d'Albert was in America, you sent me out of the *kleine Salon* in the evening in the garden to pick a few leaves to put in your letter to him. . . . Do you remember how we made *la ronde* in every room in the house in the evening, when the painters had gone?

When Puppi was born we used to lay her in the cradle on the porch stoop, and I sat by her, and kept the humming bees and flies away with a Jaeger handkerchief. And how we used to get up early and Spargelstechen [dig asparagus]. And later we used to pick strawberries and eat them with sugar and cream for dinner.

She recalls that they had their meals outdoors either on the wide lawn, or on the little platform over the ice cellar, or under a beautiful pear tree, and sometimes in the little summerhouse, or on the porch in front of the *kleine Salon,* and when d'Albert was in America they went to the circus or the zoo every single Saturday. "And then how we used to water the vegetables and the flowers and all that, all together barefoot, running around with our hair loose, and with a long hose in our hands. That must have been a sight for other people, too funny for anything."

She herself brought up a problem, suggested a new line of development, which might have resulted in a happier future for a child of her temperament. Teresita had become absorbed in the study of science. Quite rightly she feared the surplus of pianists, as much as her own nervousness in playing before others, dreading comparison with her great mother. She did not wish to become "an old piano teacher." Instead music might better be her avocation. She would like to go to Karlsruhe to study science there, were it not too much of a sacrifice for her mother. Not minding a mixture of languages she writes in April: "I love *Wissenschaft* so much as you have no idea. Everything is so logicle. Think of Mathematics, what grand logic it contends. Oh! [and this is reminiscent of the melodramatic tone of her father's letters] . . . if I could only serve the greatest of all Gods, *Wissenschaft!*" Teresita's solicitude for her mother is unaffected. She is puzzled that Carreño comes home sooner than planned. "Has it anything to do with that man I am obliged to call Father? Is it because the agents have cheated you like so many times before? I have cried so much and for the first time I have truly felt the real seriousness of your *Beruf*. Seldom tears were spilt so free from *Egoismus*."

Teresita was allowed to leave school to welcome her mother in Berlin. Science was forgotten. This may have been a major mistake. Carreño considered Teresita's progress in piano playing so remarkable that, instead, she sent her back to school to work doubly hard at the piano.

R. E. Johnston meanwhile was doing some calculating. He barely gave Carreño time to reach home before suggesting plans for another tour in America. He explains: "You see, I am taking no pianist, as I prefer to wait for the great pianist, not because she is such a great pianist, but because she is the best fellow, and the best lady to do business with that I ever encountered in the happy experience of a business association." Carreño loses no time in replying. Hers are no uncertain terms. She is willing to consider a tour of not less than eighty concerts at $500 each, clear of all expenses for two people. She will play either Knabe, Chickering, or Steinway, preferably Steinway. The contract, made with R. E. Johnston and J. W. Cochran, is to be guaranteed by the piano house.

In a long letter to Carrie Reed Carreño takes time to explain her sudden sailing back to Germany. She attributes it to her homesickness for the children, to the fact that Aachen was expecting her to take part in the music festival of the lower Rhine, and lastly to the menace of Tag. After her concert in Northampton the day before leaving she barely had time to reach the boat. On she rambles of her summer, her ill health, her hard work. Then she gives a forecast of the coming season, beginning on October 10 with a Philharmonic Concert in Berlin. From then on she is to travel through Germany, Austria, Hungary, Holland, and perhaps England before Christmas, then to Russia

with the Good Lord's help. And I begin to feel very weary of it all. I just long for a good rest, and yet, I presume, that if I got it, I would not know what to do with my life, after having worked all my life as I have. It is because I can't get it that I want it. Human all over! [And she begs Carrie to write often] Don't forget what an unhappy woman I am in reality, and in spite of all the glory, and all I may have, that my true and only happiness, besides my children and my art, is the love of those I love. . . .

From Mrs. Watson Carreño hears that the "Teresita Waltz" "has become almost as much of a universal favorite as Paderewski's Minuet at one time."

Carreño expected the same integrity from her managers that she offered them in all her own dealings. Her stand on any matter was always definite, and her rules for keeping her prestige up were simple. Never would she play in any town for a smaller fee than the one she received there before for a similar engagement, neither would she accept a call to play in a concert to replace another artist, even though it had cost her on that account a last opportunity to play the "D minor Concerto" of Rubinstein under his own leadership in Cologne the year before his death. Nor would she tolerate that untruths be printed about her. She did not hesitate, disagreeable as it was, to sue a New York journal for libelous remarks made against her, a suit later settled for cash out of court and followed by public retraction and a laudatory biographical article. On the other hand she valued the favorable repercussion in Germany of her successful season in the United States. "To disappear enhances" was as true for one side of the Atlantic as for the other.

But although she could show the world to others through her music vividly tinted as if through polaroid glass, her own sky was long drained of color. Life through much tasting had lost its flavor. Even a king or two in the audience was only a tame incident. The music itself mattered, and would have mattered more, if there were more leisure for practice. Even visiting new countries was scarcely thrilling with no more time at her disposal than to drive around the city. She submitted to official calls and receptions just as she allowed herself to be richly dressed in a manner befitting a person of her prominence. Happy from the heart she could only be with her children, and a very few intimate friends, preferably old friends whose loyalty had stood the test. There were men that would have liked to marry her, who could have freed her from financial cares. Carreño was not tempted.

ONCE again after an insufficient period of relaxation in Pertisau the winter season took its course. The "Concert Étude" of MacDowell and his "Concerto" found a place upon her programs again. In one of her own concerts with orchestra Carreño chose to play three concerti, the "Emperor Concerto" of Beethoven, the "Capriccio Brillante" of Mendelssohn, her friend of long ago, and the "Second MacDowell Concerto" toward which there seemed to be a definite change of heart. Otto Taubmann felt that she reached

the full height of her accomplishment in the interesting and valuable MacDowell *Concerto*. The very piquant *Scherzo* had to be repeated. That this *Concerto*, although treated symphonically throughout, yet furnishing the artist with so remarkably grateful if difficult and taxing a problem, has been so little noticed by pianists is striking, the more so because a superabundance of such musically worthwhile and pianistically challenging works of this kind does not exist.

The field of chamber music which Carreño had entered with her own composition proved to be an outlet that was to delight her increasingly. With d'Albert as with Sauret she had explored the intimacies of musical give and take. When Julius Klengel, noted cellist of Leipzig, asked her to play the "Sinding Quintette" with the men of his group, she accepted joyfully. In compliment her "Quartette" also had place on the program. At a later concert of the Halir Quartette Carreño again appeared, taking part in the "Sonata" of Mrs. H. H. A. Beach for violin and piano. Another pleasure awaited her. For the sixtieth-anniversary celebration in honor of Max Bruch she appeared together with Josef Hofmann in Bruch's "Fantasie," op. 11, for two pianos.

To Russia, to England, and home again the season unreeled itself. The days succeeded each other like variations on a more and more hackneyed theme. Wherever travels might take her the routine was similar. Arriving at her destination with the faithful shadow, her maid, and not forgetting to count the manifold pieces of *Handgepäck,* she at once made for the usually handsome but unhomelike suite reserved by Wolff in the best hotel of whatever the city might be. If the hour were early, a continental breakfast was served in her room. There, enveloped in her long-treasured red wrapper, she could read her letters. The blue-gray aura of the first cigarette of the morning made her feel less strange. Soon it was time to notify the local manager of her arrival, to thank the piano house for setting up a practice instrument in her parlor. There might be a rehearsal before luncheon or a walk to the hall to make the acquaintance of an unfamiliar concert grand. Nothing was permitted to interfere with the game of solitaire that ushered in the siesta. Later official guests, perhaps the mayor of the city or the heads of musical organizations, were received with the gracious remoteness that helped to shorten their visit. Only a few friends and business associates were invited to stay for tea if Carreño happened to be in the mood.

Then came the ceremony of the day, a rite which she would

concede to no other person, that of arranging her hair for the concert. In preparation the triptych mirror was flanked by twin candles. Hair pins in graduated sizes lay in military rows before it. Gradually her hair, piled high in a simple knot, took on the look of a finely grained surface, shading from onyx black to the white of marble, each strand seeming to come to rest in unintended rightness, even to the willful wisp that had escaped to curl itself tight at the nape of the neck.

The long-trained dress, be it of brocade and lace, of silk-velvet trimmed with heavy gold braid, or of elaborately embroidered chiffon, had the complicated machinery worthy of a modern motor. To put it together was the maid's affair, a task over which she perspired more than Carreño in a whole week of concerts. Putting on matching slippers that seemed too small to carry her considerable weight, Cinderella was ready for the ball.

She stepped into the carriage with the precision of a business magnate going to his office. During the concert nobody was allowed to approach her. She was alone with her music in a world that had no room even for the thought of her children or of herself. Many a time she played, and played her best, when an attack of influenza had sent her temperature up to 101 degrees. Nothing but the serious illness of a child could make her cancel a recital. At all costs she would keep faith with her audience. Then after the last encore, most often the "Teresita Waltz," the maid quickly threw a heavy embroidered shawl about her shoulders, while Carreño made ready to shake hands with those who felt impelled to express their gratitude in words, but often became tongue-tied in her presence. With ready understanding of the young students who hopefully held out programs and pencils for her autograph, she smiled winningly, asking kindly, "Where shall I put it, my dear?" Then she scrawled her name with a flourish, while her eye already welcomed the next in line, a man who put his admiration into words consistent with his gold watch chain and carefully pressed swallow-tail. Carreño seemed to grow taller as she passed him on with a formal: "You are very kind indeed, very kind." Then, recognizing a familiar face, she opened her arms wide. "My dear, my dear, how are you, and how are your precious children? You must come and see me tomorrow before I leave, and tell me all about everything. Did you really think I played well?" Then to her manager: "Your hall has admirable acoustics. I am always so glad to play here for you. Every detail is so carefully planned, and such a large audience! You are kind to take so much trouble, very kind."

A little girl attracted her attention in the background: "And who are you, my dear?" Shyly she came nearer. "I just wanted to look at you, please. I play the piano too." "Well, my dear, then we are colleagues! Marie, please take this young artist's name and address. I want to send her my photograph for her studio. You must let me know when you play in Berlin, my dear, and remember that nobody becomes an artist without hard work. It is not an easy life. Good-night, my dear. I see in your eyes that you are earnest. You have good piano hands. With courage and perseverance you will succeed. Good-night, my dear and Auf Wiedersehen!" A radiant child flew away, taking with her something more uplifting than lessons to urge her on. Finally for the last time Carreño had said a patient, "You are very kind." People were still standing about in groups: "Marie, my coat, if you please! You will excuse me if I leave you now. It is late and tomorrow I must play again. Thank you very much. You are very kind. I will come again." Preceded by ushers bearing flowers, a large bunch in her own arms, and followed by Marie, also heavily laden, Carreño made her way to the waiting carriage.

Back in the hotel Marie unhooked the gown. Madame liked to have it done quickly, for now came the culmination of the day. Another concert was wiped off the slate. At last she could relax in the comfort of her negligée for a midnight dinner. No other meal aroused such an appetite. To be invited to share it was to know Carreño in her most captivating moments. From oysters to ices with a bottle of champagne to raise her spirits she scintillated with humorous anecdotes, and unburdened her heart in reminiscence now sad, now gay. A last cigarette over a last game of solitaire and one more concert day had passed. The next might be different in setting, different in detail, But from now on her concerts were in general but the neutral background for the weaving of the patterns of her children's lives, of the lives of a few close friends. What happened to her personally ceased to be of first importance, except as it affected them. Skies were gay or gray, as she was well or ill to work for them, as they lived up to her desires for them, or failed to do so, as she was able or impotent to help. There was within her undefined a loneliness for a companion with whom she could enjoy, could advise, could forget.

For the summer of 1898 Carreño chose a new setting in Schwaz near Innsbruck. A modest and rather inconvenient castle, Schlösschen Friedheim, was her home. But there too was a deep blue lake encircled by mountains. There she could walk alone or accompanied by adoring followers. With much of her old gusto she joined in their nonsense, even played for their dancing. She allowed herself to be photographed in their midst. But into the privacy of her studio nobody, not even the children, intruded. There for hours at a time she practiced, taught, suffered, wrote, and puffed in peace. The happiness of the household depended upon the mood in which she emerged from her refuge. Eyes looked up anxiously. Would she suggest an excursion into the mountains, or as they dreaded, would she complain: "I am not feeling at all well," and disappear to have tea in miserable solitude.

Carreño's desk was as always piled high. A conservatory in Berlin made her a flattering offer to join its staff. This she declined. In one way or another she was constantly being reminded of d'Albert. He insisted upon biweekly reports concerning the health of their children. Meetings were arranged and much to Carreño's relief, postponed again. There were annoying conferences between his lawyers and hers. Carreño was human enough to be elated at the rumor that he was not playing

as well as before. Some critics even went so far as to suggest
that he marry less often and give the piano too a temporary
rest.

Then there was always a manager to scold for real or fancied
omissions. When she angrily complained that the time of an
important rehearsal in Dresden had not been imparted to her,
Hermann Wolff shook off the drops of her displeasure with one
of his tactful and merry letters.

Oh, mignonne, Reine Veuve, Impératrice-Pianiste, si vous ne saviez
nieux par cœur vos concertos que vos lettres, vous ne vous appelleriez
ni Teresa ni Carreño. Fixez vos yeux miraculeux sur la lettre du 24
mars. Vous y trouverez le passage classique et immortel: Répétition
générale—7 h. Ni Schiller, ni Goethe se sont exprimés—je connais
leurs œuvres—d'une façon plus nette et plus poétique. Répétition
générale! Comme c'est très bien dit et plein de charme. Aucun doute
de quoi il s'agit, tandis que en Faust (surtout dans la seconde partie)
vous trouvez des endroits nébuleux et beaucoup moins clairs.

7 h., naturellement du soir. Kant, le philosophe de Königsberg,
l'aurait probablement ajouté. Mais l'agent poète, s'adressant à l'artiste,
supprime ce mot, laissant à la fantaisie de la pianisticule de paraître à
7 h. du matin.

Et puis comme un petit Capriccio, comme un Intermezzo charmant
Fernow vous a chanté dans une autre lettre une admirable mélodie.
L'on désire une petite répétition a 1 h., ce qui confirmait de nouveau
l'inestimable répétition générale du soir. Conclusion: Pardonnez-
moi d'être le sacrifice d'un petit oubli de votre côté. Comme je l'adore,
ce côté!

TIME always passed on eager feet in Germany and spun itself out with nostalgic drag in America. On the day after Christmas, 1898, Carreño tore herself away once again to cross the ocean on the *Trave*. Almost everything but the sea ran smoothly. The Chickering piano house became her official manager with J. W. Cochran as personal agent. In its final form the contract, if it did not fulfill her demands, assured her of a larger income than before, and of a third again as many concerts. Accompanied by her maid and Chickering's most reliable tuner, Mr. Ruhenbeck, Carreño traveled to the Far West. She did not easily let circumstances upset her, not even when a snowslide held her train stalled in the mountains of Colorado for two whole days, preventing her from giving her first concert in San Francisco.

Instead of considering her own plight she went to see if all were well in the day coach ahead. As always the children attracted her, and she at once picked out the dirtiest and hungriest little girl. The mother had other children, and was glad to be relieved of one of them, so Carreño carried her prize off triumphantly to her stateroom, undressed and bathed her, washed her clothes and put her to bed on the sofa. What did it matter if the huge reception planned in her honor would have to be given up! For the moment nothing could be done about that; she might as well make the best of it. Of all the interludes of the trip this was the happiest. Not so for the tuner. Carreño, unmindful of the blizzard, sent him off into the town of Salida to buy the supplies she needed for her little protégée.

This arduous season had one great compensation. It reëstablished her friendship with Edward MacDowell on its old footing. The "D minor Concerto" was everywhere so well received that she thought of resurrecting the earlier one in "A minor" as well. Before making a change, which in her opinion would improve the first movement, she wrote asking the composer's permission, to which he replied in a droll letter dated March 2, 1899:

Respected Valkyrie and Grandmother: Why did you consult me about that streak of "light" you let in on that bit of dramatic depravity in the first part of my Concerto? Now that you ask me, I must admit I intended that passage to have a kind of "Atlas with a sore back" effect. I have just played it over in major and it was like dosing Atlas with vin Mariani. So there you are!—Seriously—I had planned the whole passage on the broad line of steady development from dolce to feroce—I think the triumph of the few measures in major disturbs the steadiness of the progression. Of course I can see how effective the new bit of color would be—and—you shouldn't have asked me! There are lots of things in the concerto I myself would not do as they are written (I mean of course technically and in regard to expression marks) and would give anything to hear you play it. As you know, there is nothing more despairing than trying to put certain things in black and white and this old concerto has never been revised by me since it first came out. You certainly must do wonders with it and whatever you do will be right, because it will come from the heart.—If you ask me a plain question about notes however—I've got to tell the truth, and I must admit the passage in question has a minor pug nose instead of a major straight one.—I have been studying your dates and am wondering if you will be in N. Y. between Pittsburgh and Boston (March 14–17), or between Buffalo and Pittsburgh (10–14). If so, do let me know so that I can make confessions about the concerto.—They shan't hamper you in the smallest particular— No need to say thank you!! Your faithful Grandson—

Mutual respect and modest independence speak from this very characteristic letter of Carreño's one-time pupil.

ON May 16, 1899, Carreño left for home on the S.S. *Lahn*. London claimed her for concerts in June. July was spent in Kolberg that the children might have sea bathing. Then again the homelike gates of Villa Heigl in Pertisau opened to receive her, closing to shut out the world. Carreño was free to face her personal problems. It was appalling to find them more complicated than ever. Where should she begin? To whom should she turn for advice? Chief among her obligations was always Teresita, at home since Easter. Musically she was developing astonishingly under the guidance of Josef Hofmann. Carreño was proud to admit that even she herself could not make a composition as quickly her own as Teresita. There were no difficulties that with perseverance could not easily be conquered by her gifted child.

Released from the restrictions of school, which she detested, Teresita expected to be allowed to enter unhampered upon her rights as an adult. It irked her to find that home life too demanded concessions. Learning how to manage a household was an unthinkable bore to her who had not a practical thought in her mind, quite aside from the chaos it created within that household. This tangent was quickly abandoned. Fräulein Krahl took over the tangled reins and jangling nerves were soon quieted, but, as long as Teresita was at home, never for long. When mother and daughter were together there was thunder in the air. After open clashes between them the situation always returned to the *status quo ante*. Carreño felt inadequate to deal with this child, well as she understood her, and she saw that preparing Teresita for a productive career would continue to be as difficult as compressing quicksilver into permanent shape, as teaching a darting hummingbird to plane like a sea gull. In spite of school, in spite of the remonstrance of a too anxious mother, Teresita remained undisciplined, unaccountable, more often disagreeable than friendly. She blamed everybody from God, in whom she had no real belief, to fate and her mother, the most convenient target. Money in a depression was not less stable than her own sense of values. A new dress, the gratification of a wish, could make Teresita angelically charming, when to contradict her might easily cause a family tornado. Trying to appeal to her reason was as useless as attempting to make a fingerprint on water. Carreño was in despair. She knew herself to be too temperamental to deal rightly with a daughter in whom she saw so much of herself. If only Teresita had had a wise father like her own! Finally it seemed inadvisable for both to live in the same apartment. Teresita was sent to a friend, for the moment a good solution. The thought flashed into her mother's mind more than once. "I wonder what Arturo would say." When she had failed, he had always been able to manage Teresita and Giovanni. His ideas were so sane, so practical. If only she could ask Arturo's advice!

Carreño carefully examined the receipts of her recent American tour. For a moment she dreamed of a villa of her own—it might be wise to buy this very one—where she could eventually live the unpretentious life of a private citizen. She looked forward more and more eagerly to the time when her children would be self-supporting. With a wrench she called herself back to reality. The landlord had raised the rent but she could not bear the thought of moving. She would write to Cochran that the next American tour must last eight months at the shortest, remembering also to remind him never again to allow those obnoxious three-sheet posters to advertise her as "the lioness of the piano." A lioness indeed. She a trained circus animal! It reminded her of lyceum circuits, of stuffy back bedrooms, of dirty, airless halls that smelled of beer and cowboys. Last year, whenever she saw these posters—and who could miss them—she had paid a man to tear them down.

This done and sealed with an emphatic thump, she turned to write a letter reprimanding Giovanni for playing his mouth organ in study hall. "The little Devil!" And he nearly old enough to leave school! What next? Her head ached. She would have tea in the music room alone; she would give no more lessons today. Those baths in Italy might help her rheumatism. But then what would all the students do who had spent their precious money to come to her here? She turned to the piano, her best medicine, and soon was lost in the Schumann "Fantasia," searching for new tone effects, for deeper verities.

THE fall of 1899 came almost before she was aware of it, and long before she was ready duty like an eagle was carrying her in clutching talons through Germany and Russia and back again before Christmas. She felt inwardly repaid to play in Europe again, even though financially she earned one third as much as in America.

Among the unpaid bills lay a communication from the Court of Württemberg. In return for two complimentary concerts His Majesty, the King, would be pleased to honor her with the Title: *"Pianist of the Royal Chamber."* Carreño smiled wanly; but this burdensome honor could not well be refused, and must be correctly answered. Not until she had made three drafts of her acceptance was she satisfied that all the endings were right and the word order could not be misinterpreted or improved. She, by the authority of genius Royal Chamber Musician to the Court of God and Beethoven, could not help finding all this a little silly. The comment in her diary on December 4 is an eloquent "Ouf!"

Christmas with the children was over. The new year 1900 with its new demands was upon her. Life moved too swiftly for recording. It was as if the cities passed her by while she remained standing. Each concert was brushed away with the same satisfaction that a schoolgirl takes in snipping off the heads of rows of paper dolls to mark the days before vacation. Automatically she followed her approved routine, playing for better, for worse, in sickness or in health, always insisting upon her best though caring little what the critics wrote. In spite of the pleasurable memories that almost every concert brought, she continued to find deepest comfort in the inscription a king of old had caused to be engraved upon his ring: "This too shall pass."

Carreño's friends saw the danger of strain without letup. They warned against a summer in its way as taxing as the winter, and advised against the load of teaching, rewarding as she found it. It promised a certain kind of immortality in a too transient world.

This particular summer there were other serious burdens to carry. Teresita, whose Latin temperament felt itself constricted in the stays of Berlin decorum, had taken it upon herself to go to Paris, asking posthumous permission to stay there after she was safely installed in a *pension*. Carreño was obliged to approve, and she at once made arrangements to have Teresita continue her studies with her good friend Maurice Moszkowski. Meeting her upon the street one day this witty gentleman doffed his hat and sang his "good-morning Madame Carreño," even to the turn over the n, according to musical tradition, much to their joint amusement.

Worry over Teresita weighed lightly balanced against the sudden illness of Hertha, her baby. Local doctors failed to check the fever constantly at a peak of high danger; authorities consulted by telegram were not more helpful. In desperation Carreño turned to a Berlin specialist in the nature-cure methods advocated by d'Albert. For a fabulous sum she persuaded him to visit her child for the single hour of time at his disposal. According to Fräulein Krahl the simple remedy of a clay pack hardening through the internal heat, drew out the fever and saved the life of the child. Night after night the mother watched and helped. For the period of convalescence Eugenia and Hertha were sent to the higher altitude of Merano, while Carreño, completely exhausted, recovered as she might among her duties. It was not the best of ways to prepare for a lengthy tour of the United States.

Teresita, meanwhile, found freedom to do as she liked in Paris very congenial. On the whole she made good use of her time and even gave a successful concert in Paris at the Exposition under a committee headed by Camille Saint-Saëns. In order to avoid all comparison with her mother, she appeared simply under the name T. C. Tagliapietra.

Before leaving for America Carreño made a special journey to Paris, thinking in a sudden burst of pride to take Teresita to New York, where she herself could give her lessons and for experience send her pupils. But Teresita preferred to stay where she was in the semi-Bohemian atmosphere that suited her so much better.

MR. COCHRAN had made his arrangements with the care born of real devotion to a cause in which he fervently believed. His was the full responsibility, which was materially lessened by the backing of Steinway & Sons. The tour began to unwind itself at first without incident. It took her to the Middle West, Canada, and back, then southward to New Orleans and Savannah, from where she sailed for Havana on the S.S. *Olivette*.

One of her best ideas—at least so she was convinced—had been thwarted by a too practical manager. It had pained her to see Arturo Tagliapietra patiently trudging through the streets of New York in the interest of a typewriter company, always uncomplaining, earning a sum upon which another would have found it impossible to exist. His loyalty was touching, and she felt herself in gratitude bound to him who had insisted that she take the decisive step of her life. What a good advance agent to send to Cuba and Mexico, thought Carreño! Mr. Cochran thought otherwise, going himself instead.

In Havana, the scene of a great childhood triumph, the reception to "La Duse del Piano" was as effusive but not so universal as it should have been. A ball given by the Governor as well as the great heat was brought forward in excuse. One journal stated the case frankly: "Music in Cuba is an industry not an art," and rather overstrained his imagination in comparing Carreño "in her dress of black gauze ornamented with gold sequins" to Wagner's Brünnhilde. Another critic thought that the augmented prices might have been to blame for the empty boxes and adds: "But who could buy a bottle of champagne for so little?"

Carreño herself in a letter to Carrie Reed preferred to disregard this feature of the trip. As usual every concert must appear to be a success, every event a happy one. She wrote:

The heat was so intense that I was quite overcome by it, and all I could do when people gave me an hour or two of respite was to lie down and gasp for air and breath. It was simply awful! I gave three concerts, and to this moment I do not know where I found sufficient energy to play. Well, I did, and I had a good time while I was there. All the old friends of my childhood, those still there, came to greet me in the most kind and loving manner. . . .

Her best send-off was the comment of the Havana *Post:*

Although her own magnetic personality is ever present to her listeners, she herself forgets it, and loses herself in the spirit of her author, bringing out his national characteristics, his temperament, his school, and her artistic conscience is so keen that she takes no liberties whatsoever with text or time. I was amazed to see that such effects could be accomplished by such legitimate means, but what an artist it takes to do it!

The trip to Vera Cruz on the once-good ship *Seneca*—her engines had been condemned, she no longer carried freight, nor did she carry insurance—began well enough, although she rose so high in the water that six feet of the copper bottom showed above the surface. The first hours were spent by Carreño and her manager counting boxes full of coin, the receipts of the Havana concerts, and trying to translate them into dollars and cents. It was a difficult game. After the Spanish-American War Cuban currency was in a state of chaos. In the boxes were coins of many lands, among them an oxidized Spanish doubloon, which Carreño bought to keep as a *porte bonheur*. The estimate had finally been reached and punctuated with much laughter, when a stiff Norther blew up, sending the *Seneca* pitching and rolling about in crazy gyrations. At the climax of the storm Carreño sent for Mr. Cochran. The maid lay in one berth, an hysterical Carreño in the other. She was no longer the little girl of the *Washington* whose faith comforted others. "I shall never see my children again," she moaned. Mr. Cochran himself was not sure that she would, but he managed to appear confident, and soon, danger forgotten, they were again joking with each other. The letter to Carrie Reed continues:

It took us a whole week to make a voyage that should have lasted two days, and all owing to the mismanagement of the steamship company. To begin with the steamer was an old, rickety, incapable concern, and so we had to stop at two Mexican ports, El Progreso and Campeche. It happened to be Ash Wednesday when we arrived at the first, so the natives felt that their religious conscience absolutely forbade their working on that or the following day. . . . After Campeche we had one of the worst storms that it has been my bad luck to experience at sea. How seasick I was, my darling! No name can be given to that torture, . . . and on the 31st of the month I hope to be in Chicago where I play on the first of April. (I wonder who will be fooled on that day, the public or I!)

In Mexico City, where Carreño had never been before, she found at her disposal a bungalow nestling in a sweet-smelling garden. Her coming was considered not only a musical but a social event. The Minister of Finance under the Diaz administration wished to entertain her at dinner, thus honoring the daughter of a former colleague of Venezuela. The function began at eleven at night and, interrupted by speeches and toasts, lasted interminably. Carreño had ample time to examine the elaborately embroidered tablecloth, the rows of heavy silver *épergnes* filled with flowers and tropical fruits. While they were still at table the clock struck half past four.

One of her concerts was given for the Jockey Club, after which a deputation presented her with a silver wreath resting upon a white satin pillow. Carreño accepted it with a polite speech in Spanish. Then turning to Mr. Cochran, she wailed *sotto voce:* "What am I going to do with it? I could sleep on the pillow, but no matter how famous I become, my head will never be large enough for that wreath." Until she had brought it safely to her own fireside, it seemed as if she were doing nothing but paying duty on that particular white elephant.

On the morning of her first concert in Mexico City Carreño accompanied her manager to the Teatro del Renacimiento to become familiar with the piano. It was apparent that the stage had not been cleaned for many days, and Carreño gave strict orders that the platform be thoroughly scrubbed before the performance. True to Mexican form the work was done at the last moment, and the stage was still wet when Carreño swished out upon it. As she bowed acknowledgment after the first group of solos her foot slipped. She narrowly saved herself from falling, but at the expense of an ankle that began to swell even before she reached the wings, making her faint with pain. Mr. Cochran suggested giving up the concert. Carreño refused. Out she walked upon the stage as if nothing had happened. Nobody in the audience was aware that every step was agony. The concert took place to the last encore. The story of the mishap and of her stoicism, which Mr. Cochran shared in confidence with the press, did its part to increase her popularity—and her audiences. So captivated were the Mexicans that they suggested an additional benefit performance which would undoubtedly have brought huge returns. It meant, however, the cancellation of a date in a small California town, where the fee was correspondingly low. Rather than break faith with her commitments, Carreño gave up an opportunity she greatly coveted. Money was never allowed to be a primary consideration, but she turned her back with regret upon people that spoke her language and had made her feel at home.

In Nashville she proved again that with her the audience always came first. She was about to begin her concert—the hall was filled to the last seat—when the local manager burst into the room. His box-office receipts had been attached for failure to pay a printing bill of long standing. There was no money for the artist, there could be no concert. Carreño patted him reassuringly on the back. "These people have come in good faith to hear me, I will on no account disappoint them."

In Cincinnati, a tribute that thrilled her profoundly, the entire audience rose to its feet at the end of the concerto. Critics, having no other ground for fault-finding, called attention to Carreño's size which had visibly increased since her last appearance in America. Many seconded the wish of one who said aloud: "May her shadow grow less."

In every respect the journey went from one stormy ovation to another, reaching its climax in the New York farewell concert.

Flowers in profusion, encore after encore, and at last a reception
half an hour in length made her feel certain that she had not
yet worn her welcome out.

The tour was well over with a fair profit for both the manager and the artist. As the carriage bumped along through the
desolate streets of Hoboken toward the pier, Carreño was
hardly conscious of the German band on a corner playing its
homesick folk songs. She and her manager leaned back in deep
content. On the uncomfortable bench opposite Arturo sat
drooping. Just to make conversation Mr. Cochran turned to his
artist: "There is only one thing you still need, Madame! That
is a secretary. Arturo should make a capital one. Why don't you
smuggle him along in your trunk?" Carreño took up the suggestion. "That's an idea, Arturo! If you take the next boat I
will pay your expenses, and [this with a grand theatrical ges-
ture] you may name your own salary." Arturo's blue eyes
gleamed. "Do you really mean it, Teresita?" Still in the mood
of the game Carreño answered: "Of course I do," and tapping
him lightly on the shoulder with her umbrella she declaimed in
approved Valkyrie style: "I hereby knight you my secretary."
Then, as the carriage drew up at the pier she pointed to the
door: "Arise, Sir Secretary!" Surrounded by a swarm of friends
she promptly forgot all about Arturo standing modestly on the
fringe of the circle. As the S.S. *Maria Theresia,* her namesake,
pulled out, there he was jumping up and down like a puppet
on a string, until he reached the vanishing point. Carreño turned
away from the rail. Did he really think she meant it? Would
he come? She left it to fate and quickly lost herself in the happy
thought that soon she would be seeing her children. No matter
how seasick she might be, every chug of the engine was bringing her closer to them. Laden with the good returns of her
concerts—each one had brought from $300 to $600 to add to her
reserves—she could indeed look forward into a brighter future.

At home again her first problem was as always Teresita. On
her own initiative she had once more settled in Paris, ostensibly
studying and teaching, but according to all reports leading the

disorganized life that suited her so well. It was not unusual for Teresita, returning from some pleasurable jaunt, to find the passage blocked by a student whose lesson she had conveniently forgotten. Carreño knew something must be done, and done quickly. But what? "If Arturo were here, he would know," she thought, and then her attention centered upon Giovanni idly at home since Easter.

Herr Ansfeld, the director of Schnepfenthal, advised advanced schooling and suggested Eisenach. That Giovanni's career would not be an intellectual one was obvious. His gifts were above the average, his ambition far below. The violin, for which he showed talent, seemed to present the best solution. Carreño took it upon herself to investigate the possibilities of Eisenach. On her way there she was attracted by Friedrichroda. High in the Thüringerwald, it combined a variety of the walks she loved with the pure air necessary for Hertha's well-being. There too was ample accommodation for students. She rented one of its larger villas on the Schlossweg and returned to Berlin well satisfied. Much still remained to be done before leaving.

ONE morning very early—nobody was stirring—the sound of the doorbell awakened Josephine. Looking more than ever like a frightened rabbit, she tripped to answer it, hands folded, shoulders bent as if in constant prayer, and on the way she shook her head. "Poor Madame, these awful Germans have no respect for the hours of sleep. And she sleeps so lightly. What can they be wanting now?"

As she unchained, unlocked, and unbolted the door there stood a little man, his blond mustache and goatee disheveled, his trousers unpressed, but his eyes twinkling, as he held a warning finger to his lips. "If it isn't Mr. Arturo," beamed Josephine. Arturo whispered: "It is to be a surprise so big, you have no idea. You must help to hide me." Josephine in the spirit of the game scurried away for hot water and towels, while Arturo did the best he could to repair the ravages of a night in a German third-class compartment. His coat was frayed at the collar, his trousers worn at the knee. In spite of too evident poverty, there was a certain dapper neatness about him, and as he straightened his waistcoat, the mirror answered back: "Arturo, you might look worse!" Stowed away in the room that gave directly onto the dining room he waited with what patience his pounding heart could muster for the gathering of the family at breakfast time. Carreño in her voluminous wrapper finally took her seat at the coffee urn. She replied to her children's anxious glances: "No, I am not feeling at all well today. Perhaps it would be better to give up Friedrichroda. Those Italian baths, they say, are so good for rheumatism." The children looked aghast. Carreño suddenly became aware of Josephine by her side, wringing her hands nervously, standing with an air of perpetual apology, as if asking plenary indulgence for having been born. "What is it, Josephine?" Carreño sounded impatient, and Josephine's voice rose higher and higher: "Please, Madame, there is a very large package in the next room. The man said it is important. Will Madame be so kind as to look at it now, if you please?" Carreño frowned.

What fool of a person could have thought of putting it in there! She could not remember having ordered anything large and heavy. All at once the door opened, and framed within it stood Arturo, his eyes shining points of sky blue. Forgotten was the rheumatism as Carreño enveloped her *ex*-brother-in-law in a hug of welcome. Strange that she hadn't noticed before how fine a day it was! The family barometer took a miraculous turn upward. Yes, they would go to Friedrichroda.

In a thousand little ways Arturo knew how to make himself useful. Only a week and it seemed as if he had always been a member of the household. The little room at the right of the entrance became his office. There tirelessly he made order in the business files and worked at his German so that one day he might be able to answer the telephone. Carreño sent him on the delicate mission of bringing Teresita home from Paris, where she had gone, again on her own venture, after a passably successful concert tour in Sweden. Tactfully suggesting a trip to Italy to visit her father's family, Arturo succeeded in enticing her by that roundabout way back to Berlin.

To Giovanni he appealed through their common love for taking long bicycle rides, and their friendship was cemented over the chessboard. Arturo was adept at the game. That he was careful to the point of fussiness, that nobody could pack as neatly as he, that no task was too difficult or too insignificant for him if it was she who wanted it done, Carreño soon discovered. Fräulein Krahl was the only one displeased by his coming. Meanwhile the atmosphere of the summer colony in Friedrichroda was saturated with gaiety. Even Teresita, preparing for her first long concert tour, was amenable to her mother's teaching.

BEFORE it was time to leave Friedrichroda Carreño had come to a momentous decision. Arturo must be invested with higher authority than that of uncle or secretary. His influence over the children depended upon it. As for her, she found his presence completely congenial, yes, indispensable. He knew how to soothe her nerves when they were out of tune. His companionship was diverting. Above all else here was a man whose devotion to her was established beyond fear of turning, who would even play solitaire with her. And practically and affectionately he needed her as she needed him. How often she had said to Mr. Cochran: "If I only had someone whom I could ask with the assurance of a frank answer 'How did I play last night?'" She made her decision. Arturo must travel with her, not as her secretary but as her husband. Hertha and Eugenia some months before had seriously discussed this all-important subject. Hertha opened it by saying: "It would be good if Mammie married another Papa." But Eugenia warned her: "Don't tell her that. She would feel offended. She might think we didn't have enough just with her."

In her usual direct way it was Carreño who made the advances. No aurora borealis had ever yet appeared with such terrifying beauty to mortal man as this cataclysmic proposal to the ultramodest Arturo. How could he be a fitting husband for the great Carreño! His heart said a jubilant "yes," but not without misgivings. What about the children later on? Would it be for their best? What would the world have to say? Carreño brushed aside his fears. If there were difficult moments, at least they would face them together.

At the end of September the announcement exploded with the repercussion of a major tremor throughout the world of music. To the international press it gave food for frivolous and insulting comment. In artistic circles it became the joke of the season. Carreño's friends were divided into two camps, those who abruptly chose to cancel their intimacy with a person suddenly gone mad, and those who, incredible as they found this step, decided to capitulate to a decision they could not alter. Emma Koch and her mother joined the first, while Mrs. Mac-Dowell and Mrs. Watson, after doing their best to influence Carreño not to take the irrevocable step, lined up with Mr. Cochran on the other side. Carreño looked with a heavy heart upon the havoc her coming marriage was creating in her circle.

Gathering her real friends more closely within its shrinking circumference she turned her thoughts to her children. At last they should have the father they needed.

For the sake of the children Carreño, although she still believed that ties of affection were the only binding ones, agreed that the marriage should take place according to the involved machinery of the German law. These complications combined to defer the marriage until the summer of 1902.

There was no fear in Carreño's heart that she might be making a mistake. She opened her heart as well as that of Arturo in a letter to a good friend and pupil:

You have seen enough of my life to know for yourself *how lonesome* I, in reality, was, and how *empty* my poor heart, *and can fully understand me.* That I am *happier* than I ever dreamed of being is but a short and poor description of my feelings, and even if I wrote you the longest letter and tried to convey to you what I feel, I could not tell you all I would like to tell you! As you know what I suffered and you *really are* my friend, I know that you will rejoice in my happiness, which is the happiness I *have longed for all my life,* that of possessing a true, loyal, and noble heart—who will help me through the few years that I may have to live (they cannot be many, for I am an old woman now) and who will share with me my *troubles* as well as my *joys.* This Arturo will do as my *husband,* just as he used to do when, in silence, he loved me during all these years and when I only thought that I inspired in him the greatest *sympathy* on account of the misery which I underwent with his brother. I never dreamed that he had for me any more than the affection of a brother, and not the slightest suspicion did I have that the affection which I yearned for was mine. Had I only known it! Isn't it a strange thing that all these years should have passed—he loving me devotedly all these fourteen years—I absolutely ignorant of it, and only now my eyes should have been opened? He was *too proud* to allow himself to show his true feelings to me, and only through the force of circumstances did I become aware of what he felt for me. How strange life is after all! All I had before, only flattered my vanity.—My heart took no part in it all, excepting the love I bear my children and my true and deep affection for my friends. Otherwise I was *most unhappy,* for I missed the true and loving heart which I wanted for *my own,* the companion of my lonely, sad hours. Now I *have him,* and I cannot tell you how grateful I feel for this happiness!

Arturo's world too was colored by his own unbelievable good fortune. To show his gratitude, as well as to get used to himself in this glorified role, he was glad to accompany Teresita on a tour taking her to Finland and Russia. That was no inconsiderable test. In addition to the customary details that fall to the duty of a personal manager he had to be ready to soothe, to encourage, and to see that hooks matched eyes on the intricacies of the concert dress. His own nervousness was only exceeded by Teresita's. In her first concert she began the "Toccata and Fugue in D minor" by Bach (as Tausig fitted it to a protesting piano) as if she meant to break the piano to pieces, "like a horse, who, frightened at something, suddenly runs away, not caring where he is going, or knowing." From then on she played better and better until the last encore, her own "Berceuse," brought her a real triumph. Teresita by her beauty won the hearts of all the students in her audience. They wanted to carry her through the hall on a chair; they covered her with flowers. After such an ovation it took all of Arturo's ingenuity to keep Teresita to her routine of practice and sleep. Never for all the gold in the world, said Arturo, would he accompany Teresita on tour again. He longed for Carreño and was filled with a wild jealousy of all who were privileged to be near her. She for her part complains that his letters are cold, that he does not share his thoughts with her, to which Arturo replies helplessly: "Povero me! I am not a Petrarch nor a Tasso." And he wonders that she can love a man who has such bad qualities.

Teresita returned and found her mother ecstatic over her success beyond all hopes. Had she not captivated her critics as well as her audiences? Did she not come back, wonder upon wonder, with an actual profit in her pocket? Carreño allowed happiness to cloud judgment. It seemed to her that her daughter must at once conquer Germany in her own right. She saw that notices to that effect were published in the papers. Wolff put in a deterrent word, and a friendly musician who heard Teresita in Helsingfors gave voice to his opinion in a letter he chose to send anonymously.

Your daughter has celebrated triumphs here—everybody allowed himself to be caught in the applause by her extraordinary gift, her temperament, and her lovable appearance, but everybody had to deplore that these good qualities were not blended with greater technical proficiency so that she could stand out as a fully ripened heiress of a celebrated name; this is, in short, the opinion of public criticism in every city also. Gnädige Frau, believe me, if your daughter now appears before the more satiated public and the less considerate critics in Germany there will be no end of verdicts which will be painful to you no less than to your daughter. They will not be able to refrain from showing their surprise that a mother-artist of your quality, who more than any other ever has brought technique to artistic fruition, has failed to notice lacks in this direction in her daughter, has let her remain a mediocre dilettante. You would have to bear this responsibility before the whole world, and shadow would fall upon your own name, so well known, so highly valued everywhere, which could have been so easily avoided. I ask you to examine the situation yourself. You will certainly not say that I am wrong. I would do everything to spare you and your young, inexperienced daughter any sorrow, and I wish that you might understand my fear, might listen to me, that you might do as I ask: Do not let any further tours take place at present, but let Fräulein Teresita be content until later with her success in these places, and from now on concentrate upon her complete education in every direction. If you, Gnädige Frau, do not find the time to take her artistic development under your own guidance, assign your daughter to a teacher of whom you know that he will take charge of your daughter with affectionate interest, carefully and without jealousy, without brutality, and who will in this way lead her to the artistic heights and maturity that has and shall set the name Carreño apart. Then you will have full joy in your lovable, highly talented child— Only a few words more! I must draw your attention especially to good and careful physical education of your growing daughter, for now she sits in such a bent over position at the piano, that, if care is not taken, she may do harm to her health for the rest of her life. Now I have poured out my heart to you.—May you take heed of my words. An admirer and a man of experience has spoken them, who will always count among his most enjoyable hours the very beautiful ones for which he has to thank you, and who will always follow with interest the continuation as well as the future blooming of the Carreños, and who hopes that this may become ever more brilliant and glorious.

For the moment Carreño did not allow this sane counsel to guide her. Feverishly she wrote to everyone who might have influence to launch her daughter in a serious career. To her letter asking for a higher financial rating for her own concerts the imperturbable Wolff answered, bowing to the inevitable:

Non, chère Amie, j'ai envie de vous—pour nos concerts—et mes abonnés partagent cette envie! Que faire? Ce que j'aurais fait tout de suite, si j'avais su que vous pouviez être si dure. Donc entendu, très chère amie! 800—Mais jurez sur ma tête dépourvue extérieurement de cheveux, intérieurement de cervelle, que vous ne trahirez pas à vos collègues, que vous êtes montée tant dans—mon estime. Qu'est-ce que vous jouerez? Je vous serre votre main si habile et suis votre petit jouet.

The winter's concert tour unfolded in even rhythm, to Arturo who combined the callings of secretary, companion, and maid, like a happy dream. Carreño enjoyed as much as he the hours spent in a tailor's establishment in London, from which Arturo emerged equipped with everything necessary to play the part of the intended husband of a Carreño in perfect form. Each city was a new adventure, and who could blame him for strutting a little, as he began to learn to take charge of the endless details involved in the business of giving concerts. From school Eugenia writes with childish directness: *"Wie geht es dem Onkel? Ist der Onkel schon Papa?"* Of music he knew little, although he had the instinct of every good Italian for it. And by dint of repetition—Arturo was a good listener—he even developed a critical sense of a sort. At last Carreño felt that there was someone at her side to whom, with the confidence that it would be frankly answered, she could put that question: "How did I play last night?" She had never traveled so smoothly, so gaily. Troubles and problems, aired before an understanding person, seemed to be already half solved. Most valuable of all Arturo knew by intuition when to be silent, when to disappear. So for the usual fifty concerts or so through Germany, through Holland, through Germany again, through England, Scotland, and back again to Germany with a touch of Poland, Carreño played her way in a radiant haze that gave a delicious aura to her concerts.

The climax of the tour was one devoted to compositions by Grieg with the master himself presiding over the "Grieg Concerto" in Warsaw. For him too it was a state occasion. He wrote on the first of April:

Highly esteemed Madame Carreño:—The news that you will once again do me the honor to play my *A minor Concerto* under my direction gave me colossal joy. But on the program stands besides the piano concerto my *Ballade in G minor* (*op. 24*). Should you, however, which is very probable, neither know nor play this long and complicated piece, I will of course gladly do without it, but in that case I hope that you will be so kind as to suggest instead some of my piano pieces which you may already have embodied in your repertoire. I shall be grateful for a speedy and decisive reply. My wife is heartily anticipating seeing and hearing you again, as does your old admirer

Edvard Grieg.

On the tenth he acknowledged her reply:

My hearty thanks! With the three pieces "Aus dem Volksleben" I am entirely in accord.

You call this concert a festival. Yes, when you take part in it and especially if you play the Concerto as superbly as you did in Kopenhagen—(do you see how infamous I am!)—then at any rate it becomes a festival!

Meanwhile the formidable array of documents required for marriage in Germany was collecting upon Carreño's desk, and the wedding day could finally be set for June 30, 1902. Teresita

1902

*Arturo Tagliapietra and Teresa Carreño*

and Giovanni attended the simple ceremony. An elaborate dinner at which champagne flowed generously was shared by a small circle of friends in the dining room of Kurfürstendamm 28. It was natural that Italy should be the destination for their wedding journey. In Tavernola by the cool waters of the lake of Iseo they took a house, where later the family joined them. Teresa Carreño was once more Teresa Carreño Tagliapietra.

# PART IV

# VISTA

Es giebt nichts höheres, als sich der Gottheit mehr als andere Menschen
nähern und von hier aus die Strahlen der Gottheit unter das Menschen-
geschlecht zu verbreiten.

(Beethooven)

Das, meine geliebte Teresa Carenno, haben Sie erreicht,
Gott erhalt's Ihnen und uns noch lange!
In alter herzlicher Verehrung und Liebe, Ihre alte

Grunewald-Berlin          Lilli Lehmann.          21-12-1912.

TEN years passed. It was the evening of November 21, 1912, half a century since a tiny prodigy had promised, not knowing what it meant, "I shall be an artist all my life"; twenty-three years since a Venezuelan amazon had first flooded a Germany grown cold and conventional with the sunshine of a new spontaneity in music. Today she stood unrivaled, the empress of pianists.

In the foyer of the grand banquet hall of the Kaiserhof in Berlin more than two hundred associates and friends were assembled to do Teresa Carreño honor. They had answered the call of Artur Nikisch and his committee to celebrate her golden anniversary as an artist. The atmosphere was vibrant. The occasion was one to evoke high enthusiasm and most gay attire, most precious jewels.

Impatiently attention wandered from neighbor to neighbor, finally centering in the empty arch through which Carreño must enter. At last by common instinct came a hush, then a wild welcoming wave of applause. Teresa Carreño, more straight, more regal than ever was making her way along the improvised aisle on the arm of Arturo Tagliapietra who, flushed and uncomfortable, passed stiffly by her side. Ten years had made little outward difference in Carreño's appearance. Her hair, still shading from coal to snow, followed its former impulsive curves, framing as becomingly as ever a profile as finely sculptured as before. Her eyes held the wisdom that time and suffering bring and glowed with the light of old, generated within. In her dress of silvery blue silk she moved slowly to the ballroom.

At the center of the long table, raised to dominate the hall, Carreño and her suffering husband sat enthroned with Hertha and Eugenia their unwilling neighbors. Had they been consulted the daughters would have chosen to sit more humbly among their contemporaries. Eugenia nervously wondered what she could find to say to the pale young man at her right, what language she should use. It did not help matters when she discovered that he was the Ambassador from Venezuela, and that the speech he was to give made him momentarily an unresponsive companion. Hertha was equally at a loss. At her left presided the Wagnerian soprano, Lilli Lehmann, so like her mother in style and appearance. Yet glacier and geyser were not more opposite than they. All at once Eugenia and Hertha pricked up their ears. Somewhere out of sight an orchestra was tuning. Dinner music would make the evening pass less tediously. Up went their spirits only to fall with sickening speed at the loud, unanimous "sch" that after the first phrase reduced the discouraged players to silence. They were not impressed by the fact that gathered here was a representative cross section of musical Germany, including famous artists, delegates from exclusive organizations, and those who, be it artistically or commercially, were responsible for the smooth running of the concert mechanism. At Carreño's table sat Christian Sinding, some of whose compositions were a part of Carreño's standing repertoire and next to Sinding's wife Emil Paur, under whose baton Carreño had often played concertos, among them his own.

And there near the end of the important table was "dear Louise." Before her eyes too there must be passing, headed by the genial Hermann, a procession of those of another day, who should have graced this occasion by privilege of friendship and distinction: Edvard Grieg, Johannes Brahms, Hans von Bülow, Anton Rubinstein! How she missed them, all those who had helped to crystallize her standards. As she caught the eye of Louise Wolff Carreño raised her glass in a message they both understood.

All at once Lilli Lehmann was the focus of attention as she rose from her chair. With a gesture worthy of an Isolde she drank a toast to her sister Walküre and to their future *"Brüderschaft"* (brotherhood), a rite by virtue of which the brilliant butterfly of the Andes and the great silver moth of Nordic moonlight authorized each other to use the intimate "Du," which to a German is the open sesame to his most sacred loyalties.

The endless reading of telegrams from fellow musicians, from friends of many lands, from royalty as from former servants filled the intermission between courses. There were speeches yet to follow, a poem by the brother of Maurice Moszkowski, the more literary if not more witty Alexander, in which he welcomed Teresa as tenth to the company of the nine Muses. The hour grew late. As the master of ceremonies presented Dr. Santos Dominici, Carreño's compatriot, the audience seemed little inclined to give him ear. Only diplomatic tact and a vital interest in his subject saved the day. Lyrically, intimately he carried his listeners back to the Venezuela of Carreño's childhood, tried to make it vivid to them as it meant home to him. Carreño leaned forward captivated. His touching picture of the background against which her genius had flowered so prematurely was holding enthralled a company surfeited and fatigued by a banquet that had lasted too long. No one was more profoundly stirred than Carreño herself. Forgetting that it was of her the Envoy was speaking she joined in the applause as enthusiastically as the rest.

In climax Carreño rose among her flowers to thank her composite host. Spanish-American German never rang out more clearly. "You know that I do not speak good German, but one language we all speak, that is the language of the heart," she began. Movingly she paid her debt of gratitude in words that caused her more nervousness in the speaking than a whole winter full of concerts.

Eugenia and Hertha sighed with relief. Even Arturo unbent. That patient look of proud embarrassment had not once left his face. Did anyone realize how difficult it was to be the husband of a Carreño, he wondered. After an endless reception in the foyer Carreño could at last return from her golden jubilee to the place that Arturo had made home, and to the game of solitaire which alone could induce a restful night.

CARREÑO awoke in a mood of depression to a world steeped in gloom. Buffeted by winds sometimes too strong for her steady feet she stood alone on the heights. Looking far down into the misty distance from which she had ascended she examined once more the ledges which had nearly spelled disaster in the climbing. What more was there left to live for, what greater summits for her to scale? Looking ahead she saw a level road, curving gradually downward in the distance. The prospect was dull, tame, uninviting. Yet she had ample cause to go on, for Arturo's sake, for her children who, one and all, still leaned upon her for support. Until Hertha and Eugenia were safely married or established in productive careers she must keep on "with the dear Father's help."

Ten years of matrimony stretched behind Carreño like many-colored streamers from a maypole, each ribbon representing a life close to hers. Woven together in haphazard pattern they made up her own much more truly than the events that shaped it. Negligible in comparison was the round of concert giving that each year for fifty years had turned like a phonograph record, stopping only when the season ran down. That everlasting sameness of enforced variety which others might stupidly envy was becoming more and more irksome. Her own inner tempo was slowing down, she felt, to a congenial andante. Yet outwardly she must not fail, as she never had failed, until the last note. What if she did draw upon her reserve capital of strength, there would yet be enough in her store to last as long as needed.

From 1902 to 1912 the graph of Carreño's concerts still shows, with pockets here and there, a gentle trend upward. The death of Hermann Wolff in 1901, a heavy personal blow, created new problems. Of the managers who were tried and found wanting in one vital respect or another, there was none she could so entirely respect, none with whom she could laugh so merrily in the midst of a quarrel both enjoyed as a sport because they were so evenly matched. The season of 1902–3 had been the leanest of all in the German period. It added up to twenty-seven engagements only, the customary average being twice that. Car-

*Walküre*

reño lost no time in advising Herr Fernow, now in charge of the "Konzertdirektion Wolff" in a letter that was politely to the point, that, unless he found more time to devote to her interests, she would be obliged to relieve him of his duties as her agent. Herr Fernow heeded the warning, for the year following was a banner one.

In the spring of 1903 Carreño yielded to an urge of long standing to visit her Mother Country Spain, where piano recitals were the exception. Her local manager was somewhat worried about the outcome of his enterprise, and as a concession to Spanish taste proposed programs of lighter character than those usually chosen by Carreño for her concerts in Germany. With categorical directness Carreño replied:

The artist who presents himself for the first time in a country ought, before everything, to show what he can do with the repertoire that makes him best understood by his public, and so should try to gain its approval not for what he plays, but for how he plays. That is my case, and thus I shall be obliged to proceed with Barcelona and the other places in Spain where I shall have the honor of presenting myself just as in London, Paris, etc., and if the audience is not content, it will be my fault and not that of my programs. One can never hear too much of the good and great works of art, and however much one hears an A flat Polonaise of Chopin, one cannot cease admiring it. So my good friend, Barcelona will have to bear with my programs as they are!

And that city as well as others did so without a murmur of complaint. Lisbon, for instance, was moved to a frenzy of excitement. Ladies threw upon the stage the flowers they wore. Carreño played enough encores to fill another entire program, among them her own "Danza Venezolana." She returned with another triumph and 12,000 francs to her credit, quite ready for a summer on the island of Wyk, where she once again proved to herself that it was the mountains she really preferred. Here she prepared the "D minor Concerto" of Brahms for public performance, perhaps in answer to the demand made public by certain critics that she enrich her programs with new works. For some unexplained reason it soon disappeared from the list. It may be that Carreño shared von Bülow's point of view. Approached by a reporter, who wished to know what changes he would make in the repertoire of an orchestra he had been appointed to conduct, he answered: "Gentlemen, we shall play the same music, but we shall try to play it better." Or, more probably, time and health forbade that she spend all of each summer increasing her repertoire. Carreño did make a point of bringing something new on the programs of the first of her yearly Berlin recitals, and on occasion a work of small or large dimension by a minor prophet gave encouragement and prestige to the author she sponsored, Poldini, Cowen, Mrs. Beach, and even Max Reger in his "salad days" among them. Her own words are applicable here. Audiences continued to swarm to hear her, not for what she did as much as for how she did it. She drew them more magnetically than ever. There were more fees in the 1,000 m. class, less in the 400 m. brackets to be entered in the book of accounts kept by Arturo with such painstaking accuracy and neatness that it became one of the family jokes.

Carreño's relations with her managers had always been based upon the best mutual interest. It was not in her to accept an engagement at so high a figure that in her judgment it precluded the making of expenses on the part of the impresario. On one occasion she refused an engagement in Leipzig at an enormous figure giving as her reason: "Since I have never previously been able to earn the sum that Mr. Eulenburg offers me for three recitals in Leipzig, that would be a loss for him which I cannot permit. That feeling would be intolerable to me."

Neither would she be railroaded into making compromises of which she disapproved, although they might possibly be of practical advantage. So in a letter to Mr. Adams, who advised a placating attitude toward a gentleman believing himself entitled to a commission on one of her concert tours, she wrote:

As to the matter of Mr. C., I am sorry to say I cannot accept an amicable settlement of it, as Mr. C.'s letters are absolutely of such an offensive character that it is impossible for me to accept any visit from him. He has no more and no less than called me a liar in his last letter, and I do not allow any living being to tax me of untruth unpunished. Kind as your advice is in regard to the matter between Mr. C. and myself, and much as I agree with what you write that "it is much easier to make an enemy than a friend," I am of the opinion (and always have been) that a friendship which one has to pay for is not worth keeping.

For five consecutive years after her marriage Carreño made European countries her territory, as much for the sake of her children as to let the notoriety of which she was the object because of her fourth marriage quiet down. Not until the spring of 1907 did she leave this well-combed area. However, rumors had persistently reached her of untold riches waiting to fall into the lap of musicians adventurous enough to gather them in Australia and New Zealand. To prove this Paderewski's bewildering success was cited. Benno Scherek, as good a pianist as he was an impresario, offered himself as representative for the tour. Arturo was more than ready to be an even more personal one. For him the joys of travel could never reach the saturation point. There were other angles in favor of such a voyage. It would be of benefit to Teresita, and Carreño herself would be relieved to have her younger daughters safely out of reach of their father.

Definite plans were accordingly made. Carreño found a governess trustworthy and young enough to be a companion for the two adolescents. Eugenia and Hertha welcomed the change from the discipline of school to the leisurely pleasures of a first sea voyage. Fearing that d'Albert might take steps to prevent the departure of his children preparations were made with all secrecy. It seemed safer for that reason to embark at Naples. Hardly had they arrived at this port, when they heard to their dismay that d'Albert had taken rooms in a neighboring hotel. Carreño was in a panic. Instead of being allowed to see the sights of the city, the children were kept indoors. Meals were served in private. Then hastily one dark night Carreño with her retinue of family and of trunks and bags boarded the waiting *Oruba*. Not until the ship was safely out of harbor could she bring herself to laugh at the danger they had circumvented. It did not occur to her that, as it actually turned out to be, d'Albert might have been totally unaware of their plans as of their presence.

Arrived in Melbourne after a voyage that was restful even for as poor a sailor as Carreño, the tour unwound itself in general much like any other, except that the coming of a great artist was much more of an event in Australia than in Europe. Five concerts in each of the larger cities became the rule. Carreño strained her memory to resurrect from the long ago compositions she had outgrown. Gottschalk, Vogrich, even her own "Revue à Prague" once more showed their heads sheepishly above the surface.

There was another difficulty. The islands could boast of but few orchestras worthy of accompanying a Carreño. A whole repertoire of concerti would have been lying useless had it not been for Carreño's resourcefulness. She decided to incorporate one in each of her recital programs, enlisting the versatile Scherek to substitute for the orchestra at a second piano. It was a happy solution. A concerto in any form was a novelty in most of the smaller places, and in spite of tropical downpours and intense heat the concert halls were always well filled.

There was only one mishap to record. During the second Melbourne concert a slight injury to the little finger of the right hand became increasingly painful to Carreño during the course of the evening. An infection set in, and only the utmost stoicism enabled her to finish a program whose every chord spelled torture. Her doctor advised that the finger be lanced. "Go ahead," said the Spartan, proceeding to entertain the surgeon with her most witty stories, and while he operated upon the precious member, she wiped off the beads of perspiration rolling down his face.

Australian society took Carreño to its bosom. It had not known that a great artist could be so unaffected, so approachable. A little mixed in geography, it found "no frill, no fuss about this Sicilian lady." If she chose to wear an elaborate robe en train of black velvet embroidered in gold for a matinée concert, that, all agreed, was her affair. It was hard to make time for all the interviews and auditions that Carreño granted and Arturo knew how to cut short at the right moment by entering the room on one pretext or another. The necessary hours of practice with Scherek were frequently interrupted by aristocratic callers, by the autograph seekers whom Carreño seldom denied, and by reporters who wanted to know whether she was to wear her frock of gray satin with slashed elbow sleeves of chiffon, or her favorite one of black tulle covered with blue-green paillettes, among which seed pearls meandered in delicate tracery, the whole over mermaid-green silk veiled by white chiffon.

No detail of this artist's life was too insignificant to appear in print. Carreño was bombarded with invitations, only a few of which she accepted, and never without consulting her manager who knew his Australia. One morning she found herself receiving in the alien setting of the Ladies' Patriotic Club of Sydney. Holding a bouquet of orchids tied with the red and yellow of Spain which her hostesses deemed appropriate, she stood for hours before the huge bare fireplace, into which the throng threatened to push her. They made a wall through which only the most aggressive could make their way. Local talent lent its indifferent gifts to compositions by Chopin and Moszkowski that fortunately could only faintly penetrate the incessant buzz of conversation, of which anything from politics to corsets was the topic. At last this function too was over, a tribute to the cause if only another chore to the guest of honor, and Carreño could enjoy in more congenial and cool company a launch luncheon along the coast line of the harbor.

Quite different was an entertainment offered Carreño and Arturo by Maggie and Bella Papakura in Rotorua, New Zealand. The two sisters could be counted upon to provide a good show. Beginning with the poi dancers and ending with choruses by the children of the native school there was not a dull moment. In the bare and dusky hall of Whakarewarewa the natives had gathered on one side, the foreigners or *paheka* distinguished by an invitation at the other. Meta Tawpopoki, a chief of the Arawas, gave the address of welcome in flowery Maori language. The translation of the Rev. F. A. Bennett made the musical words intelligible to the guests. In conclusion the chief asked Carreño to show her *paheka* accomplishments as his people had shown theirs. A second chief voiced the same wish on the part of his numerous progeny huddled in a wriggling group upon the floor, "that they might also sometime become learned in the *paheka* art." He then called upon the young men standing along the wall to join with him in a dance in celebration of this their noted guest. Discarding first his coat and then even his shirt he urged them on, while the natives clapped and cheered in rhythm, and Carreño joined in as if she were one of them. Then, not to be outdone by her hosts, she walked to the piano so strangely out of place in this setting and began to play, while the exhausted old chief still lay panting in the middle of the floor. She played on and on, not with perfunctory politeness, but with the thrilling realization that she and her native friends after all spoke and understood a common language in music and the dance. It was late in the night when Carreño and Arturo, laden with native treasures and blessings, took their departure.

Carreño chose to consider this trip to a new land a kind of vacation before the really serious business of the eighty concerts booked for her in the United States by R. E. Johnston and the John Church Company. This strenuous holiday was complicated on the return trip by the fact that Eugenia fell ill on the steamer with a case of intermittent fever about which the ship's doctor seemed able to do nothing. Tired from nights of sleeplessness and in fear of losing her child she interrupted the journey in the Fiji Islands. As soon as it was known that a renowned pianist had reached Suva, petitions begging for a concert came in such number that it seemed expedient to arrange for one. There was only one piano worthy of the name and that was woefully off pitch. No tuner was in sight, but

*Teresa Carreño Tagliapietra*

what did that matter! Carreño quite enjoyed the morning that she spent putting the instrument into passable shape with a pair of pliers. The concert was a triumph, and in a surprisingly short time, thanks to good medical attention and the doglike devotion of a native who camped on the mat before her door, Eugenia recovered in time for the next boat, the last possible one which would bring them to America for Carreño's first engagement. Three days after her arrival in Chicago Carreño, who had not really practiced for months, and had contracted to play the Everett, a piano unfamiliar to her, celebrated another signal triumph in Orchestra Hall.

One cloud hung low in Carreño's sky, as in 1907 it darkened the horizon of all musical America. It was the tragedy of the slow, irrevocable fading of Edward MacDowell, the lovable friend and pupil of Carreño's youth, the respected colleague of her wiser years, the first American to be admitted to German programs on equal terms with its own composers, the one before all others who had given dignity to the profession of music in the United States by earning for it full academic recognition as a subject worthy of higher study like any other on the University curriculum! Carreño saw Edward for a last time during the Christmas holidays in New York. He was apathetically playing with his toys. Once she caught his eye, shining with the momentary gladness of recognition, then returning almost instantaneously to the dullness of inner withdrawal. Shortly after this visit she was playing the MacDowell "Concerto" with the Boston Symphony Orchestra. Still with the pathos of this meeting in mind she suddenly forgot what she was supposed to be playing and floundered noticeably before finding her way, a rare happening indeed.

That Edward, too, fitfully remembered is shown in a letter penned by Marian MacDowell, Edward's wife, who wrote to Carreño in December:

I am sitting beside Edward, and I said to him a minute ago, "I am writing to Teresita, shall I send her your love?" His face brightened as it had not all day, and he said "Yes." A few memories remain with him, and you are one of them— It is all misty but I know you will be touched when I tell you the only name he ever calls me by save my own is Teresita! In the summer half the time he used that name for me—he said so little in the old days—but quite aside from his affection, he never forgot how loyally you helped him and how much he owed you.

After the final catastrophe, less sad than the living death preceding it, Carreño more ardently than ever put herself at the service of MacDowell's compositions. No longer, as Marian MacDowell wrote in an earlier year, was she "the only great artist who has had the courage and the will to actually play his music" but it was she who was fittingly chosen to play his "Second Concerto," so particularly hers as well, in the great Memorial Concert in New York on March 31, 1908. From now on the "Keltic Sonata" and later the "Tragica," too, were frequently heard in her concerts.

Carreño was traveling in the West at the time of the funeral. She felt driven by her so readily overflowing sympathy to do something for the comfort of Edward MacDowell's parents and hit upon what she thought was a perfect plan. Arturo took a strong stand against it, eventually converting her to his way of thinking. He reminded her that what she needed rather than a summer of sight-seeing in Italy with the Thomas MacDowells as her guests—after a long series of concerts at $400 each she could afford such a luxury—was a period of complete rest in preparation for a season that promised to be doubly strenuous after long absence from Germany. It was vital that she come back to her adopted country with her powers unimpaired. Arturo was perfectly right. The question was closed.

When later in March Carreño returned to New York, the first one to greet her as she stepped from her carriage at the door of the Netherland was Mrs. MacDowell. With a fresh surge of pity, Carreño impulsively poured out her plan for the very trip she had so definitely given up, not only asking the MacDowells but their grandson, and Juan Buitrago, to accompany them, all as her guests. The dazed Arturo stood help-lessly by.

Two people ill with sorrow were not calculated to affect heal-ingly nerves that were raw after seventeen months of almost continuous concertizing. The trip was not the success it was meant to be. The MacDowells found that the comforts of Italian hotels compared unfavorably with those to be had in their own four walls. Carreño, disappointed that drives and her favorite museums could not cure her friends of homesickness, at last left them under the care of Arturo, while she withdrew to the simple Hotel Panorama high above the little town of Oberstdorf in Upper Bavaria.

Here she found in the proprietor, the jovial Herr Theater-direktor Grassl, a man who could make her laugh without half trying. Her room had an exquisite view of snow-covered moun-tains in a chain. Every night as she mounted the stairs, bran-dishing her long gaslighter and singing Brünnhilde's Ho-jo-to-ho, she knew that she might count upon a restful night. In a tiny house near-by stood her piano. She spent all of every morning in undisturbed practice.

Carreño and Mrs. Watson conceived the idea in almost tele-pathic coincidence not uncommon between them, that the elder MacDowells, the Watsons, and the Tagliapietras should spend the following summer together in the Catskills. This was not to be. The death of Mrs. MacDowell cut the knot life could not loosen. Carreño wrote to their common friend Adelaide Okell:

In my heart, in my mind she lives and will live as long as I live. As she believed so thoroughly in an after life, I feel as if she really were around me and her beloved spirit near me, and that she knows now, better than when she was living, how deeply and tenderly I have loved her in the twenty-six years of our friendship.

OVERWORK, worry, and sorrow undermined Carreño's vigor, like termites gnawing at the beams that support a well-built house. She was obliged to seek the health-giving waters of Bad

Gastein, where she became a noticeable figure. Even those who failed to recognize her knew that only a celebrity would walk so proudly, so indifferently in stout boots, a high-necked white shirtwaist, and the same old skirt she loved the better for every added cigarette hole which punctured it. The broad brim of a finely woven Panama encircled by a plain black band shaded her face as she strode down the street among more worldly minded mortals, rhythmically swinging her cane. People remarked to each other as she passed: Could this stocky, serious woman be the beloved Walküre who looked so majestically happy and tall upon the concert stage?

As Oberstdorf the year before had helped to guide to a successful close a European tour that broke all records with seventy-six concerts, so Gastein fulfilled its mission by putting Carreño into shape for the most stupendous effort of all. Beginning in Finland she went by way of a crowded winter season in the United States to Australia, New Zealand, and South Africa, then back by way of Egypt and Italy to Germany again. From home to home the journey lasted eighteen months. A total of one hundred and thirty-two concerts surpassed that of the first Australian tour. Financially Carreño, who besides Arturo and Mr. Scherek had again taken the two younger children and their governess along, barely broke even. Yet the journey had its compensations. Carreño's old wish raised its head to have a piece of land that she might call her own, as an investment first of all, and perhaps as the place where she might build herself the home to which she would ultimately retire. It was an important moment for her when she gave bold signature to the deed that made her owner of a thirty-acre tract of land at Grossmont near San Diego next to that belonging to her good friend, Ernestine Schumann-Heink.

In this second visit to the antipodes the element of novelty which packed the houses before was lacking, and in South Africa, unused to solo recitals, five concerts at a stretch were a heavy diet. It was nevertheless an interesting new experience, even if occasionally the call of a fire sprinkler drifted into the quiet of a Beethoven Andante in an alien key, and the curfew call for the Kafirs blended weirdly with the strains of the "Keltic Sonata." The obligatory round of parties varied the routine of concert playing. For the first time in her life Carreño was called upon to dedicate a golf course in Johannesburg. With the club especially inscribed and presented to her she was expected to send the first ball out upon the green. This she did to such good effect that a whole army of caddies was unable to find it.

More than once an insistent sore throat and attendant rheumatism threatened to put an end to the tour. On the way home, when a last concert had been given in Cairo under acute discomfort, Carreño sought remedy by taking a trip on camel back into the desert sands. But not until the baths of Italy had exerted their curative power did Carreño lose the last trace of lameness. It was an exhausted artist who returned to Kurfürstendamm 28 for the summer.

Before it ended the doctor prescribed a month of solitude in Oberstdorf. No member of her family and only one pupil was allowed to accompany her. Every morning the strains of the piano part of the Taneieff or the César Franck "Quintette," of Liszt's *"Feux follets"* or the "B minor Sonate" of Chopin floated across the meadows behind the practice cabin into the woods beyond, and often Carreño smiled to see her pupil in a light-blue dress, set in relief against the dark of the fir trees, listening and learning by the hour. She too was studying the Chopin "Sonate." In the middle of the next lesson Carreño suddenly burst out laughing. "Very good, very good, my dear! You have caught my tricks." Then, more seriously, she reminded her: "Copying another easily turns into caricature. What is right for me is not necessarily right for you. Interpretation must spring from the heart. Nevertheless you have done very well, my dear. Now go and find yourself in the 'Sonate,' and bring it to me again next time."

For four weeks Carreño enjoyed the walks along the narrow wooded paths she knew so well, and watched from her high window the evening mists drifting over Oberstdorf as the lights were being turned on, the deeply etched mountains turning to rose in the afterglow. This was solitude in its most exquisite essence. By chance, however, one acquaintance or another had wind of Carreño's whereabouts. She was never free from danger of intrusion. Herr Grassl was a good buffer. He loved nothing better than to make excuses for her according to the best tradition of the German theater. While Carreño quickly dressed in her walking clothes to make truth out of fiction, Herr Grassl with a flourishing bow and elaborate apology convincingly deplored:

Madame will be desolate. Not long ago she left for a walk, a long walk. No, Madame did not tell me where she meant to go. Probably she will not return for dinner, and it is such a good dinner too! She would so have delighted to have you share it with her. I shall most certainly give her your messages. No, she is not at all well. She suffers from acute headache. *Auf Wiedersehen, meine Herrschaften! Grüss Gott!* Madame will be inconsolable.

Meanwhile Carreño, setting out for the walk she was supposed to be taking, stopped at the door to listen, then, thoroughly relishing the comedy, slipped away by the back door.

AND soon the leaves were falling. It was time to prepare for another European winter, opened by a joint tour with Mischa Elman through the British Isles. Eugenia had begged to be taken along instead of Arturo. She looked forward to it as a delightful vacation, not realizing the duties it involved. Counting baggage—Carreño traveled with no less than ten trunks and as many packages—laying out the proper clothes, making calls, attending parties that lasted late at night after the concert she could only hear from the green room, all this was preliminary to the routine of almost daily packing while the town slept. Carreño, still on top of the wave, was at last obliged to send her daughter to bed, while she played her favorite part, that of nurse to one of her children.

One mishap nearly ruined the trip. Carreño had allowed herself a great luxury. A small suitcase of alligator skin had been made for her according to her own specifications. It was designed to hold all the fittings given her in the course of time by pupils and friends. There was a special corner reserved for the pincushion Teresita had made for her mother at the age of six. Everything about this bag was perfect even to the protective covering of light-brown fabric with corners and initials of darker leather. It was intended to last a lifetime and would have added prestige to any traveler.

One night on the point of leaving London, Carreño had arranged her things in the compartment of the train and, as was her habit, went outside to walk up and down the platform for a last moment of exercise. When she returned to her seat her bag, her precious bag, was nowhere to be found. All the proverbial efficiency of the English police system failed to unearth any trace of the suitcase or of the articles within it. The most valuable one was a pin made of the brightly scintillating blue wings of a South American butterfly with jeweled antennae, covered with glass and set in gold. It had become practically the only ornament she liked to wear. But the loss which touched her to the heart was the tiny pincushion with its large uneven stitching.

After disaster and near-disaster Carreño was glad to return to her own apartment. There also things sometimes disappeared, but one always knew where they were and how to get them back. It was only necessary to call poor old Josephine: "Josephine, I have lost my silver paper-cutter. You are clever at finding things. Please see that it is put back in its place. I need it before tomorrow." Invariably the lost was found. Josephine had one single obsession, the fear of being left penniless to starve. Against this evil day she stowed away anything that happened to attract her, from ash trays to coffee grounds. The family good-naturedly bore with this idiosyncrasy. After all who could tell fortunes from molten lead on a New Year's eve more vividly than she, and who at heart could be more devoted!

Although Carreño's concerts overreached the fifty mark in the season of 1911 she seemed to have more time at home than usual. Friends who dropped in at the tea hour often found her at the head of the long table. One afternoon Frau Leonard, whose husband was entrusted with the partial management of Carreño's concert business, was the principal guest. Bruno Gortatowsky, Carreño's assistant, an almost daily visitor, and the pupil who had just finished her lesson were the only ones outside of the family circle on this day. Frau Leonard was a relatively new friend. Carreño wished to show her special courtesy. She was never at a loss for vocabulary, but occasionally the convolutions of German word order were too much for her. As Frau Leonard was leaving Carreño accompanied her to the door. Hertha, always the first to enjoy a ludicrous situation, laughed aloud to hear her mother say: "Then I shall have the pleasure of not seeing you until April?" As she reëntered the room, Carreño found the others in gales of merriment. Not one to permit a joke at her expense, unless it were initiated by herself, she abruptly left the room.

But Giovanni's vagaries always amused her. His gift of mimicry was nearly as good as her own. Curiosity prompting him to find out just what went on in the salon when his mother gave interviews, he disguised himself one day as a reporter, made an appointment by telephone, and rang his own front doorbell. Carreño received him formally, and it was ten minutes before the light in his eyes, so like hers, made her aware that she was speaking to her own son.

Another year flew by—on swifter wings than ever, it seemed to Carreño—and soon Hertha and Eugenia were again impatiently waiting for the all-important decision. Where would their mother decide to spend the summer of 1912? Young girls of eighteen and twenty did not look for a quiet retreat with an inspiring view. Their requirements were simple: lots of company and lots of tennis! A friend had scoured Switzerland for the ideal spot and finally found it, she thought, in Grindelwald. The Chalet Burgner stood high at the end of a long street.

From the veranda the eye was led over the valley to the gleaming Grindelwald glacier field nestling in the bare arms of the mountain. The house was much like the Villa Waltenberger on the Salzberg, or the Hotel Panorama in Oberstdorf. It was spacious and homelike and simple. Along the main street which it dominated there was accommodation for the pupils and their instruments in peasant houses and *pensions*. The conditions were equally auspicious for those seeking solitude and for the socially inclined. The prospect enchanted Eugenia and Hertha, and Carreño with her thirty-odd pieces of baggage, her husband, and one pupil too impatient to wait for the rest, set out to pave the way for the coming of the family and the musical colony.

Immediately there was something distasteful to her in the atmosphere of the place. The air was invigorating, and yet she felt ill, depressed. At last she found the explanation. It was the glacier. It held her with its spell. Look at it she must, even against her will, and every day it appeared to be coming closer. The students worked feverishly, on pins and needles for fear that their maestra would abandon this queerly assorted group. They did not breathe freely until one morning Hertha and Eugenia zigzagged down the street to spread the glad news that their mother was feeling better and had decided to stay. She had even joked about that archhypnotist, the glacier. It would not surprise her, so she said, to see that clammy thing confront her eye, slowly making its way up the aisle, as she stepped upon the platform at her Berlin concert. Might it be well to send it an invitation as Don Giovanni had summoned the cold statue of the Commendatore to his party? All was well. Carreño once more was pouring tea for the chosen, giving lessons, taking her morning walks. Arturo again trundled his bicycle up the hill, reading his *Corriere*. The colony celebrated and joined together in early morning tramps that began in drizzling rain and ended on crisp, crackling fields of snow.

A high moment came when Wilhelm Backhaus arrived to practice with Carreño for their coming tour of Great Britain in two-piano ensemble. However much they liked each other as people, there was not enough time to make a pretense of blending two individuals, artistically as far apart as they were in age. Musically speaking, Carreño was relieved when this tournament came to an outwardly passable end.

Mentally Carreño's barometric pressure registered an all-time low. Truly appalling was the prospect of her golden jubilee as an artist. It also brought its complications. To her horror she discovered that her naïve and faithful assistant Bruno Gortatowsky was taking up a collection of money to be presented to her on that occasion. Although by tactful persuasion he was brought to abandon the project, she could not keep him from using the savings he had accumulated bit by bit to buy himself the Bechstein he coveted and needed, in order to present her instead with a costly tea service of solid silver.

One morning Carreño was walking with one of her pupils along a Grindelwald path. She stopped to look at the mountains, at their peaks of blinding white against unbroken blue, as if to measure her own stature against their immensity. She spoke as if to herself: "What have I still to live for? After this anniversary celebration I shall have had all that an artist can desire. No matter how long I may live, I cannot expect to reap higher honor, greater glory, or more wealth than are mine today. And they call it a jubilee!" For a time there was silence. The only sound the dull thud of the cane in its even rhythm. And once more she halted to let her eye travel across to an almost invisible trail, a light, jagged line engraved upon gray stone. "There still is one thing I can do. I can teach. If a mountain climber who has scaled dangerous heights meets another looking for the way up, is it not his duty to show him the shortest, easiest, safest path?" She went on with a firmer, faster step, a clearer tapping of her cane. She still had a mission to perform.

HER mind turned to the past. Shocking was the havoc that a fourth marriage had created in Carreño's inner circle those long ten years ago. She was not one to tolerate disrespect of the husband she had chosen, and even her lawyer, Justizrath Michaelis, and the genial Mr. Cochran had been under suspicion of disloyalty, and were nearly cut from her list like many others. Mrs. Watson and Mrs. MacDowell, who had been frank in opposing this union while there were still time, resigned themselves to the inevitable, and received Arturo as a fourth in their respective quartettes. Mrs. MacDowell wrote wistfully: "I never thought it would fall to my lot to defend your fourth husband." That he grew in her affection to the end a letter, probably her last, written to Carreño on February 1, 1909, shows very definitely:

I am so happy that you have such a dear, devoted husband who makes your busy life more restful, contented, and happy. God bless him for it too. We all love him. Who could help it who knows him as we do, the loveliness of his daily life—so unspoiled by prosperity, so faithful, so delicate in his feelings—and we are all so happy that you have him in your long journey to smooth all the rough places for you that he can.

Carreño was without doubt. In marrying blond, blue-eyed Arturo she had made no mistake. What if he had added another name to the long list depending upon her for support! What did it matter that she had lost the 7,500 m. she had invested in the business which Arturo had founded with such high hopes! It was the fault of his Italian associate that the enterprise had failed. For the two short years that it lasted they had sold good Italian wines and the best salted almonds to be had in Berlin at their store, Uhlandstrasse 48. But how could Arturo, careful though he was as a keeper of books, be expected to have the necessary business acumen to hold his own against an ill-chosen partner! Carreño entered her loss and quickly forgot about it. Secretly she was glad that Arturo was again free to devote himself to her interests alone. When the bustle of an apartment full of children unnerved her, it was a refreshing change to go off to an Italian restaurant close at hand with Arturo. There they refurbished old jokes, renewed memories of the days they had shared years ago, over a delicious dinner made festive with a bottle of the best dry champagne.

For Arturo it was enough just to sit or to walk by her side. His place in her heart had made him feel that he was of importance in the scheme of things, and this he prized more than the worldly comforts he now was permitted to enjoy, his handsome clothes, his good cigars. There was no doubt that he exerted a beneficent influence over the two older children. He was of their own blood. Arturo had been the friend of their childhood. They understood each other.

It was different with the little d'Alberts. As their own father became a known factor in their lives, they quite naturally resented the control that Arturo—called Papa to distinguish him from d'Albert, always referred to as "our father"—had over their own actions. It seemed sometimes as if they could not reach their mother except through him. The older they grew the more complicated was this relationship to become. The tact that never failed Arturo in dealing with Teresita and Giovanni forsook him hopelessly where these two little girls were concerned. They stood against him, strong in union, a formidable pair. Violent scoldings so congenial to the Southern temperament faced in repercussion the telling weapon of silence. There were weeks when the opposing camps were not on speaking terms.

And still Carreño knew that she had made no mistake. She loved Arturo, trusted his judgment, and occasionally he even caused her unwitting flurries of jealousy. On one of their ocean voyages Arturo's chair happened to stand next to that of a very personable young woman. They talked and laughed together in the way of steamer acquaintances. Carreño came upon them just as Arturo was picking up a book for his neighbor. It needed no more than that to make his wife stalk off to her cabin in anger, followed by a puzzled husband—how was he to know that Eugenia had been joking about "Papa's love affair?"—who reached the door only to have it slammed in his face. "Don't you dare to come in here," shouted an irate voice, and poor Arturo went out upon the deck to meditate upon the ways of an artist and to await the return of a more conciliatory state of mind.

Whenever Carreño went on tour with her personal maid, Marie, instead of Arturo by her side, she took comfort in writing letters to her husband at every breathing point. Thus from Amsterdam in one of those rare moments when she considered her reactions to her own concerts worth mentioning:

Since yesterday evening I am here playing the part of a great lady without taking in even a penny.—I have the same rooms we had together—do you remember?—and it makes me sick at heart that you are not here, Turo mio!! This morning I stayed in bed, and after my breakfast I did my accounts with the result that I lacked one gulden and 83 cents.—I am more relieved than I can tell you not to have to play either today or tomorrow. I feel like another person when I haven't another program before me. Yesterday for instance, when I had played really well, I had a great joy. When I don't play as I wish, I could hit myself and send the piano and all concerts to the inferno.

Carreño was not an artist given to stage fright. She had her superstitions, but these she generally left outside at the door of the concert hall. There was only one recital that she regularly dreaded every year, the first Berlin *Klavierabend* of the season. "Turo mio," she might be heard to say almost in tears: "I know I shall play badly, I feel that it will be a complete fiasco." Arturo knew how to strike the right note, how to bring a smile to those tightly set lips: "Teresita, have you ever made a failure in Berlin?—No?—Well, then it is about time you did. Everybody has to play badly sometimes." His methods worked. He well knew that not even the glacier of Grindelwald making its dripping way to the front row could affect the composure of the Walküre once seated before her Bechstein. With every year of companionship Carreño became more certain that Arturo's protecting nearness was her great necessity, of which nothing could deprive her save death.

CARREÑO turned in thought to the child of her worries, Teresita. However indefatigably the mother tried to iron out her jumble of difficulties, there was no use. Teresita remained an undisciplined child of genius, a veritable Peter Pan living a whimsical life in which adult reasoning played no part and awakened no response. The family could not feel at peace in the apartment unless Teresita were out of it or shut up in her room with a headache that was real or improvised as it happened.

Following the advice of her anonymous counselor in Finland Carreño had come to see that it was not for the best to push Teresita into a premature concert career. She was willing to let her filter into public consciousness, giving a concert here or there as occasion presented itself. Meanwhile she gave her daughter invaluable but irregular lessons. They convinced her that here was the dust that stars are made of. The family learned to dread these lessons. When Carreño announced at the luncheon table: "Teresita, I want to see you at three o'clock today," they shivered. These torrid temperaments were bound to clash in disagreement, the lessons sure to end in a double headache.

It was the mother's plan that they appear in two-piano concerts together. The idea had public appeal. Nevertheless, this combination did not last. Carreño for once was the more nervous of the two, and the quality of her own solo groups suffered in consequence. Besides, she could never be sure that Teresita would play until she was actually on the platform. Speaking of such a concert the *Neueste Nachrichten* of Chemnitz noted that

Fr. Carreño was not at her best this time; the palm went incontestably to her daughter, Teresita Carreño Tagliapietra, who since the last time she played in Chemnitz has come into gorgeous bloom both bodily and musically, and who gave proof yesterday in the "E minor Concerto" of Chopin of well-ripened artistry. I cannot remember ever having heard this concerto—or Chopin in any form at that—played so beautifully and with such comprehension of his own inner meaning.

Finally, in 1906, Carreño found her daughter ready for a concert with orchestra. The Singakademie, she hoped, would prove a setting of as good omen for her daughter as it had been for herself in 1889. Teresita presented herself in three concerti, each one an old favorite on the slate of the great Brünnhilde. On the evening of the ordeal Carreño, who faced thousands at a time without a tremor, was too nervously upset to attend the performance. Teresita felt more at ease for her absence. This examination earned her a good *cum laude*. The *Berliner Lokal Anzeiger* admitted that "she had success, but she would perhaps have had a greater one if she did not carry the name which on the other hand again wakened an interest in her appearance at the very outset. For Teresita has an intensively musical nature together with individuality and wild temperament.

Her managers were to find out to their cost that this temperament was apt to trickle into her business relations. They learned not to count her concerts before they were given. If she appeared for rehearsal at all, she came half an hour late without apology. Or she would telephone to her agent in Frankfurt, postponing a concert she was to give that evening, simply because she had found something more interesting to do in Cologne. Concert agents, who had at first taken her seriously for the sake of her mother and her promise, after Teresita had defaulted once too often, began to withdraw from the scene. When she did play the result was not to be foretold. She might choose to thrill her audience with delicate, insinuating melodies, or it might be her night for deafening their ears with the noise of the mob storming the Bastille. But no matter how much she annoyed them, conductors, critics, agents, and the public conceded that she could play the piano—if and when she felt inclined. That was not often, for there was little ambition in her. She preferred to lie indolently upon her uncomfortable laurels rather than let them prick her into activity uncongenial to her nature. And with teaching the situation was much the same. She was a good teacher when it pleased her to be. If she preferred to go shopping instead of giving her lesson, she did not think it necessary to notify her students first. Let them wait by twos and threes if they cared to.

Teresita's will-o'-the-wispish charm was attractive to the young men of her acquaintance, among them a would-be singer, conductor, composer, or whatever the fates would lead him to become, from England. A broad, tall, and likable young man, Teresita found him amusing, tolerable, or irritating according to her mood. He fell irreparably in love with this tousle-curled, trouble-making beauty who could on occasion turn into a sleek bobbed-haired demon with bangs overnight. Teresita considered him a plaything, not caring particularly whether he came or went. It was not Teresita's lovers but her health that bothered Carreño at this moment. Since she could not be left alone in the apartment while her mother traveled in Australia, Carreño decided to take her along. Teresita fell in with the idea. There was just a chance that this adventuring might brighten the dull life that she found so desolate. Besides, she liked being with Arturo.

Melbourne was the first objective. One morning there came a knock at the door: "A gentleman to see you, Miss, from Berlin." Teresita clapped her hands: "Mammie, what do you think? That crazy boy has followed me all the way here, but I didn't believe he would do it." And to the boy: "I shall be down directly," which meant a good half hour in Teresita language. This time when he asked her to marry him she saw no reason for refusing. Was he not her Lohengrin come to fight her battles, to free her from the intolerable monotony of being her mother's shadow? Why had she never thought of it before? She could lead her own life, be her own free self like any other girl of twenty-five. Carreño agreed. What a relief to delegate the responsibility of Teresita to this strong, solid Englishman. They might even be happy together. The wedding took place simply in church on the fifth of June, 1907, and Teresita for the first time was to know the joy of living in her own house, of being her own mistress to ride and swim or just dream at will with the smoke rings wreathing above her. The pair eventually followed Carreño's route home by way of the Fiji Islands. Suva was the place which in all their adventuring suited them best.

When Carreño returned to Berlin after the disenchanting summer of 1908 in Italy and Oberstdorf, she found Teresita established in an apartment of the Kaiserin Augustastrasse 74. It was not Teresita who notified her mother that there would be a baby in the fall, but the mother of her husband, who casually mentioned it in a letter written to ask Carreño to settle a certain sum upon Teresita until her son should have finished his musical studies. Carreño saw with a sinking heart that the burden of Teresita's support was still to rest mainly upon her shoulders, and answered in a typical letter:

I wish it were in my power to do as you ask me. Alas! I cannot, for my only resources are my work, which unfortunately I cannot so safely rely on (no artist ever can) as to enable me to settle any fixed sum on Teresita for one year or any part of it. That I am ready to do what I can, and as much as it is in my power, I hardly need to mention, for to help our children is not only the mother's privilege but her greatest pleasure.

Meanwhile Teresita had turned from her piano to composition, samples of which she sent to her mother in Oberstdorf. Carreño took time to criticize them in detail in a letter which shows how ready she always was to ignore previous disappointments in the dawning of the slightest hope.

. . . It was impossible for me to answer your first letter, because I was stupid enough to try to cut out a sliver which had become imbedded in the flesh of the little finger of my right hand, and the same thing happened as in Melbourne. Now, God be thanked, I am better, and in a few days I shall not even remember what I endured.

Your Sonata has many very good things, and I took much pleasure in playing it. As I told you when I read it over superficially on the day you showed it to me, it is not good that the first part should be in

E, and the second in D major. The Scherzo, too, ought to stay in the principal key just like the last movement, or at least in some related one. The development of the first part is not well-made, and the Scherzo is too short. All these defects however are just the result of your inexperience. With the next Sonata everything will be much better. Your last composition (that which you do not know how to name) I was unable to play. When I shall do so I will tell you more about it. Your idea of modernizing that Bach Fugue pleases me very much. It will be a good study for you, and will be a good thing for the piano if you adapt it better to our instrument of today. I am very glad that the things for the "Killiwillie" had already come and amuse you. I believe I have not forgotten anything; but ask your nurse, and tell me if anything is lacking and I will send it to you.

In October the baby was born. Teresita, the mother, was almost as helpless as her daughter Suva. When the baby cried so did the mother. Teresita, the housekeeper, fared no better. Seventeen-year-old Eugenia was shocked by the size of Teresita's meat bill, and would have liked to show her how to manage as thriftily as she did for her mother, a duty she only recently assumed. Both Teresita and her husband were unhappy. Was this the freedom for which they had forsaken their homes? Was it for this they had abandoned their music studies? When Teresita's mother-in-law stepped in, offering to take the baby while her parents went on with their professions, both jumped at the chance.

Teresita left for Paris accompanied by Josephine, this time to study singing and acting. She bid for her mother's sympathy by describing her lonely Christmas in one little room "like Mimi in La Bohème. . . . If you had let me study the ballet when I was nine or ten years old, things would be much easier for me. . . . People expect so much of an artist, a wonderful voice, good diction, and the facility of a ballet dancer, to be Sarah Bernhardts, Duses, Strausses, and Debussys all in one," she laments. In a peculiar manner she loved her mother. "I wish I could do something to help in some way, as it seems you were born to work for other people," she affectionately wrote more than once, yet without energy enough to put her thought into action. She shared with her mother the new discovery of a miraculous toothpaste called Kolynos, and asked her to try it on the "kids," and then in the same breath she suggested that her mother open a piano school in Paris, London, and New York all at once, because people are becoming interested in *"la nouvelle méthode allemande par laquelle on arrive à bien jouer sans beaucoup étudier."* Even Breithaupt's revolutionary book, *Die Natürliche Klaviertechnik,* dedicated to Carreño, was being translated into French.

And on she went at random, adding violin and wind instruments to her studies in order to write a fairy opera, buying expensive clothes while her mother footed the bills. Then, tiring of Paris, Teresita left for Levanto to study singing with Braggiotti, and finding him much like Lilli Lehmann in his style of voice production, she changed to Grazziani in Florence, who taught in the good old Italian way more to her liking.

Teresita is a hard person to keep track of. She lives now under Josephine's name, now under her own. Sometimes she turns up in Paris where the floods bring the smells of disinfectants into her window and works spasmodically at score reading with the thought of becoming a conductor. Again, the fact that she is able to crescendo from a pianissimo to a good forte on high C makes her decide that singing is her calling after all. Money drifts through her fingers like the white sand of the Riviera. When there is no more, she pawns the clothes she dislikes and writes for a new supply of funds. Now and then she sees her husband only to quarrel at the slightest provocation or none at all. Amicably enough they decide to separate, not yet a year after the child's birth. Again she moves on from place to place. Her husband seeks her out in Jersey only to find that she is back in Paris. Eager to marry a young girl of recent acquaintance who will make him a better wife, he now desires a divorce, which on her mother's advice Teresita refuses to grant. Josephine once more comes to live with her favorite among Carreño's children, this time in a Milan apartment, where Teresita continues to disown her name. She is afraid of something, of anything, even of people on the street. But when Josephine falls ill with a third attack of double pneumonia, she nurses her day and night, substituting the medicines she believes in for those the doctor prescribes. Worse comes to worst when the landlord suddenly sells the building, and orders them to leave at the end of the week. Teresita fights for a reprieve. Moving Josephine just then would be fatal. Several weeks of grace are granted, during which a chimney fire nearly smothers them both. Yet Josephine miraculously recovers, thanks to the devoted care of one who, like Scarlett O'Hara, only in a rare moment thinks first of anyone but herself.

Tired of Milan Teresita accepts an invitation to visit a friend in Norway. It is a happy vacation, the nicest part of which is the time spent alone as Miss de Paul in Aasgaard: "I feel so much happier and quieter when people know nothing about me, and I can pass unobserved through the crowds," she writes.

A new city now lures her. She returns to Berlin to ask that Arturo accompany her to Rome where Maestro Villa will do wonders for her voice. She sees it with clarity. The piano will always wait for her. For singing it will soon be too late. Arturo is not free to join her as she begged, and Teresita leaves for Rome, only to abandon it again for Naples against her mother's wishes.

With Teresita, Carreño would always be beyond her depth. Her resources were exhausted. How could she be shielded, kept safe among the dreadful people she chose to cultivate as her friends! Yet Teresita proved more than once that she could handle an emergency. Not many days before, Teresita had pushed away only just in time the point of a dagger meant for the heart of the medical student at her side. It fell from the hand of a jealous rival. Carreño read the letter telling of this episode with horror and sent up a silent prayer to the Dear Father for the one who, with all her vagaries, was most like herself.

*Giovanni and Teresita*

CARREÑO never admitted to herself that her children could be grown men and women. Giovanni, even at thirty, was still her "beloved baby boy." His mother liked to think of him so, liked to manage his life. In great part this attitude helped to keep him dependent, kept him from making the most of his gifts. He had inherited something of the *laissez aller* nature of his father, the baritone, his love of a game of chance, as well as a paler reflection of his talent, but he looked like his mother, with the same cameo-cut-in-onyx profile, the same proud bearing of hidalgo ancestors. He was witty, he was clever, he could be the life of the party. Yet, unlike his mother, his joyousness seldom rang true. It displayed itself against a backdrop of pessimism at first assumed—the sophisticated veneer of the very young—then gradually becoming ingrained.

Far from intending to stand in his way, it was important to Carreño that her only son should find himself. His talent for the violin was already somewhat developed. To use it as a means to this end seemed worth the trial, and Carreño unhesitatingly spent 2,000 m. for a good violin and much more for the best of teaching. However, long hours of intensive practice were not for Giovanni. He would have reveled in that short-cut method "by which one arrives at superlative results without much study." Thoroughly annoyed by an instrument which would not at once respond to his thought and fingers, he turned to shorthand and typing, learning the bare essentials necessary for the position offered him in a business office in Paris. The *sine qua non* of alertness and care for detail had not been acquired in his course, and this opening, too, soon closed against him.

There was one field in which he might succeed with a minimum of effort, given the prerequisite which Giovanni felt he had. He could sing in his beguiling high baritone to the tinkle of the guitar so as to enrapture his friends. With practically no study at all he joined a light opera company in London for a season, then toured all over Great Britain taking a minor part in that popular success, "The Merry Widow." He found but slight reward in this dull routine, in this music distasteful to one who had been fed on richer fare, but he did like to sing. That he knew.

Carreño believed in the possibilities of his voice and was willing to meet the expense of study with the best masters Italy afforded. Giovanni accordingly settled in Rome with friends. From there he wrote to his mother: "The Signora is more like Teresita than anybody else. She lets her husband do the work. She stays in bed and complains, when it is she who is late, that the dinner is cold." The expense of daily lessons and comfortable living were a great drain on Carreño's purse. Leaving for her second Australian tour she carefully set aside the allowance she felt she could afford, to be sent to Giovanni in monthly installments. To his letter of thanks Carreño answered encouragingly, understandingly, revealingly:

My own beloved baby boy: Your dear letters have come and have rejoiced our hearts. . . . You must have been very much "down in the dumps" when you wrote, as Arturo received a letter by the same mail as yours to me from Signor Villa in which he speaks most encouragingly about your progress and the development of your voice. I was very much surprised at what you write.

Do not get down-hearted, darling, as even though your voice might not develop to be a very wonderful voice, the quality of it is beautiful, and if you become a true, great artist you will carry everything through with your great art; but it must be truly great art! It is not the large quantity of voice which makes the success: it is the great art. I could name to you a whole row of great singers whose voices were not large. In fact some of them had small voices as for instance my old teacher Delle Sedie. . . . Take Maurel as another example. His voice was not large and not so very sympathetic and yet what a great artist he is even as an old man now! He must be nearly seventy years old, yet he is great as an artist, though his voice is a thing of the past. Take Wüllner; did he ever have a voice? I don't think he ever had as much as he has now. What he possesses is mighty little but more than he ever had, and what a career he has made with his great art, his temperament, his wonderful diction and interpretation. Did you ever hear him? He has made a sensation in the United States and his houses have been crowded to overflowing for his Liederabende in every city in which he has appeared in America, and that also singing in German.

So, darling baby boy mine, do not worry and do not get discouraged. Work hard and aim at the highest in our art and you will come out with flying colors. It needs a lot of work, of thought; in fact more mind-work than technical work, a great deal of self-abnegation in every respect. But the results, when you have attained that height in art which every true artist must aim for, are most satisfactory, and one feels entirely compensated by the happiness which achieving something of what we hoped for in our art brings to us. No one knows that better than your mother, my darling blessed baby boy! So then, courage, and work for the highest!

Your sarcastic remarks about the money matters and your being afraid of being left to suffer for want of money in case you are ill I do not think I deserve. Will you look back into all your life and tell me whether my help has ever failed you. As you must acknowledge to yourself that I have always been there to see to your wants and to get you out of things which were far from being "wants," you need not fear that you may now come to grief for want of my help. As long as I can work and earn, and you are not yet ready to take up the burden of your self-support as an artist (which I know how anxious you are to do!) I will be there, sweetheart. If through illness or accident I am taken away, then will be the time when you will not have your mother to look after you.

Arturo was delighted with your Italian letter, and we both were very happy to see how much you have learned. Keep on studying and improving, my darling. Languages are of great importance and utility in life, especially to an artist who must travel all over the world to earn his living.

I get letters pretty regularly from Teresita who is still in Paris and seems satisfied with her progress. Let us hope that she will succeed with her purpose. Josephine is with her, as you know, and is well, I am happy to say. Whether she also is studying singing and acting or not, that I don't know. Teresita does not mention anything about it, and as I have not received the bills for Josephine's tuition, I suppose that she—Josephine—has withstood the temptation.

Things with us are going less well in a business way than they did three years ago, and Heaven knows they were weak enough. Of course this is quite *entre nous,* as it will not do for people to think that I am doing anything else but brilliant business. Should anyone ask you, say that you presume that business is good. In almost every city I have had half the houses which I had the last time I was here, and as the enthusiasm is if anything greater than before and the press is still more enthusiastic than ever, I can't explain it in any other way but that the people are not musical enough to wish to hear me play again, and only those who are really interested in music and true lovers of it come to my recitals, and they are a very small number. So far I am not losing money—*es fehlte noch*—but I am not making any more than just expenses. It is rather discouraging, isn't it? If the enthusiasm were not as it is I would give it up and take a rest before going to South Africa. My health is also not as I should like it, as I have all sorts of ailings which make life not sweet; but as long as it remains within these limits I suffer and go on doing my different duties.

Back again a year later on Italian soil, Carreño visited both Giovanni in Rome and Teresita in Milan. From there she wrote in a letter that gives much of her simple philosophy:

It is just one week today since we parted with you at the station in Rome and with what a heavy and sad heart did I leave you, my own darling! I felt as though I wanted either to stay with my boy or take him along! What a sad fate it is, after all, a mother's! She brings her babies up and they grow nearer and dearer to her heart as the years come and go, and then she must part with them at the time of life when age weighs upon her and she needs them and their love more than ever. But if her babies are happy and contented, and she sees that they are making a way towards a position which may bring them all they themselves wish to possess, she cheerfully submits, thanks God that her darlings are doing well, and builds her happiness on her own unhappiness. Queer, is it not?

Well, never mind! Such is life, such is nature and above all, such is God's own will and we must submit and be resigned.

Once having bought real estate in California Carreño thought seriously of investing in property in Italy. But her sound business instincts once more held her back from doing the imprudent thing with hard-earned money. She writes to Giovanni soon after her arrival in Berlin,

Thank you a thousand times for your dear letter, the last one received only yesterday owing to the fact that Arturo and I took a trip to Oneglia (on the Italian Riviera) to look at a property which—as far as the description and the photographs which were sent to us by the agent in Venice went—seemed the very thing which I have wanted to buy as a speculation for many years. . . . In order not to keep you in suspense about it, I will tell you right now that it was not what we expected and of course we did not buy it. It is beautifully situated on a high mountain and the view (all around are olive tree mountains) is most beautiful. If I had money I would buy it at once as a place where we could go every summer for pleasure and enjoy the gorgeous scenery and the pure mountain air! I haven't the shekels and so I will enjoy the high altitude of 28 Kurfürstendamm if I can't afford to hire some place for the summer.

Another matter which we have settled is about our apartment. We will stay right here where we are although I found one apartment which I would love to have had, the price of it being 1300 m. more than this one per year, and taking that into consideration, the large expense of moving and a very large sum which would have to be spent to get the other apartment in order, we have weighed our poverty against all other probabilities and possibilities and decided that the most reasonable all around was to remain where we are. I know that you will not be sorry to hear that we remain in the old home.

We are very sorry to hear about your tooth, my darling baby boy. How on earth did you break it? You have such splendid teeth that you ought to be very careful of them. Did you try to bite anyone's head off, and was it a head of iron? . . .

Enclosed you will find a bill for one hundred marks which I want you to use for a trip to the sea-side. You must not stay in Rome during these hot weeks. The sea air will do your voice and your general health a lot of good. So please, darling baby boy mine, take the next train after you get this letter and go anywhere near the sea where it is cool and where the air is invigorating. If you need more money, let me know.

In August of 1911 Giovanni was obliged to confess that he had gambled away most of his allowance. "My cursed, my damned bad luck has proven itself once more, and was mocking me," he pleads, and adds as an afterthought, "I know I am an awful burden to you." Carreño had a temperament that could flare, but in forgiveness too she was never halfhearted.

The reason I did not answer you sooner after receiving your former letter was that I felt really grieved and awfully disappointed in you. I have such confidence in your sound common sense and in your power of will that to learn that you had again succumbed to the temptation of gambling was a great blow to me and to my trust in your strength of will. Had I written you under the impression which your letter made upon me I would have added to your feelings of unhappiness, and I preferred to wait until the first impression had somewhat subsided and I felt less unhappy. As I see how well you recognize your own folly, I am not going to say any more about it. Let it be a life-lesson to you, darling baby boy!

Who is that idiot Fano? Has he the long ears which befit his brain condition? If he hasn't it is certainly a mistake of nature. He should have four legs, long ears and be called by the befitting name "Asino."

I had to smile at what you write was his opinion of your voice. If you had offered him a thousand Lire to get you an engagement in grand opera you would have seen how much better he found your voice immediately. Italy is simply a débauché country in art, and I shall be glad when you are ready to get out of it.—Don't you let anyone interfere with your tone production which is most excellent. You really sing, not bellow as is the fashion now in Italy. That jackass called Fano didn't think your voice large enough to sing in grand opera! The ignorant fool! At any rate you are not the first instance of being told by a manager that the voice was not large enough: Your father was told the same thing: de Reszke (the tenor) was told to give up singing as he had no voice: Pauline Lucca was sent away from a conservatory in Vienna because she had no voice, and hundred other examples I could cite you if I only remembered them now. As you see, Asini are a common animal and not specially Italian.

I enclose here two hundred marks, all I have with me, and please let me know at once how much money you need to accomplish your object, so that I can tell Schickler to send it to you.

And so she stands as fiercely maternal as any mother bear, ready to growl at anyone who dares to attack her offspring. Giovanni went on singing from one impresario to another, not knowing which criticism to take to heart. According to one his placement was wrong, while another advised musical comedy in America because of its less exacting standards, and a third declared that *"Baritono Tagliapietra ha una voce bellissima ma e nervoso come un diavolo."*

At last the longed-for chance was his. He had a real engagement to sing in *Il Barbiere de Sevilla* in Vignola near Modena on Christmas Day. "You will understand that your baby boy is in awful agonies," he wrote. "Think of me at nine o'clock on Sunday." At Kurfürstendamm 28 nobody thought of going to bed before the coming of the telegram for better or worse. The bell rang; Carreño unfolded the piece of buff paper hardly daring to read its message. The others held their breath. "A great success! It was a great success," shouted the mother.

Long after the others had gone to bed a happy mother sat writing to her son from the fullness of her pride:

My own beloved baby boy: Just now your telegram has come and our joy over the good news it has brought to us I cannot tell you in words. We all have jumped for joy and oh! how thankful your old mother feels that this, your first trial in your career has brought you satisfaction and joy and also the encouragement which the good results of this your first appearance, the first step in your career, must be to you! I am awfully happy over it, my own darling. My prayers were with you as also my heart and my thoughts. I kept watching the clock in our dining room as we sat there for supper, calculating the time at which you made your entrance and followed you with my imagination from one scene to the other, praying that success might be yours. My prayers were heard, and how grateful am I for this! Keep on working, my beloved boy! Do not lose a moment of study and improvement and aim at the highest pinnacle of your art. Be a true, honest, real artist, and this can only be achieved by hard and continued work. Nobody knows this better than your mother. Art is such infinite joy to the artist and such a generous repayer for all the work we have to perform and all the sacrifices we bring to it! The satisfaction and the happiness that it brings us in return no one but an artist can know. Those who serve their art honestly and not for their own glory, those are the chosen ones, the truly great, and to those only does art give back thousandfold the compensation for all their hours days, months, and years of striving for the highest ideal. With true greatness in art also comes the remuneration of making yourself an independent position in life. I have written down now, my beloved darling, in these lines my creed and my experience. Following these firm convictions even though it may not be as great as I had dreamed it in my youth, has yet enabled me to make my way, establish for myself a position in art, and also has brought me the material remuneration which has helped me to help my babies. Above all this has stood my firm belief in God and in his help without which I could have done nothing. Without God there can be no true, great art.

We have missed you awfully, my own precious darling, and your mother has longed and longed for her beloved baby boy. Twenty times a day at least I wanted to write and send you the money to come and spend the Christmas days with us, and the only thing which kept me back from doing it has been the thought that perhaps in coming away just now you might miss a chance of presenting yourself and giving yourself a chance of making a start in your career and judging for yourself on the stage what you can do. I am glad now that I withstood the temptation and sacrificed my own pleasure.

The Christmas has been the same as of old to us. The tree is in my study here, the presents on the table, pianos, sofas just as you so well know it. I—well, darling, my heart was heavy, for you and Teresita were not here. My mind went back to the years when I had you all around me. I saw you in my heart's memory, first with your knickerbockers, then your first long trousers, your getting taller and taller, your voice changing, your hands becoming those of a man, the boy disappearing, and then I saw you as you are, a tall, splendid, manly man. Teresita, the darling child, wayward but sweet with all her great charm and her beauty developing, her great, great talent also developing and being neglected by her and making me so unhappy because of this neglect of a great gift which God had given her—then all my worry about her—well, darling, this all made my heart feel heavy.

Well, there is so much that I have which makes me feel so deeply grateful to Him who has granted it to me, that I made myself no end of reproaches for allowing any other thoughts but those of gratitude to occupy my thoughts and my heart, and when your telegram came it lifted all that was a weight from my heart and dispelled all that might have been a regret of the times gone by. I am now happy and only gratitude fills my poor old heart, for though I know well enough what you still have to do, this good beginning is a good omen and makes me see better than ever that I made no mistake in advising you as I did when you sang for me in London for the first time some four years ago now.

Arturo and I returned yesterday afternoon from Budapest and Vienna where I had been playing. Thank Heaven that I have ten days of rest before me! I have worked awfully hard in England and here, but I am glad that I did it, as it has brought me good results. . . .

Giovanni did not have the push to follow up his success at once. He contented himself with singing in small towns to good effect in *Don Pasquale* and *Faust*. The ability to keep his temper was not one of his qualities, and it did not ingratiate him with an impresario to have him slam the door in his face. It was Carreño who kept his courage up through her unbreakable faith. She offered him the chance to sing in her concerts, to study for opera in Germany, anything he really wanted, and unflaggingly she wrote giving him advice from the deep well of her own experience, as in the letter from Lissa:

Here is your mother in a little bit of a place where she plays this evening (Heaven knows why!)—and where she feels just as lonesome and as hungry for a sight of her beloved son as she does no matter where she is and where she goes!

From your letter to Arturo I see that you did not get my telegram on your birthday and that makes me feel very badly. I sent it on the seventh in the morning from Göttingen (where I was playing that evening) and I cannot understand why it did not reach you. I feel awfully over it, for I did so want that you should get a loving greeting from me on that day! My thoughts and my blessings were with you as they ever are, but I wanted to remind you that your mother had been there at your birth and was so happy when she held her baby boy in her arms! God bless you, my own darling, and keep healthy and happy for many and many years to come!—

I am continually playing and travelling. Since years I have not had so much work on hand, I mean so many concerts following each other here in Europe, and though I am glad to earn the money, it keeps me a slave to the work and does not allow me to do any writing or anything else which I would like to do excepting of course solitaire and reading in the trains. . . .

The notices about your performance are on the whole, though short, very good—I am sorry that you did not send the names of the paper and the date. You must collect all these notices with the titles of the paper and the dates, and keep them to send to the agents, as they always need them and want them to send to managers. You must get yourself several copies and keep one for your own private collection, one for me, and the other for the "Reklame."

In talking to Leonard (one of my agents) about you and your success, he asked me whether you did not care to sing in German. When I told him that you could do so as you spoke the language perfectly, he asked me why you did not come to Germany. He thinks that you could do well and find an engagement in a theatre here. I told him that you wished to make first your career in Italian Opera before you tried anything else. If you came to Germany you would have to study first with a Kapellmeister the German operas. Would you care to do this? I must now come to the end of this scrawl as I am afraid of straining my hand and must look out for my recital this evening. Night before last I played in Posen; tomorrow I play in Breslau and on Wednesday the 14th in Prag. From Prag I return home to Berlin where I shall be until the eighteenth, starting on that day for Vienna where I play on the 19th and then come home again to stay until the twenty-seventh. I play with Nikisch at the Philharmonic Concerts on the 25th (public rehearsal) and on the 26th (Concert). Then comes Gewandhaus, Leipzig, and then I continue my wanderings to München, Halle, Köln, Bonn, Frankfurt a/M., Wiesbaden, Neustadt, Karlsruhe, Stuttgart, Saarbrücken, Greiz, Leipzig, Berlin (Élite Concert), Riga, Königsberg, and on the fourth of April Paris. On the 27th of April I play again in London and on the 7th of May I give my first summer recital in London. Would you like to sing in my recital in London? How jolly that would be! Let me know, darling, if you feel at all inclined to do so.

She was not to have the pleasure of presenting her son in one of her own concerts. Discouraged that Giovanni leaned upon her more exactingly than ever and that for three months he had not troubled to write, she finally reminds him that she is no longer young, that she does not feel well enough to carry the burden after the current year, much to her sorrow, "sorrow because I feel my physical health disappearing, and sorrow because I cannot help you and Teresita until you are on top of the hill. You will have, both of you, to do the climbing on your own feet." Teresita had incurred her displeasure by leaving Rome, her teacher Villa, and the singing career, to go to Naples for purpose of her own without caring to notify her mother, whose patience had reached the snapping point. However, it was not in her to abandon the children to their fate. Her threat had frightened them into good behavior, and she went on as before.

So Carreño with all the hope of her believing affection lived on for the day when Giovanni's best would be recognized by the public and the press. Since he preferred to remain in Italy, good fortune attend him there!

For Carreño motherhood had found its fullest reward in the two daughters of d'Albert. They were the ones to draw profit from the haphazard upbringing to which Teresita and Giovanni had been subjected. Carreño had learned much at their expense. Eugenia and Hertha were not burdened with the handicap of poor inheritance. Their mother resolved that they should develop normally and wholesomely, much like any other young girls of their age.

When Carreño left Coswig for Berlin, she entrusted the full care for her little girls to Fräulein Krahl, "*die gute* Krahl." She was devotion itself, beside being a thrifty housekeeper and a person who knew her own mind. The domestic mechanism ran smoothly under her supervision. But soon after Arturo's first surprise appearance it became evident that he disliked Krahl as cordially as she looked upon his coming as an intolerable intrusion. His marriage brought the strain of their relation to early explosion. A slight error of judgment was magnified in importance until Carreño was brought to the point of dismissing her faithful helper in anger. It was not easy for Carreño to sever her connection with one who had stood by while she was steering her way through the rapids of despair to happier waters. This shows through in her parting letter:

I should like to do everything, everything for you to show you how I feel with you with my whole heart and how full I am with gratitude for the love you bear me and my children. Only one thing I cannot do, much as I should like to, that is to keep you with me. That is quite impossible after all that has happened between us. During the seven years that we have been together we have both grown older, I have even grown *old* and the consideration which I took for your very marked touchiness and independence until the last moment of your being here I can take no longer, because I must have peace and freedom in my home.

You say that you have stood a great deal from me. You will never know, for I cannot express it, how much I have suffered through your lack of respect and consideration for me. From no one on earth, excepting those three horrible men to whom I was married before I married my present husband, have I stood what I have stood from you. Only by thinking of your great qualities have I managed to be patient with you, to find excuses for you myself in my heart, and so to get along with you without daily friction! You don't realize it, because that is the way you are and you can't help it; but I can no longer live that way and have grown too old for that. Even if it had been my fault—and I admit that I may be to blame—I must stay as I am and have the right like any person on earth to do what I like in my home and to have my freedom.

Believe me, my good Krahl, when I resign myself to the sad necessity of giving you up, I am the loser, not you! But, alas! there is no other way. Perhaps in time we shall come together again, when the past has been forgotten. I cannot tell you enough how grateful I am for your feelings towards me and my children. And my friendship, as well as the love of the children, I am certain you will have for life, no matter what the circumstances.

Ever since the separation d'Albert had periodically threatened to take advantage of the clause in the divorce agreement which gave him the right to visit their children. Each time the meeting was postponed for one reason or another. When Arturo had taken his place at Carreño's side, d'Albert again entered an intruding wedge through his lawyer, who wrote asking that Carreño dispose the minds of Eugenia and Hertha favorably for the coming of their father. To this she replied:

It is unfortunately not possible to comply with Herr d'Albert's wish and that for educational as well as health reasons. Herr d'Albert seems to forget that his children know nothing of him, and that he is a perfect stranger to the little ones. If I may remind him that he left his children when the elder was two years old and the younger only five months, he can explain to himself why the children know nothing. I have thought it right to keep them as long as possible in ignorance of the fact that their father left them without any reason which could justify him in their eyes. The children are so sensitive that I let them go nowhere for fear of their becoming ill in air that is not quite pure. Therefore I must insist that the children meet their father either at your house as you so kindly suggest or at that of Frau Direktor Wolff, and that whosoever accompanies them stays with the children during the whole of the time. But for the moment Eugenia has a bad attack of bronchitis and Hertha too is ill with a cold, so that the doctor has strictly forbidden their going outdoors.

This visit was put off again, and in reply to another letter repeating d'Albert's wish that the children be notified of his existence, Carreño wrote once more. She does not know how to prepare the children for seeing the father who until now has treated them with disregard. "Lies are unfortunately much too hard for me, and are neither to my taste nor in my character. He must find a way to their hearts himself and obtain their pardon." To Carreño's extreme relief this visit also did not materialize.

Not until both little girls were away at school in Neu Wat-
zum in 1904 were they to make the acquaintance of their father.
At least nothing had been done to prejudice them against
d'Albert, and at first they were thrilled to go to this intimate
stranger who had known them well before they knew themselves. In their imagination he was a kind of Siegfried as stately
as their mother. They knocked at his door in a hotel of Braunschweig with eager knuckles.

The high-pitched, weak *"Herein"* was not the rich, deep-
voiced welcome they expected, nor did this narrow-chested,
dwarflike person, who looked at them peeringly through com-
pressed slits, come up in any way to the ideal of their imagination. Worst of all he wore his hair long and an unfashionably
broad-brimmed hat on top of it. Eugenia especially dreaded the
moment when she would have to present him to her school-
mates. Disappointment kept them unresponsive, and d'Albert on
his part was at a loss to find words to reach these hostile little
girls whose only wish from the moment of their entrance was
to be gone again. Nevertheless, from then on the father made a
point of keeping in closer touch with his daughters, partly because he took pleasure in annoying Carreño whenever he could.
Eugenia little by little cultivated a certain liking for him. Hertha with instinctive loyalty to her mother held herself strictly
aloof.

Although they dressed alike in their blue Peter Thompsons,
aprons and hair ribbons helped to accentuate the difference between the two sisters. Eugenia's hair was dark with a coppery
sheen as the sun fell upon it. There was a glint of copper, too,
in her brown eyes. In temperament and looks she vaguely suggested a much improved d'Albert. Blue-eyed Hertha's hair was
golden. Her profile and her fearless, straight thinking were her
mother's. Eugenia was the more reserved, Hertha sunnily outgoing. Every gesture was ample. The motion of her walk took
in all of the surrounding territory as she threw her body from
side to side, not to make faster progress as much as just for joy
in action. When something amused her she threw back her

head, opened her mouth wide, and shouted aloud. There were no mezzotints in Hertha's makeup.

Of the two Eugenia was the more practical, the more conventional. It bothered her that she was almost the smallest one in the whole school, that her pet name was *"Liliputchen."* No exercise was too hard provided it might help to make her taller, while Hertha in a halfhearted way did what she could to grow thin. For her it added to the zest of life to shock others by her antics, although Eugenia, the conformist, called her to task for it with a reproving "Aber Hertha!" Eugenia would have had her mother be like the ordinary mothers of her friends. Once she called her to task for addressing the letters she wrote to them jointly to "Fräuleinen" instead of "Fräulein." She went further, admonishing her: "But when you come to the station to meet us, please don't call our names out loud, for everyone will repeat them then, and say them so very wrongly because they can't pronounce them. But please above all don't wear that jacket, you know which one I mean, the one I can't bear. Even if it is fashionable, it is unfashionable for me." At another time, upon hearing of a rumor that d'Albert will marry again, she exclaims in despair: "I feel so ashamed of my father. Why can't he ever think of his children who carry his name? It is a disgrace to us, especially in Berlin, where people are so particular about the names." Being the children of artists had its shadows.

All that was less vital to Hertha. She was at the age when everything was either *"tragisch"* or *"pompös."* When she heard her father's opera *Flauto Solo* in Braunschweig that was *pompös,* when she had a poor report it was *tragisch,* but it did not keep her unhappy for long. What really upset her was apt to be something quite different. "When other people write 'Berlin mother,' then it is absolutely necessary that I write something also in that style," and she begins a letter: "My own darling Australian, American, European mother." From the depths of her affection she complains: "It's already bad when you can't be there Christmas, Easter or New Year, but when it comes to birthdays, my own private days, it is bad luck!" Hertha's letters are generally playful. She is fond of teasing her mother: "I nearly play as well as you do. I thought you might get jealous, so I never practice more than two hours. I might play better if I did, so I won't. I play your waltz now, the one you composed in Sidney [the "Valse Gayo," last of Carreño's published compositions] only it sounds a little different."

Whether they were at school in Wolfenbüttel, in Chicago, with their governess in Melbourne and in Durban, or on vacation in Oberstdorf, Ober-Salzberg, and Friedrichroda, the lives of Hertha and Eugenia ran parallel. They quarreled as sisters do. "You know that contradicting each other is the family crest," confesses Hertha. But let anybody dare to attack one, the other was sure to take a formidable stand in her defense.

Eugenia was a versatile person. Her talents were many but not driving. She played nicely—her hands were curiously like her father's—could cook a good dinner, and sew a neat seam, and play a game of tennis of which any young girl might be proud. In fact she became expert in sports of many kinds, of which horseback-riding was her favorite. In 1911 d'Albert made her a present of a horse, as much for the pleasure of adding its upkeep to Carreño's already heavy burdens as for that of delighting his namesake. Eugenia was the *persona grata* of the moment. All the good things of life appealed to her strongly, but she had days of reflective melancholy in which she took her future under microscopic consideration, threatening by turns to become a nurse, a suffragette, or a nun. After her confirmation in the Protestant Kaiser Wilhelm Gedächtniskirche she fell naturally into the groove waiting for her coming, one which suited her well and eased Carreño's shoulders. Eugenia who had a tendency toward order and thrift soon made herself at home in the intricacies of the art of keeping house. She also became her mother's right hand in initiating new pupils into the technical fundamentals of Carreño's way of teaching.

Hertha's leanings and gifts were artistic along two possible lines not incompatible with each other. She could cultivate painting, drawing, or singing with promising result, and she studied earnestly but with that exuberance which makes work seem play.

Carreño could look with just pride upon these two daughters. She had brought them to this point by giving them the advantages of discipline, education, and travel. Her hopes for them were of the highest. "I must go on working until Hertha is married," she reminded herself.

In her eldest daughter Carreño was never to take much comfort. As soon as she heard of the death of Mrs. Bischoff in 1902, she sent word to Emilita through Mrs. MacDowell that, if she needed it, a mother's love still existed for her. It was not until three years later that Emilita asked her mother for a meeting in Frankfurt, where Carreño happened to have a concert engagement. Clear-sighted Arturo put in his word of warning. He was sure it would prove to be another trouble escaped from her Pandora's box already overfilled. Carreño refused to listen. All at once she felt she could not wait until the appointed time to see this child, now a married woman thirty-one years old. Her incorrigibly maternal nature prevailed, and with a singing of the heart she made ready for the meeting.

It did not measure up to expectation. Arturo was right. The motives which brought Emilita to the point of seeking out her mother were not alone the promptings of affection. Before an hour had passed it was obvious that "Lita" looked upon her mother as the plentiful source of wealth from which she too might draw her share. Instead of the 5,000 marks for which she frankly asked on this afternoon she left with 500, and in parting begged Carreño to keep the meeting secret for fear of its reaction upon Sauret, her father. The mother in Carreño could survive even this disappointment. She recognized understandingly that Lita had been spoiled by an overindulgent foster mother, whose fortune she had inherited and brought to her husband, a young captain of the German army. This money had depreciated, leaving barely enough for living in the style demanded by army etiquette. Feeling herself not without responsibility toward her daughter Carreño decided to take on Lita and her many wants. Every letter kept her duly informed of them, even reminding the grandmother of the birthdays of her three grandchildren, of the most acceptable presents for every occasion. Naïvely she asked for jewelry and a fur coat for herself, for money that would spell a vacation for her son Walter. Or Lisbeth needed a change; it would be ideal if she could visit at Kurfürstendamm 28. Even as Carreño tried to gratify Lita's inexhaustible wishes to the limit of her powers, a voice cried within her—"this child is none of mine."

Taking all in all Carreño, surveying the past decade from the perspective of the jubilee year could find them good, could still write: "I am so grateful to our good Father in Heaven that He has granted me so much joy in life which has helped me so much to stand the deep sufferings which I have also had in it."

As Carreño turned from the clear vista of her past to the future which Providence in its kindliness and wisdom shrouded in mist, she knew that for years her chief suffering had come from being inadequate to the task of helping Teresita realize her great potentialities. After the strain and excitement of her anniversary year came the inevitable reaction.

Angered by Teresita's active opposition to her wishes and by her neglect in writing—"she only remembers my existence when she is in trouble and needs my help and the only address she gives me, her mother, is c/o Cooks"—, Carreño informs Giovanni that Teresita is not to be allowed to spend the summer in Salzberg. "My health has to be considered, as it is necessary for you all that I can keep on working and Teresita would make me so ill that I would be totally unfit for my next winter's work or to give the many lessons which I shall have to give in Salzberg in order to be able to pay the expenses of our living there. If I did not take the pupils we could not allow ourselves the summer in Salzberg or anywhere else but at home."

A month later she writes again:

You will find here if they all come, twenty pupils of mine. How is this for a rest? It is not much of a rest, you will say, and I know it; but we could not have been able to afford the trip here and the hiring of the Villa, and in one way we have a rest, for we all can enjoy this beautiful air, and I know that we need not worry about the expenses connected with our being here.—Eugenia and Herta will be as happy as can be to see you and are both looking forward to your visit. They both love you dearly, and if you teased them less their happiness would be untroubled. Please, darling baby boy, do not tease them so much and for my sake leave the question of fathers at rest. I wish you all, my beloved darlings, would only remember me in the parent question, and as I have been both mother and father to you all, it ought to be easy for you all to forget that there ever was a father in question.

Carreño went ahead for a few days of solitude on the Salzberg before the influx of family and pupils. Their sixteen pianos were distributed in every available peasant house on the mountain side. All was blissfully peaceful. The clouds that shrouded the summits overlooking Berchtesgaden nestling below were not yet clouds of war. No passport was needed to climb the road leading up the mountain, and Carreño enjoyed her walks in the rain which the salty mountain was miraculously able to soak in, as hour upon hour it descended in drenching sheets. The Villa Waltenberger cuddled against the woods halfway up the steep incline. This was the third return to its harboring walls, almost as congenial to Carreño's soul as Oberstdorf and the Pertisau of other years. From the toy village at the foot of the mountain through wooded paths, across flower-dotted fields to the breathtaking view of higher mountains still, dusted with snow, everything awakened a health-giving response in Carreño. But this year the twinges of rheumatism were particularly stubborn. The pupils arrived before Carreño was in shape for teaching.

One evening the family was finishing a late supper. From far away, then closer and circling around the house, came the sound of a guitar. It was "poor old Josephine" who knew even before a tenor voice broke into an Italian folk song, who it was that so romantically announced himself in a serenade: "It's Giovanni," she called out and hurried as fast as her shuffling feet would allow to open the door. And with the coming of Giovanni, the romantic reincarnation of the troubadour, life had new zest for the Carreño colony. Whether he was staging a mock auction of one of Hertha's latest paintings or singing *"Vorrei bacciarti"* in his melting baritone from the balcony railing to the accompaniment of his beribboned guitar, everybody stopped to listen. His joviality was contagious, but though it could raise his mother's spirits, it was not effective against rheumatism and gout. Carreño decided one morning that she must go at once to Italy for the good of her health, and it was a dejected group of pupils who watched the vanishing train carrying their teacher away, the one for whose instructions some had come from Finland, some from Australia, some from Turkey. Would she come back in two weeks as she had promised? Those who chose to stay on the chance of a return bombarded the Villa Waltenberger daily for news of Carreño's health, of her plans, and drowned their disappointment in dogged hard work in the morning, in rainy walks to Berchtesgaden at tea time, and in games of charades or cards at night. They had their reward. Carreño rejoined her family at the end of the third week almost her old, energetic self; but the relief was only temporary.

News came by cable one morning of the death of Mrs. Watson, in which her husband had preceded her the year before. A few days later, like a message from another world, came her parting letter, adding a second shock to the impact of the first. In spite of a trip alone to Oberstdorf before the beginning of the season Carreño was in no condition to face the exigencies of an American tour, always so much more arduous than a European one.

There was always Teresita to add to her depression. Teresita had been ill. As soon as she was able to leave the nuns in the nursing home in Florence, Carreño sent her to Lucerne to regain her strength. There too she could not find rest. Penniless as usual Teresita borrowed from a casual acquaintance, played the races, and won enough for third-class transportation to Brussels. From there she called to her mother for help, and once more not in vain.

Carreño on tour in England visited her daughter in London before embarking for the United States in the fall of 1913. She listened once again to Teresita's distorted views of life, heard herself blamed for not ever having tried to understand her, for being thirty thousand years behind the times in her outlook. After Teresita had left the hotel that evening, Carreño let herself go in one of her most severe attacks of hysterics; then, pulling herself together, she went for a long walk, not knowing or caring where it took her. Teresita, too, spent the next day in tears, then tried her best to placate her mother in a lovable, contrite letter. She deplores the trouble she is always causing, vows to do better, and advises her mother to take bromides instead of Fellow's Syrup. Unable to see herself as the cause of her mother's ill health, Teresita preferred to attribute it to lack of oil in the air of Europe. She should, prescribed Teresita, wrap up in wool soaked in oil to grease her joints "still tuned to the oily air of Caracas." Might it be that a potential doctor or nurse was lost in her as in her mother?

With a large sum of money at her disposal once more Teresita felt better. She would, she decided, return to the piano, give concerts, and teach, but not in London. And so before the new year made its entrance Teresita was once more discussing her future with her brother, this time in Milan. Before tea was served she was sure she wished to try her luck as an artist in Greece, and as she buttered her toast she changed to the idea of teaching the secrets of Carreño technique from a South American angle in Paris, then before the cups were removed she dreamed herself in Algiers. When they parted, neither knew what she really meant to do.

For Carreño herself the winter of 1913 could not have begun worse. The sea voyage was not long enough to soothe nerves jangled askew. Soon after landing Carreño fell easy prey to one of her chronic colds which developed into influenza and then into bronchitis. Physicians called in for advice in nearly every city en route tried one and all to persuade her to abandon the tour. They made graphic pictures of the dangers of a complete nervous breakdown, and did their best to frighten her into taking a year at least of concertless, studentless rest. It sounded appealing. But what of her manager Mr. Adams of the Wolfsohn bureau, who had worked hard and successfully to fill her calendar of dates! What of the John Church Company who were counting upon her to lend the weight of her approval and prestige to the Everett piano which she was playing in her concerts! No, she would see it through to the end. By a sheer miracle she survived and that with canceling only one single concert in all of the more than fifty on her roster.

Neither public nor critics knew that she was feeling unfit, dragging her way by force of will from town to town. On the

1916

*Carreño*

1913

platform she still appeared the Walküre whom mortal ills could not touch. There was in her playing a new aura of detached, visionary unworldliness that, if it no longer drove her hearers to excess with excitement as of old, did bring whole audiences to their feet in spontaneous expression of the veneration which awed and united them for this rare moment. They unconsciously felt in her music as they listened the wisdom and measure of long, rich living. It pointed the way with the clarity of deep insight to purer heights of serene enjoyment beyond the knowledge of man, but not beyond his capacity of feeling. Her appeal was perhaps less for the young than before. Those whose lives had passed the middle distance, or those who had through suffering lived much in a short span of time understood her meaning best. There were some who, openly disappointed, missed the fire of the old Carreño, and did not know how to find the new in her more softly voiced world-mindedness. Even the shopworn "Liebestraum" in her hands became a thing of elusive loveliness. People stopped breathing in order not to lose the point where sound merged into silence, whose very emptiness was charged with significance. Many who came to hear Carreño with the sole idea of being entertained left with the feeling of having shared in a religious experience. Carreño and the music she played were still indivisibly one and the same. She had never tried to look or to be younger than she was. So in simple honesty she disdained to assume the dash and passion natural to her in the days of her prime. Instead she rose on lighter wings into the rarer atmosphere of clairvoyance where now she felt at home. No less honestly could she say now as before: "I am Carreño!" So Dr. Walter Niemann comparing the Carreño of the Eighties with the Carreño in 1913 understandingly drew her musical likeness in an article published in *Reklam's Universum*, in honor of her sixtieth birthday. (See Postlude.)

In high spirits and proud of the crowning of her efforts with good returns and better health, Carreño looked forward eagerly to her home and her children. Hertha and Eugenia had been leading busy and normal lives at Kurfürstendamm 28, Hertha dividing her interests between painting and singing. The latter she seriously considered adopting as her profession until a cable from Carreño demanded that she stop her lessons at once. A casual remark, quite unintentionally made, had frightened her. Hertha's voice, Eugenia had written, sounded husky. Just that was enough to make the mother fear that the teaching might be at fault. It never occurred to either of the younger daughters to disobey. There was nothing for it but to concentrate with double energy on painting in which Hertha had been making noteworthy progress. Eugenia meanwhile kept house, studied, and taught in preparation for her mother's homecoming.

THE season was at last safely over, and Carreño as a concession to her physicians gave up teaching for the summer. Trouble loomed on the horizon with new and dramatic variations on the Teresita theme. From Milan she had set out in search of her Eldorado and found it in the warmer, freer air of Kram near Tunis. She wrote, filled with new peace, of the happiness she had found in her little apartment of the Arab quarter near the sea. Carreño's hair rose as she read. The European colony might be shocked, the police might look upon her with suspicion, although a perfectly respectable Neapolitan had come with her as her companion; Teresita for once was in her element. "I am really happy in the bottom of my heart," her letter fairly shouted. And not the least of her reasons for this was Mohammed, a romantic young Arab ten years her junior in front of whose cabin she went swimming every day. "There is youth for you," she exulted and described to her horrified mother how Mohammed, angry at not being able to open the door of his cabin, smashed the window and lifted her through it in his arms. Then she capped all with the climax of a Liszt "Polonaise": "He is just the sort of one I should like to bring to you as a son-in-law." Carreño turned cold at heart while Teresita's letter warbled on. Little does it matter to her that they meet only on the grounds of very limited French on his part, nor does she care especially that he already has four wives, since he makes no secret of it.

The dread with which her mother awaited the next letter can well be imagined. Could there be worse news still? There could and there was.

Teresita had fallen critically ill with an eruption and a fever which made her turn entirely black. Her Neapolitan companion took the first possible conveyance for home. It was Mohammed who cared for her and brought a nurse from Tunis. To make matters worse yet, the police were asking for her birth certificate and Teresita frantically wrote to her mother for it. Meanwhile a young German doctor, the same whose life Teresita had saved from the point of a hostile dagger, recommended her to the good offices of the German Consul. She begged to return home, to which her mother cabled an emphatic "no." From Malta, which she managed to reach without her birth certificate, she wrote one of her most pitiful, childish letters in her almost illegible hand:

. . . I really do not understand you. I expect somebody has been telling lies about me to you, and of course as usual you believe them —just as you used to believe Fräulein Krahl. . . . I have quite out-grown the influence Naples had on me. Please be kind and change your mind. I want so much to come to you. I want to work and study with you and give lessons. I give you my word of honor that if you take me back I will behave beautifully and you will not regret it.

Carreño replied with an ample cheque. For the sake of her own health she could not afford another set-to with Teresita.

Meanwhile the threatening rumble of war was becoming more and more insistent until one day it exploded with catastrophic detonation. It caught Carreño, returned home from her American tour, alone in Oberstdorf. In the heat of mobilization it took Arturo five days to reach his wife from Berlin, and not until the end of September was Carreño in possession of the passport without which henceforth one could not live or leave anywhere in Europe.

Once more at home, Arturo told her of a new disaster which had overwhelmed Teresita. She had left Malta on the *Trieste,* an Austrian vessel, on July 31, 1914, which, upon declaration of war, put in at Bône harbor, Algeria. In Batna near-by that very evening Teresita was arrested as a spy, not being in possession of any papers of identification, not knowing whether she should consider herself an American or an English citizen, whether she were divorced or not. Things looked hopeless for her in the dirty dungeon she shared with two German wild-beast tamers and two Arab women, one who had killed her husband, the other her child. The fact that she was in command of the German language, that she had known the German consul in Tunis, and worse, that she had landed just before the Germans shelled Bône harbor, militated against her. Her picture appeared in the papers as that of the one who had given the signal which launched the attack. From hour to hour Teresita expected to be shot. Happily she managed to get a message through to her old singing teacher, Signor Villa, who sent it on to Berlin, and soon the American Embassy, later joined by the English, was enlisted in her defense. However the Algerian authorities refused to free her, and three months and a half passed before Teresita had permission to leave for the island of Mallorca. There at the Hotel Catala seven kilometers from Palma she reassembled her shattered nerves as best she could after an experience which might have driven the most level-headed person to insanity. Pine-covered mountains made a protecting screen against the north winds, and open country stretched before her to the sea beyond, as she spent day upon day lounging on the wide terrace, waiting for permission to leave the island of her refuge and detention.

At the outbreak of the war Carreño, like everyone else in Germany, felt sure that victory would be on the German side. She refused to take Arturo's advice and remove her money out of the hands of Schickler's private bank for deposit in Switzerland. Unlike d'Albert who, good German that he was, had found it expedient to become a Swiss citizen at the first moment of conflagration, she preferred to stand or fall with the country of her adoption. In September she wrote to Giovanni, studying in Milan, from whom she had not heard for three months:

I have to give you very unpleasant news, I am sorry to say. Through this terrible war we find ourselves in most serious financial trouble. The little money I have been able to set aside is all tied up, and all I can get is a loan on it to enable us to live, and that depriving us of every comfort. We have to do without servants and must content ourselves with barely enough so as not to starve. I can only send 150 marks, and you will have to see what you can do to earn your bread and butter for alas! I cannot help you any more. All engagements for the winter are being cancelled, and I fear there will be nothing for me to earn either with concerts or with pupils. Who wants lessons under these terrible circumstances?

If Carreño painted conditions in what proved to be colors of somewhat exaggerated gloom, telegrams which canceled one after another of the fifty-five engagements already on her list seemed to justify her in so doing. Life at home ran along in much the same orderly groove with only one servant at 25 marks a month to do heavy cleaning, and Josephine to help where she could. Eugenia and Hertha manfully did their part and managed to find time for a course in nursing, working for war relief wherever they were allowed. The problem of their status of nationality worried the authorities. For a time they were obliged to present themselves at police headquarters daily until some official had the clever idea of having them declared not alien but homeless. These girls without a country were allowed to travel in Germany on English passports, suffering outside of red tape no other particular inconvenience on that account.

Later in October Germany once more began to insist upon the solace of music without which there is no living for a Teuton, although making it as difficult as possible for the artist who was expected to provide it. On every provocation in every city passports had to be presented and studied at length, questions had to be answered that pried into one's very reason for being born. Hours that should have been spent preparing in quiet for the evening were used up standing in line at the Consulate or at the police station until there was barely time for dressing. Letters from those high in authority availed nothing against the intrusive stupidity of some of the inquisitors, one of whom wished to know why Carreño could not give her concerts by letter. Crossing frontiers was worse. Now and then she found an inspector who could be counted among her admirers and was only too glad to smooth the way. More often she was obliged to let herself be herded, pushed, and insulted like everyone else in this orgy of hatred and suspicion. She made the best of it because she felt now, as she was too young to realize in 1863, that she could bring a measure of comfort more real than material help to thousands whom hope had forsaken. For this it was worth while to cross the sealed borders of Holland, Denmark, and Sweden with all the hardships it entailed.

In one way it was a relief to be on tour rather than at home. Italy's entrance into the conflict on the side of the allies brought disharmony into this cosmopolitan household. That Arturo's sympathies were ranged on the side of the country of his birth was natural. Yet he was obliged to live among those who thrilled to every German victory. Loud disagreement often ended in the deadlock of silence charged with tension. Mealtimes became the dreaded parts of the day. With actual relief Carreño left for Madrid alone to give three concerts under the auspices of the Philharmonic Society there, and to pilot Teresita back from Barcelona. In one of the luxurious apartments of the Palace Hotel she prepared for these all-important functions. The Society was the most exclusive of all Spain, only members having entrance to the concerts from which even the usual critics were debarred. One of Carreño's most absorbed listeners was the Infanta Isabel, aunt of the King, by far the most musical member of the royal household.

By ill luck Carreño contracted a cold on the night of her first concert. She played between spells of coughing. Bronchitis developed, and for more than a week she was forced to stay in bed. Her second concert, played before she had recovered strength sapped by high fever, was nevertheless received with universal enthusiasm which outlived even the third to such an extent that an extra concert was called for by petition and unanimously voted by the directorate. All this was tremendously gratifying. But Carreño longed for home, no news of which had reached her during the two months of her stay. She was packing, impatient to be on her way, when the Major Domo of the Court called upon her with great ceremony, bringing an invitation from Queen Victoria to play a week later at the Palace. The request honored her too much to be denied.

On the evening of May 31, 1915, a festal equipage pranced up to the door of the hotel to take her to the Queen. As she entered the hall where the ladies of the royal family and of the Court were standing about in groups, the Queen stepped forward to greet the guest who was her match in bearing. Diamonds glittered under crystal chandeliers like fireflies under the stars. After Carreño had been presented to the Queen Mother María Christina and to a bevy of Princesses, King Alfonso himself entered the hall attended by Gentlemen of the Court. He welcomed Carreño with genial cordiality to which he added: "Señora Carreño, I have known you very well since my boyhood. Your picture hangs in my mother's boudoir." Then while the others were taking their seats, Carreño was escorted to the piano. Her sweeping bow was the gracious salutation of one queen to another. Carreño smiled. She was suddenly reminded of the little Teresita of long ago whose curtsy had been her downfall. For more than an hour she played whatever one or another of the group called for. Last of all the Queen Mother asked for the "Marche Militaire." This the King really appreciated. "Oh, Señora," he said, "if you only knew what suffering this composition has caused me! My mother insisted that I learn to play the piano. I have no ear for music and nothing on earth could give me an understanding of it. I remember with agony that she would make me play this march with her for four hands. She was dreadfully strict about time, and made me count aloud one, two; one, two, until I was hoarse."

As Carreño shook hands with the Queen in leaving she was honored by another invitation to play, this time in the rooms of the Queen Mother, on the following Thursday afternoon. Flattering as it was, Carreño accepted with reluctance. There had still been no word from home. The days dragged on.

This second appearance at Court had a more intimate setting. The Queen Mother received her guest very simply, inquired for her family, her children, and apologized for asking Carreño to defer her playing until the coming of King Alfonso. He had refused to be left out. "It is the greatest compliment he could pay you, my dear Señora," said the Queen Mother. Again it was a request program. At its end tea was served at two tables, one for the royal family, one for the artist and members of the Court circle. A chair opposite Carreño was vacant. Seeing this the King himself took his seat there and began to talk vivaciously with this artist, whom he liked in spite of her playing rather than because of it. Carreño was as much touched by this courtesy as by the gifts of jeweled brooches presented to her by the Queen, the Queen Mother, and the Infanta Isabel.

After this Carreño left at once for Barcelona, settled Teresita's affairs, secured her English passport, and managed to cross the borders in safety. She rejoiced to Arturo,

At last I am on the way home, and I can't tell you how happy I am! It seemed to me that I should never return to you or the children, and the unbearable thing was not to have any word of you. The despatch from Eugenia in answer to mine came as if from Heaven. Thank God that you are well, and that I can again hear from you!

Near Lausanne Teresita found a place where she could try to regain control of herself under the care of an eminent nerve specialist, who advised temporary rest and no idea of a musical career for a long time to come. The influence of North Africa and the mental torture of imprisonment had left Teresita passive, devoid of the little initiative she once had. She waited for fate to do its worst, relegated every decision to her mother, and yearned for the happy days in Africa with Mohammed. If only she could earn enough money to go to Tangiers and live in a little cottage by the sea, married to somebody, anybody who would protect her, own a little low Arab horse, and ride and walk and live! She blames her mother for her unhappy state and hits the point in self-analysis:

You see, I can't rely upon myself or upon my capacities. The latter come and go according to the emotions of my soul. I would not care if I did not have your name. If I had a name of my own to play with in my musical eccentricities I should not mind in the least, and would go concertizing around the whole world. But as it is I am afraid of putting a stain on that, your beautifully polished name.

She recognizes that "to make a name in Europe you do not need to be young, you only need to be great"—yet, too tired to take up the challenge, she lapses into lethargy and leaves all to Allah and to her mother.

But Carreño had not yet reached home. In Bern she drove to the American Embassy for the necessary formalities and was received by an uncouth man who did not think it worth while to rise from the chair in which he was comfortably sprawling. "If I had been the laundress bringing his collars back badly ironed, he could not have been less courteous," commented Carreño. Between yawns he informed her that she would have to have a birth certificate in addition to her passport to prove that she was really an American citizen. Those were the latest orders. Then he withdrew his attention in favor of a newspaper. A day and a half passed in negotiation before she was able to leave for Basle and there she was held up for three more days, this time by German officials, until she could prove herself a bona fide resident of Berlin. A letter to Mr. Cochran summed up the experience of this trip from the haven of home, concluding:

Well, now I have taken you to Spain and to the Royal Family there, and have made you travel through France and Switzerland (whether you were willing or not) and brought you into Germany and into our home. I will allow you to rest a while—I think you need it badly —to remain at your own dear home, and as you are there, I will now bring you back to business and in doing so will end my letter as I began it. This is according to all musical rules. And yet they say we women are not logical!

You are quite right about the advisability of my placing myself in America at the earliest opportunity and (as often it has happened) your thoughts and mine were running in the same channel. From what you write the United States will be overrun next season by musical attractions and specially by pianists of more or less popularity. In view of this I have asked myself and am now putting the question before you whether it would not be advisable to postpone my tour, "our tour," until the season 1916/17, provided I am still an inhabitant of this planet. My prospects here even with this terrible war and in spite of it are very good. Already I have many offers for next season, not only from the different musical societies in Germany but also from those of Scandinavia, Holland, Switzerland, and Spain, which again wishes to have me. Even admitting that circumstances would be such that some of those offers might not take effect, I would still have enough engagements to make my season a profitable one. Also with pupils I would be able to make a good income. All this would happen without my having to incur any extra expense and I would remain at home or within easy reach of my family.

AND so it was decided. The summer passed busily. Carreño added Beethoven's "G major Concerto," which had tempted her since she first heard it under d'Albert's fingers, to her repertoire, and began to make plans for her treatise on "Possibilities of Tone Color by the Artistic Use of the Pedal." Her style was by no means literary, but she had something authoritative to contribute on this subject.

It looked as if the season could begin with tranquillity when one morning the newspapers brought word that Giovanni, too, had been arrested as a German spy in Milan, where his voice was undergoing the changes from baritone to tenor. Letters from Germany in German had attracted the curiosity of the Government, especially a postcard in which Carreño harmlessly asked how his "work" was progressing. The quotation marks looked suspicious. It was his interest in guns, however, that led to his undoing. Lunching one day in a public restaurant with a friend, Giovanni's attention was arrested by a passing column of soldiers. He casually inquired whether the guns they carried were

Vetterli guns. The remark was overheard by a zealous patriot, and that evening soldiers came to the pension with a warrant for his arrest. They gave him the alternative of taking a cab to the police station at his own expense or of submitting to the indignity of walking handcuffed between them. There his money and other property were taken from him, then every article of clothing, in place of which he was required to put on prison garments stained with blood and unwashed since the last user had been released to freedom or death. He shared his cell, six paces long by four in width, with an ordinary thief. Two filthy mattresses directly on the floor masqueraded as beds. Food consisted of bread and a dish of thin soup served in containers so dirty that for three days Giovanni was unable to bring himself to eat. But for a friend whose anxiety led her to arouse the American consul from his apathy by continuous prodding, Giovanni might have remained in prison for the rest of the war. She was permitted to supply him with books, food cooked in the *pension,* and money with which he bribed an official to move him to a slightly cleaner cell of his own. There nights continued to be more unbearable than the days. Every two hours a guard unlocked the cell door, turned the light of a lantern full upon him, and locked him in again with a bang and a jangle of keys. Even within these intervals of solitude there was no peace. The *Sentinella alerta* of the guards, repeated every fifteen minutes by these potential opera singers in fortissimo, made the fitful sleeper jump to wakefulness. It was easier to rest by day. After eighteen days Giovanni was given his liberty and his property on condition that he would leave the country at once. He had no greater wish. From Lugano, his first stop, he made his way to Frankfurt, there to adjust his rising voice to tenor level, quality, and repertoire under the guidance of Herr Bellwidt. Carreño as well as her son could breathe freely once more.

THIS shock at the beginning of a taxing season helped to undermine her shaky health, but it was not her own condition that upset her most. From Stockholm she wrote to Arturo:

Only a few lines to tell you everything goes well although as usual I have a cold. But after Dr. Rystedt gave me those old cough powders it has improved. I hope that you received my telegrams. Both concerts here and in Upsala were sold out. Was that not nice? All our dear friends here are grieved that you did not come with me and send you their hearty greetings. Frau Hofmann who declared that you are her special favorite (the dear old friend!) asked particularly about your health. When I told her about your sciatica she said to tell you that there is a famous doctor here whose specialty is sciatica. He says the only way to cure it is to stay in bed two weeks, but not less, and then take massage. Not before! He says no other cure is useful. The sciatic nerve must have complete rest and then you get well. That sounds very sensible and I urge you to do this.

Again and again Carreño complains that Arturo writes nothing about his own condition. "That after all is the most important thing," she reiterates. From Stavanger she finds time for a really long letter that gives insight into the uncertainties of the life of a concert artist during the war.

. . . You will be surprised to have a letter from this place, I know. An engagement for 400 crowns was offered me here by Hals, and I accepted it, very especially because it could take place between the two concerts in Bergen. I played here night before last and was supposed to leave for my second concert in Bergen this evening. Last night when I was ready and packed to take the night boat to Bergen, I had a telegram from Harloff in which he told me that the prospects for today's concert were so bad that he advised me not to give the concert. After the enthusiasm of the audience and, as I am told, the splendid criticisms in the papers, this news was a great surprise and certainly not a pleasant one. Of course I cancelled the concert, and go on to Bergen to night to take the night train to Kristiania tomorrow, then on to Göteborg on the eighteenth. As one says: "Everything has its bright side." I felt so badly—I caught cold again on the way here—and just before Harloff's telegram came I had decided not to leave for Bergen until this morning. We had such a storm all day yesterday and way into the night that I was afraid I might become seriously ill if I went out in such awful weather.

And then came Harloff's telegram and I could stay right here, which was best for my health.

Business in Kristiania was not good either. The first concert brought me 700 crowns and in the second I lost nearly 200 crowns. So the first paid for the last and I had 427 crowns left. The reason is said to be that the critic of the most-read paper wrote so dreadfully about me that people after reading it did not come to hear me. The musicians in Kristiania, so I am told, were outraged and wrote letters to the editor of the paper demanding that he be dismissed. In any case the audience made a real demonstration in the second concert, and as I stepped out upon the platform I found upon my chair in front of the piano a huge laurel wreath tied with Norwegian colors with an inscription which read: "In greatest esteem from the pianists and pianistes of Kristiania." The applause did not wish to end, and I had to stand there in order to respond gratefully for five minutes before I was allowed to sit down to play. Since I knew nothing of the criticism this reception was somewhat surprising to me. The next day Hals told me about the criticism, and then I understood the reason for the ovation. It was a nice way for the musicians and the audience to punish the critic, and I was very much touched and grateful, but I lost money through this *Herr Kritiker,* in spite of everything.

Frau Sinding (not Frau Christian but our old friend in Kristiania) told me just on the day of my departure that a letter had been made public which read: The admirers of Frau Carreño ask her to give one more Popular Concert in Kristiania. That was nice and flattering too, was it not? Harloff in Bergen was the one who told me that this bad criticism was responsible for the small attendance. Could one think of anything more stupid? All the other critics wrote beautiful notices, I was told in Kristiania, and just this one had more influence than all the others together. It doesn't flatter the intelligence and the musical taste of the Norwegian Public.

The concert in Tonsberg was delightful and the people were charming. It was sold out. So the great? critic of Kristiania must have had no influence there. . . .

Now, my beloved, I have told you everything that has happened so far. All our friends regret very much that you did not come along, and send you their greetings. In Kristiania with the Sindings—do you remember when we were there together and the chauffeur could not find the house?—I was asked for dinner, and Herr Sinding drank to your health and everyone followed suit. That gave me particularly great pleasure. Neither were our children forgotten. They are really dear good people and true friends. I also had the pleasure of seeing Christian Sinding and his beautiful lovable wife. They send you, Eugenia, and Hertha their greetings. . . .

And so I hope with God's help to be with you and my "Babies" on the fifth. Your old wife, Teresa.

As Carreño wove her way from Scandinavia to Rumania in more than forty concerts she could look back upon 1915 artistically with satisfaction. More and more she was drawn to Beethoven. His "G major Concerto" found a place on a Berlin program which she devoted to three of his concerti. With Rosé she appeared in three Beethoven sonatas for violin and piano. An outstanding event of the early part of the year was a concert shared with Lilli Lehmann. It was one of the memorable events of the musical season. For a night they appeared with rejuvenated freshness, exuberantly temperamental as in the old days. No, her powers were not waning. "Do you never grow tired?" someone asked the timeworn question. And her answer was an exultant fanfare: "When I do I shall stop playing." In Bucharest bronchitis threatened and was subdued without causing the loss of a single concert. She remembered the doctor's warning: "A year of complete rest or else a nervous collapse," only to put it contemptuously aside.

Again and again Carreño had reason to be glad that she was still in Europe where concerts were surprisingly plentiful. She was relieved to assure herself in person that Giovanni was improving in health and voice, that he was in good hands, and above all that he was working, "trying to enter into the spirit of the great Beethoven." Here and there an engagement to sing in opera in small cities brought him returns in experience rather than in money. It was gratifying, too, that she could pass approvingly upon the engagement of Eugenia to a young German lieutenant, and upon the teachers Hertha had chosen to help her with her singing and painting in Munich. For the time being Teresita also was not in active eruption. The anxious mother sent Arturo, whose sciatica was still the great anxiety of the moment, to Switzerland armed with a letter of credit which would make if possible for Teresita to go to South America for a concert tour, as she had begged to do long before. When it came to the point of making definite arrangements for sailing, courage forsook her. She refused to go without Arturo for a manager as once in Finland. How could she, she argued rightly, take charge of her own business when she had never been able to do mathematics in any form. Arturo categorically refused, and Carreño was as glad to see Teresita come to the sensible conclusion of abandoning the tour as she was to see the letter of credit returned intact. Instead Teresita changed her quarters to Berne, while at Carreño's suggestion Arturo remained in Chêxbres for treatment.

The cure seemed to have been effective. Together Arturo and Teresa once more faced the hardships of a journey to Spain for three highly remunerative concerts under the auspices of the Philharmonic Society as before. The French Government again created difficulties which hampered the return to Berlin so seriously that they were obliged to retrace their steps from the French border to Madrid to ask for the intercession of the Infanta Isabel in their behalf. Upon her insistent demand permission was granted them to pass through French territory only after precious weeks had been spent in besieging one office after another. Safely at home once more, dangers and annoyances of the past were quickly crowded out by the exigencies of each day.

One morning came news of the death of Manuel after prolonged illness. Devotedly Rosie had cared for him and supported them both by turning to the breeding of dogs. Handsome Manuel gone, his life a wasted promise! Carreño could not let herself go in the luxurious indulgence of grief. There were concerts to be played. She must spare herself for what lay before her. Nevertheless each shock took its toll of strength!

Of all the concerts during this season the ones to which she contributed her participation for the benefit of war relief gave her the deepest satisfaction. When the Crown Princess of Germany called her to the royal box to thank her in person for aiding a cause under her patronage, Carreño esteemed it an honor. But she was just as mindful of her own dignity as an artist. On one occasion she had given her services for the benefit of the widows and orphans of fallen soldiers in a concert at Kroll's under the auspices of Excellenz von Bülow. After the performance an Adjutant appeared to ask that Carreño accompany him to the box of His Excellency who desired to express his gratitude. Carreño drew herself up to her full stature, unhesitatingly rejecting the distinction. "Please tell His Excellency that no thanks are necessary. I did it for the soldiers." And she could not refrain from adding: "Besides, if Excellenz von Bülow wishes to express his appreciation he should come to me. I am a woman."

Art admits of no compromise. It was Carreño's sense of the dignity of her calling which would not allow her to accept a financially breath-taking offer to play every evening for a week in this same setting of Kroll's Theater for 2,500 marks a night, she to play for one hour only. Then, after an intermission the rest of the evening was to be given over to vaudeville. In order not to be tempted, in order to keep faith with herself as a musician, she, a little ruefully to be sure, sent in a prompt refusal.

WORD from Mr. Cochran seemed to point the way to a successful season in the United States, still unscathed by war and its repercussions. That the Steinway Company was willing to coöperate was an additional inducement, and Carreño in spite of the remonstrance of Eugenia and Hertha, in spite of the advice of Arturo, provisionally agreed to brave the new terrors of the ocean, reserving however the right to cancel the trip should there be too few concerts to warrant it.

With Eugenia soon to be married, Hertha in Munich, Giovanni in Frankfurt, Teresita in Switzerland, and Arturo with her in America, keeping the apartment at Kurfürstendamm 28 would have been an inexcusable extravagance. Poor old Josephine could go with Eugenia. There began the sad business of dismantling the home, of storing furniture. As she waited while the movers carried out the last boxes, Carreño was assailed by a premonition: "I feel that I shall not come back again," she confided to Hertha. It would not have been a great disappointment had Mr. Cochran sent word that the tour should be abandoned, but when instead a cable came announcing thirty fixed engagements, common sense dictated immediate departure.

Carreño and Arturo took passage for September 7 on the steamer *Oskar II,* sailing from Denmark. Crossing the border at Warnemünde with eight trunks and more pieces of hand luggage was no laughing matter. There was no detail of equipment which customs officials did not find worthy of suspicious scrutiny. The dresses, carefully packed by Arturo with tissue paper between the folds, were deprived of this protection. Labels were removed from all bottles, and a whole supply of calling cards was confiscated. Only after page-by-page examination was Carreño permitted to take her music and her books out of the country under seal. Arrived in Kopenhagen completely exhausted, it was found necessary to repack every trunk anew. No danger of mines at sea could match the terrors of travel on land at this time, Carreño decided. There was no fear in her as she embarked, and in fact the journey proved to be unexpectedly eventless and pleasurable, potential peril merely adding a stimulating tang.

Of her arrival in New York Carreño tells in a letter to one of her students.

Your dear letter welcoming us to America was such a dear welcome and gave both your Berlin Daddy and your Berlin Mother such a great pleasure! Thank you a thousand times for the dear kind message, my darling child! We arrived on the nineteenth instant after having a most pleasant journey. We met no mines, no U-boats, no submarines, and altogether had as quiet a trip (sea and all other elements!) as could have been wished. As soon as we could we started looking for an apartment, as we intend making a home for ourselves here in New York for some time to come. I find that I will have time to teach whilst I am here (for which I am awfully glad) and therefore, we want more privacy and independence than we have in a hotel. Until now, though we have seen a great number of apartments more or less suitable, we have not found just what we wish to have. There are so many sides to this important question! First of all the price, then the location, the size, the freedom of playing the piano when and as I feel like it, which means of course at reasonable hours. And in order to find all these conditions we are yet hunting. Let us hope we will have the good luck to find just the treasure for which we are looking. . . .

I will tell you just a little of the happenings which may be of a little interest to you as my child. First of all Eugenia married on the ninth of last month Lieutenant Jörn Duske. He is a very charming and energetic young man twenty-five years old. They are devoted to each other, and though neither one of them has much of the "worldly goods," I think they will be very happy in their married life. The wedding was a 'Kriegsheirath' and consequently very simple and quiet. . . .

Before leaving Berlin we gave up our apartment in Kurfürstendamm 28. This has been a sorrow to me as you can imagine. Twenty-two years of my life were spent there. My babies came as babies and small children to this home, grew up in it, became grown-ups. . . . So much joy and sorrow did I go through at 28 Kurfüstendamm! I felt as though I were parting with a large share of my heart by leaving our old home! I will not say any more about it, darling, for my heart grows sadder and sadder when I speak of it all, and I have made up my mind to use all that I possess of will-power to fight my feelings.

This letter is growing to such dimensions that in kindness to you, my sweet child, I will come to an end. . . . Auf baldiges und gesundes Wiedersehen, darling child, and with a heart full of love I remain your affectionate "Berlin Mother."

P.S. Sept. 29th. I just found an apartment, thank Heaven!! From tomorrow on our address will be the "Della Robbia," 740 West End Ave. This will be your New York home.

ONE of the chief compensations of the American tour of 1916 was to be the renewed opportunity for teaching. In Germany that part of Carreño's profession had lately been at a standstill, and she had missed it, the more because it was the only corner of her art still unexplored in fullness.

Carreño taught according to three simple rules: "1. Master the fundamentals. 2. Know what to do. 3. Do it." Like other creative teachers she disliked the word *method*. It suggested constraining walls, not opening ways. As she required freedom for herself, freedom in self-expression, freedom on occasion to change her mind, so she insisted that her students take advantage of their right to blaze their own trails. She was always open-eared to follow an interpretation widely divergent from her own to the end, if she found in it something significant, something sincerely personal, and her praise was apt to be as extravagant as her blame. At no time was a student in doubt as to his rating, but neither was there a guarantee that the performance which found favor today might not meet with disapproval tomorrow. A pupil who expected systematic step-by-step training, a Jacob's ladder leading to the paradise of art according to a black-and-white right and wrong, clear as the Commandments, soon left in utter confusion to seek another master. Those independent enough, imaginative enough to penetrate the brambles of contradiction to the clearing, discovered that the principles upon which their musical beliefs were grounded finally tallied with Carreño's own. In their essence they were definite as the Constitution.

Until German standards had caused Carreño to reëvaluate her playing she had continued to teach as her father instructed her, using the material she had inherited from him in the somewhat stereotyped way which had imitation and repetition as its pedagogical basis. She encouraged her disciples to copy her, and in turn presented them with a caricature of their own performance to the life. She was an active listener, and if the *modus operandi* failed in result there was always the experimental approach: "Try it this way. Perhaps this will work better." Until Carreño had come into her own in Germany, the quality of her pupils had been uninspiring, a strain to the patience of one to whom difficulties presented no problem. The door often closed with a "thank goodness that's over."

Germany revolutionized this attitude. When young boys and girls came to Carreño for help that seemed to mean life or death, she began to give closer thought to her responsibilities as a teacher. What did she have to give in return for their investment in money and in faith? Detailed analysis was not for her. She gladly left it to people like Rudolf Maria Breithaupt who had found the tenets of his book, *Die Natürliche Klaviertechnik,* confirmed by her playing. *Weight* and *relaxation* were the recent bywords of pianistic vocabulary. That they were more often misapplied than comprehended was an unfortunate by-product. Good-by to the superannuated Breslauer, to Kullak, and those of his kind! Good-by to the finger methods by whose limited lights, like the ghostly ones of the marshes, countless potential virtuosos had sought technical perfection and found instead the end of a promising career in the quicksands of neuritis. Newly aware of reserves of power, of stronger muscles ready to take the burden from the weaker, Germany splashed, rolled, and pounded to its heart's content. The Liszt pupil had paved the way, and the weight-technicians followed suit with uncontrolled abandon, in joyous confidence that they had found the combinations to the safe where the secret of genius lay hidden, the simple solution to the riddle: "How can the extraordinary be accomplished without hard work"? In their intoxication at finding piano playing suddenly made easier they forgot that it is not a system but the person who succeeds, that Carreño had found the opening key by virtue of three small words: "I am Carreño" long before she was eight years old. Naïvely they acclaimed her: "Here is the one who adopts and proves our theories." Whether she liked it or not Carreño saw herself saddled with a method.

Together with a feeling of responsibility the years brought another revelation. Teaching had its moments even as playing. There were facets in the musical profession that sparkled freshly by reflected illumination. The development of a student could be as important, as exciting as her own, might even arm her against the stagnation of unrelieved routine. Passing on convictions, putting beliefs into words, striking responsive chords, that too was necessary, never forgetting that music itself, not talking about it is the thing. How many times she was heard to insist: "To understand music you must hear it, to love music you must hear it, to believe in music you must hear it." Her disciples were taught to listen well.

Beyond duty, beyond pleasure Carreño saw in music a way of life, demanding full dedication. She made her pupils aware that the most beautiful piece of craftsmanship is not necessarily art, that art means selfless surrender to the cause of the composer by a soul that is stirred. "It is a serious thing to me to play Beethoven," Carreño once said. "When I play one of his Sonates, I say a prayer with every phrase, that I may be guided to interpret it as he meant it to be." She had no patience with those who looked for other than inner rewards in music, who entered upon this calling in a spirit of self-seeking. To such she gave warning: "Art and commercialism are born enemies, far more than England and Germany. They never shake hands."

Art as a way of life led to a more universal conception still. It was a religion to which in all faith she was consecrated.

"Without God there can be no true great art," Carreño once quoted in a letter to her son, and it was not in ritual but in art that she found her God.

Guiding principles of so inclusive dimensions were hard indeed to compress into outline form for a student. It was not in Carreño to try to do it. Nothing could be less congenial to her than the academic way. According to the inspiration of the moment she permitted visions of her inner world to sift through, radiant, treasurable particles among more practical, less colorful grains. It was left to the student to choose and sort and carry away what he found useful. The supply was unfathomable.

High moments are likely to bring balancing pits of depression. There was, alas, no regular weekly lesson hour for the Carreño student. It was not unusual for him to wait anxiously for a month before being summoned for a hearing, or to be called at too short notice only to be met at the door by Josephine with a contrite: "I'm so sorry, but Madame is unable to teach this afternoon. She is suffering from a very severe headache." On one occasion Carreño and one of her students were on the train homeward bound after a hard-working summer. "My dear," said Carreño, "it just occurs to me that we have never studied a Beethoven sonate together. Bring me the opus 110 next Thursday." Rather than lose the opportunity the pupil rushed from the station to the apartment, worked day and night, even allowing herself to be fed at the piano, and finally appeared with her sonate for a lesson that lasted through the morning and proved to be the most profitable of them all.

As there was no fixed weekly lesson hour, so there was no timing of the lesson itself. Carreño taught as long or as briefly as she pleased, sometimes even by correspondence. If absorbed, two hours might pass without a break, while the teakettle sang in the dining room, and the family awaited the opening of the door patiently. They found amusement in the interim by ridiculing the remarks and mistakes that filtered through. On the other hand a lesson not fully prepared, or one to which Carreño was unsympathetically inclined, might terminate in less than half of the usual hour. One young aspirant, coming for a first audition, failed completely to measure up to standard. After twenty minutes the door closed behind her. The customary bill for a regular lesson was sent and promptly contested by the young girl: "Kindly state what Madame Carreño charges for a twenty minute talk?" The reply, sent by Arturo, was equally brief. "Your mother asked Madame Carreño to give you a lesson which she did. Madame Carreño's time in music is not measured by minutes but by the lesson." The bill was paid under further protest.

What would happen in the lesson was quite as unpredictable. Carreño felt no obligation to cover assigned ground. Sometimes the hour passed in the minute consideration of a page or two of a composition which an ambitious student had prepared in full. Sometimes a technical detail that needed righting showed her in relentless vein, hammering at the problem with patience that outlasted her pupil's, unmindful of tears shed in the process, until it had been mastered once and for all. Lessons like these were not the least valuable ones. Then again there were times when, sitting at the far end of the room, Carreño listened without a word while a whole movement unfolded itself. Then might come the moment which meant compensation for long hours of floundering. "You played that like an angel, my darling child, like a real artist."

More often than not Carreño allowed herself to react spontaneously without continuity of plan, throwing in a suggestion here, illustrating a point there, indicating the orchestral part for the Concerto on the second piano (while the cigarette glowed on between her small, white teeth), leaving it to the student to draw the inferences, make the connections later on at home. By instinct she felt her way into the recesses of a student's personality. Pedagogically she was a democrat and refrained from imposing her established individuality upon one still in process of formation. She was sincere in saying: "It is no compliment to the teacher to be told that her pupil plays as he does." Rather should he be the clarifying mirror in which the student sees himself as he is.

So recognizing the relation between teacher and student as a very personal one, Carreño frankly admitted that her way of teaching might not be right for every student. She grew to be more and more careful in her choice. A student lacking in advancement but otherwise well taught was advised to continue with his former teacher; to another she recommended study with Leschetitzky, although his ideas were different from her own, because she felt that this person would be more easily at home in his method. For drill in the fundamentals of her technical principles she sent pupils to her understudy, Bruno Gortatowsky, and later on to Eugenia. A person for whom she felt an intuitive dislike was refused admittance to her class no matter how well he played.

Once the pupil was accepted, Carreño expected complete responsiveness. A young American girl came for a first lesson. Technically maladjusted, she was initiated into Carreño's way of doing, very unlike her own. "But Madame," she pleaded, "you are not going to change my technique, are you?" "Don't worry, my dear," Carreño reassured her. "I am not going to change your technique. I am going to give you some."

Disregarding the laws of professional etiquette always ended in abrupt dismissal. As she would not receive as her student one who was still officially under the direction of another, so she refused to see again a girl who, she discovered, in order to double results, was studying with two teachers at the same time. On one point especially she was adamant. No one had the right to advertise herself a Carreño pupil without her sanction. It enraged her to hear that a certain Fräulein was giving lectures on the "Carreño Method" before one of the outstanding musical organizations in Berlin when, in Carreño's opinion, she could not have had enough lessons to master her ideas. A letter to the president of this *Verein* put a sudden end to the series. On another occasion, Carreño was giving a concert in a small mid-Western town. In passing the local manager happened to mention: "Madame, one of your most enthusiastic pupils is teaching your method here." Carreño could not remember the name, though she had an almost infallible memory for names. So she asked that the young lady be brought to the green room. Neither was it a face she remembered, and Carreño had an equally infallible memory for faces. "When did you study with me, Miss B?" asked Carreño. "My memory is so poor." "Madame, I really must confess that I never had a formal lesson. But when you were in Italy one summer I used to sit beneath the window when you were practicing. I learned more from you then than from any other teacher I ever had." "It takes an artist to learn from hearing an artist," was Carreño's comment as she turned away disgusted. Again in San Francisco she was to play the Tschaikowsky "Concerto." The rehearsal went badly. The conductor took strange liberties. When Carreño frankly expressed her displeasure, he explained to her hearty amusement: "You see it was this way, Madame. I wanted particularly to be ready for your coming. A young pianist, your devoted pupil, told me that he knew exactly how you wished the Concerto to be interpreted. So I asked him to rehearse it with the orchestra several times last week." "And who may this young man be?" asked Carreño. "Mr. C? Yes, I remember him perfectly. I cannot have given him more than three lessons in all. Do ask him to call upon me at my hotel." Needless to say, Mr. C. thought it the better part of valor to stay away.

Once adopted as a "Berlin son or daughter" the student had Carreño's full backing. Her propaganda was forceful and unreserved, couched in superlatives in keeping with her enthusiasm. That her satellites adored her was common knowledge in musical circles. They arranged concerts for her, often created the background for a successful appearance through the atmosphere of eagerness they radiated within their communities. This give and take with her musical children was no small compensation in Carreño's life of trouble, especially during the later years.

In Carreño's teaching there were points that she considered

worthy of plentiful repetition. The most important one was physical fitness. Steady nerves, strength and quiet, fresh air and exercise in it were to her the *sine qua non* of success. She was radical enough to say: "It is better to work too little than too much." In the summer she might knock at the door of an over-conscientious plodder. "I am going for a walk, my dear. Will you come with me? It will do you good. You can do twice as much in half the time later on." Nobody would have thought of refusing such an invitation, even if the heavens were behaving in the approved Upper Bavarian manner, disgorging water-falls upon the great and the ungreat, obscuring vision until one might as well have been in Illinois for all the sense there was of mountains capped with snow. Enshrouded like monks in water-shedding capes of *Loden* cloth, heavy shoes thoroughly oiled, they went on and on for hours. Is there anything more restful to tired nerves than the rain? It is the nearest we shall come to wearing the *Tarnkappe* which made Siegfried invisible. To walk silently by her side on days like these was to know Carreño well.

True to her reputation as the most universal of pianists Carreño insisted again and again that every composition be treated as a whole. Music and gesture should be at one. As strongly as Wagner she dwelt upon this. Interpretation meant revealing the essential no more than subordinating the unessential. Freedom therefore was artistic economy in its truest sense. *"Le trop est ennemi du bien,"* said Rubinstein. Could there be anything more ridiculous than an exaggerated flourish of the arm at the end of a Beethoven Andante? Could the ideal of every serious pianist, that the performer be forgotten in the music he plays, be attained without self-abnegating oneness of music and motion? As a case in point Carreño insisted that the holding of a chord must not be left to the pedal alone, while the hands lie idle in the lap, as if the piano were a mechanical one playing on alone. To achieve unity inwardly and outwardly in architectural proportion, this should be the aim of the coming artist.

Simplicity was another keynote of her teaching. A great composition does not become greater by distortion. Lack of mannerism, accurate adherence to the spirit of a composition, without pedantic enslavement to the letter of a particular edition—although she had her favorites—she considered fundamental. If a student after sufficient study developed a conviction contrary to the indications of the composer or to her own Carreño made no objection. She remembered that as a child of fourteen she had played a certain passage *forte* where *piano* was noted. Matthias, her teacher at that time, drew attention to the mistake. At the next repetition the same thing occurred. Manuel Antonio, always a silent observer at these lessons, scolded her for her supposed inattention. Teresita answered: "But I can't play it that way. I don't feel it that way." Matthias wisely put in his word. "Let her play it as she likes. Later she may change and do it in my way of her own accord." And she admitted long after, "So I did."

Neither was Carreño fussy about fingerings. She urged each student to study her own hand, to find for herself the fingering that suited it best, and then to stick to it. In case of difficulty she recommended practicing passages with different fingerings to iron out the trouble, as well as transposing them into other keys, keeping the fingering the same.

*"El todo para el pianista es el colorido,"* Carreño is reported to have said. This may be an editorial overstatement. It is true, however, that above everything she valued variety in interpretation, this rather to be achieved by changes of tone effect than by rhythmic shiftings. Cultivating differences of touch in staccato and legato, increasing the dynamic range at both ends, was as much her ambition for the student as keeping tone always within the margin of the beautiful, never allowing it to overreach the limitations of the piano mechanism. As she believed in making the most of a roaring climax, so she did in the effective value of exploring the softest depths to the last whisper. That she considered the pedal a most important aid in achieving shading is proved by the fact that the only work ever written by her was on that subject. In it she made clear not only its great possi-

bilities, but also cautioned against its abuse. Like fire and water she esteemed it a good servant but a bad master, and as strongly as Clara Schumann herself she stood out against the pseudo-artists who wallow in *"Pedalgerassel und Verschiebungsgefühl"* (pedal rattling and soft-pedal feeling).

Carreño was by intuition an excellent psychologist. Difficulties, she counseled, become easy by thinking them so. The student found it true. She urged on the timid, pinned down the inaccurate, and made the overconfident aware of his weaknesses. When confronted by that common phenomenon, the nervous pupil, she quieted him by making light of his obsession. "Do you prefer that I go into the garden, my dear, while you play?" Or she quoted Gottschalk, who advised his own disciples: "Never be afraid to play before an artist. The artist listens for that which is well done, the person who knows nothing listens for the faults." She made him transcend the mechanism of the instrument, and even his less reliable self, by bringing him to experience the joy she felt in playing to others. She brought him for the time to forget that he was a learner, to shake off the chains that forged him to the teacher, to play simply, directly; she taught him to respect his inner man as his only dictator. When in a lesson repetition had called for more repetition, punctuated with an inexorable: "No, my child, that is not it at all! Relax, my dear, do not articulate. You are playing the piano, not shoveling snow"; the hour was not allowed to end with minor inflection but on an ascending note of encouragement: "That was not bad at all, my child, not bad at all. And now you shall have a cup of tea to make up for the trouble your severe old teacher gives you." Supposing that in spite of her prodding the difficulty under consideration had not been mastered beyond possibility of future error, instead of attacking it again the next time in the same passage, another similar one was substituted to clinch the matter. For example a student was assigned the "Concert Study in D flat" by Liszt. She reacted to it negatively, consequently playing it badly, perfunctorily. "Why, my darling child, it sounds as if you had just come out

of a convent. Let's try the one in F minor for next time. I think
you practice too long at a time. I must send Hertha to you tomorrow for a game of tennis." That did not seem to help. Relentlessly Liszt followed upon Liszt until Grindelwald and
Liszt could never again exist apart in the mind of the student.
One day confronted by yet another composition of this composer she exploded, "I can't bear another thing of his. I hate
every note he wrote. It's sugar and water." "Splendid, my child,
you are showing signs of just the temperament it takes to play
Liszt well. If, detesting Liszt as you do, you play him beautifully notwithstanding, how much more of an artist you will be!
Bring me "Mazeppa" next time, if you please." The student survived the heroic treatment, learned to understand the greater
Liszt, and lived to earn the seal of approval for her reading of
the "Liszt Sonate." Not until then was she permitted to turn
to other more congenial tasks.

Ten Carreño pupils meeting together would agree only upon
this—that they had been taught in ten different ways. But not
one would have exchanged that experience, unorganized as it
was, for another. What after all is great teaching but bringing
the student alive to the beautiful in music and making him
conscious of his mission to keep it so with everything within his
power. In that sense Carreño was a great teacher.

THE first business talk with Mr. Cochran had revealed a startling state of things. It came to light that instead of thirty concerts there were only three that could be counted upon at the
moment. The cable had been garbled in the sending. Carreño
was deeply indignant. She might then have stayed near her
children in her own apartment. With the utmost difficulty she
brought herself to consider the other side of the medal. Eventually she might be glad she had come away. There would be
plenty of leisure for teaching. Only a short declaration of intention in the musical journals, and students would come swarm-
ing as they always had without resorting even to such means.
Now that she was really in the United States there would also

be other calls for her participation. Yet the blow was a vital one. She would not be able to afford the comfort of Arturo's protecting presence on her journeys, or the services of a personal maid. In their apartment they must now content themselves with only one helper. On the maid's free afternoons Carreño herself did the cooking, washed the dishes, and thought nothing of welcoming guests at the door enveloped in a kitchen apron. Some of her happiest moments were spent in this domestic way. But she could not dust away her anxiety about the children from whom there was no word for two long months. At the sight of a photograph of Hertha placed upon her dressing table by a friend who thought it would please her, she burst into a fit of uncontrolled weeping.

This worry was consigned to the background to make way for a more tangible one. Just as she was about to step out upon the platform to begin her Boston recital on October 22, Carreño received word of the illness of Arturo, laid low by an attack of acute appendicitis. Only force of will made her go through with the performance, kept her from infecting her audience with her own restlessness. A few days of surpassing length and the danger was past, the operation avoided. Carreño, again at home for a breathing space, hovered over her husband, showered him with delicacies she ought not to have afforded, and touched his heart with the gift of a very comfortable and expensive armchair in which to spend the tedious hours of convalescence. When finally she tore herself away to fulfill her engagements in the Middle West, she wrote from every possible stopping place in words that were full of affectionate concern. From Duluth came a solicitous letter, as usual in Italian:

Most beloved and most dear Turo mio: I cannot tell you the joy which your dear, dear letter gave me. A thousand times thousand thanks, Turo mio. I understand that you are not yet capable of writing long letters, and I do not wish that you should tire yourself giving me more than the news of how you are feeling. For the time being I shall content myself with this, and I can't tell you how grateful I am to the good God who had helped you to regain your health and your strength! What a fright you gave me, Turo mio! Don't do it again, I beg of you! Be very careful and do nothing that might cause you the slightest disturbance, for the love of God!—That for today, my well-beloved! Take good care of yourself and remember that your health is my necessity and my joy and comfort. A million tender kisses from your old wife Teresa.

Ten days later she wrote from Chicago:

My most dear and most beloved husband: Thousands and thousands of thanks for your two dear letters with which you gave me most great pleasure, Turo mio! My thoughts are always with you, and my prayers for your health fly to God with every thought, and you can imagine how happy I am to feel that you are improving and recovering completely. God be thanked thousands and thousands of times! You can imagine too the joy I had in receiving the letter of our Eugenia!! It was a real feast to have the good news of you and our children! How I thank the good God for having also granted me this boon. Don't be worried about my cold, *"ma guarda e passa."* I feel better, thank God. You should be accustomed to these colds of mine by now, which, as you know, keep company with me all winter. Aside from that everything goes well.

So she characteristically made light of her own troubles.

On December 11, 1916, Carreño returned to Arturo for the Christmas hiatus, spent gaily enough among friends who did their best to distract her from thought of the double distance war had created between her and her children, from the ominous vastness of empty silence. It made little impression that she played to Woodrow Wilson in the White House where once she had thought as little of playing to Lincoln. Neither did it reach beneath the surface, although for the moment she was touched by it, that the orchestra in Kansas City greeted her entrance upon the stage with a rousing fanfare, and that the whole audience rose to its feet by automatic impulse. These things had ceased to matter. She had drunk to the full from the chalice of ovations. Her real happiness lay in her playing and in solitude shared with Arturo, her hope in reunion with her children.

One afternoon in Carreño's music room, where a photograph

of Liszt presided on the open Steinway, twilight was inviting reminiscence. A circle of friends from Caracas sat listening as she described her visit to the Court of Spain, while they cozily stirred their tea and looked far down upon the dreamy Hudson. J. Perez Lee, a journalist, eager to know what her feelings were about the land of her birth, turned conversation back to her Venezuelan past. Carreño lowered her voice and spoke with slow emphasis. "Sometimes I cherished her for her misfortunes, sometimes for the generosity of her nature, always as an irreplaceable mother. Upon her bosom I wish to sleep the dream of earth. It is there that I wish my ashes to rest." Then simply and naturally without trace of dread she talked on about death as fulfillment, death as a friend, and so they sat together for a long time in deepening darkness.

As the season began, concerts popped up like puffballs where they were least expected. There would be in all as many as Mr. Cochran had cabled in the first place, even if at fees somewhat lower than those anticipated. Besides, there was abundance of private teaching in odd moments and flourishing classes at the American Institute of Applied Music. During the past years in Germany, Carreño had pioneered in the making of rolls for the Duo-Art, the Welte, the Ampico. Reproducing mechanisms had brought her little satisfaction. In the first place the ordeal of playing for the making of the master roll was nerve-racking. She was overcome by stage fright unknown in a whole lifetime of concerts. Hertha once had accompanied her for moral support on such an occasion. The lights which went on and off, the three men who sat busily taking notes, the mystifying machinery, all combined to upset her, so that the initial roll was a complete failure. When finally with perspiration standing out in beads from every pore she had completed her work, her relief was such that she suggested a pleasure trip on the Rhine for recuperation. The results of her recordings all disappointed her. In spite of hours spent in revision she found them far from true to her style. She tried to have a number recalled from publication, unwilling to allow experimentation at such a price.

Strangely enough she made no phonograph records. At the request of an English publisher, she did undertake the drudgery of editing some of the pieces in her repertoire according to her own interpretation. The book on the use of the pedal was in its final stages. Carreño worked without wasting a minute, as if against time. And yet, all told, the year brought the leanest of harvests.

Since the entrance of the United States into the war in the spring of 1917, news from Germany could come by way of neutral countries only. Frau Sinding volunteered to act as transmitter for the Carreños. From the sketchy words which passed the censor the anxious mother could gather little that was personal or heartening. In reply to a cable in which Hertha asked permission to marry Louis Weber, a young engineer from Reutlingen, then in the army, Carreño sent her blessing. Did she remember that this, according to her own setting, was to give the signal for her retirement? If so she repudiated it.

The far-off horizon glowed with promise of activity. The Chicago Musical College was engaging her for a lucrative summer session of teaching. After that a South American tour was in prospect beginning with Brazil. On the way back she planned to show Venezuela to Arturo and Arturo to Venezuela. This time it should be a different homecoming. The winter concerts in North America were to be in the hands of Winston & Livingston and were already being widely advertised. This was no time to rest upon her laurels. "Indeed not!"

In good spirits Carreño set out for Havana, where her contract called for three concerts, by way of St. Petersburg, Florida. There the Carreño Club, still flourishing today, did her honor; there she played a final recital in the United States before sailing on the *Olivette* from Tampa. Arturo accompanied her mainly for the sake of his health. Her own seemed neither better nor worse than usual. Shortly before landing she was sitting on the forward deck of the steamer. Arturo noticed his wife rubbing her eyes as if to get rid of an irritation. "What on earth do you suppose is the matter with my eyes, Arturo?" she asked without special concern. "I see two of you, two of the chair, two of everything." Arturo tried to reassure her, but the condition persisted. At the pier a host of old friends and new received her with bouquets of Havana's most precious roses. They too were doubled in her sight.

As soon as she was safely established in the Hotel Trotcha she decided to consult the best available oculist, Señor Desvernine. He proved to be one who as a little boy had been chosen to crown Teresita the prodigy with a wreath of gold in this same city. Carreño refused as ridiculous his advice that she leave at once for New York. She must not fail her audience. If necessary she could play, as she often did, with eyes closed. Meanwhile the glasses prescribed for her needed changing after a few hours of use. The evening came. Carreño played in masterly manner as usual, wearing a dress of light-blue satin embroidered in a beaded pattern. It seemed to make no difference that she saw two keyboards instead of one, that the hall was half empty; she had the satisfaction of having done her duty. But for the command of her doctors that she return to New York, she might have attempted a second concert. On the following morning before her departure she called upon an old lady whose visit she had missed the day before. There was no indication that she realized the seriousness of her condition until her first words to Mr. Cochran who met her at the train. Quite simply she warned him: "You have seen your old friend for the last time."

Meanwhile in Havana there were those who attributed Carreño's departure to unmotivated wilfullness due to the disappointment at having so small an audience to welcome her. *La Noche* indulged in sarcasm. "Singular coincidence! Like Paderewski Teresa Carreño is prevented from giving the concerts she announced. Both artists became ill in our healthful pure climate. We hope that Mme. Carreño grows better shortly and can still give in spite of her great age many concerts . . . in New York."

Three eminent New York physicians, including a nerve and a heart specialist, did everything that could be done. They agreed that the trouble was a grave one, diplopia, a partial paralysis of the optic nerve which threatened to go farther. Complete quiet and a strict diet were prescribed. Arturo, despair in his heart, watched by her side and kept hope alive. Medicines which might have helped, Carreño was unable to assimilate. General nervous prostration, developing unrecognized through years of overstrain without adequate relief, had finally found this local outlet. The capital of strength upon which Carreño had too recklessly drawn was drained. Once more she sat down at her Steinway to play the "Harmonious Blacksmith" variations, the last encore of her Havana recital, holding out with difficulty to the end. It was to be the last tryst with music.

News of her illness, spreading through the United States, reached as far as Teresita in London, but not to her children in Germany. With satisfaction Carreño read the short letter that told of Hertha's wedding in Munich on April 2. It had after all been the signal from a higher source for her retirement and not alone from the concert platform. She understood and was not afraid, only tired, too tired even to send messages to her children. At seven o'clock in the evening on June 12, 1917, the Walküre entered Walhalla.

*"It came to pass that after a time the artist was forgotten, but the work lived."*
OLIVE SCHREINER

AFTERGLOW

NOTHING could be less of Carreño than the conventional funeral services. Flowers that once became more alive in her vital hands drooped beneath the suffocating weight of her absence. She who once spoke to her "dear Father" in music, and to whom he gave answer quite as directly in the voice of nature, would have looked pityingly from the place of her liberation upon a group of mortals, celebrated mortals to be sure, huddled too closely together in too small a space, to do honor in the presence of that material shell from which the pearl of great price had escaped to fuse its iridescence with that of the sunset. How useless the tears of this sad company come to bid farewell after the hostess had gone. A giant fanfare in the open, a moment of universal silence, each one alone with his thoughts! That would have been the perfect tribute.

But even death, the bridge that each must cross alone, has its social obligations. On the morning of Thursday, June 14, 1917, as the hour neared eleven, Carreño's colleagues, friends, and students filled her living room. None of the many artists who had had close association with her felt equal to making music for this occasion. Strangers intoned "Nearer, my God, to Thee" and "Oh, rest in the Lord." Dr. Louis K. Anspacher of Columbia gave the commemorative address.

The honorary pallbearers were Ignace Jan Paderewski, Ernest Hutcheson, Walter Damrosch, Walter Rothwell, Josef Stransky, Mischa Elman, Franz Kneisel, Albert Spalding, and Charles Steinway.

After the services a few friends accompanied Arturo to Union Hill, N.J., where, according to the wish of the Walküre, and most fittingly, her body was consigned to the encircling flames, an act which in welcoming salute Heaven itself punctuated by a crash of thunder.

IN the summer of 1935 this biographer took a trip to Venezuela in the interest of her book. Except for a painting of Carreño in the early years hanging in the Teatro Municipal, and an unrecognizable bust standing neglected and in need of dusting on the floor of a room of the Academia de Música, she found little external evidence that this great artist was appreciated by her own people. Among the musicians and scholars of Caracas the eager response whenever her name was mentioned was all the more surprising. That her ashes had not yet found a definitive place of rest after so many years aroused consternation. Carreño's own wish that she be buried in her mother country, although several times published, had failed to draw attention. Now a few words only, and the proper authorities wakened to action. Mr. Rudolf Dolge became the moving spirit of the undertaking to bring about the repatriation of the ashes of Venezuela's great daughter. In this he was seconded by Señor Don Salvador Llamozas, the Dean of pianists in Caracas, and one who had been among those chosen to welcome Carreño home in 1885.

Arturo Tagliapietra was readily convinced that no more fitting honor could be offered the memory of his wife. The death of President Gomez delayed the execution of the plan, and not until February, 1938, were the ashes, housed in a dignified urn of greenish bronze which the Venezuelan sculptor, Nicholás Veloz, had fashioned, brought home on the S.S. *Santa Paula*. That the event might not take place without the presence of at least one member of Carreño's immediate family, Teresita was invited to come to Caracas from London as guest of the Government. Together with a deputation of distinguished citizens she waited at La Guaira to receive the urn which was immediately taken to the chapel of the Cementerio del Sur in Caracas. After a brief religious service in this place it was set upon the marble pedestal erected for it in the poets' corner. There, just as the sun was setting, while the Military Band of Caracas played Beethoven's "Funeral March," President Contreras, in the presence of Carreño's relatives, of members of the diplomatic corps, and of representatives of societies who laid their wreaths around the pedestal, unveiled the urn draped in the colors of Venezuela and of the United States. In brief but moving words José Antonio Calcaño made the address of dedication with which the ceremony closed.

That evening in the Teatro Municipal, once the Teatro Guzman Blanco where Carreño was so often heard, a great concert took place in her memory. It lasted over two hours. There sounded once again Cayetano Carreño's Mass, "La Oración en el Huerto," Carreño's "String Quartette," and her "Hymn to Bolívar." Fittingly Juan Bautista Plaza, who now fills the post of Maestro de Capilla once held by Carreño's ancestors, was chosen to give the comprehensive and eminently appropriate address of the evening. At this time a stamp was also issued in her honor. This indeed was a worthy homecoming. Carreño would not have been indifferent to it.

CARACAS 1938

*Teresa Carreño repatriated*

So it is best to leave her. Since her last flight it has not been permitted that any other reach her universal height, that any take her place. She is a memory, an influence, a belief, a legend. Such are the steep steps to oblivion. In essence she exists wherever great music sounds, wherever her artistic credo strikes a responsive chord.

To the young musicians of Venezuela her life will remain a guiding torch. Whether her ashes stand beneath the stars or are moved in due time to a shadowy recess of the Panteón to keep august company with Bolívar, so many of whose traits she shared, wherever music is loved, a voice will still be heard by those attuned to listen, saying, "I am Carreño."

# POSTLUDE

## Teresa Carreño

An article in honor of Carreño's Sixtieth Birthday
by
Dr. Walter Niemann
from Reclam's Universum, December 1, 1913

I PAINT two pictures of Carreño's playing. It has never seen its equal in fascinating virility and hypnotic power among the maestros of piano virtuosity. The first is the Carreño of the 1880's and 1890's, the second the Carreño of today.

A Carreño evening in the wonderful Empire styled hall of the *Kurtheater* in Wiesbaden, tuned to white, gold, sparkling crystal chandeliers and heavy pillars of marble! A brilliant, cosmopolitan gathering, the hall completely sold out, high and stormy waves of enthusiasm, encore after encore—that was its setting. The enthusiasm was the spontaneous honoring by the artistically imaginative people of Germany for a very great personality, for her conquering force, glowing with temperament, for her regally proud and thoroughbred individuality.

The playing of Carreño combines extreme exploitation of force, masculine sense of sculpture in the modeling of the tone, with the utmost lightness and elasticity in the working of the entire play mechanism. Hence her unbelievable endurance and joy in playing, her enormous strength which knows no exhaustion. Her genuine, thundering octaves, which she shakes out of her sleeve, her staccato filed to the sharpest, the sheen, the intensity, and the evenness of her passages, the iron heaviness of her chord and mass effects (introduction of the *B flat minor Concerto* of Tschaikowsky) incomparable, and of its kind, inspired by fieriest temperament most hot-blooded feeling, quite inimitable.

Whoever is acquainted with the hard, stinging, and pointed fortes of so many of our younger and young pianists—the concert tone of Liszt misunderstood—breathes afresh when he hears a fortissimo of iron power, yet of absolute beauty and fullness. Royal dignity, aristocratic pride, that is the realm in which this queen of pianists reigns most freely. The great heroic Concerti (Beethoven E flat, Liszt E, Rubenstein D minor, Tschaikowsky B flat minor), the Polonaises of Chopin and Liszt, the great heroic Sonatas from Beethoven to Chopin, Liszt, and MacDowell, the Erlking of Schubert-Liszt, Schubert-Tausig's Marche Militaire, Chopin's great Concert Etudes are therefore the most blazing highlights of a Carreño evening. The stern defiance which burrows its way through the rarely heard Polonaises in E flat minor and F sharp minor Carreño brings out in stirring verity; the firm tread of the Polonaise rhythm transforms the Chopin salon under her hands into a lofty marble hall of kings, and of Polish petty aristocrats she makes a festal military procession of rulers, great and small.

Outside of the standard works of piano literature from Beethoven to Schumann and Liszt, these latter conceived with authentically romantic feeling—before all in Schumann's Fantasia in C major—there was generally little or no place left in her repertoire for the new or the contemporary. This was characteristic of the Carreño evenings of the Eighties or Nineties. In them the name of Carreño shone over the whole world.

During the years of her marriage to d'Albert something new and unique was added to this; the playing of two magnitudes upon two grand pianos. And again an unforgettable impression takes memory back to that same hall in Wiesbaden. There they played together the virile Variations in E flat minor by Sinding. Could it be that their human harmony was perhaps no longer completely tuned to that soft E flat major? Or what could it have been? In short, never was a Nordically heroic dramatist of the piano recreated more heroically and dramatically, never was he more explosive with Promethean defiance, each wishing to outdo, to vanquish the other. Here anything technical and mechanical was forced into the background, here the head was bowed before that divine something which, through the volcanic eruptions of two temperaments of equal stature, overflowed and poured down upon lowly humanity gathered in the concert hall.

The Carreño of today has become a different but not a lesser person. D'Albert appears to have signed himself over to pianistic pugilism, since, after having exhausted success in opera with *Tiefland,* he again exchanged the desk for the piano, probably after too long an intermission. How differently, how much more wholly and existentially the playing of Carreño has ripened up to the time of golden autumn! Clarified maturity, human as well as artistic, sublimates her playing in a wonderfully appealing and personal way. Today she delights in quiet breadth, still, thoughtful contemplation, loving care for detail, fine technical polish, measure and harmony in everything. Expert drawing overrules glowing color and shows itself, particularly in the interweaving polyphony of Bach, the later Beethoven and Schumann, in utmost refinement of musical pastel. Her incomparable and unexcelled sense of architecture and proportion asks for and gives only the extreme of the plastic and well-defined. The melodic line has perhaps noticeably suffered the loss of former sensuous warmth and soulfulness, its poetic fragrance, her temperament now perhaps appreciably lacks the old hot fire, but substituted for it is a dusky chiaroscuro in piano and pianissimo that ravishes in equal measure.

The Carreño program gradually follows the modern trend to the new. MacDowell from now appears with his four great Sonatas, his Witches' Dance, the Barcarolle, the Orientales, the Concert Studies. And in conjunction piquant gew-gaws of the witty Hungarian satirist, the charming conversationalist of Lake Geneva, Eduard Poldini, and of others who are "made" if Carreño but mentions their name.

This heavy, golden harvest of autumn shows its fruits in manifold lights. Pieces of grand style like Chopin's Ballade in G minor, like the second movement of Schumann's Fantasia in C major show, even in respect to temperament, the Carreño of old. Chopin remains the master in the playing of whose music natural lessening of temperament and fire is yet compensated for by inner intensity of feeling. It is Beethoven who shows the most decided clarification in the playing of the artiste to the limit of the strictest objectivation, bordering upon the classical. Lyric melodiousness stays under cover, reticent, subdued. Even a predominantly brilliant and exuberant Sonata like the one in E flat from Op. 31 by Beethoven is perceived in intimate twilight. One cannot help noting a hint of the didactic in her playing. The blooming, warm sensuousness of the piano tone gives way to almost bitter reticence, interpretation to peaceful, superior serenity.

Between the mysterious delicacy of tone coloring and the heavy pathos of the fortissimo there lies a middle kingdom whose somewhat arid ground falls off to both sides perhaps a little abruptly. The large all-comprehensive drive has given place to most clear, impersonal analysis, to the sublimation of a life filled with profound inner experience.

That is the Carreño of today. The Carreño of once upon a time, mistress of the musical alfresco, was the darling of the masses. The Carreño of today, mistress of the landscape, of intimate story telling, is the darling of connoisseurs and gourmets of the piano. And that is no step backward but forward, which may have been bought with much resignation and sacrifice of concert mob applause, for whom strength is all, refinement nothing. And so Carreño of today remains equally to be honored as the Carreño of old, whose volcanic temperament forced the old and new world into the spell of her enchantment. We greet you the Maestra and Queen of all pianistes, from the heart!

DR. WALTER NIEMANN

# CHRONOLOGY

| | |
|---|---|
| Birth of Emilita Sauret | March 23, 1874 |
| Death of Manuel Antonio Carreño | Late August, 1874 |

## IN THE UNITED STATES                    *1874–1889*

| | |
|---|---|
| Tour with Ilma di Murska | 1874–1875 |
| Separation from Sauret | Spring, 1875 |
| In Boston studying to be a singer | 1875–1876 |
| Operatic débuts in New York and Boston | Spring, 1876 |
| New Rochelle | 1876–1889 |
|    Marriage with Giovanni Tagliapietra | 1876 |
|    Lulu Tagliapietra | born 1878–died 1881 |
|    Birth of Teresita Tagliapietra | December 24, 1882 |
|    Birth of Giovanni Tagliapietra | January 7, 1885 |
|    Venezuelan Concert Tour | October, 1885–September, 1886 |
|    Venezuelan Operatic Venture | February–May, 1887 |
|    Departure for Europe | July 3, 1889 |

## IN GERMANY                    *October, 1889–October, 1916*

| | |
|---|---|
| Berlin début | November 18, 1889 |
| Carreño and d'Albert | 1891–1894 |
|    Birth of Eugenia d'Albert | September 27, 1892 |
|    Two-piano ensemble | 1893–1894 |
|    Birth of Hertha d'Albert | September 26, 1894 |
|    Divorce | October, 1895 |
| Berlin, Kurfürstendamm 28 | May, 1895–October, 1916 |
|    Summer in Pertisau, Achensee | 1895 |
|    European Concerts | 1895–1896 |
|    Summer teaching in Pertisau | 1896 |
|    European Concerts | Autumn, 1896 |
|    Tour of the United States | December 22, 1896–May 28, 1897 |

| | |
|---|---|
| Summer teaching in Pertisau | 1897 |
| European Concerts | 1897–1898 |
| Summer in Schwaz, Tyrol | 1898 |
| Tour of the United States | December 27, 1898–May 16, 1899 |
| Summer in Kolberg and Pertisau | 1899 |
| European Concerts | 1899–1900 |
| Summer in Pertisau and Merano | 1900 |
| Tour of the United States, Havana, and Mexico | October 30, 1900–May 15, 1901 |
| Summer in Friedrichroda | 1901 |
| Concerts in Europe | 1901–1902 |
| Marriage with Arturo Tagliapietra June 30, 1902 | June 30, 1902 |
| Summer in Tavernola, Italy | 1902 |
| Concerts in Europe | 1902–1903 |
| Summer in Wyk a / Föhr | 1903 |
| Concerts in Europe | 1903–1904 |
| Summer in Obersalzberg | 1904 |
| Concerts in Europe | 1904–1905 |
| Summer in Friedrichroda | 1905 |
| Concerts in Europe | 1905–1906 |
| Summer in Wyk a / Föhr | 1906 |
| Concerts in Europe | 1906–1907 |
| Tour of Australia, New Zealand, and the United States | April, 1907–April, 1908 |
| Summer in Italy and Obersalzberg | 1908 |
| Concerts in Europe | 1908–1909 |
| Summer in Bad Gastein and Obersalzberg | 1909 |
| Tour of the United States, Australia, New Zealand, and South Africa | November, 1909–April, 1911 |

| | |
|---|---|
| Fall in Oberstdorf | 1911 |
| Concerts in Europe | 1911–1912 |
| Summer in Grindelwald, Switzerland | 1912 |
| Concerts in Europe | 1912–1913 |
| Golden Jubilee | December 21, 1912 |
| Summer in Obersalzberg | 1913 |
| Tour of the United States | October, 1913–May, 1914 |
| Summer in Oberstdorf | 1914 |
| Concerts in Europe | 1914–1915 |
| Summer in Berlin | 1915 |
| Concerts in Europe | 1915–1916 |
| Summer in Berlin | 1916 |

| | |
|---|---|
| *IN THE UNITED STATES* | *October, 1916–June, 1917* |
| On tour | October, 1916–March, 1917 |
| Last Concert in Havana | March 21, 1917 |
| Death | June 12, 1917 |

| | |
|---|---|
| Repatriation of the ashes of Teresa Carreño in Caracas by the Government of Venezuela | February 15, 1938 |

# SOURCES

The most vital of all records are the intangible, vanishing ones of personal intercourse. Hours spent with Carreño, with members of her family, and with friends of long standing have been fertile for insight as for information. By courtesy of the Executors of the Estate of Teresa Carreño, Arturo Tagliapietra, and Clarence M. Woolley, access has been given to letters, concert records, articles, criticisms, programs, and compositions in their custody.

It is neither feasible nor necessary to list all the books and articles consulted. Newspapers and musical journals of many countries, only the most important of which are listed, have furnished a liberal share of material.

## MANUSCRIPTS

CALCAÑO, JOSÉ ANTONIO. *Palabras pronunciadas por J. A. Calcaño en el Cementerio General del Sur, al Ser Repatriados las Cenizas de Teresa Carreño el 15 de Febrero de 1938.*

CARREÑO, TERESA. "War Time Experiences of a Concert Artist Touring Europe."

COCHRAN, J. W. "Teresa Carreño as I knew her." Told to Ray C. B. Brown.

COHEN, NATHANIEL H. "Excerpts from the Memoirs of Nathaniel H. Cohen."

FRANCIA, FELIPE. *"Bautismos, Matrimonios y Entierros en Caracas."* Letra F. Libretas 9, 10, 11. Tomo XIX. Academia de la Historia, Caracas.

LLAMOZAS, SALVADOR. *"La Vuelta a la Patria de la célebre Pianista Teresa Carreño en 1885."*

OKELL, ADELAIDE C. Teresa Carreño. Memorial address made at Wesley College Conservatory, Grand Forks, S.D., May 15, 1918.

PONCE, RAFAEL MIRÁBAL. *"Apuntes Históricos sobre la Familia Carreño."*

## BOOKS

ARONSON, RUDOLPH. *Theatrical and Musical Memoirs.* New York, 1913.

BERMÚDEZ, JUAN AUGUSTIN. *Diccionario Histórico*. Madrid, 1800.

BREITHAUPT, RUDOLF M. *Die Natürliche Klaviertechnik*. Der Meisterin Teresa Carreño gewidmet. Leipzig, 1905.

BROWN, ABBIE FARWELL. *The Boyhood of Edward MacDowell*. New York, 1924.

VON BÜLOW, HANS GUIDO. *Briefe und Schriften Hans von Bülows*. Ed. by Marie von Bülow. vol. 8. Leipzig, 1908.

CAMACHO, SIMÓN (*pseud*. NAZARENO). *Cosas de los Estados Unidos*. New York, 1864.

CARRAFFA, ALBERTO y ARTURO. *Enciclopedia Heráldica y Genealógica Hispano-Americana*. Tomo 24 (with bibliography and plates). Madrid, 1926.

CARREÑO, MANUEL ANTONIO. *Manual de Urbanidad y Buenas Maneras para Uso de la Juventud De Ambos Sexos*. New York, Lima, 1859. Paris, 1920.

—— TERESA. *Possibilities of Tone Color by Artistic Use of the Pedals*. Cincinnati, New York, London, 1919.

COOKE, JAMES FRANCIS. *Great Pianists on Piano Playing*. Philadelphia, 1913.

L. CORTIJO, ALAHIJA. *La Música Popular y Los Músicos Célebres de la América Latina*. Barcelona, 1917.

COWEN, SIR FREDERIC HYMEN. *My Art and my Friends*. London, 1913.

CHARNACÉ, GUY DE. *Les Etoiles du Chant* (Adelina Patti). Paris, 1866.

DALTON, LEONARD V. *Venezuela*. New York, 1925.

DAMROSCH, WALTER JOHANNES. *My Musical Life*. New York, 1923.

EHRLICH, A. *Berühmte Klavierspieler der Vergangenheit und Gegenwart*. Leipzig, 1898.

—— *Berühmte Sängerinnern*. Leipzig, 1896.

ELSON, ARTHUR. *Woman's Work in Music*. Boston, 1904.

FINCK, HENRY T. *My Adventures in the Golden Age of Music*. New York, 1926.

FORS, LUIS RICARDO. *Gottschalk*. Havana, 1880.

GERHARDI, DR. KARL AUGUST. *Das Wesen des Genies*. Jauer, 1907.

GILMAN, LAWRENCE. *Edward MacDowell*. London, New York, 1906.

GOTTSCHALK, LOUIS MOREAU. *Notes of a Pianist*. Ed. by Clara Gottschalk; translated from the French by Robert E. Peterson. Philadelphia, 1881.

LORENO DE GUERRA Y ALONSO, JUAN. *Guía de la Grandeza. Titulos y Caballeros de España*. Madrid, 1917.

GUINÁN, FRANCISCO GONZALES. *História Contemporanea de Venezuela.* Caracas, 1924.

HEGERMANN-LINDENCRONE, L. DE. *The Sunny Side of Diplomatic Life.* New York, London, 1914.

Collection of the Hispanic Society of America. *Carreño de Miranda.* New York, 1928.

KIENZL, WILHELM. *Lebenswanderung.* Stuttgart, 1926.

KOEHLER, ELSA VON HASE. *Briefe eines deutschen Meisters, Max Reger.* Leipzig, 1928.

LAHEE, HENRY C. *Grand Opera in America.* Boston, 1902.

LEHMANN, LILLI. *My Path through Life.* Translated by Alice Benedict Seligman. London, 1914.

LIPSIUS, IDA MARIA. *La Mara (pseud.).*
*Musikalische Studienköpfe,* V. Die Frauen im Tonleben der Gegenwart. Leipzig, 1902.

LOZANO Y LOZANO, FABIO. *El Maestro del Libertador.* Paris, 1913.

MAPLESON, JAMES HENRY. *Memoirs.* 2 vols. London, 1888.

MASON, WILLIAM. *Memoirs of a Musical Life.* New York, 1901.

MORSCH, ANNA. *Deutschland's Tonkünstlerinnen.* Berlin, 1893.

PEREZ BALSERA, JOSÉ. *Los Caballeros de Santiago.* 7 vols. Madrid, 1936.

PIFERRER, FRANCISCO. *Nobiliario de los Reines y Señoríos de España.* Madrid, 1859.

PLAZA, JUAN BAUTISTA. *Teresa Carreño.* Caracas, 1938.

PLAZA, RAMÓN DE LA. *Ensayos sobre el Arte en Venezuela.* Caracas, 1883.

PORTE, JOHN F. *Edward MacDowell.* London, 1922.

RAUPP, WILHELM. *Eugen d'Albert, ein Künstler und Menschenschicksal.* Leipzig, 1930.

RIVIÈRE, JULES. *My Musical Life and Recollections.* London, 1893.

ROJAS, ARISTIDES. *Estudios Históricos.* 3 vols. Caracas, 1927.

ROURKE, THOMAS. *Man of Glory, Simón Bolívar.* New York, 1939.

RUBINSTEIN, ANTON. *Erinnerungen aus 50 Yahren.* Leipzig, 1893.

—— *Anton Rubinsteins Gedankenkorb.* Mit einem Vorwort von Hermann Wolff. Leipzig, 1897.

RYAN, THOMAS. *Recollections of an Old Musician.* New York, 1899.

SILVA, ANDRÉS A. *Hojas de Todas Colores.* Caracas, 1883.

VON STEIN, RICHARD. *Grieg.* Leipzig, 1921.

STRAKOSCH, MAURICE. *Souvenirs d'un Impresario.* Deuxième édition. Paris, 1887.

THOMAS, ROSE FAY. *Memoirs of Theodore Thomas*. New York, 1911.
—— THEODORE. *A Musical Autobiography*. Ed. by George P. Upton. Chicago, 1905.
TOYE, FRANCIS. *Rossini, A Study in Tragi-Comedy*. London, 1934.
UPTON, GEORGE P. *Musical Memories 1850–1900*. Chicago, 1908.
VAUCAIRE, MICHEL. *Bolívar*. Paris, 1928.
WILSTACH, PAUL. *Richard Mansfield*. New York, 1908.

## ARTICLES

AMPHION (*pseud.*). MARÍA TERESA CARREÑO. *El Buen Senrido*. Caracas, December 5, 1862.
ARMSTRONG, WILLIAM. The Best Musical Investment. An interview with Teresa Carreño. *The Musician,* March, 1917.
—— Teresa Carreño's Reminiscences. *Musical Courier*. Pt. I. June 28, 1917. Pt. II. July 6, 1917.
ARRIETA, D. A. Teresa Carreño. *El Cojo Ilustrado*. Caracas, July 1, 1893.
Bei TERESA CARREÑO, "der Titanin der Tasten." *New Yorker Herold*. December 24, 1916.
BOLLING, ERNEST L. Our first Musical Ambassador, Louis Moreau Gottschalk. *The Etude,* February, 1932.
BROWER, HARRIETTE. Carreño's Technic a Parental Gift. *Musical America*. December 8, 1913.
—— Memories of Leslie Hodgson: Teresa Carreño. *Musical America*. July 14, 1917.
BURGESS, RUTH PAYNE. Teresa Carreño como Professora. *El Universal*. Caracas, August 14, 1935.
CAMACHO, SIMÓN. NAZARENO (*pseud.*). El Album de Teresa Carreño. *Diario de la Marina*. Havana, March 17, 1863.
Carreño in Cuba. *Musical Age*. New York, March 28, 1901.
Celebridades Contemporaneas: Teresa Carreño. *La Regeneración*. Madrid, November 28, 1866.
CHORLEY, HENRY F. A Spanish American Pianiste. *The Athenaeum*. London, January 28, 1872.
GIFFEN, YETTA DOROTHEA. Wisdom and Wit from the Lips of Teresa Carreño. *Musical Courier*. March 8, 1917.
GUTIERREZ, RAFAEL HERNANDEZ. Triunfo del Genio. *El Porvenir*. Caracas, June 30, 1866.

Idealism in Music Study: An interview with Teresa Carreño. *The Etude*. Philadelphia, June, 1917.

JACOB, O. P. Berlin a Musical Dictator—Why? *Musical America*. June, 1912.

Living Stage Folk who knew and cheered Lincoln. *The New York Times*. February 12, 1911.

LARRAZÁBAL, FELIPE. Tributo de Justizia al Mérito. *El Independiente*. Caracas, May 26, 1862.

LUNT, CORNELIA G. Teresa Carreño: An Appreciation. *The Musical Monitor*. New York, July, 1917.

MATHEWS, W. S. B. Personal Glimpses of Teresa Carreño. *Music*. New York, 1897.

NIEMANN, DR. WALTER. Teresa Carreño. *Reclam's Universum*. 30 Yhrg. Heft 10. December, 1913.

PARDO, MIGUEL EDUARDO. Mujer y Artista. *El Cojo Ilustrado*. Caracas, May 15, 1903.

PLUMMER, HARRY CHAPIN. Venezuela. Pays Honor to Memory of Carreño. *Musical Courier*. March 25, 1938.

POMBO, RAFAEL. Teresa Carreño. *La Crónica*. New York, March 12, 1863.

SCHULTZE, ADOLF. Teresa Carreño. *Neue Musik-Zeitung*. Stuttgart-Leipzig, November 13, 1902.

SILVA, ANDRÉS A. Celebridades Artísticas de Venezuela: María Teresa Carreño. *Museo Venezolano*. December 1, 1865.

Teresa Carreño's Death ends Notable Career. *Musical America*. June 23, 1917.

Teresa Carreño. *The Lady*. London, June 5, 1896.

Teresa Carreño, "Lioness of the Piano." *The World*. New York, March 14, 1897.

Troubles of a Feminine Impresario. *Musical America*. November 6, 1909.

Un Bautismo de Gloria. *El Continental*. New York, January 1, 1863.

# INDEX